THE WORLD'S BEST BOOKS

Homer to Hemingway

Other Books by Asa Don Dickinson

———————

One Thousand Best Books
Best Books of Our Time
Best Books of the Decade 1926-35
Best Books of the Decade 1936-45

THE WORLD'S BEST BOOKS

Homer to Hemingway

3000 Books of 3000 Years
1050 B. C. to 1950 A. D.
Selected on the Basis of a
Consensus of Expert Opinion

By

Asa Don Dickinson

THE H · W · WILSON COMPANY

NEW YORK   1953

AF Technical Book

"In the multitude of counsellors there is safety."

Proverbs XI: 14

PREFACE

This is my fifth *and final* published clue to the literary labyrinth.*
For more than thirty years I have been exploring this fascinating maze
in spare time, so I can now claim some familiarity with it. The results
of these long-continued gropings are presented herewith. This book
is a unification, a condensation and a revision of, as well as an addition
to, its four predecessors. Herein I have dared to list the best books
from Homer to Hemingway, 1050 B.C. to 1950 A.D., three thousand
books of three thousand years.

Let me hasten to add that the choice of titles, as hitherto, has been
based on a consensus of expert opinion. But, as everyone knows, the
world has changed enormously in thirty years. Public opinion and
critical opinion have changed with it. Some, but by no means all, of
the books highly regarded by Grandfather and his teachers evoke only
boredom or derision in today's readers. A few seemingly moribund
books have won a new lease of life. While other volumes—some old,
some new—from which Grandmother would have shrunk in horror
are accepted without a qualm by the present generation. We elders
often sigh for the good old days of our youth, yet incline to the belief
that today's readers may have gained in honesty as much as they have
lost in delicacy.

These reflections have influenced to some extent the selection of
the authors and titles here presented. In some instances the body of
ancient critical opinion has been weighed and measured less meticu-
lously and mechanically than in the four previous volumes. But the
author still asks his readers to remember that "the word *best* in his title
means *selected on the basis of a consensus of expert opinion as most
worthy of the attention of today's intelligent American readers who
are equipped with at least a high school education or its equivalent.*"

Titles described in the main text of this volume, which have also
appeared in one or other of its four predecessors may be distinguished
by one of the Roman numerals, I, II, III, or IV, following the date of
publication. These are a means of referring to the earlier volume
wherein the title in question has probably received somewhat fuller
treatment. As the most recently published of those guides, however,
carries its survey only through the books of 1945, publications of later
date have no previous listing to which reference can be made.

The main body of the work consists of a single arrangement, al-
phabetical by authors, of all the 3000 titles included in the book. There

---

* The strange figure on the back-strip of this book was copied from an ancient Cretan coin.
There is basis of fact for the legend of King Minos of Crete and his *labyrinth*.

will be found the most essential, identifying facts about each author, as well as a thumbnail description or evaluation of each book. The Table of Contents is a key to other groupings of titles and authors according to form, subject matter, nationality and date.

So many works have been consulted in the preparation of this book that it would be tedious to list them. But special mention is due *Good Reading*, 1947, compiled by The Committee on College Reading, sponsored by The National Council of Teachers of English, and published by Penguin Books, Inc. (It is now issued as a Mentor Book by the New American Library of World Literature.) In it more than 1000 titles are listed and briefly described. I have found these pithy characterizations so irresistible that about two score of them have been transcribed (with due credit) in these pages.

A. D. D.

CONTENTS

"May blessings be upon the head of Cadmus, the Phoenicians, or whoever it was invented books."—Thomas Carlyle.

THE WORLD'S BEST BOOKS

Homer to Hemingway

———•———

"A. E.," pseudonym *See* Russell, George William.

à Kempis *See* Thomas à Kempis.

Adams, Franklin Pierce ("F. P. A.") 1881- American journalist and wit. Best known for his column, *The Conning Tower*, and for his part in the radio program *Information Please.*

INNOCENT MERRIMENT; AN ANTHOLOGY OF LIGHT VERSE. 1942. (IV) Burlesque, parody, nonsense rhymes and satire; translation, paraphrase, song and story.

Adams, Henry 1838-1918 American author; descendant of two presidents of the United States; Boston Brahmin; member of the American Academy of Arts and Letters.

EDUCATION OF HENRY ADAMS. 1918. (I and II) This autobiography is chiefly a somewhat jaundiced criticism of American institutions as they affected a brilliant but disappointed man who had been offered every advantage they could give. A very important book.

MONT ST. MICHEL AND CHARTRES. 1913. (II) Study of "the spiritual significance of medievalism as typified in two great cathedrals"; a picture of Thirteenth Century unity which the author wishes us to contrast with the description of Twentieth Century multiplicity in his *Education of Henry Adams.* (Neither book will be enjoyed by immature minds.)

HENRY ADAMS AND HIS FRIENDS; A COLLECTION OF HIS UNPUBLISHED LETTERS. 1947. Some 650 letters to his friends: 1858-1918. A thoughtful man, dowered with ample leisure, Adams was one of the great letter-writers. His pessimism is to be expected, discounted and enjoyed.

Adams, James Truslow   1878-1949   American historian. Pulitzer prize-winner. Member, American Academy of Arts and Letters.

Epic of America. 1931. (III) We are led again along the trail our fathers travelled. The Promised Land of democracy at which they aimed is pointed out, and we are shown how far from their destination we still are.

March of Democracy. 2v. 1932-33. (III) Spirited factual narrative of our country's history. Addressed to the average citizen who will like it the better for its wealth of illustrations.

New England in the Republic, 1776-1850. 1926. (III) Another American historian, Allan Nevins, once called this the best single volume of American history in existence.

Our Business Civilization. 1929. (III) Convincing statement of the case against American materialism.

Provincial Society, 1690-1763. 1927. (III) Readable and highly competent narrative, enlivened by many illustrations and racy extracts from diaries and newspapers of the day.

Adams, Samuel Hopkins   1871-   American author of many books dealing with the American scene.

A. Woollcott, His Life and His World. 1945. (IV) A lively book, worthy of its sprightly subject.

Addams, Jane   1860-1935   Her settlement work in Chicago made her one of the most distinguished and revered of American women.

Twenty Years at Hull House. 1910. (II) This record of accomplishment is still a source of inspiration and suggestion to social reformers.

Addison, Joseph   1672-1719   English author, whose graceful contributions to *The Spectator* and *The Tatler* have inspired imitation from his time to ours.

Essays. (I) The charming pieces about Sir Roger de Coverley, which appeared in *The Spectator*, have been said to contain the seed from which developed the English novel.

Ade, George 1866-1944 American humorist, whose slangy "fables," once immensely popular, portray in an amusing way life among the Hoosiers at the turn of the century.

The Permanent Ade. 1947. (II) Much of his best and most characteristic work has been gathered here between a single pair of covers.

Adler, Mortimer James 1902- American college professor; an apostle of the study of Great Books as a means for acquiring a liberal education.

How to Read a Book. 1940. (IV) Four hundred pages about learning and thinking, how and what to read, and the why of it; about the obligations of citizens in a democracy.

Æschylus 525-456 B.C. Greek dramatist—the "Father of Tragedy."

Tragedies (I) (Available in Everyman's Library or World's Classics editions.) Of his 72 plays whose titles we know, only seven have survived. These comprise the House of Atreus trilogy (*Agamemnon, Choephori, Eumenides*), and *The Suppliants, The Persians, Seven against Thebes* and *Prometheus Bound*. The magic of the Greek dramatists casts strange gleams into the shadowy corners of Greek mythology. After 2400 years we are using the names of some of their characters to typify the concepts of a new science—psychology.

Æsop 6th Century B.C. A semi-legendary Greek slave, to whom have been attributed many of the folktales about animals who think and speak like men. The beast-fable is a literary type whose history can be traced back to the childhood of the race.

Fables. (I) Æsop's tales have been translated into many tongues and have appeared in innumerable editions, including Everyman's Library.

Agar, Herbert 1897- American author of books on American public affairs; a Pulitzer prize-winner in 1934.

Price of Union. 1950. History, from the Revolution to 1909, of American political parties, presidential campaigns and the presidency—to "illustrate the growth of a unique political system."

Aiken, Conrad 1889- American poet and fictionist. "Though his reputation has been largely based on his poetry, Aiken will be remembered most for his short stories."—*Time*.

SELECTED POEMS. 1929. He won the Pulitzer prize for poetry in 1930.

SHORT STORIES. 1950. Like his poems, these are strongly tinctured by his keen interest in psychoanalysis.

Ainsworth, Harrison 1805-82 English historical novelist whose hair-raising tales of England in the times of the Tudor and Stuart kings owed much of their former popularity to the grotesque illustrations of Cruikshank.

OLD ST. PAUL'S. 1841. (I) A story of the Great Plague and Fire of London in 1666.

TOWER OF LONDON. 1840. (I) The tragic story of Lady Jane Grey.

WINDSOR CASTLE. 1843. (I) A Bluebeard tale of Henry the Eighth and his wives.

Akins, Zoë 1886- American playwright.

THE OLD MAID. 1934. New York in the Repressed Fifties. Won Pulitzer prize for drama in 1935. Adapted from Edith Wharton's novelette with the same title.

Alcott, Amos Bronson 1799-1888 American educator and transcendentalist.

JOURNALS. 1938. (IV) The student of American literature should at least skim through these journals, for their author was an active member of the Concord group which played so large a part in *The Flowering of New England*.

Alcott, Louisa May 1832-88 This industrious and soberly gifted daughter of an impractical father (Bronson Alcott) wrote the best known and best loved books for girls in the English language.

LITTLE WOMEN. 1869. (I) Based upon the family life of the author and her sisters in old Concord.

Aldington, Richard   1892-   English novelist and poet. Served in World War I; married Hilda Doolittle, "H. D.," American imagist poet (*q.v.*).

VIKING BOOK OF POETRY OF THE ENGLISH-SPEAKING WORLD. 1941. (IV) An excellent anthology; 1300 poems by 300 poets of the last thousand years.

D. H. LAWRENCE; PORTRAIT OF A GENIUS BUT . . . 1950. "Objective portrait painted twenty years after the subject's death. . . . Will doubtless stand the test of time better than anything else so far in print."—*New York Herald Tribune.*

Aldrich, Thomas Bailey   1836-1907   American man of letters.

ℓ STORY OF A BAD BOY. 1868. (I) Partly autobiographical tale of a "mischievous but truly good, natural New England boy." Translated into six European languages, it has been enjoyed by adults no less than by boys and girls.

Allen, Frederick Lewis   1890-   American editor, who has worked in turn for *The Atlantic, The Century* and *Harper's.*

ONLY YESTERDAY; AN INFORMAL HISTORY OF THE NINETEEN-TWENTIES. 1931. (III) Graybeards, especially, enjoy books like this one. It is an exceptionally good example of its kind.

THE GREAT PIERPONT MORGAN. 1949. "Friendly but honest," this is "more a character study than a detailed narrative."

Allen, Mrs Frederick Lewis   *See* Rogers, Agnes.

Allen, Hervey   1889-1949   American author, teacher, soldier (seriously wounded in World War I).

ISRAFEL; LIFE AND TIMES OF EDGAR ALLAN POE.   2v.   1926. (III) Scholarly, satisfying, sympathetic—yet objective—life of the unhappiest genius of American letters. Largely based on original, contemporary material, mostly hitherto unused.

ANTHONY ADVERSE. 1933. (III) A historical romance. In 1224 pages the gorgeous hero's history is set down from his conception in 1775 to his death in 1825—fifty years of adventurous life in far-flung corners of the globe.

Amiel, Henri Frédéric   1821-81   Swiss professor of philosophy.

PRIVATE JOURNAL . . . translated by Van Wyck Brooks and Charles Van Wyck Brooks. 1935. (I) This so-called journal is a collection of detached meditations—philosophic, religious, descriptive or personal in tone; lucid and aphoristic in style. A good bedside book. (There is also a translation by Mrs. Humphrey Ward.)

Amundsen, Roald   1872-1928   Norwegian polar explorer. He disappeared in 1928 on a rescue mission to the North Pole.

SOUTH POLE. 1913. (II) Its discoverer's story of his great achievement.

Andersen, Hans Christian   1805-75   Danish man of letters; best known to the English-speaking world for his

FAIRY TALES. (I) A good translation is the one by Mrs. E. Lucas, illustrated by Charles and Robinson. Among books for children these tales enjoy a world-wide reputation for their humor, imagination and simplicity.

Anderson, Maxwell   1889-   American dramatist. Among his most successful plays are the following:

WHAT PRICE GLORY? 1924. A powerful, grim and ugly play about World War I; written with Laurence Stallings.

SATURDAY'S CHILDREN. 1927. A comedy of modern life in New York.

ELIZABETH THE QUEEN. 1930. Historical drama.

BOTH YOUR HOUSES. 1933. Satire on political corruption in Congress. Won Pulitzer prize in 1934.

MARY OF SCOTLAND. 1934. Historical play.

WINTERSET. 1935. Drama in verse, based on the Sacco-Vanzetti case.

HIGH TOR. 1936. In verse. Won a Critics' prize. "A fantasy of many virtues."—Stark Young, in *New Republic*.

Anderson, Sherwood   1876-1941   This man of the Middle West was in turn a worker at odd jobs, a soldier, a businessman, an author and a small town journalist. He had, says John Farrar, "a curious ability to give voice to the tragedies of small lives."

WINESBURG, OHIO. 1919. (II) Collection of tales of small town life. Perhaps his best known and most characteristic book.

TRIUMPH OF THE EGG. 1921. (II) Tales of misery and despair which, said Carl Van Doren, excel "even *Winesburg* in both poetry and truth."

DARK LAUGHTER. 1925. (II) An escape story which perhaps was particularly in mind when Carl Van Doren said that Anderson's novels "ache with the sense of a dumb confusion in America."

STORY TELLER'S STORY. 1924. (II) A long autobiography containing the recognizable embryos of many of his stories.

TAR; A MIDWEST CHILDHOOD. 1926. (III) Recollections and imaginative recreation of his American boyhood from the age of four to early adolescence.

PORTABLE SHERWOOD ANDERSON; edited with an introduction by Horace Gregory. 1949. The "best of his writings"—631 pages of them. Includes all of *Poor White*, much of *Winesburg, Ohio*, six short stories, some letters, etc.

Andrews, Roy Chapman 1884- American explorer, zoologist, anthropologist.

ON THE TRAIL OF ANCIENT MAN. 1926. (III) Popularization of scientific news about dinosaurs' eggs and such, from the paleontological front in the Gobi desert, in east Asia.

UNDER A LUCKY STAR; A LIFETIME OF ADVENTURE. 1943. (IV) Not just a scientist's stuffy memoirs, but good-humored recollections of adventurous travel, written for the general reader.

Andreyev, Leonid Nikolaevich 1871-1919 Russian fictionist and dramatist of the old regime. Despairing fatalism was his chosen companion.

HE WHO GETS SLAPPED. 1922. (II) Story of a philosopher who seeks escape from *Weltschmerz* in the life of a clown at the circus.

LIFE OF MAN. 1907. (II) A drama of unrelieved pessimism which is said to have led many Russian students to suicide.

SEVEN WHO WERE HANGED. 1908. (II) This story is a sympathetic study of the humanness of criminals condemned to death.

THE RED LAUGH. 1904. (II) Bleeding human bodies constitute the *red laugh* in this narrative describing horrors of the Russo-Japanese War.

Angle, Paul M.   1900-   Editor.   Historical scholar and Lincoln specialist.

LINCOLN READER. 1947. A Lincoln anthology: 179 selections, by 65 authors. "The most completely satisfactory one-volume biography thus far."

Anglo-Saxon Chronicle.   9th (?) to 12th Centuries.   An important source-book for the early history of England. The period included is nominally that from the birth of Christ to 1154, but the Seventh to Ninth Centuries are the ones most fully covered. The names of the Venerable Bede (673-735) and Alfred the Great (841-901) are associated with the authorship of this composite monkish record. The best edition is that of C. Plummer in 2 volumes, 1892-99. The latest translation (1909) is that by E. E. C. Gomme.

Anglo-Saxon Poetry: 650-1000 A.D.; edited by R. K. Gordon. Everyman's Library. This good selection of translations includes *Beowulf, Widsith, Judith,* and six other titles.

Annunzio, Gabriele d'   1863-1938   Italian poet, warrior, politician, lover.

FLAME OF LIFE. 1899. (II) Novel inspired by the author's affair with Duse, tragedy queen. It is famed for its magnificent descriptions of Venice.

LA GIOCONDA. 1901. (II) Play about a faithless husband and a self-sacrificing wife.

DAUGHTER OF JORIO. 1904. (II) Harrowing melodrama in beautiful verse, full of splendid imagery and passionate fire.

Anthony, Katherine   1877-   American biographer.

CATHERINE THE GREAT. 1925. Life of the once obscure German woman who became an empress and ruled supreme in Eighteenth-Century Russia. She won lasting fame both for her brains and her many lovers. A masterly psychoanalytic biography.

Antin, Mary (Mrs. M. A. Grabau)   1881-   Russian immigrant.

THE PROMISED LAND. 1912. Ranked by *The Nation* with the autobiographies of Benjamin Franklin, Jacob Riis, and Booker Washington.

Antoninus, Marcus Aurelius *See* Aurelius Antoninus, Marcus.

Apuleius, Lucius   Born about 124 A.D.   Roman philosopher and satirist.

THE GOLDEN ASS. Fantastic romance written in the Second Century. The hero is transformed, by magic, into an ass and has many lusty adventures. This picaresque tale is one of the first milestones on the long road of prose fiction. An excellent new translation, called *Transformations of Lucius*, by Robert Graves, was published in 1951.

Aquinas, St. Thomas   1225(?)-74   Italian scholastic philosopher and teacher, from whose doctrine the term Thomism is derived.

SUMMA THEOLOGIAE. This systematic survey of Catholic theology has caused its author to be accorded philosophical rank with St. Augustine and Aristotle, and has even won him a place on the lists of the Great Books enthusiasts.

Arabian Nights' Entertainments. (I) Traceable to the Tenth Century or earlier, the "modern" collection of these Eastern folk tales, chiefly Indian or Persian, was assembled in the Fourteenth or Fifteenth Century. There are innumerable editions for young and old, of varying degrees of sophistication. The standard English translations are by E. W. Lane (1840), John Payne (1884), and the definitive, monumental version in 16 volumes by Sir Richard Burton, published 1885-88. Andrew Lang's selection of the tales is a good one for children, but there are many others, some charmingly illustrated.

Arblay, Mme. d' *See* Burney, Frances.

Ariosto, Ludovico   1474-1533   Italian poet.

ORLANDO FURIOSO. 1512-32. (I) Epic poem recounting the fabulous deeds of Charlemagne and his knights—especially Roland (Orlando)—against the Saracens. There are English translations by Sir John Harington (1591); and W. S. Rose, New Edition, 1892.

Aristophanes   448(?)-380(?) B.C.   Greek author of comedies, some of which satirize the godless, leveling radicals of his day, including Socrates.

THE BIRDS. 414 B.C. (I) In this extravaganza two disgruntled Athenians emigrate to the country of the birds, where is built a walled city, Cloud-Cuckoo Land, from which it is hoped to shut out the gods and foster bird-power.

THE CLOUDS. 423 B.C. (I) A pitiless satire against Socrates and the Sophists and their manner of argument.

THE FROGS. 405 B.C. (I) Describes the descent of Dionysus, patron of the drama, to the dark realm of Pluto, to bring back Euripides. After much squabbling in the lower regions, it is Æschylus who is deemed more worthy to return to daylight.

Aristotle   384-322 B.C.   Greek philosopher; pupil of Plato and tutor of Alexander the Great. His influence on the development of philosophy and science was great until the comparatively recent rise of scientific method.

WORKS. (I) Among the most important of these are his *Metaphysics, Politics, Nicomachian Ethics, Poetics, History of Animals, On the Soul, Rhetoric* and *Aesthetics.* A good selection in English is the *Basic Works*, edited by McKeon and published by Random House in 1941.

Armstrong, Margaret   1867-1944   American artist and illustrator till 1930; thereafter, biographer and writer of mysteries.

FANNY KEMBLE: A PASSIONATE VICTORIAN. 1938. (IV) Fanny Kemble (1809-93), famous British actress, spent half her life in America. It was a most interesting life and this book is a masterly telling of its story. (See also the subject's own published letters and memoirs.)

Arnold, Sir Edwin   1832-1904   English poet and Orientalist, well versed in the ancient history, literature, and religion of the Hindus.

LIGHT OF ASIA. 1878. (I) Poetical exposition of the life and teachings of Gautama (Buddha). A popular introduction, in blank verse, for Western minds to Eastern manners and ways of thinking.

SONG CELESTIAL. Paraphrase from the Sanskrit of the Hindu *Bhagavad-Gita*, beloved of Mahatma Gandhi. (See also *Mahabharata* and *Ramayana*.)

Arnold, Henry H. 1886-1950 General, United States Army Air Force.

GLOBAL MISSION. 1949. Autobiography, combined with a history of American military aviation. "An important book and an easy one to read."—*New Yorker*.

Arnold, Matthew 1822-88 English poet, essayist, critic, and classical scholar.

COLLECTED POEMS. (I) Includes *Sohrab and Rustum,* a narrative of a fight to the death of a father and son unknown to one another: *Thyrsis*, a monody on the death of the poet Clough; and the classical *Empedocles on Etna*.

CULTURE AND ANARCHY. 1869. (I) This essay in social criticism is an attempt to define pure culture and to show what it could do for social England in the Victorian Age.

ESSAYS IN CRITICISM. 2v. 1865-68. (I) In their day these essays were pronounced "the most important utterances on criticism in modern times." They are still of far more than historical interest and value.

Arnold, Thurman 1891- American lawyer, writer on economics and government, and Federal official—especially United States Assistant Attorney-General in charge of antitrust prosecutions, 1938-43.

FOLKLORE OF CAPITALISM. 1937. "A lively attack on some revered catch phrases of traditional economics."—*Good Reading*.

Arvin, Newton 1900- American biographer and critic, in the field of American literature.

HERMAN MELVILLE. 1950. "Arvin's short literary biography is the wisest and most balanced single piece of writing on Melville I have seen."—A. Kazin, in *New York Times*. "Let's be blunt; this is not just a first-rate book on the life and art of Melville; it is also a superb exercise of critical scholarship and an ornament to American letters."—H. P. Vincent, in *Saturday Review of Literature*.

WHITMAN. 1938. (IV) Less a biography of the author of *Leaves of Grass* than an able critical, social, and political interpretation of the book. Has some left-wing coloration.

Asch, Sholem   1880-   American author.   Born   in   Poland;
naturalized in 1920; writes his books in Yiddish.

THE NAZARENE. 1939. (IV) Christians are enthusiastic in
their praise of this scholarly story of the life and times of Jesus.

THE APOSTLE. 1943. (IV) A reverent and deeply felt novel
about St. Paul; sequel to *The Nazarene.*

MARY. 1949. "Sholem Asch's finished trilogy is an epic
work in the grand tradition intellectually, spiritually, and in literary stature."—Edmund Fuller, in *Saturday Review of Literature.*

Atherton, Gertrude   1857-1938   Californian novelist who might
be described as a radical aristocrat.   She was a great-grandniece
of Benjamin Franklin.

THE CONQUEROR. 1902. (II) Well-documented novel about
Alexander Hamilton. It may fairly be called Miss Atherton's best
as well as her most successful book.

Aubry, G. J. *See* Conrad, Joseph.

Aucassin and Nicolette.   Twelfth Century.   This charming
French folktale is a love story of the days of the troubadours. It
is what the French call a *"conte-fable,"* with passages alternating in
prose and verse. A good translation (1887) by Andrew Lang was
reprinted by Holiday House in 1936.

Auden, Wystan Hugh   1907-   English-born poet, now a citizen
of the United States.

COLLECTED POETRY. 1945. (IV) "This volume firmly estab-
lishes Mr. Auden as the most exciting poet of his generation."—
Atlantic.

AGE OF ANXIETY. 1947. This long poem—called "a bleak and
pessimistic New York eclogue"—is in fact "a morality play, showing
us the route to hope and health: a deep and fresh piece of work."

Audubon, John James   1785-1851   Franco-American artist and
ornithologist.

BIRDS OF AMERICA; introduction and descriptive text by William Vogt. 1937. (Popular reprint, 1947.) (IV) Five hundred
superb reproductions of the most famous bird-paintings ever made.

AUDUBON'S AMERICA: NARRATIVES AND EXPERIENCES; edited by Donald Culross Peattie. 1940. (IV) The freshest and liveliest of Audubon's impressions, selected from his numerous memoirs and journals.

Augustine, Saint 354-430 After a profligate youth this son of a pagan father and Christian mother was converted to Christianity at thirty-two, to become eventually one of the four great fathers of the early church.

CONFESSIONS. 397. (I) It has been said that this constitutes "the first completely honest self-analysis in the history of literature."

CITY OF GOD. 426. (I) A learned, eloquent and pious defense of the rising Christian civilization against the pagan civilization which it was succeeding.

Aurelius Antoninus, Marcus 121-180 Emperor of Rome (161-180); philosopher.

MEDITATIONS. (I) The finest flower of Stoic philosophy. Detached paragraphs on life and death, logic, virtue, etc. There are satisfactory versions in *Everyman's Library, World's Classics* and *Classics Club* editions.

Auslander, Joseph 1897- American poet, scholar, teacher.

WINGED HORSE; THE STORY OF THE POETS AND THEIR POETRY. 1927. (III) Written with F. E. Hill. Not an anthology, but a history, though there is also a *Winged Horse Anthology*, by the same hands.

Austen, Jane 1775-1817 English novelist. She wrote only six books, died at forty-two, and had no formal education worth mentioning. Yet most critics would pronounce her the world's best woman novelist. Her field is quiet satire and social comedy in the only world she knew—English provincial society in the Nineteenth Century's first quarter.

PRIDE AND PREJUDICE. 1813. (I) Her masterpiece. Almost as delightfully rewarding is

SENSE AND SENSIBILITY. 1811. (I) Then came, perhaps in order of merit:

EMMA. 1816. (I) The heroine is a well-meaning, though blundering, matchmaker.

MANSFIELD PARK. 1814. (I) Concerns the troubles of a poor relation.

NORTHANGER ABBEY. 1818. (I) A satire on the "Gothic Romances."

PERSUASION. 1818. (I) The discerning reader will enjoy them all, especially if an edition with illustrations by Hugh Thomson or C. E. Brock is available. One of the Modern Library Giants includes all six titles.

Austin, Mary 1868-1934 American author and loving student of the Southwest.

LAND OF LITTLE RAIN. 1903. Descriptive and interpretative study of the American desert country and its people.

THE ARROW MAKER. 1911. (II) Serious play, illustrating Indian life in the Southwest.

EARTH HORIZON. 1932. (III) An autobiography; detached, impersonal, competent, and so, characteristic.

Babbitt, Irving 1865-1933 Deploring the romantic spirit as typified by Rousseau in both life and letters, this American scholar preached a doctrine of humanism ("nothing too much—decorum—restraint"), which is sometimes, unhappily, confused with humanitarianism.

NEW LAOKOÖN, AN ESSAY ON THE CONFUSION OF THE ARTS. 1910.

ROUSSEAU AND ROMANTICISM. 1919.

Bacchelli, Riccardo 1891- Italian novelist.

MILL ON THE PO. 1950. "A massive, agrarian epic in the tradition of Rölvaag, Hamsun, and Nexö."—*Chicago Tribune.* "Regarded in Italy as the Italian equivalent of *War and peace.*"—*Library Journal.*

Bacon, Francis (Viscount St. Albans) 1561-1626 British philosopher, essayist, statesman.

ESSAYS. 1597-1625. (I) In these "he talks to plain men in language everybody understands, about things in which everybody is interested." Few books are more often quoted.

ADVANCEMENT OF LEARNING. 1605. (I) A plea for scientific method and a blast against medieval scholasticism.

NOVUM ORGANUM. 1620. (I) Explains his inductive system of reasoning—the philosophical and scientific method which based all knowledge on experiment or experience.

NEW ATLANTIS. 1624. (I) An allegorical romance, named for its scene—the fabled continent sunk in the Atlantic ocean.

Bainton, Roland H. 1894-   American professor of church history at Yale. Born in England; member of the Society of Friends.

HERE I STAND; A LIFE OF MARTIN LUTHER. 1950. Illustrated with contemporary woodcuts and engravings. "Readable and authoritative."—*Christian Science Monitor.*

Baker, Dorothy   1907-   American author.

YOUNG MAN WITH A HORN. 1938. (IV) The author's first novel, this "strangely touching story of a swing musician," based upon the life of Bix Beiderbecke, was greeted with enthusiasm by many competent critics.

Baker, Ray Stannard   1870-1946   American author and editor; beloved by thousands for his friendly philosophizing under the pseudonym David Grayson.

ADVENTURES OF DAVID GRAYSON. 1925. (II) Includes *Adventures in Contentment* (1907), *Adventures in Friendship* (1910), *The Friendly Road* (1913), *Great Possessions* (1917).

WOODROW WILSON; LIFE AND LETTERS. 1927-39. (III) The authorized biography, from original sources; awarded Pulitzer prize, 1940.

Ballantyne, Robert M.   1825-94   Almost forgotten Scottish writer of excellent adventure stories for young people.

CORAL ISLAND. 1857. Appears on the list of "representative English classics" deemed worthy of translation, drawn up for Unesco by a committee of competent English bookmen.

GORILLA HUNTERS. 1861. The only Ballantyne title listed in Benét's *Reader's Encyclopaedia.*

Balzac, Honoré de 1799-1850 French realist; author of the enormous series of novels he called *The Human Comedy*. At his death it included 92 titles with about 2000 characters.

PÈRE GORIOT. 1834 (I) The French *Lear*. Story of the ingratitude of his children toward a fatuously devoted parent.

EUGÉNIE GRANDET. 1834. (I) Middle-class family pride and middle-class hunger for money are this book's themes.

COUNTRY DOCTOR. 1833. (I) Portrait of a physician who functioned as the good angel of his community.

COUSIN BETTE. 1846. (I)

COUSIN PONS. 1847. (I) Both are pictures of lower-class Parisian life a century ago. Bette is a poor relation the keynote of whose character is jealousy. Pons is a poor simple-minded old man, crushed by humiliations, but forgiving all and revenging himself only by benefits.

Bancroft, George 1800-91 American historian, statesman, diplomat.

HISTORY OF THE UNITED STATES. 10v. 1834-74. (I) The standard history of our grandfathers. Still valuable as a statement of the American side of mooted questions, especially in its account of the American Revolution. The final volume closes with the year 1799.

Barbellion, W. N. P., (pseudonym of Bruce Cummings) 1889-1919 British biologist.

JOURNAL OF A DISAPPOINTED MAN. 1919. Despite its repellent title, this book has been described as one of the world's great autobiographies.

Barbusse, Henri 1874-1935 French novelist and pacifist.

UNDER FIRE. 1917. (II) Novel which describes the life of the common soldier in wartime. The pacifist classic of World War I. Won the Prix Goncourt, 1917.

Barham, R. H. (Thomas Ingoldsby, pseudonym) 1788-1845 Jovial English parson, and Dean of St. Paul's, London.

INGOLDSBY LEGENDS. 1840-47. (I) Tales in verse and prose, mostly "of superstition and diablerie touched by uproarious humor"; also many travesties of medieval legends.

Barnes, Margaret Ayer   1886-   American student, wife, and mother till forty. Thereafter, chiefly a writer of excellent fiction which justifies her belief that a brilliant character study of an individual is the most vital thing in literature.

Within This Present. 1933. (III) Mirror of one family's life in Chicago from Civil War to New Deal.

Years of Grace. 1930. (III) A Chicago matron, born during the "years of grace," observes in maturity the phenomena of the jazz age. Pulitzer prize, 1931.

Barnett, Lincoln K.   1909-

Universe of Dr. Einstein. 1948. "A popular exposition of contemporary theories of quanta, relativity and cosmology." Einstein has endorsed it as "a valuable contribution to popular scientific writing."

Baroja, Pio   1873-   Spanish novelist. "He stands for the Spanish mind at its most enlightened."—H. L. Mencken.

Tree of Knowledge. 1928. A pitiless picture of Twentieth-Century life in Spain.

Baron, Alexander, (pseudonym of Alec Bernstein)   English novelist.
From the City, from the Plough. 1949. "In its quiet way, in only a few pages, this book says as much about war as have many larger, less mature, and more popular American novels."— *Yale Review.*

Barr, Stringfellow   1897-   American Rhodes scholar; editor; president, St. John's College (1937-46); president, Foundation for World Government, 1948-.

Pilgrimage of Western Man. 1949. A history of modern Europe. "As a guide to understanding the historical background of our age it is worth a dozen books like Toynbee's *Study of History.*"—*Annals of the American Academy of Political and Social Science.*

Barrie, Sir James M.   1860-1937   British novelist and dramatist. Laughter and tears were ever at his command. On many of his pages both appear companionably together.

Little Minister. 1890. (I) Charming story of a strait-laced young minister's love for a gypsy with rowans in her hair.

SENTIMENTAL TOMMY. 1896. (I) Story of a fascinating, exasperating Scottish boy who, like his namesake in Missouri, was blessed and cursed by an alarmingly exuberant imagination.

MARGARET OGILVY. 1896. (I) Barrie's touching but at times embarrassingly intimate tribute to his mother, born Margaret Ogilvy.

THE ADMIRABLE CRICHTON. 1903. (I) A satiric comedy. Capable butler becomes guide, guardian, and master of a company of aristocrats who are wrecked on a desert island.

ALICE SIT-BY-THE-FIRE. 1905. (II) In this play a mother, still young and charming, returns from India and is dismayed to find that her children—almost strangers to her—are grown up and that she is expected to sit quietly in the chimney-corner henceforth and forevermore.

DEAR BRUTUS. 1922. (II) Guests at the house-party in this play are magically allowed a second chance, only to find themselves no wiser, better, or happier than before.

> "The fault, dear Brutus, is not in our stars
> But in ourselves, that we are underlings."

PETER PAN. 1904. (II) This child's play, a masterpiece of tender, wistful fooling, is one of the best loved of modern dramas, both on stage and screen.

WHAT EVERY WOMAN KNOWS. 1908. (II) The testing of a clever, self-effacing wife.

QUALITY STREET. 1903. (II) A comedy of manners—the dashing soldier and the tired schoolmistress.

Barry, Philip 1896-1949 American playwright. His work has been "presented more often outside New York than that of any other American playwright except Eugene O'Neill."

HOTEL UNIVERSE. 1930. Psychological play. The problems of frustrated house-party guests are solved, but not without tragedy.

HOLIDAY. 1928. "His finest comedy . . . where his skill at fantastic verbal foolery reached perfection."

PHILADELPHIA STORY. 1939. "Combines the shimmering wit and beauty of 'Holiday' with a more searching and important psychological study."—F. B. Millet.

Barton, Margaret   1897-   English writer whose main interest is Eighteenth-Century England. She sometimes collaborates with Sir Osbert Sitwell.

GARRICK. 1949. Life of the great English player; "fountainhead of modern acting," and friend of Dr. Johnson.

Barzun, Jacques Martin   1907-   Professor of history at Columbia University since 1929. Born in Paris, he came to the United States in 1919; became a citizen in 1933.

TEACHER IN AMERICA. 1945. (IV) Really a book about teaching rather than teachers; what is taught and why and how, and what can be done to improve teaching. There is not a dull page in it.

Bashkirtseff, Marie   1860-84   Brilliant Russian art student of noble family. She died of consumption at twenty-four.

JOURNAL. 1885. (I) The author cunningly described her book as "the record of a woman's life, written down day by day without any attempt at concealment, as if no one in the world were to read it, yet with the purpose of being read."

Bates, Ernest Sutherland   1879-1939   American writer and educator.

BIBLE DESIGNED TO BE READ AS LIVING LITERATURE. 1936. Largely the King James Version text, with modern spelling and punctuation, logical arrangement of the parts, and normal paragraphing instead of the traditional "verses."

Baudelaire, Pierre Charles   1821-67   French poet and critic. A leader of the Decadents. Debauchee, mystic, admirer and translator of Poe, he was attracted strangely by both Catholicism and diabolism.

FLOWERS OF EVIL. 1857. Poems admired for their beauty but prosecuted for their immorality.

Beaconsfield, Earl of *See* Disraeli, Benjamin.

Beard, Charles Austin   1874-1948   American college professor, publicist and writer on American history, in which he stressed economic influences. Member, American Institute of Arts and Letters. Many of his books were written in collaboration with his wife, Mary Ritter Beard (1876-1946).

ECONOMIC INTERPRETATION OF THE CONSTITUTION OF THE UNITED STATES. 1913. In this book were first developed many of the ideas which are prominent in his later works.

RISE OF AMERICAN CIVILIZATION. 2v. 1927. (III) A full, scholarly, modern, enlightened and eminently readable book; most critics would call it his best.

AMERICAN LEVIATHAN; THE REPUBLIC IN THE MACHINE AGE. 1930. (III) Anatomy and physiology of the many-armed monster that is the American Federal Government—mainly an objective description of its qualities, functions, methods, and habits. Written with William Beard.

THE REPUBLIC: CONVERSATIONS ON FUNDAMENTALS. 1939. (IV) A course of twenty-one lectures on the basic issues of government and democracy.

AMERICA IN MIDPASSAGE. 1939. (IV) This is a continuation of *The Rise of American Civilization* (1927). It covers our history from 1924 to 1938.

BASIC HISTORY OF THE UNITED STATES. 1944. (IV) "Perhaps, all in all, the best one-volume history that has ever been written about the United States."—*The New Yorker.*

Beard, Charles Austin, editor.

WHITHER MANKIND; A PANORAMA OF MODERN CIVILIZATION. 1928. (III) Sixteen authorities survey sixteen aspects of our civilization, under the chairmanship of Professor Beard. It is interesting to compare these summaries with the state of affairs some decades later.

Beard, Mary Ritter *See* Beard, Charles Austin.

Beard, Miriam (Mrs. Alfred Vagts) 1901- Daughter of C. A. Beard and M. R. Beard.

HISTORY OF THE BUSINESS MAN. 1938. (IV) An important book; well written, readable, and sometimes amusing.

Beaumarchais, P. A. C. de 1732-99 French clockmaker, controversialist, dramatist; friend and financial backer of the American Revolution.

BARBER OF SEVILLE. 1775. Comedy satirizing the privileged classes, wherein the character of Figaro, sprightly master of intrigue, is first introduced.

MARRIAGE OF FIGARO. 1784. Distinguished for ingenuity of intrigue, brilliant dialog, and masterly character-drawing. "Figaro's denunciation of aristocratic pretensions definitely foreshadows the French Revolution."

Beaumont, Francis (1584-1616) and **Fletcher, John** (1579-1625) Elizabethan dramatists of the Mermaid Tavern group. Theirs is probably the most famous collaboration in English literature.

PLAYS: especially *Philaster* (1620)—a romantic drama with an elaborate plot, complete with the ubiquitous woman-page; *Maid's Tragedy* (1619)—their most powerful play, including "situations not only of tremendous theatrical effect but of real, tragic pathos and horror"; and *Knight of the Burning Pestle* (1607)—a mock-heroic cockney drama, probably inspired by the current vogue of *Don Quixote*.

Beckford, William 1759-1844 British author; son of a Lord Mayor of London, Member of Parliament, and reckless spendthrift.

VATHEK. 1784. (I) This gorgeous Eastern fairy tale—"the finest oriental tale ever written by an Englishman," said Professor Raleigh—is something of a literary curiosity. Originally written in French, the English version—first to be published—is by another hand.

Beddoes, Thomas Lovell 1803-49 English dramatist and poet.

DEATH'S JEST BOOK. 1850. A tragedy which tells a true story of the Thirteenth Century—the stabbing of a duke by his court fool.

Bede, The Venerable 673-735 Anglo-Saxon historian and monkish scholar.

ECCLESIASTICAL HISTORY OF THE ENGLISH NATION. (I) Written in Latin and translated into Anglo-Saxon by Alfred the Great, Bede's great work is by no means confined to ecclesiastical matters, but is a general history of England down to the Eighth Century against a background of the known world of that time.

Beebe, William 1877- American biologist and nature writer.

JUNGLE PEACE. 1918. (II) A trained observer's record, set down with "charming literary style, genial humor and scientific accuracy."

EDGE OF THE JUNGLE. 1921. (II) More of the same. Heywood Broun liked it so well that he nominated it "book of the season."

ARCTURUS ADVENTURE. 1926. (III). Account of an expedition to the Sargasso Sea and the Galapagos region of the Pacific. Many marvels were witnessed, including the birth of a volcano.

BENEATH TROPIC SEAS; A RECORD OF DIVING AMONG THE CORAL REEFS OFF HAITI. 1928. (III) The author sits or walks about the sea-floor in his diving-helmet and tells us what he sees.

BOOK OF NATURALISTS; AN ANTHOLOGY OF THE BEST NATURAL HISTORY. 1944. Selections—from Aristotle to writers of today.

HIGH JUNGLE. 1949. The product of three expeditions to the Venezuelan Andes. "His latest book stands very high, indeed, on that ridge where literature and natural history meet."—E. W. Teale, in *New York Herald Tribune*.

Beer, Thomas 1889-1940 American author. A private in World War I, he won a commission and served in France.

MAUVE DECADE; AMERICAN LIFE AT THE END OF THE NINETEENTH CENTURY. 1926. (III) Here is no jig-time rendering of the days known as the "gay nineties," but the opulent orchestration of many instruments, with wisdom dominant as often as wit.

Beerbohm, Sir Max 1872- English satirist, parodist, and caricaturist. Shaw called him "the incomparable Max."

CHRISTMAS GARLAND. 1912. (II) Parodies of the contemporary masters of English prose. "A classic that no household should be without."—*New York Times*.

AND EVEN NOW. 1920. (II) "Familiar essays characterized by whimsical, yet almost sardonic satire."—*Good Reading*.

ZULEIKA DOBSON. 1911. (II) Love story of an undergraduate duke and a maddeningly beautiful vaudeville actress. The spirit of the Oxford of its day is inimitably caught in this most amusing of extravaganzas.

SEVEN MEN. 1919. (I and II) Brilliantly witty short stories.

Behrman, Samuel Nathaniel 1893- American playwright; author of witty, sophisticated comedies.

SECOND MAN. 1927. Shrewd psychology and good dialog make this social comedy successful.

BIOGRAPHY. 1932. A worldly wise and witty heroine is the star of this light comedy.

Beith, John Hay   *See* Hay, Ian.

Bell, Eric Temple   1883-   Professor of Mathematics at the California Institute of Technology.

MEN OF MATHEMATICS. 1937. Readable survey of the lives and achievements of great mathematicians from Zeno to Poincaré.

Bell, Gertrude   1868-1926   English scholar, traveler, mountaineer, archaeologist, explorer, expert on Arabia and "distinguished servant of the State."

LETTERS; edited by Lady Bell. 2v. 1927. The extraordinarily interesting letters of a remarkable woman.

Bellamy, Edward   1850-98   American author.

LOOKING BACKWARD: 2000-1887. 1888. Description of an excellently organized Utopia—the United States in the year 2000. Less than half a century remains in which to make the author's dream come true.

Belloc, Hilaire   1870-   English writer, born in France; known for both liberal and Catholic sympathies.

ROBESPIERRE. 1901. (I and II) A striking portrait, highlighting the lurid background of the French Revolution.

EMMANUEL BURDEN, MERCHANT. 1904. (II) The strongest of his novels—a political satire and tragedy.

PATH TO ROME. 1902. (II) A zestful book of travel.

ON NOTHING AND KINDRED SUBJECTS. 1908. (II) Charming essays in his best vein.

Bemis, Samuel Flagg   1891-   American professor of diplomatic history at Yale and writer on American history.

JOHN QUINCY ADAMS AND THE FOUNDATIONS OF AMERICAN FOREIGN POLICY. 1949. Won the Pulitzer prize for biography. "A fresh and major contribution to the literature of the period . . . 1795-1825."—*Quarterly Booklist.*

Benavente, Jacinto 1866- A Spanish dramatist who wears no rose-colored spectacles. He won a Nobel prize in 1922 and has been called the Spanish Shakespeare.

PLAYS. 4v. 1917. Among these "vivid pictures of Spanish life," *Bonds of Interest* (1907) deserves special mention: "with it he attained the pinnacle of his fame."

Benchley, Robert Charles 1889-1945 American humorist. "He is at his best, perhaps, in his depictions of the struggles of the human animal in the minor crises of human experience."—F. B. Millet. "As a writer of nonsense . . . he is unsurpassed."—Stephen Leacock.

20,000 LEAGUES UNDER THE SEA, OR DAVID COPPERFIELD. 1928. "The collaboration of Benchley and [his illustrator] Gluyas Williams has produced a hilariously entertaining book."—*Book Review Digest.*

BENCHLEY BESIDE HIMSELF. 1943. "Chuckling essays on how to react to the oppression of irritating trifles."—*Good Reading.*

TREASURER'S REPORT AND OTHER ASPECTS OF COMMUNITY SINGING. 1930.

OF ALL THINGS. 1921.

Most of Benchley's books are illustrated by Gluyas Williams. These are the ones to seek out, for the pictures are quite as amusing as the text.

Benét, Stephen Vincent 1898-1943 American poet and fictionist. Member, American Academy of Arts and Letters.

JOHN BROWN'S BODY. 1928. (III) Long story about the Civil War. It is in rhymed and blank verse, with prose interludes. Won Pulitzer prize, 1929.

WESTERN STAR. 1943. (IV) The beginning of a great epic poem (cut short by the author's death) of the westward migration of those who founded this nation. The tale is here told only so far as the settlings at Jamestown and Plymouth. Won Pulitzer prize, 1944.

THIRTEEN O'CLOCK. 1937. Short stories, including his most popular production, *The Devil and Daniel Webster.*

Benét, William Rose   1886-1950   American poet; elder brother of Stephen Vincent Benét; his second wife was the poet Elinor Wylie (1885-1928). He was an editor of the *Saturday Review of Literature* from its inception till his death. Member, National Institute of Arts and Letters.

Dust Which Is God. 1941. (IV) Autobiographical novel in verse which presents a detailed picture of the first four decades of this century. It won the Pulitzer prize in 1942.

Benjamin, René   1885-   French novelist.

Private Gaspard. 1916. (II) The hero of this tale of World War I—a gamin of Paris—is the incarnation of *esprit*—the Gallic cock unconquerable. The book won the Goncourt prize.

Bennett, Arnold   1867-1931   English novelist.

Old Wives' Tale. 1908. (I and II) This book is generally conceded to be Bennett's masterpiece. It is the story of the lives of two middle-class sisters who came from the Five Towns—the pottery district of England. This novel is as devoid of glamor as it is full of interest.

Clayhanger Trilogy. (I and II) Published in one volume in 1925, this consists of *Clayhanger* (1910), *Hilda Lessways* (1911), and *These Twain* (1916). These novels also are about the people of the Five Towns. They are of the same genre and hardly less successful than *The Old Wives' Tale*.

Buried Alive. 1908. (I and II) Fantastic tale of a very shy but eminent British artist who tries to evade his admirers by "dying" and being buried in Westminster Abbey in the person of his valet. As *The Great Adventure* (and later as *Holy Matrimony*) it was successful both as play and moving picture.

Milestones. 1912. (I and II) Bennett's most successful play. The milestones are three generations which flourished respectively in 1860, 1885, and 1912; and the play sets forth strikingly the difference in their ideals and standards. (Written with Edward Knoblauch.)

Riceyman Steps. 1923. (II) Tale of a bookseller, his wife and their little servant. Again he "translates the commonplace from dullness to dignity by lifting it to the plane of the universal."

Imperial Palace. 1930. (III) Long novel about a big hotel. There are a hundred characters, but the chief one is the hotel itself.

LITERARY TASTE, edited and revised by Frank Swinnerton. 1937. Simple guide to good reading that has helped thousands to the enjoyment of good books.

Bent, Silas   1882-   American publicist.

JUSTICE OLIVER WENDELL HOLMES. 1932. (III) Life of "the Autocrat's" son, who was thrice wounded in the Civil War before starting the career which ended with thirty years of service in the United States Supreme Court. Wherever possible the story is told in the subject's own words.

Bentham, Jeremy   1748-1832   British jurist and utilitarian philosopher, the key to whose judgments was always "the greatest good to the greatest number."

INTRODUCTION TO THE PRINCIPLES OF MORALS AND LEGISLATION. 1789. This book is generally regarded as the master work.

Bentley, Eric R.   1916-   Anglo-American author and editor.

BERNARD SHAW. 1948. "To my way of thinking, the fairest, the most illuminating, and the best analysis so far . . . of Shaw's beliefs, his methods, and his meaning."—John Mason Brown, in *Saturday Review of Literature.*

Bentley, Phyllis   1894-   English novelist.

INHERITANCE. 1932. (IV) Story about six generations of the Oldroyds, Yorkshire weavers and mill-owners, and the struggle between capital and labor during the last hundred years.

Beowulf. (I) Anonymous folk-epic of the Seventh or Eighth Century. The dragon-slaying hero is of Scandinavian origin. The language is Old English (Anglo-Saxon). Translations of this work—the first milestone along the highway of English literature—have been made by F. B. Gummere, C. B. Tinker and many others. (*See also* Anglo-Saxon Poetry.)

Berenson, Bernhard   1865-   Russian-born, American-educated art critic, long resident in Italy. "The greatest living connoisseur of Italian Renaissance art." Member, American Academy of Arts and Letters.

ITALIAN PAINTERS OF THE RENAISSANCE. 1932.

SKETCH FOR A SELF-PORTRAIT. 1949. "Intellectual autobiography of one of the most brilliant conversationalists of our time."— *New York Times.*

AESTHETICS AND HISTORY IN THE VISUAL ARTS. 1948. "No dry and scholarly speculation, but the outcome of a life of the closest intimacy with art of every kind."—*School and Society.*

Bergson, Henri 1859-1941 French philosopher.

CREATIVE EVOLUTION. 1911. (French edition, 1907.) (I and II) It may still be said that no philosophical work published since this one has attracted so much attention. Rejecting monism, the author conceived the universe "as neither all spirit nor all matter, but as an eternal process, a *becoming*, which preserves the past and creates the future."

Berkeley, George 1685-1753 English bishop and philosopher. From 1729 to 1732 he lived in the colony of Rhode Island. A metaphysical idealist, he believed that "the objects of sense perception are only ideas in our mind . . . and that the whole of reality consists only of ideas in the mind of God."

PRINCIPLES OF HUMAN KNOWLEDGE. 1710. (I) "A last stand to reconcile empiricism with idealism."—*Good Reading.*

Bernstein, Alec *See* Baron, Alexander, pseudonym.

Besant, Sir Walter 1836-1901 English author. His novels were very popular among the later Victorians.

ALL SORTS AND CONDITIONS OF MEN. 1882. (I) A novel which described the social conditions of that day in London's East End and brought about the building of the People's Palace, an early settlement house.

Besier, Rudolph 1878- English dramatist.

BARRETTS OF WIMPOLE STREET. 1930. (III) A dramatization, which has won high praise on stage and screen, of the true love story of Robert Browning and Elizabeth Barrett.

Bevan, Edwyn Robert 1870- English author of books on religion.

CHRISTIANITY. 1932. To write upon Christianity in 240 small pages is a task not to be entrusted to many authors. Mr. Bevan's success is brilliant.

SYMBOLISM AND BELIEF. 1938. "Charming, clarifying exposition of certain essentials of religion in theory and practice."—*Good Reading.*

Beveridge, Albert   1862-1927   Orator, statesman and biographer, from Indiana.

JOHN MARSHALL. 4v. 1919-22. (II) The definitive life of the great Chief Justice of the United States Supreme Court, whose decisions established the principles of constitutional interpretation.

ABRAHAM LINCOLN, 1809-58. 2v. 1928. (III) This fine, detailed biography, cut short by the author's death, ends with his account of Lincoln's debate with Douglas. Even so, it was awarded the Pulitzer prize for American history.

Beyle, Marie Henri   *See* Stendhal, pseudonym.

Bhagavadgita   *See* Mahabharata; *see also* Arnold, Sir Edwin.

Bible.   (I)

The various parts of the Bible are supposed to have been composed between the beginning of the Thirteenth Century B.C. and the end of the First Century A.D. The earliest manuscripts now known of the Old and New Testaments are of the Ninth and Third Centuries A.D. respectively, though fragmentary Old Testament texts dating from as early as the Second Century B.C. were discovered near the Red Sea in 1947 to 1949. The first book printed from movable type was probably Gutenberg's Bible of 1455 in the Latin tongue. Coverdale's Bible (probably printed in Antwerp in 1535) was the first complete Bible printed in English. It was translated "Out of Douche and Latyn." (Wycliffe had completed his translation in 1382, but it was not printed till 1850.) Tyndale's was the first English translation of the New Testament directly from the Greek. It was printed at Cologne in 1526 and all later versions are based upon it. Thomas Matthew's translation, based on Tyndale and Coverdale, was the first English Bible printed (1538) in England. The King James or Authorized Version, of 1611, presents the text which is still the one most familiar to modern ears, though the Revised Version of 1885 and the American Revised Version of 1901, now supplemented by the American Revised Standard Version of the whole Bible (1952), embody indisputable improvements and are gradually winning general acceptance. (Roman Catholics however, do not accept the Authorized Version or its derivatives, but cling to the Rheims-Douai Version, an English translation made about 1600 directly from the Vulgate—St. Jerome's Latin version of 385-405. This too is now being revised.)

Bible *See also* Bates, Ernest Sutherland.

Bierce, Ambrose 1842-1914(?) Untamed American writer who specialized in realistic fiction with horror sauce. He disappeared into Mexico, at seventy-two, in the wild days of Pancho Villa.

IN THE MIDST OF LIFE. 1898. Among these "tales of soldiers and civilians" are to be found, say the critics, some of the best short stories ever published in the United States.

CAN SUCH THINGS BE? 1893. "Stories of the supernatural, the ghostly or the inexplicable mysterious."

Birrell, Sir Augustine 1850-1933 English statesman and author of graceful essays.

OBITER DICTA. 1884 More Obiter Dicta. 1887. These books established his reputation as critic and humorist. The essays are bright, graceful, and urbane.

Bishop, Elizabeth American poet.

NORTH AND SOUTH. 1946. Called "a distinct literary event," this first book of poems won a substantial prize for which eight hundred poets contended.

Bishop, Morris Gilbert 1893- American professor of romance languages.

CHAMPLAIN; THE LIFE OF FORTITUDE. 1948. "Eminently readable . . . a shining example of how the most scholarly work can be set forth in a manner that appeals to the lay reader."—*Canadian Historical Review.*

Björnson, Björnstjerne 1832-1910 Norwegian novelist and dramatist.

SYNNÖVE SOLBAKKEN (1857), ARNE (1858) (I), AND THE FISHER MAIDEN (1868) (I), are all fresh, wholesome stories of Norwegian peasant life.

THE GAUNTLET (1883) (I), is his best known play and has been called his masterpiece. It deals with the "double standard."

Blackmore, Richard Doddridge   1825-1900   English novelist.

LORNA DOONE. 1869. (I) Thousands of love stories have been written but only one *Lorna Doone*. It has everything—except *contemporaneousness* and *sophistication*.

Blackstone, Sir William   1723-80   English jurist.

COMMENTARIES ON THE LAWS OF ENGLAND. 1765. A curiosity of literature as well as a landmark of English history. "The only lawbook that by its literary quality holds an unquestioned position in English literature. . . . The complacent, often naïve tone of fervent admiration betrays the attitude of an urbane, Tory gentleman of the Eighteenth Century."

Blair, Eric *See* Orwell, George, pseudonym.

Blake, William   1757-1827   English poet, mystic, engraver, illustrator. Few literary figures of the Eighteenth Century are as interesting to modern students. The vogue and the puzzle of Blake continue, and books about him increase in number.

POETICAL WORKS. (I) These fall into two groups: the comparatively simple *Songs of Innocence* and *Songs of Experience*; and the series of *Prophetic Books*, beginning with *The Book of Thel* (1787). Many of the poems are illustrated by his own unearthly engravings.

Blasco-Ibáñez, Vicente   1867-1928   Spanish author of melodramatic novels.

FOUR HORSEMEN OF THE APOCALYPSE. 1918. (II) This immensely popular novel of World War I is most interesting perhaps in its dramatic contrasting of French and German racial psychology under the stress of war.

MARE NOSTRUM. 1919. (II) Tragic tale of a simple and susceptible Spanish sailor who becomes the tool of a female German spy and so aids the German submarines that have slipped into the Mediterranean (Mare Nostrum).

BLOOD AND SAND. 1919. Novel of the bull-ring, depicting the romantic, stylistic horrors which appeal so irresistibly to the Spanish people.

SHADOW OF THE CATHEDRAL. 1919. (II) This novel might be described as a biography of the great church at Toledo. It is also "a powerful indictment of the misrule" of Spanish Catholicism.

Blixen, Baroness K. *See* Dinesen, Isak, pseudonym.

Blodget, Mrs. A. S. *See* Skinner, Cornelia Otis.

Blunden, Edmund C. 1896-   English poet, critic, biographer.

SHELLEY: A LIFE STORY. 1947. "Nowhere else is Shelley's story presented more precisely, more accurately, or more convincingly."—*Saturday Review of Literature.*

LEIGH HUNT AND HIS CIRCLE. 1930. "At once good narrative, good portraits, and good criticism."—*Times* (London).

Boas, Franz   1858-1942   American anthropologist, born in Germany.

ANTHROPOLOGY AND MODERN LIFE. Revised edition, 1938. Valuable for the general reader, this book should have corrosive action on many popular social prejudices.

MIND OF PRIMITIVE MAN. Revised edition, 1938. Study of the influence of heredity, environment, evolution, cultural traits, racial prejudice.

Boccaccio, Giovanni   1313-75   Italian scholar and writer; a great figure of Renaissance Italy; friend of Petrarch and biographer of Dante.

THE DECAMERON. 1353. (I) Collection of 100 tales, many of clerical and feminine guile. They are often humorous and indecent. Chaucer, Shakespeare, Dryden, and Molière borrowed many of the plots. In old age Boccaccio deplored the licentiousness of this, the only book which brought him lasting fame.

Boethius   480(?)-525(?)   Roman philosopher and Aristotelian scholar.

CONSOLATION OF PHILOSOPHY. 525(?) His swan song, written before his execution which was ordered by Theodoric, the emperor he had served. The book was a favorite with scholars during the Middle Ages and later. In it philosophy becomes the handmaid of religion. Alfred the Great translated it and so did Queen Elizabeth. Chaucer paid it the compliment of imitation.

Boileau, Nicolas   1636-1711   French poet and critic. Hopelessly out of date as he is today, one must know something of this Neoclassic, conservative "pope" to understand French literature.

ART OF POETRY. 1674. Didactic poem in which he inculcates the avoidance of modern or national themes and urges adherence to the timeworn inspiration of Greece and Rome.

Boissier, Gaston   1823-1908   French classical scholar, historian and critic.

CICERO AND HIS FRIENDS. 1865. (I)   Roman society, as well as the great advocate himself, is made to live again in this study of Cicero's letters.

Bojer, Johan   1872-   Norwegian novelist.

GREAT HUNGER. 1919. (II)   A moving tale of a Norwegian peasant and the satisfaction of his soul's hunger through suffering. A *Boston Transcript* reviewer declared that this book "comes nearer the dignity and power of Greek drama in its perfection than any other novel I have read since Hardy's *Jude the Obscure.*"

Bok, Edward   1863-1930   American editor. Hogarth's industrious apprentice comes inevitably to mind when one contemplates the career of the Dutch immigrant boy who became the editor and practically the creator of the *Ladies' Home Journal.*

AMERICANIZATION OF EDWARD BOK. 1920. (I and II)   Lord Northcliffe called this "the best autobiography of the time."

Bonnet, Theodore   American author.

THE MUDLARK. 1949.   A dirty little slum urchin in this story wanted to see his queen, Victoria, "the mother of England." So he did. "Quite effortless to read. The courtly, sensitive relationship between Dizzy and his Queen is as Victorian as it is plausible; so too the rivalry between the other councilors and that reckless Highlander, Mr. Brown."—Edward Weeks, in *Atlantic.*

Boothe, Clare (Mrs. Henry R. Luce)   1903-   American actress, journalist, playwright, and member of Congress.

EUROPE IN THE SPRING. 1940. (IV)   A sensitive traveler's harrowing picture of London, Paris, Amsterdam, and Brussels on the eve of catastrophe.

Borgese, Giuseppe Antonio   1882-   Poet and university professor in Italy and the United States. In 1931 he came from Italy to America to escape Fascism.

GOLIATH; THE MARCH OF FASCISM. 1937. (IV)   "History of Italian culture and politics from Dante to Mussolini, portraying the background and rise of modern Fascism."—*Book Review Digest.*

Borrow, George 1803-81 English writer, traveler, philologist.

LAVENGRO. 1851. (I) ROMANY RYE. 1857. (I) Half fiction, half autobiography, these two books are specially fascinating to the reader who yearns for the open road and is curious about gypsies. With one or both of them in his hands he may sit snug in his armchair and enjoy the fun without fear of bad weather, hunger, or police.

BIBLE IN SPAIN. 1843. (I) An account of the five years the author spent in Spain as an agent of the English Bible Society. His travels are interesting, though the Bible is not always in evidence.

Boswell, James 1740-95 Scottish biographer and diarist; exemplar of the Eighteenth-Century Briton.

LIFE OF JOHNSON. 1791-93. (I) This book about the sententious dictionary-maker is generally thought to be the best biography ever written. Macaulay's comment is striking: "Boswell is the first of biographers. He has no second. . . . Many of the greatest men . . . have written biography. Boswell was one of the smallest men who ever lived and he has beaten them all."

LONDON JOURNAL, 1762-63. 1950. "One of the most fascinating and illuminating records of human peculiarity that ever ran down the nib of a pen."—*Saturday Review of Literature.*

Botkin, Benjamin Albert, editor 1901- American folklore specialist.

TREASURY OF AMERICAN FOLKLORE; STORIES, BALLADS AND TRADITIONS OF THE PEOPLE. 1944. (IV) "The general impression one gets is of the sheer lustiness of Americans. Cowboys, bad men, lumberjacks and big Negro laborers rollick through its pages."— *Christian Science Monitor.*

Bourget, Paul 1852-1935 French author.

THE DISCIPLE. 1889. (I) Early psychological novel. The scene is Paris after the Franco-Prussian War, where the author was a member of the "lost generation" of that day, with which he later became impatient. This book is the author's warning to his former godless associates.

Bowen, Catherine Drinker (Mrs. T. M. Downs) 1897- American biographer, usually of musicians or American statesmen.

JOHN ADAMS AND THE AMERICAN REVOLUTION. 1950. "It is a great achievement to have re-created Adams so faithfully, to have re-created the era of the American Revolution."—H. S. Commager.

Bowen, Elizabeth 1899- Anglo-Irish novelist.

DEATH OF THE HEART. 1939 (IV) Distinguished novel in the tradition of Henry James and Proust: her middle-class English family's disharmonies dismay the heroine. "By far her best book and as satisfying a novel as has come out of England in some time."—*The New Yorker.*

IVY GRIPS THE STEPS, AND OTHER STORIES. 1946. "These twelve beautifully written stories . . . are an emphatically successful demonstration of what war did to the mind and spirit of the English people."—*The New Yorker.*

HEAT OF THE DAY. 1949. Novel about London after Dunkirk, and peaceful Ireland. "Miss Bowen at her best."—*Time.*

Bowers, Claude G. 1879- American historian and diplomat.

JEFFERSON AND HAMILTON, THE STRUGGLE FOR AMERICA. 1925. (II) The spirit of that stormy age lives again in these pages.

JEFFERSON IN POWER: THE DEATH STRUGGLE WITH THE FEDERALISTS. 1936. (IV) Covers the eight years of Jefferson's presidency. J. T. Adams considered this Bowers's best book.

YOUNG JEFFERSON: 1743-1789. 1945. (IV) From his birth to his return from Europe to become Washington's Secretary of State.

BEVERIDGE AND THE PROGRESSIVE ERA. 1932. (III) This is really a political history of the United States from the War with Spain till after World War I—till "Progressive" idealism had given place first to the "normalcy" of Harding and then to the laconic respectability of Coolidge.

THE TRAGIC ERA: THE REVOLUTION AFTER LINCOLN. 1929. (IV) Review of the politically scandalous years that followed Lincoln's assassination. Includes a vindication of Andrew Johnson.

Bowman, Peter 1917- American author and mechanical engineer.

BEACH RED. 1945. (IV) Something of a literary curiosity— a war book describing a landing on a Pacific island, with one line to the second, one chapter to the minute. Praised by many reviewers.

Boyd, James 1888-1944 American novelist.

DRUMS. 1925. (II) A novel describing the days of '76 in a Southern colony. Called "the finest novel of the American Revolution which has yet been written." Paul Jones figures prominently in its pages.

MARCHING ON. 1927. (III) A poor boy's adventures in the ranks of the Confederate army and in a Federal prison. An excellent historical novel.

Boyd, Thomas 1898-1935 American writer who won the *Croix de Guerre* as a marine in World War I.

THROUGH THE WHEAT. 1923. (II) Fictional description (written at twenty-three) of the horrors of the trenches. *The Bookman* called it a far truer picture of war than Dos Passos' *Three Soldiers*.

Boyle, Kay 1903- American writer of fiction who has lived much in France.

PLAGUED BY THE NIGHTINGALE. 1931. Her first novel. Provincial France is the scene.

THIRTY STORIES, 1927-46. 1946. "Miss Boyle is a storyteller, a superb one; by and large, the best in the country and one of the best now living. This . . . emerges clearly . . . in this present volume of her collected tales."—Struthers Burt, in *Saturday Review of Literature*.

Boyle, Robert 1627-91 English scientist and theologian. Discoverer of "Boyle's Law" in physics and founder of "Boyle's Lectures" on Christianity.

SKEPTICAL CHYMIST. 1661. He purged British chemistry of alchemy and helped to make it a modern science.

Brace, Gerald Warner   1901-   American novelist.

GARRETSON CHRONICLE. 1947. Pictures the decline of a New England family through three generations. "The quiet, graceful style is admirably suited to this thought-provoking novel; its characters fully and richly conceived."—*Quarterly Booklist.*

Bradford, Gamaliel   1863-1932 This author of what he called psychographs was a New Englander of the eighth generation and almost a lifelong invalid. H. L. Mencken said, "I like these Bradford books. They make dead men seem real to me—and often surprisingly likable."

LEE THE AMERICAN. 1912. (II) Interesting and well-documented study of the great Confederate's personality.

CONFEDERATE PORTRAITS. 1914. (II) Eight Southern soldiers are "psychographed"—and so is the Battle of Gettysburg. A much better job than Matthew Brady could have done.

UNION PORTRAITS. 1916. (II) Similar studies of nine Northern leaders.

PORTRAITS OF AMERICAN WOMEN. 1919. (II) From Abigail Adams to Emily Dickinson, eight subjects are shrewdly and humorously analyzed.

DAMAGED SOULS. 1923. (II) Psychographs of seven more or less imperfect American heroes from Tom Paine to Ben Butler.

AMERICAN PORTRAITS, 1875-1900. 1922. (II) Character studies of nine Americans prominent in the last century. All are as interesting as good fiction, humorous, and of high critical quality.

BARE SOULS. 1924. (II) Some critics consider this the author's best book. Voltaire, Gray, Walpole, Cowper, Lamb, Keats, Flaubert and Fitzgerald are the "souls" studied: all *literary* figures.

DARWIN. 1926. (III) The author concludes that Darwin was "one of the simplest, purest, noblest, most candid, most lovable, most Christian souls that ever lived."

Bradford, Roark   1896-1948 Author, chiefly, of supposedly Negro versions of stories from the Bible.

OL' MAN ADAM AND HIS CHILLUN. 1928. This is the best known of Bradford's yarns, probably because it was the seed from which sprang Marc Connelly's most successful play, *Green Pastures,* 1929.

Bradley, John Hodgdon, Jr. 1898- American geologist.

PARADE OF THE LIVING. 1930. (III) Describes interestingly for the general reader the procession and succession of living creatures that have passed across the face of the earth since the dawn of geological time, leaving their lasting shadows on the rocks. In short, this is an introduction to paleontology.

Brandes, Georg 1842-1927 Danish critic and scholar. "One of the great systematic critics . . . worthy to rank with Sainte-Beuve, Taine and Brunetière."—*New International Encyclopaedia.*

MAIN CURRENTS IN NINETEENTH CENTURY LITERATURE. 6v. 1901-05. (I and II) A monumental work for the scholarly student.

CREATIVE SPIRITS OF THE NINETEENTH CENTURY. 1923. (II) A revision and enlargement of his *Eminent Authors.* . . . He is careful to describe in this masterly analysis the most important and individual characteristics of each writer's work.

Breasted, James H. 1865-1935 American orientalist, archaeologist, and historian.

ANCIENT TIMES. Revised edition, 1935. Textbook by a competent scholar. But it is more than that, for it is delightfully written and profusely illustrated. A book for the general reader.

CONQUEST OF CIVILIZATION. 1926. The story of its development from the Stone Age to the period of Rome's ascendancy.

HISTORY OF EGYPT. Revised edition, 1942. Accords with recent archaeological discoveries.

Bridges, Robert 1844-1930 British poet; Poet Laureate, 1913-30.

POETICAL WORKS. 1936. (II) "Much of his work makes me think of the old Japanese color prints."—Lafcadio Hearn.

TESTAMENT OF BEAUTY. 1926. "A poet's philosophy, calmly, artistically and beautifully expressed."—*Good Reading.*

Brieux, Eugène 1858-1932 French dramatist and social reformer. Member, French Academy.

DAMAGED GOODS. 1901. (II) Created a furor when produced in the United States because of what was then considered its sensationally frank treatment of a sex problem.

RED ROBE. 1900. (II) This play dealing with the abuse of legal power is in France considered Brieux's masterpiece.

Briffault, Robert Stephen   1876-1948   British anthropologist and novelist.

THE MOTHERS; A STUDY OF THE ORIGINS OF SENTIMENTS AND INSTITUTIONS. 3v. 1927. A *tour de force* of scholarship, worthy to rank with Frazer's *Golden Bough.* The author accepts "a matriarchal theory of social evolution."

EUROPA. 1935. "This long novel is a social document. The author has a knowledge of the great forces which bring about the decay of civilizations and he uses it in *Europa* to show in what direction the world is perhaps headed."—*Boston Transcript.*

Brinton, Crane   1898-   American Rhodes Scholar; professor of history at Harvard University.

FROM MANY ONE; THE PROCESS OF POLITICAL INTEGRATION. 1948. The problem of world government. "It will be difficult at best to live sanely in our insecure age. Illusions are . . . dangerous. This is why this little book is an important contribution to the counsels of the nation."—Reinhold Niebuhr, in *Nation.*

IDEAS AND MEN, THE STORY OF WESTERN THOUGHT. 1950. "Only a leisurely reading of this scholarly, sane and stimulating survey can give a really just idea of its vitality, freshness, originality and charm."—Geoffrey Bruun, in *Saturday Review of Literature.*

Brittain, Vera   1893(?)-   English writer.

TESTAMENT OF YOUTH; AN AUTOBIOGRAPHICAL STUDY OF THE YEARS 1900-25. 1933. (III) "This is how it was," she says. A very popular book after the First World War, its message might well be read again and pondered after the Second.

Brogan, Denis W.   1900-   British professor of political science, who has written much on American history and government.

AMERICAN CHARACTER. 1944. (IV) Knowing more about the United States than most Americans, he has written this book to explain to fellow Britons certain American principles and attitudes.

AMERICAN THEMES. 1949. Forty essays from the output of eighteen years. "Essays by a Scotsman who not only is a brilliant

and exciting writer but has taken time and trouble to inform
himself about this country's history and folkways. . . . He makes
observations that are witty, and, most of the time, wise."—*New
Yorker.*

Bromfield, Louis   1896-   American novelist, agriculturist and
cosmopolite.   Member, National Academy of Arts and Letters.

GREEN BAY TREE.   1924.   "Story of life in an American steel
town. . . .   Expression of the author's reaction against the usual
drab presentation of middle western subjects."—F. B. Millet.   The
author's first book, and one of his most successful ones.

POSSESSION.   1925.   (II)   Chronicles the escape of a musical
genius from a middle-west town to New York, Paris, and the world.

EARLY AUTUMN; A STORY OF A LADY.   1926.   (III)   The Puritan repressions that surround her have their way in the end with
the warm-blooded heroine.   Won Pulitzer prize in 1927.

GOOD WOMAN.   1927.   (III)   Story of the tragic results of a
domineering woman's desire for spiritual regeneration—in others.
These four novels all deal with a theme which the author calls
"escape."   It is concerned with the decay of the Puritan tradition
in New England and the rise of western industrialism.

PLEASANT VALLEY.   1945.   (IV)   In part reminiscences of sophisticated life in cities of America, France, and India, and in part
exposition of the author's theories of farming and the blessedness
of American farm life.   This book is "straight from the heart with
no eye on the box office," says the *Saturday Review of Literature.*

Brontë, Charlotte   1816-55   English novelist.

JANE EYRE.   1847.   (I)   The hero is not handsome, the heroine
is a plain-faced governess, the plot is melodramatic; yet this novel,
the author's masterpiece, took England and America by storm a
century ago.

SHIRLEY.   1849.   (I)   The heroine of this novel is an idealized
portrait of the author's strange sister, Emily.   The scene is their
native Yorkshire and its mills, during the riots which flared upon
the introduction of improved machinery.

Brontë, Charlotte; Brontë, Emily; and Brontë, Anne

POEMS BY CURRER, ELLIS AND ACTON BELL. 1846. This first printed book by the three famed sisters will well repay examination. The best poems are from the hand of Emily, the most gifted, least normal, and least prolific of the group.

Brontë, Emily 1818-48 English novelist and poet; sister of Charlotte.

WUTHERING HEIGHTS. 1848. (I) Haunting tale of brutal, frightening horror on the Yorkshire moors. The greatest artistic triumph of that unhappy but gifted family.

Brooke, Rupert 1887-1915 "The ideal image of English youth." —Henry James.

COLLECTED POEMS. 1918. (II) The sonnet sequence "1914" marks the summit of his genius.

Brooks, Van Wyck 1886- Critic and historian of American literature. Member, American Academy of Arts and Letters.

ORDEAL OF MARK TWAIN. 1919. (II) To many this book is a disturbing interpretation of an old favorite, not to be accepted with complacency.

AMERICA'S COMING OF AGE. 1915. (II) In this book the author considers two primal urges in American life—the pursuit of money and the pursuit of culture. He believes he has found in their conflict the explanation for America's alleged aesthetic sterility.

LIFE OF EMERSON. 1932. (III) Straightforward biography: what Emerson did and thought—how he lived.

FLOWERING OF NEW ENGLAND, 1815-1865. 1936. (IV) About the men whose portraits still decorate schoolroom walls throughout the nation: Longfellow, Emerson, Hawthorne, Thoreau, Lowell, etc. Won a Pulitzer prize, 1937, and was designated "the most distinguished non-fiction book of 1936" by the American Booksellers Association. (Vol. 2 of *The Writer in America, 1800-1915.*)

NEW ENGLAND: INDIAN SUMMER, 1865-1915. 1940. (IV) The critics vied with one another in their praise of this book which, among the hundreds of authors considered, highlights four: Henry Adams, Henry James, Parkman, and Howells. (Vol. 4 of *The Writer in America, 1800-1915.*)

WORLD OF WASHINGTON IRVING. 1944. (IV) This title in the series on American literary history covers 1800 to 1840, for the whole United States except New England. (Vol. 1 of *The Writer in America, 1800-1915.*)

TIMES OF MELVILLE AND WHITMAN. 1947. Covers the period from the Forties to the Eighties. "In his treatment of Whitman and Mark Twain Mr. Brooks is at his best and his best is very good indeed. . . . No other historian of American letters has succeeded so brilliantly in giving us the complete history of a literary period." —*Commonweal.* (Vol. 3 of *The Writer in America, 1800-1915.*)*

OPINIONS OF OLIVER ALLSTON. 1941. (IV) The opinions mostly have to do with literature. Allston is a transparent mask for Brooks. "Because this book plumbs the depths and shallows of vital problems, it should be widely, slowly and thoughtfully read."—*Saturday Review of Literature.*

Broun, Heywood   1888-1939   American journalist: an aggressive liberal.

COLLECTED EDITION. 1941. "The best of Broun's essays and other writings. . . . Mirrors vividly a keen mind and a fine soul."—*Good Reading.*

Brown, Harry Peter M'Nab   1917-   American author who served in World War II, part of the time on the staff of *Yank.*

WALK IN THE SUN. 1944. (IV) "This short novel describes a few hours with a few men on a beachhead in Italy. . . . It is very good indeed."—John Hersey.

Brown, Ivor   1891-   English dramatic critic, novelist, essayist.

SHAKESPEARE. 1949. A study of Shakespeare's life and works which provides a compendium of recorded fact and opinion. "One of the sanest and most satisfying books ever written about Shakespeare."—*Manchester Guardian.* "This book will be deservedly popular with the general reader, and the specialist will enjoy quarreling with the author."—*Spectator.*

Brown, John Mason   1900-   American dramatic critic, lecturer, and war correspondent; served in United States Navy, 1942-44.

MANY A WATCHFUL NIGHT. 1944. (IV) Personal account of pre-invasion England and the events up to D-Day, of the landing in Normandy and the subsequent battles.

* The fifth and last volume of *The Writer in America, 1800-1915* is *The Confident Years, 1885-1915.* 1952.

Brown, Lloyd Arnold   1907-   Librarian and cartographer.

STORY OF MAPS. 1949. "This is a work of scholarship, but its biographical method, its style and its subject . . . should make it widely popular."—*Library Journal.* "Adroitly seasoned with drama, the book is logical, balanced and excellently illustrated."—*Quarterly Booklist.*

Browne, Lewis   1897-1949   Jewish author, chiefly of books on religion. He came to America from London at fifteen.

THIS BELIEVING WORLD; A SIMPLE ACCOUNT OF THE GREAT RELIGIONS OF MANKIND. 1926. (III) A scholar's *interesting* story of the evolution and transmission of religious beliefs throughout the world.

Browne, Sir Thomas   1603-82   English physician who was also one of the greatest English prose-writers. He who has read *with enjoyment* the works of this author may consider himself a full-fledged citizen of the Republic of Letters.

RELIGIO MEDICI. 1643. (I) "Profoundly religious meditations, interspersed with a physician's realism. Mellow, sonorous style."— *Good Reading.*

HYDROTAPHIA, OR URN BURIAL. 1658. (I) "A descant on the vanity of human life, based on the discovery of certain cinerary urns in Norfolk."

Brownell, W. C.   1851-1928   Member, American Academy of Arts and Letters. In his lifetime he was often referred to as the dean of American critics, which moved Mencken to allude to him as "the Amherst Aristotle . . . a worthy if somewhat gummy man."

VICTORIAN PROSE MASTERS. 1901. (I and II) A book of information and excellent taste and geniality. His subjects are Thackeray, Carlyle, George Eliot, Arnold, Ruskin, and Meredith.

AMERICAN PROSE MASTERS. 1909. (I and II) Incisive estimates of Cooper, Hawthorne, Emerson, Poe, Lowell, and Henry James.

Browning, Elizabeth Barrett   1806-61   English poet; wife of Robert Browning. Poe declared that she "had done more in poetry than any other woman living or dead."

POETICAL WORKS. 1889. (I) *Sonnets from the Portuguese* (1850) is justly considered her best work. They are not really translations but original love poems addressed to her husband. E. C. Stedman declared them to be the "most exquisite poetry hitherto written by a woman."

AURORA LEIGH (1857), a novel in blank verse, is little read today, though it was praised to the skies by other Victorian writers. *Casa Guidi Windows* (1851) and *Prometheus Bound* (1833)—a translation from Æschylus—are among her best known other works. (See also Besier, R., *The Barretts of Wimpole Street*.)

Browning, Robert 1812-89 British poet; husband of Elizabeth Barrett Browning. "Surely the brawniest neo-Elizabethan Titan whom our age has seen."—J. A. Symonds.

WORKS. (I) Browning's obscurity has been overemphasized and exaggerated. Readers accustomed to modern poetry will encounter so few difficulties that they will wonder what all the fuss was about. Space is lacking in which to list even the more important of Browning's poems, but mention must be made of *The Ring and the Book*, his most famous and most ambitious work.

Bryant, William Cullen 1794-1878 American poet; editor, *New York Evening Post*, 1829-78.

POEMS. (I) His best verse, usually inspired by nature—American nature at first hand—was written in youth, though the thought of mortality is generally present. See especially *Thanatopsis*, *To a Waterfowl*, *The Death of the Flowers*, *The Flood of Years*. His excellent blank verse translations of *The Iliad* and *The Odyssey* were made during his last decade.

Bryce, James (Viscount Bryce) 1838-1922 British author and statesman; ambassador to the United States, 1907-13.

AMERICAN COMMONWEALTH. 1888. (I) In its day this book was easily the best of all descriptions and criticisms of American political and social institutions. It is still historically valuable and indeed is often cited by contemporary writers.

MODERN DEMOCRACIES. 2v. 1921. (II) These descriptions and comparisons of democratic government in the United States, Canada, Australia, New Zealand, France, and Switzerland are still of interest and value to students of democracy.

Buchan, John (Lord Tweedsmuir)   1875-1940   British historian, biographer, novelist; Member of Parliament; Governor-General of Canada.

OLIVER CROMWELL. 1934. (III) Old-fashioned biography at its best: straightforward, full, readable, well documented. Though the portrait is sympathetic, *the wart is still there.*

SIR WALTER SCOTT. 1934. (III) A study of the man and the competently told story of his life; together with a budget of the best modern criticism of his works.

PILGRIM'S WAY; AN ESSAY IN RECOLLECTION. 1940. (IV) A really first-rate autobiography—one of the few in the English language. A readable and important book. The title in England is *Memory Hold the Door.*

Buck, Paul   1899-   American historian.

ROAD TO REUNION: 1865-1900. 1937. (IV) How the United States, riven by the Civil War, became whole again. Awarded Pulitzer prize for history, 1938.

Buck, Pearl (Mrs R. J. Walsh)   1892-   American novelist. Much of her youth was spent in China, close to the Chinese peasants. Awarded Nobel prize, 1938. Member, National Institute of Arts and Letters.

GOOD EARTH. 1931. (III) Masterly revelation of Chinese life and character—strong, simple, elemental. Won Pulitzer prize for fiction, 1932. The best-selling novel in the United States in both 1931 and 1932.

SONS. 1932. (III) A not unworthy sequel to *The Good Earth*; richer in incident and action.

HOUSE DIVIDED. 1935. (III) Concluding novel in the *Good Earth* trilogy. Tells the story of Wang's grandson, who, after his student life in America, returns home to find China rent by revolution.

THE MOTHER. 1934. (III) Story of a daughter of the Chinese soil. The same scriptural rhythms are resorted to again in describing the body, mind, and soul of an elemental human being.

DRAGON SEED. 1942. (IV) Story of China under the Japanese invader. "I doubt if Pearl Buck was ever better than in . . . *Dragon Seed.*"—Edward Weeks in *Atlantic.*

THE PATRIOT. 1939. (IV) A tale of twelve years in the life of a young Chinese: experience with Communists; sojourn in Japan; return to China to fight under the Generalissimo.

FIGHTING ANGEL: PORTRAIT OF A SOUL. 1939. (IV) Admirable and sympathetic account of Mrs. Buck's missionary father—his stalwart faith and indefatigable labors, both in scholarship and evangelism.

Buckle, Henry T. 1821-62 British historian.

HISTORY OF CIVILIZATION IN ENGLAND. 2v. 1857-61. The author argues with boldness and vigor that climate, soil, food, and the aspects of nature are the determining factors in intellectual progress. Though but a fragment of the exhaustive work he did not live to finish, these volumes produced a sensation in Europe and America. The incisiveness of the style and the broad sweep of the generalizations make them still not only readable but well worth reading.

Buley, R. Carlyle 1893- Professor of American history at the University of Indiana.

THE OLD NORTHWEST: PIONEER PERIOD, 1815-40. 2v. 1950. Covers only the Lake States—Ohio to Wisconsin—with emphasis on their social history. Won a Pulitzer prize in 1951.

Bulfinch, Thomas 1796-1867 American mythologist; son of the architect, Charles Bulfinch.

AGE OF FABLE. 1855; revised edition, edited by E. E. Hale, 1862. (I) The beauties of classical mythology, tastefully set forth for both young and old.

AGE OF CHIVALRY. 1858; revised edition, edited by E. E. Hale, 1879. (I) Legends of King Arthur, from the Mabinogion, etc., and tales of Robin Hood, Richard the Lion Heart, the Black Prince, and other British heroes.

Bullen, Frank T. 1857-1915 English sailor and writer of sea tales.

CRUISE OF THE CACHALOT. 1898. A classic story of whale-fishing.

Bulwer-Lytton, Edward *See* Lytton, Edward Bulwer- (Lord Lytton).

**Bunin, Ivan   1870-   Russian poet and novelist.

THE VILLAGE. 1920. Tragic tale of two brothers, with a background of village life under the Czars.

GENTLEMAN FROM SAN FRANCISCO. 1923. It was largely for this book of stories that the author was awarded the Nobel prize.

Bunyan, John   1628-88   British Puritan preacher and author.

PILGRIM'S PROGRESS FROM THIS WORLD TO THAT WHICH IS TO COME. 1678-84. (I) This pious allegory is the most famous of the many books written in prison. No work except the Bible has been so much read by the English peoples and it has been translated into scores of different tongues. Its sincerity, no less than its homely style, has won for it millions of friends, young and old, learned and simple.

GRACE ABOUNDING TO THE CHIEF OF SINNERS. 1666. Autobiographical record of the spiritual experiences which preceded and accompanied the author's conversion.

LIFE AND DEATH OF MR. BADMAN. 1680. The folly of wickedness demonstrated in an allegorical dialog.

Burke, Edmund   1729-97   British statesman, orator and writer. He was friendly to the cause of the rebellious American colonists, but shocked by the excesses of the French Revolution.

ON AMERICAN TAXATION. 1774. (I)

ON CONCILIATION WITH THE AMERICAN COLONIES. 1775. (I) Plea for granting a regulated autonomy to the Colonies as a means of preventing their defection. His speech remains a definitive pronouncement of the principles of colonial government.

REFLECTIONS ON THE REVOLUTION IN FRANCE. 1790. (I) He was an ardent champion of liberty, but it must be a "manly, moral, regulated liberty." The revolutionists in France were demanding the wholesale abolition of old institutions and moral safeguards.

Burman, Ben Lucien   1895-   American author and journalist. "The man who made America river-conscious."

BIG RIVER TO CROSS: MISSISSIPPI LIFE TODAY. 1940. (IV) "Brings Mark Twain up to date. . . . Local stuff at its most ingratiating."—*New Yorker.*

Burnet, Gilbert   1643-1715   British prelate and statesman. Accompanied William III to England in 1688 as his chaplain, and was made a bishop the following year.

History of My Own Times. 1723. The true story of the English Revolution of 1688, as seen by an eye-witness who was an able writer.

Burney, Frances (Madame d'Arblay)   1752-1840   English novelist and diarist; friend of Dr. Johnson; maid-of-honor to Queen Charlotte.

Evelina. 1778. (I)   Cecilia. 1782. (I)   Edmund Gosse sums up Twentieth-Century critical opinion of Miss Burney as follows: "She is a social satirist of a very high order, whose early *Evelina* and *Cecilia* were written with an ease which she afterwards unluckily abandoned for an aping of the pomposity of her favorite lexicographer."

Journal and Letters. 7v. 1742-46 (I) These outpourings are lively, gossipy and full of prejudices. They afford numberless glimpses of great events and small in high places.

Burnham, James   1905-   American professor of philosophy and student of public affairs; a former Marxist.

Managerial Revolution. 1941. (IV) We are, he thinks, in the midst of a social revolution. Power is passing from the capitalists to the *administrators*, both in business and government.

Burns, John Horne   1916-   American teacher; served in the North African and Italian campaigns of World War II.

The Gallery. 1947. A novel about Americans and Italians in Naples in 1944. "He shows the Americans behaving, with a few honorable exceptions, as pitiless conquerors of a hungry and helpless people."—*Library Journal.*

Burns, Robert   1759-96   Scottish poet. He wrote mostly in dialect, like the inspired peasant that he was. It has been said that he had little power of invention but was content to better the work of other men. Even so, in large measure, was Shakespeare.

Works. (I) Even his best lyrical gems and ballads are too numerous to mention separately. Among his longer productions *The Cotter's Saturday Night* and *Tam o' Shanter* are among the most famous.

Burroughs, John 1837-1921 American naturalist and writer.

Accepting the Universe. 1910. (I) Herein, following in Margaret Fuller's footsteps, Burroughs gives the universe a philosophical going-over and finds it good.

Wake-Robin (1871) (I) and Locusts and Wild Honey (1879) (I) are generally listed among his most rewarding titles.

Pepacton. 1881. (I) Papers on such outdoor subjects as springs, and his holiday trip down the Pepacton (Indian name for a branch of the Delaware) in a homemade skiff.

Summit of the Years. 1913. (II) Here the garnered treasure of a lifetime's observation is illumined by the radiance of an old man's mellowed fancy and time-ripened sagacity.

Burt, Maxwell Struthers 1882- American fictionist, with a background of Philadelphia, Princeton, Oxford, and Wyoming.

Interpreter's House. 1924. (II and III) Brilliant, readable and thoughtful story of a New York family.

Delectable Mountains. 1927. (III) Competent, sophisticated, yet wholesome story of modern married life.

Burton, Sir Richard 1821-90 British author, philologist, and explorer of Africa, India, Arabia, Brazil, etc.

Personal Narrative of a Pilgrimage to El Medinah and Mecca. 1855. He went disguised as an Arab. If his identity had been discovered he would have been killed.

He is best known in libraries for his translations of *The Arabian Nights* and *The Lusiad*—Portuguese epic of the poet Camöens. (Burton spoke twenty-nine languages.)

Burton, Robert 1577-1640 English antiquary and monster of classical erudition.

Anatomy of Melancholy. 1621. (I) A curious grab-bag of more or less interesting, seldom useful, but always ancient esoterica. A book often referred to, but seldom read.

Bury, Richard de See Richard de Bury

Bush, Vannevar 1890- Electrical engineer; administrator; president, Carnegie Institution; member, American Academy of Arts and Sciences.

MODERN ARMS AND FREE MEN . . . THE ROLE OF SCIENCE IN PRESERVING DEMOCRACY. 1949. "It is a book which should be read wherever doubts persist and faith falters. It is not an opiate. It is a call to free men to be worthy of their heritage."—*Atlantic*.

Butcher, Harry C. 1901- American radio executive; naval aide to General Eisenhower, 1942-45.

MY THREE YEARS WITH EISENHOWER. 1946. Informal diary of "Ike's" admiring friend. Both personal and military events are recorded. "Consciously written for posterity."—*Library Journal*.

Butcher, Samuel Henry, translator *See* Homer.

Butler, Joseph (Bishop Butler) 1692-1752 English theologian.

ANALOGY OF RELIGION. 1736. (I) Attempt to answer the objections of the Eighteenth Century deists to Christianity. Not easy reading.

Butler, Nicholas Murray 1862-1947 American educator. He lived, learned, taught, and administered at Columbia University from 1882 until his death as President Emeritus.

ACROSS THE BUSY YEARS. 2v. 1939-40. (IV) "Invaluable to the social historian, these memoirs of the great and the prominent are designedly and frankly full-dress."—*New Yorker*.

Butler, Samuel 1612-80 British satirist.

HUDIBRAS. 1663. (I) A mock-epic of knight errantry, satirizing the Puritans with puns, facetious epigrams, and pseudo-theological hair-splitting. Mrs. Browning called Butler "the genius of his class; a natural enemy to poetry under the form of a poet."

Butler, Samuel 1835-1902 English novelist, satirist, and scholar; also a painter, composer, sheep-farmer in Australia, and grandson of a bishop.

WAY OF ALL FLESH. 1903. (I and II) A caustic novel, partly autobiographical, which satirizes the Victorian ikons in general and family relationships in particular. A mordant commentary on the perennial frailties of human nature.

EREWHON. 1872. (I) That is, *Nowhere*; a tale of an Utopia, whence all machines have been cast out, and where to be ill is considered vicious and to be well, virtuous.

NOTE BOOKS. 1912. (II) "Ironic and witty flashes from the mind of an acute thinker. . . . Newcomers to this rich field might read the essay *'Quis Desiderio?'*, describing Butler's troubles in the reading-room of the British Museum."

Butler, Samuel   (1835-1902), translator *See also* Homer.

Butterfield, Roger Place   1907-

AMERICAN PAST. 1947. History of the United States from Concord to Hiroshima, told with the aid of 1000 pictures.

Buxton-Forman, H., editor   *See* Keats, John.

Bynner, Witter   1881-   American poet, interpreter of the Hispano-Indian culture of the Southwest, translator of Chinese poetry.

SELECTED POEMS. 1936. "Impossible to read without being touched by his humanity, his warm openness."

WAY OF LIFE. 1944. "Compact interpretation for Western readers of Taoism, the teaching of Lao-Tsze."—*Good Reading*

Byrd, Richard Evelyn   1888-   American admiral, naval aviator and polar explorer.

SKYWARD. 1928. (III) Interesting account of the author's spectacular career in aviation.

LITTLE AMERICA, AERIAL EXPLORATION IN THE ANTARCTIC; THE FLIGHT TO THE SOUTH POLE. 1930. (III) The book is named after the base camp established on the Ross Ice Barrier.

ALONE. 1938. (IV) Account of his self-imposed isolation at Advance Base in the Antarctic in 1934. "If it took courage to survive the ordeal, it has likewise taken courage to tell about it."

Byrne, Donn   1889-1928   Irish romancer; born in New York and educated in Europe.

MESSER MARCO POLO. 1921. (II) James Branch Cabell called this love story of Marco Polo and the daughter of Kubla Khan "a very magically beautiful book."

BLIND RAFTERY. 1924. (II) Love and springtime in Ireland. "It's a lovely tale with magic in it," says one critic; " 'Tis a masterpiece," says another; "It should be read aloud," says a third.

HANGMAN'S HOUSE. 1926. (IV) Tale of true love in a glamorous Ireland of a generation ago.

Byrnes, James Francis 1879- American Justice of the Supreme Court; "Assistant President"; and Secretary of State.

SPEAKING FRANKLY. 1947. The story of his journeys (1945-46) —77,000 miles "in search of peace." "If there were a prize for the most nationally useful book of the year, the 1947 prize should be awarded without a moment's hesitation to former Secretary of State Byrnes."—*Saturday Review of Literature.*

Byron, George Gordon Noel (Lord Byron) 1788-1824 British poet and eternal rebel. To him all the world was a stage, with himself always cast as the star-crossed hero. Yet Goethe said, shortly after his death, "I never saw true poetical power greater in any man."

POEMS. (I) *Childe Harold* (1812-17) is the poem which made him famous. Its hero is extremely "Byronic." *Don Juan,* begun in 1818, is often called his masterpiece, though a brother poet, Southey, pronounced it "a foul blot on the literature of his country." Among his other important titles are *Manfred* (1817), *A Vision of Judgment* (1822), *The Giaour* (1813), *The Two Foscari* (1821), *The Prisoner of Chillon* (1816), and *Marino Faliero* (1820).

Cabell, James Branch 1879- American romantic novelist and satirist. Gentleman and scholar of Virginia. Mencken called him a lingering survivor of the *ancien régime.* Member, National Institute of Arts and Letters.

RIVET IN GRANDFATHER'S NECK. 1915. (II) Ironical scrutiny of the Old South and its stiff-necked loyalty to its traditions. "Irony is the worm at the root of Cabell's romanticism."

CREAM OF THE JEST. 1917. (II) In this amazing fantasy the story swings between two existences of the hero. He sometimes finds a path of escape from modern banality into an ancient realm of "Old unhappy far-off things and battles long ago."

JURGEN. 1919. (II) "This epic of eroticism is classic in form, romantic in style, and wittily satirical in diction."—Keller. The hero wanders at will among the personages of classical and medieval mythology, to say nothing of the denizens of Heaven and Hell. His adventures are recorded with a phallic candor which caused the book to be banned for a time by the law.

BEYOND LIFE. 1919. (II)   These essays are planks in Cabell's literary platform. Romanticism, he says, is the quality which makes literature durable, while contemporary realism leads to a fade-out.

STRAWS AND PRAYERBOOKS. 1924. More essays expressing a cynic's views on life and art.

Cable, George W.   1844-1925   Author of charming sketches and romances, generally about old Creole life in Louisiana. Member, American Academy of Arts and Letters.

OLD CREOLE DAYS. 1879. (I)   Short stories.

THE GRANDISSIMES. 1880. (I)   New Orleans just after the Louisiana Purchase. Cable's first novel.

DR. SEVIER. 1885. (I)   Story of New Orleans just before the Civil War.

THE CAVALIER. 1901. (I and II)   Very popular story of love and adventure in the South during the Civil War.

Cabot, Richard C.   1868-1939   American physician and sociologist.

WHAT MEN LIVE BY. 1914.   He chooses work, play, love, and worship as the four cornerstones on which to build a good life.

Caesar, Caius Julius   100-44 B.C.   Roman general, statesman, and historian.

COMMENTARIES ON THE GALLIC AND CIVIL WARS. 51 B.C. (I) A general's report to the people back home of his successes in Gaul, Germany, and Britain. Said Cicero, "It is as unadorned as an ancient statue; and it owes its beauty and its grace to its nudity."

Cahan, Abraham   1860-1951   Russian-American novelist and editor.

RISE OF DAVID LEVINSKY. 1917. (II)   A picture of conditions in New York's clothing industry. It has been called the best of all immigrant novels.

Caine, Sir Hall 1853-1931 Sensational British novelist from the Isle of Man. Though derided by the critics, his work was so popular that many of his novels were quickly dramatized and repeated their successes at the box-office.

THE DEEMSTER. 1887. This early product of his talent is characteristically somber and very Manx-y. Dramatized as *Ben-ma'-Chree*.

Calderón de la Barca, Pedro 1600-81 Classic Spanish dramatist and ecclesiastic. He acknowledged writing more than a hundred plays and about as many religious "autos."

WONDERFUL MAGICIAN. (I) Religious drama that suggests *Faust*, on the martyrdom of St. Cyprian and St. Justina.

LIFE IS A DREAM. (I) Selected by President Eliot for inclusion in the *Harvard Classics*.

Caldwell, Erskine 1903- American author of "realistically" earthy novels and short stories, dealing usually with degenerate proletarians of the South.

TOBACCO ROAD. 1932. GOD'S LITTLE ACRE. 1933. "The horror . . . is much more easily detected than the mirth, but such novels . . . are sufficient indications that laughter can arise from an unabashed exhibition of degradation and degeneracy."—F. B. Millet.

YOU HAVE SEEN THEIR FACES. 1937. (IV) Stirring commentary and striking photographs of Southern sharecroppers, black and white. Photographs are by Margaret Bourke-White.

Calvin, John 1509-44 French Protestant reformer whose theological doctrines strongly influenced Puritanism in England and America, as exemplified by Milton, Bunyan, and Jonathan Edwards.

INSTITUTES OF THE CHRISTIAN RELIGION. 1536 (Latin version). 1540 (French version). Widely accepted in the Sixteenth Century as the standard of reformed theology.

Camden, William 1551-1623 English antiquarian, historian and schoolmaster.

BRITANNIA. 1586 (Latin version). 1610 (English version). A survey and description of the British Isles, based upon extensive travels by the author.

Cameron, Mrs. A. C. *See* Bowen, Elizabeth.

Camöens, Luiz Vaz de 1524(?)-1580(?) Portuguese poet.

LUSIAD. 1572. The national epic of Portugal, celebrating chiefly the conquest of the Portuguese East Indies. It was written during the author's banishment to and imprisonment in that part of the world. There have been several English translations, including one by Sir Richard Burton.

Campbell, Thomas 1777-1844 English poet.

POEMS. (I) *Ye Mariners of England* and *The Battle of the Baltic* are said to be unequaled in English for their stirring patriotism. Americans should read *Gertrude of Wyoming*, with its tragic story of murder and ruin in Coleridge's "terrestrial paradise" on the Susquehanna, which Campbell and Coleridge never saw.

Camus, Albert 1913- French journalist, born in Algiers; a leader of the Resistance.

THE STRANGER. 1946. "Reminiscent of Kafka." A clerk in Algiers shoots an Arab and is condemned to die. (Published in England as *The Outsider*.)

THE PLAGUE. 1948. Novel about an epidemic of plague in a modern city. "A first rate novel. . . . A perfect achievement which, despite the unrelieved grimness of the theme, contains great variety, gay humor and stimulating philosophy."—*New Republic*.

Canby, Henry Seidel 1878- American critic. Taught English at Yale; edited literary journals; secretary, National Institute of Arts and Letters.

DEFINITIONS; ESSAYS IN CONTEMPORARY CRITICISM. 2v. 1922-24. (II) Analyses of books and writers. Interesting, and scholarly without heaviness.

CLASSIC AMERICANS . . . WITH SURVEY OF THE COLONIAL BACKGROUND OF OUR NATIONAL LITERATURE. 1931. (III) Analyses, estimates and interpretations of Irving, Cooper, Emerson, Thoreau, Hawthorne, Melville, Poe, and Whitman.

THOREAU. 1939. (IV) "One of the very best of recent literary biographies . . . a book that without any question will remain the standard life for a long time to come."—*New York Herald Tribune*.

WALT WHITMAN, AN AMERICAN. 1943. (IV) "Study of Whitman as artist and personality, and particularly of his grandeur and limitations as a pioneer spokesman of American democracy."—*New Yorker*.

AMERICAN MEMOIR. 1947. "No editor of our time has written so acutely and so vivaciously of those who have worked with him in the literary field. . . . The values, like the humor which glints through these pages, are those of a sane and likable American editor, still candid and unafraid."—Edward Weeks, in *Atlantic*.

Canby, Henry Seidel, editor *See* Thoreau, Henry David.

Canfield, Dorothy *See* Fisher, Dorothy Canfield.

Capek, Karel 1890-1938 Czech dramatist.

R.U.R. 1923. This is the fantastic melodrama which gave the English language a new word: *robot*. *R.U.R.* stands for *Rossum's Universal Robots*, the name of the company which manufactures mechanical men by the millions. As human beings diminish in numbers, the Robots increase. There is a revolt, the Robots take over the world and finally achieve humanity themselves, just as they begin to wear out. (*Robot* derives from the Czech word *robotnik*, meaning serf.)

Capote, Truman 1923- American novelist; born in New Orleans.

OTHER VOICES, OTHER ROOMS. 1948. A curious and decadent novel, chiefly concerned with the abnormal maturing of an adolescent.

Carlson, John Roy, (pseudonym of Arthur Derounian) 1909- Born in Greece; came to the United States in 1921; naturalized in 1926.

UNDER COVER. 1943. (IV) A professional observer's sensational exposure of Fascist activities in the United States during World War II.

Carlyle, Thomas 1795-1881 Scottish man of letters. "The finest appreciation of Carlyle . . . was uttered by an inspired loafer [Whitman] in Camden, New Jersey."—A. T. Quiller-Couch, 1892. "Altogether Gothic. Rugged, mountainous, volcanic, he was himself more a French Revolution than any of his volumes."—Walt Whitman, 1881.

SARTOR RESARTUS (THE TAILOR REPATCHED). 1835. (I) A philosophic and symbolic satire on Man, the clothed animal. Frederic Harrison considered it "the most original, the most characteristic, the deepest and most lyrical of his productions."

FRENCH REVOLUTION. 1837. (I) Dramatic and impressionistic—one of the world's truly great books. But historians tell students that if they wish to see this great event steadily and to see it whole—rather than by flashes of lightning—they had better read this work in connection with another and more commonplace treatment of the subject.

HEROES AND HERO WORSHIP. 1941. (I) This, perhaps, is the book of Carlyle's to begin on. It is easier going than most of his work, yet "displays a mastery of our language as splendid as anything in our prose literature." One wonders: Did Hitler ever read this book? Or did the Nazis work up their enthusiasm for *Der Führer Prinzep* all by themselves?

PAST AND PRESENT. 1843. (I) Here the author contrasts the England of the Twelfth Century with that of the Nineteenth—to the disadvantage of the latter.

OLIVER CROMWELL'S LETTERS AND SPEECHES. 1845. (I) With an elaborate introduction and commentary. In 1884 Froude called this work "by far the most important contribution to English history which has been made in the present century."

FREDERICK THE GREAT. 1858-65. (I) Emerson, surprisingly, declared this to be "infinitely the wittiest book that ever was written." C. K. Adams called it "a work of superlative genius which defies every canon of criticism and sets at nought every rule of historical composition."

Carmer, Carl 1893-   American author; teacher of college English, 1915-27.

STARS FELL ON ALABAMA. 1934. (III) Tales and sketches of life in Alabama. A Northerner's impressions of black and white in the Deep South.

THE HUDSON. 1939. (IV) Collection of Hudson facts and stories of Hudson folk, their lore and ways.

Carpio, Lope Félix de Vega *See* Vega Carpio, Lope Félix de.

Carr, John Dickson 1905-   Anglo-American fictionist.

LIFE OF SIR ARTHUR CONAN DOYLE. 1949. Lively, readable biography of the creator of Sherlock Holmes. Generously illustrated.

Carrel, Alexis 1873-1944 Franco-American biologist. Awarded Nobel prize for surgery in 1912. Originated Carrel-Dakin solution for wound antisepsis.

MAN THE UNKNOWN. 1935. (III) Speculations on the nature and destiny of man. Books by such an author are commonly praised by scientists and ignored by religionists. It has been the other way about with this one. Many have read it to find out why.

Carroll, Gladys Hasty 1904- American novelist, who writes in and of the New England tradition.

AS THE EARTH TURNS. 1933. (III) Unusually competent first novel: the homely and wholesome spectacle of a year on a Maine farm. Written with wisdom and sincerity, out of ample knowledge of place and people.

Carroll, Lewis, (pseudonym of C. L. Dodgson) 1832-98 English mathematician.

ALICE IN WONDERLAND. (1865) and its sequel, THROUGH THE LOOKING-GLASS (1871). (I and II) Professedly children's books, these fairy tales, for three generations, have fascinated human beings of all ages. The original illustrations, by Sir John Tenniel, have never been equaled.

Carryl, Charles Edward 1842-1920 American financier and author of children's books.

DAVY AND THE GOBLIN. 1886. Alice-in-Wonderland type of story for children. It is slowly but steadily achieving recognition as a children's classic.

Cary, Joyce 1888- Anglo-Irish novelist, poet, writer on political science.

TO BE A PILGRIM. 1949. "Mr. Cary weaves some more of his spidery, almost neo-classic prose around a few quietly decadent English gentlefolk. . . . His exploration of the vagaries of an elderly and sick mind is a minor *tour de force.*"—*New Yorker.*

THE HORSE'S MOUTH. 1950. "The best thing of its kind America has imported in forty years."—*New York Times.* "A laughing, scampish novel about a London artist too old to pay his way in Bohemia."—*Atlantic.*

FEARFUL JOY. 1950. Story of the times and of a woman's life in England from birth to old age: social revelation in fictional guise. "Has the usual Cary warmth, charm and high humor, enhanced by excellent writing."—*Library Journal.*

Casanova de Seingalt, Giovanni Jacopo   1725-98   Italian-born European adventurer, great lover, and librarian.

MEMOIRS. 12v. 1826-38. "They are clever, well written and, above all, cynical, and interesting as a trustworthy picture of the morals and manners of the time."—*Encyclopaedia Britannica.*

Castiglione, Count Baldassare de   1478-1529   Distinguished courtier and diplomat in the days of the Italian Renaissance.

THE COURTIER. 1528. (English translation by Hoby, 1561 and 1900.) Treatise, in dialog, on the qualities and ideals of a gentleman. The characteristics considered include his dress, bearing, amusements, conversation, behavior, ethics, culture, etc.

Cather, Willa Sibert   1875-1947   American novelist. Born in Virginia, reared and educated in Nebraska. Then came newspaper work and teaching in Pennsylvania, followed by editing (*McClure's Magazine*) in New York. Member, American Academy of Arts and Letters. "Her heroines are among the most convincing women in the entire range of American fiction."—Carl Van Doren.

O PIONEERS. 1913. (II) Powerful yet simple novel, telling of the settlement of Nebraska by Swedes, French and Bohemians.

SONG OF THE LARK. 1915. (II) This novel tells in detailed, leisurely fashion the life story of a poor young girl who became an opera star.

MY ANTONIA. 1918. (II) This unforgettable story of a Bohemian immigrant girl is often spoken of as Miss Cather's masterpiece. H. L. Mencken says that it is "a great deal more than simply a good novel. It is a document in the history of American literature. . . . No *romantic* novel ever written in America, by man or woman, is one half so beautiful."

ONE OF OURS. 1922. (II) A war novel which won the Pulitzer prize in 1923. The early chapters, describing the hero's boyhood on the broad Nebraska prairie, are more convincing than the later ones which deal with his ordeal by battle on the fields of France.

Lost Lady. 1923. (II) The theme of this book is the moral disintegration of a lovable woman. H. S. Canby says that though it is "the slenderest of Miss Cather's novels, it is also, I think, the most perfect."

Professor's House. 1925. (II) The professor built a new house only to find that his heart remained behind in the old one with his youth, and the memories of his happier though less prosperous early career.

Death Comes for the Archbishop. 1927. (III) Beautiful story of two French priests—true men of God—who journeyed to the New Mexican wilderness over a century ago, won the loving reverence of Spanish, Indians, and Americans through their faith and works, and built a cathedral. Spirit and color of the sun-drenched Southwest are rendered with truth and vividness.

Shadows on the Rock. 1931. (III) Here is Quebec in the days of Frontenac; but with no bold, strong rendering of the high lights and black depths of character. The "shadows" are delicate, pastel shades. What Miss Cather has chosen to do, however, she has done very beautifully.

Obscure Destinies. 1932. (III) Three masterly long short stories of the West.

Sapphira and the Slave Girl. 1940. (III) Virginia before the Civil War. "One finds in this novel that delicate yet powerful art of brief and significant narrative, where all that is needed is included and all that is needless is left out. It is the French art of the *nouvelle*. . . ."—H. S. Canby.

Catullus, Caius Valerius   87-54 B.C.   Roman lyric poet.

Poems; translated by Francis Cornish for the Loeb Library. (I) For Catullus the virile Latin tongue assumes a truly Grecian sweetness, grace and melody.

Cecil, Lord David   1902-   English critic who has specialized in the Victorian age of English literature.

Hardy the Novelist. 1946. "Vividly painted and subtle portrait of a great artist in fiction."—*Yale Review*.

Poets and Story-tellers; a Book of Critical Essays. 1949. "Eight critical essays by one of the most sensitive, as well as sensible, literary critics of our day, who follows faithfully the dictum of Hazlitt that genuine criticism should . . . reflect the colors, the light and shade, the soul and body of a work."—*New Yorker*.

Two Quiet Lives; Dorothy Osborne and Thomas Gray. 1948. (Dorothy Osborne was the wife of Sir William Temple.) "This is the kind of book that the English do so brilliantly well: literary biography that is factually impeccable . . . and at the same time gracious, warming and truly illuminating—so that reading is like listening to superb and friendly conversation."—*Catholic World.*

Cellini, Benvenuto   1500-71   Italian sculptor and worker in precious metals.

Autobiography.   Written, 1558-62; printed, 1730;   best English version is that by J. A. Symonds, 1887.   (I)   This frank revelation of the life and deeds of a wicked superman in the golden days of the Italian Renaissance is one of the world's great autobiographies.

Cervantes Saavedra, Miguel de   1547-1616   Spanish novelist and soldier.

Adventures of Don Quixote.   1605-15.   (I)   This book, which has been called the greatest comic novel ever written, laughed away the outworn convention of chivalry's knights errant.   The poor Don, mad from reading romances, sallies forth to tilt at windmills, slay giants, rescue maidens in distress, etc.   By these fantastic attempts at knightly service he brings ludicrous mischances upon the heads of himself and his bumpkin squire.

There have been ten or a dozen English translations since that of Shelton (1612-20).   The latest one is probably the best of all— that by the late Samuel Putnam, published in 1949.

Chamberlain, John Rensselaer   1903-   American author, editor and critic.

American Stakes.   1940.   (III)   A liberal's essays on American problems in politics and economics.   Conservative reviewers compliment him on his sanity, fairness, and good humor.

Chamberlin, William Henry   1897-   American newspaper correspondent who spent seven years in Russia.   His wife is a native Russian.

Russian Revolution, 1917-1921, 2v. 1935.   (III)   A sound, fair, full history, with ample documentation and bibliography.   It is not hard reading.

Chambers, Sir E. K. 1866- British essayist and critic.

WILLIAM SHAKESPEARE: A STUDY OF FACTS AND PROBLEMS. 1930. (Abridged by C. Williams and called *A Short Life of Shakespeare.* 1933.)

SHAKESPEARE: A SURVEY. 1925 (Reissued, 1951). Essays, written 1904-08, as prefaces to the plays.

Chambers, Robert W. 1865-1933 Prolific and popular American novelist. His best book was probably

CARDIGAN. 1901. (II) Romance of the American Revolution: the Mohawk Valley, Pittsburgh, and Lexington.

Chambers, Whittaker, translator *See* Salten, Felix.

Channing, Edward 1856-1931 Professor of history at Harvard University.

HISTORY OF THE UNITED STATES. 8v. 1905-26. (II) Comprehensive work covering the social as well as the political and military aspects. "Not only an admirable specimen of historical scholarship, but a successful effort to present the results of research in an attractive form."—*American Historical Review.*

Chanson de Roland. 11th Century. (I) This is the most famous of the *chansons de geste,* written by the *trouvéres* of northern France and chanted by minstrels or *jongleurs.* English chroniclers state that it was sung at the Battle of Hastings (1066). The epic of about 6000 lines tells the story of the fight and death of Roland at the Pyrenean pass of Roncesvalles. Good English translations are those by A. S. Way (1913) and Leonard Bacon (1914). The perhaps legendary hero is supposed to have been a champion, and perhaps nephew, of the Emperor Charlemagne. (See also *Orlando Furioso,* by Ariosto.)

Chapman, F. S. 1907- English lieutenant-colonel in World War II.

THE JUNGLE IS NEUTRAL. 1949. For three years, cut off from the outside world, Chapman lived in the Malay jungle, as an irregular fighter behind the Japanese lines. "Scholar, scientist, and biographer, he has produced a splendid book of war and travel." —*Manchester Guardian.*

Chapman, George, translator   *See* Homer.

Chapman, John Jay   1862-1933   American man of letters, crusader, and "aristophile." To guide his pen he framed the homely maxim: "What don't bite ain't right."

JOHN JAY CHAPMAN AND HIS LETTERS; edited by M. A. De Wolfe Howe. 1937. (IV) "Whoever misses this biography loses hours of enjoyment. . . . Don't do it, even if you think biography does not interest you. This one will."—*Boston Transcript.*

Chapman, Maristan   1895-   The pen name of Mr. and Mrs. J. S. H. Chapman, who have written many stories of the Southern hill people.

HAPPY MOUNTAIN. 1927. (III) A hill boy goes forth to see men and cities and seek his fortune in the big world "far 'n' beyond." He returns when the right time comes. A dialect story—and a good one.

Charnwood, Lord (Godfrey Rathbone Benson)   1864-1925   English biographer.

ABRAHAM LINCOLN. 1916. (I and II) Many consider this attempt by an English author to portray the Great American the most successful interpretation of his character achieved up to the time of its publication.

Chase, Mary Ellen   1887-   American novelist and teacher of college English. She can boast a fine heritage from her forebears —hardy sailors and farmers of the state of Maine.

MARY PETERS. 1934. (III) Beautifully written novel about a woman of Maine whose childhood was spent aboard a sailing-vessel trading to far places. Maturity brought anxiety and sorrow and loneliness—but also serenity, in a Maine village.

GOODLY FELLOWSHIP. 1939. (IV) These autobiographical chapters recount experiences from Maine to Montana, chiefly as a teacher of English. It is an inspiring book.

WINDSWEPT. 1941. (IV) Story of three generations (1880-1939) of the Marston family in their big stone house on the Maine coast. Full of courage and vitality, this is probably Miss Chase's finest novel.

BIBLE AND THE COMMON READER. 1942. An interesting, inspiring and informing introduction to the Bible as rewarding literature.

Chase, Stuart 1888- Prolific author of books that deal as a rule with American public affairs. He says, "Fun for me is economic research and writing about it."

YOUR MONEY'S WORTH; A STUDY OF THE WASTE OF THE CONSUMER'S DOLLAR. 1927. (III) About costs and prices. How they are affected by advertising, adulteration, competition, etc.

MEN AND MACHINES. 1929. (III) A casting up of accounts between Man and the man-made Monsters who serve him and are served by him: what the latter have done for their creator: what they have done to him.

MEXICO; A STUDY OF TWO AMERICAS. 1931. (III) A comparison of ways of life in Tepoztlan, a Mexican village, and in "Middletown," typical American community. One exemplifies the age of handicraft, the other the age of the machine.

RICH LAND, POOR LAND; A STUDY OF WASTE IN THE NATURAL RESOURCES OF AMERICA. 1936. (IV) Profoundly disturbing book on the disastrous effects of erosion by wind and water. "A grand book by a man who knows what he is talking about."—*Forum.*

PROPER STUDY OF MANKIND; AN INQUIRY INTO SCIENCE OF HUMAN RELATIONS. 1948. Critics describe this as "perhaps his most important book," and say that "it may be one of the most influential books of the decade."

Chatrian, Alexandre, joint author *See* Erckmann, Émile.

Chaucer, Geoffrey 1340-1400 English poet: called the Father of English Poetry. The greatest literary figure of his age. London's Middle English dialect, in which he wrote, became the basis of the English tongue we know today. He was a prolific writer during most of his life, at first under the influence of Froissart and other French authors; then for a time he followed Boccaccio; and finally came his truly English period during which, with the *Canterbury Tales* at least, he far surpassed his former models. Through all his works, as Coleridge says, "there reigns a cheerfulness, a manly hilarity, which makes it almost impossible to doubt a correspondent habit of feeling in the author himself."

CANTERBURY TALES. 1386-1400. "Masterpieces of narrative art, revealing the author's close observation of men and women, his delight in the process, his ready human sympathy, and his elusive humor."—Keller.

Of the *Tales* read first the *Prologue, Knight's Tale, Clerk's Tale,* and *Pardoner's Tale.* Of Chaucer's other works those perhaps most deserving attention are *Troilus and Cressida, Legend of Good Women, Boece* (translation of Boethius, *q.v.*), and *House of Fame.* If the poet's archaisms are found too troublesome the reader may have recourse to the *Modern Reader's Chaucer,* published by Macmillan.

Chekhov, Anton 1860-1904 Russian dramatist and fictionist. His stories, packed with irony, pathos, or humor, or sometimes with all three, are masterpieces of concentrated narrative. His slow-paced plays are full of realism, and of a timeless truth to humanity.

CHERRY ORCHARD. 1903. (I and II) This, his last and best play, is a tragicomic picture of the passing of the old order of Russian aristocracy.

UNCLE VANYA. 1912. (I and II) Published with *Ivanoff, The Sea-Gull,* and *The Swan Song*—all translated by Marian Fell. They are tragedies of the pre-Revolution upper classes, a prey to the boredom which was the accompaniment of their idle, fatuous lives.

LITTLE DARLING AND OTHER STORIES. (I and II) All these stories are about women. None of them is happy and only a few are nice.

THE BISHOP AND OTHER STORIES. 1919. (II) Here is social history made easy. "There is almost magic in the way he contrives to draw a picture in a few seemingly simple lines. He is never tiresome."—M. J. Olgin.

LETTERS TO HIS FAMILY AND FRIENDS. 1920. (I and II) "Illustrate various phases of his life and character, and present fascinating scenes of Russian life."—*A.L.A. Catalog,* 1926.

There are good collections of Chekhov's best writings in some of the series of reprints, for example, *The Portable Chekhov,* published by Viking in 1947.

Cheney, Sheldon 1886- American exponent of art and the theatre. His emphasis is on the modern in both fields.

NEW WORLD ARCHITECTURE, WITH 389 ILLUSTRATIONS. 1930. (III) Sympathetic interpretation with decided stress on the first word in the title. Sullivan and Wright might be called his heroes.

WORLD HISTORY OF ART. 1947. All-inclusive; copiously illustrated. "There is a freshness and vividness about the whole book that are characteristic of a task done for the first time."—*New York Times.*

STORY OF MODERN ART. Revised and enlarged edition. 1945. This book is double-starred in the *Standard Catalog,* 1949.

Chesterfield, Earl of (Philip Dormer Stanhope) 1694-1773 English politician and aristocratic worldling.

LETTERS TO HIS SON. 1774. (I) With their painstaking instruction on manners, and hints on "uniting wickedness with the graces," they mirror the lax morality of the time with taste and gentility. Dickens is said, however, to have maligned Chesterfield in his portrait of the villainous Mr. Chester in *Barnaby Rudge.*

Chesterton, Gilbert K. 1874-1936 Prolific British author who was journalist, dramatist, poet, novelist, and critic; Prince of Paradox; zealous Catholic and medievalist; to say nothing of being a physical reincarnation of Jack Falstaff.

HERETICS. 1905. (I and II) The worth-while ones, like Kipling, Shaw, Wells, George Moore and G. Lowes Dickinson, he tells us, are really orthodox—though each in his own way.

ORTHODOXY. 1908. (I and II) Definite convictions and a serious theory of the universe, as every good Catholic knows, are essential to a sane and happy life.

CHARLES DICKENS, A CRITICAL STUDY. 1906. (I and II) "Characteristically frolicsome"; suggestive, appreciative, brilliant, illuminating and entertaining; "the very last book one would go to sleep over."

VICTORIAN AGE IN ENGLISH LITERATURE. 1913. (I and II) "Sane and refreshing, as well as brilliant."—*The Independent.*

AUTOBIOGRAPHY. 1936 and 1939. (IV) "The mind behind this book must be praised. It is one of the most attractive minds of our time, and this book is one of its completest expressions."—Mark Van Doren.

THE MAN WHO WAS CHESTERTON; edited by R. T. Bond. 1937. "The best of the laughing philosopher's essays and a selection of his verse."—*English Library.*

Childs, Marquis W. 1903- American correspondent and author of political and economic best-sellers.

SWEDEN: THE MIDDLE WAY. 1936 and 3rd ed., 1947. (IV) How limited socialism works in Sweden.

Christensen, E. O. 1890- Director of the Index, housed in the National Gallery of Art in Washington.

INDEX OF AMERICAN DESIGN. 1950. The Index is a tremendously valuable cultural stock-pile of the American people. It originated in a Federal Art project of the WPA. "A picture book of great charm."—*Saturday Review of Literature.*

"The range and scope of the book are remarkable. . . . An important step in the understanding of American culture."—*New York Times.*

"This superb book brings together in one binding the folk-art heritage of our country."—*School Arts.*

Churchill, Winston 1871-1947 American novelist. His earlier books, based on a colorful background of history, are his most successful ones. His later stories, dealing with political, economic or social themes, though written with the best intentions and founded on personal observation and experience, failed to gain much favor.

RICHARD CARVEL. 1899. (I) A story with a quite credible and well-characterized hero, of the days before and during the American Revolution.

THE CRISIS. 1901. (I) Excellent story of the Civil War, with well-drawn characters and many dramatic situations.

THE CROSSING. 1904. (I) Describes the beginning of the Western migration. Hero is a drummer-boy with George Rogers Clark's expedition against the British, in the later years of the Revolution.

Churchill, Winston Spencer 1874- British statesman, whose mother was an American. After Munich (1940), England called Churchill at sixty-six to head the Government. The rest is history. He saved England and the world from the impending catastrophe, only to be retired from office when the fighting—for a time—was over.

WORLD CRISIS. 3v. 1923-29. Resumé of World War I.

MARLBOROUGH, HIS LIFE AND TIMES. 6v. 1933-38 (II) This life of the great Duke (1650-1722) is an example of biography on a grand scale. Its author, a descendant of the Duke, has inherited many of the latter's superb qualities without his defects. Moreover, Churchill's long and vigorous life as student of history, author, soldier and statesman, has furnished him with extraordinarily complete equipment for undertaking this particular task.

BLOOD, SWEAT AND TEARS. 1941. (IV) Speeches of the Prime Minister during the terrible days from May 1938, to February 1941. "This is the voice of a great leader and a great fighter for democracy, standing alone in one of the greatest crises in the history of the world."—Walter Millis. "Churchill has earned the right to be called the best public speaker in the world today."—*New Republic.*

THE GATHERING STORM. 1948. (Vol. 1 of *Second World War.*) "How the English-speaking peoples through their unwisdom, carelessness and good nature allowed the wicked to re-arm."

THEIR FINEST HOUR. 1949. (Vol. 2 of *Second World War.*) "Because the British people had faith in themselves their darkest hour became their finest. And in Winston Churchill they found not only the leader they deserved but a chronicler worthy of their deeds."—*Nation.* *Their Finest Hour* is written with simplicity and gusto. But when the great phrase is needed Churchill has it. . . . This book is history. It is also adventure—adventure for a man, a nation and a way of life."—Drew Middleton, in *New York Times.*

GRAND ALLIANCE. 1950. (Vol. 3 of *Second World War.*) "If anything, more absorbing than its predecessors. . . . The reader will find in these pages an abundance of fascinating disclosures." —*Atlantic.* "It is, of course, wonderful stuff—a masterly piece of historical writing, rich, savory, and complete with humor and wit." —*New Yorker.*

HINGE OF FATE. 1950. (Vol. 4 of *Second World War.*) Covers the period from January 1942 to May 1943. "One of the major pieces of writing of our time."—Crane Brinton, in *Saturday Review of Literature.* "A superlative book. No memoirs by generals, or politicians, no studies of battles or conferences are in the same class."—Drew Middleton, in *New York Times.*

Chute, Marchette Gaylord   1909-

GEOFFREY CHAUCER OF ENGLAND. 1946. Biography and criticism. "Miss Chute has analyzed Chaucer's writings with understanding."—*Library Journal.* "Its readers will be eager to read Chaucer."—*Yale Review.*

SHAKESPEARE OF LONDON. 1950. Based entirely on contemporary evidence. "Excellent book about Shakespeare—clear, interesting, reliable, every page bearing evidence to her competence and care."—*Nation.*

Cibber, Colley   1671-1757   Actor and dramatist; Poet Laureate.

APOLOGY FOR HIS LIFE. 1740. Brander Matthews declared this autobiography one of the best books ever written about the stage. Full of good-humored personal gossip about Mrs. Oldfield, Mrs. Bracegirdle, Betterton, and the other luminaries of the London stage in its colorful post-Restoration days.

Cicero, Marcus Tullius   106-43 B.C.   Roman orator, man of letters, statesman.

WORKS. (I) Of the orations among the most famous are those against Catiline, against Verres, and against Mark Antony. Of the essays, mostly philosophical, see those on friendship, old age, rhetoric, oratory, the nature of the gods. For Cicero, the letter-writer, see Boissier's *Cicero and His Friends,* which is based upon his letters, especially those to Atticus, Caelius, Julius Caesar, Brutus, and Octavius.

Clarendon, Earl of (Edward Hyde)   1609-74   English statesman and historian. Adviser of Charles I during the Civil War; Lord Chancellor of England, 1660-67; impeached and banished by Parliament, 1667.

HISTORY OF THE REBELLION. 1702-04. "It is his great distinction that, living in an age of pedants, he had the courage to write history . . . in a spirit of complete simplicity. The diction . . . is curiously modern; we may read pages of his great book without lighting upon a single word now no longer in use."— Sir Edmund Gosse.

Clark, Walter Van Tilburg 1909-   American novelist, born in Maine, but reared and educated in Nevada.

Ox-Bow Incident. 1940. (IV) This first novel is a rousing tale of the cattle country in the Eighties. There are rustlers and a lynching. But the characters are not mere appendages to shooting-irons. They seem real people.

Claudel, Paul 1868-   French poet, dramatist, diplomat, Catholic mystic.

Tidings Brought to Mary. 1916. Reverent and beautiful miracle play which attracted world-wide attention.

Clemens, Samuel L. (Mark Twain) 1835-1910   Born in Missouri; became pilot on the Mississippi (1857); went to Nevada (1861); in San Francisco (1865); Sandwich Islands (1866); Europe and the Near East (1867); married (1870); thereafter lived in or not very far from New York, with long sojourns in Europe.

Huckleberry Finn. 1884. (I) Undoubtedly Mark Twain's masterpiece. This tale of pioneer life on the Mississippi had by mid-century delighted three generations of Americans of all ages. Some critics say it is the best book written by an American.

Tom Sawyer. 1876. (I) Preceded its sequel, *Huckleberry Finn*, by eight years. It is a story with more plot and excitement but far less charm and substance than the picaresque sequel.

Innocents Abroad. 1869. (I) Describes humorously and brashly an excursion with a boatload of conventional Christians to Europe, the Holy Land, and Egypt.

Roughing It. 1872. (I) Covers his trip, in pioneer days, to the mining-camps of Nevada; life in those frenzied camps; San Francisco and an earthquake; and finally the voyage to and life in the Hawaiian Islands.

Life on the Mississippi. 1883. (I) In these recollections of his early years on the river as a pilot he records an epoch in the country's growth which has passed into history. The second half of the book—written twenty years after the first—is largely filler material, much less interesting than the first part.

PRINCE AND THE PAUPER. 1882. (I) Prince Edward of England and Tom Canty, the beggar-boy, look very much alike. The story tells how, just for fun, they change clothes, and what happens thereafter.

CONNECTICUT YANKEE AT KING ARTHUR'S COURT. 1889. Satirical romance. It recounts the adventures of a Nineteenth-Century American who, after a blow on the head, finds himself back in the days of medieval chivalry. The knights are of course no less shocked and astonished at his ignorance of court life and his knowledge of modern gadgets, than he is with them and their, to him, nonsensical, highfalutin ways, and their deplorable ignorance.

MYSTERIOUS STRANGER. 1916. (II) The pessimism that, after many bereavements, darkened the old jester's later years, is poured forth in this devastating satire on the weakness and stupidity of the human race and on the futility of human existence. It could never have been published during the lifetime of his beloved wife.

MARK TWAIN'S AUTOBIOGRAPHY. 2v. 1924. (II) A hodgepodge that is also a great book, for it is full of fine things—vivid flashes emanating from an extraordinary personality.

MARK TWAIN'S LETTERS. 2v. 1917. (II) His admirers will find endless pleasure in these letters, edited by his devoted friend and biographer, Albert Bigelow Paine.

PERSONAL RECOLLECTIONS OF JOAN OF ARC. 1896. (I) The author's most serious and conscientious work. He had unbounded reverence and admiration for Joan—"the most noble life that was ever born into this world"—and her story was probably the only subject he treated with which he took no liberties.

Clendening, Logan　　1884-1945　　American physician and teacher of medicine.

HUMAN BODY. 4th edition, 1945. (III) A book about the human body in health and disease that is up-to-date, reliable, outspoken, and not at all solemn and preachy. It may have caused some restlessness in Victorian graveyards.

Clodd, Edward　　1840-1930　　British scientist.

STORY OF THE ALPHABET. New edition, 1938. Able book on a subject of interest to every reader.

Cobb, Humphrey 1899- American author and soldier in World War I.

PATHS OF GLORY. 1935. (III) About a French regiment in World War I. The story scored a real success, not only as anti-war propaganda and as a thrilling tale, but as literature.

Cobb, Irvin S. 1876-1944 American humorist.

OLD JUDGE PRIEST. 1915. (II) His stories about the wise old Kentucky judge are probably his best—very human and very American.

Cobbett, William (Peter Porcupine, pseudonym) 1766-1835 British political journalist.

RURAL RIDES. 1830. Describes political tours on horseback through the English countryside. "A vivid picture of the life of a certain stratum of society at a particular epoch. . . . It is one of the best examples of the use of terse, vigorous, direct and unadorned Anglo-Saxon which the language has to show."

Coffin, Robert Peter Tristram 1892- American author. His reputation is based on his poetry, even as his poetry is based on the rock-ribbed state of Maine, its folk and their ways.

COLLECTED POEMS. 1939. Contains *Strange Holiness* (1935), which was awarded Pulitzer prize for 1936.

Cohen, Morris R. 1880-1947 Revered teacher of philosophy at City College, New York, who began life as the son of Russian-Jewish immigrants.

A DREAMER'S JOURNEY. 1949. "The book not only gives insight into the making of a significant mind; it also gives another deep glimpse into the makings of America. It joins Jacob Riis' *Making of an American*, Booker Washington's *Up from Slavery*, and Mary Antin's *Promised Land*."—Felix Frankfurter, in *New York Times*.

Coit, Margaret L. 1919-

JOHN C. CALHOUN: AN AMERICAN PORTRAIT. 1950. Pulitzer prize biography. "A brilliant achievement, scholarly and at the same time a work of art steeped in charm, an important contribution to history, a new illumination of a great career."—Claude G. Bowers, in *New York Times*.

Coleridge, Samuel Taylor   1772-1834   British poet, critic, philosopher.

Works. (I) "All that he did excellently might be bound up in twenty pages, but it should be bound in pure gold." In these pages would certainly be found his three great poems: *Rime of the Ancient Mariner, Kubla Khan* and *Christabel.* His *Lectures on Shakespeare* laid the foundations of modern Shakespeare criticism; *Biographia Literaria*—a loose-knit miscellany—autobiographical, philosophical and literary—enriched English criticism with some fundamental principles and judgments.

Colette (Sidonie Gabrielle Claudine Colette)   1873-   French novelist. Called "the outstanding living French novelist" and, by Paul Claudel, "the greatest living writer" in France. President of the Goncourt Academy. Among her best novels, most of which are analytical studies of women, are

The Vagrant. 1910.

Chéri. 1929.

Gentle Libertine. 1931.

Last of Chéri. 1932.

Collins, Wilkie   1824-89   Earliest English writer of first-rate mystery stories.

Woman in White. 1860. (I) and The Moonstone. 1868. (I) These are his best books. The plot of the latter has been called the best ever contrived. Though excellent at plots, Collins was rather weak in character delineation.

Colum, Padraic   1881-   Irish poet, dramatist, novelist. A founder of the Irish National Theatre. He has lived mostly in the United States since 1914.

King of Ireland's Son. 1916. (II) Fairy story, telling how the prince wooed the wizard's daughter. "A book of uncommon beauty."

Road Round Ireland. 1933. (III) There are cabinet officers and facts in this book, but there are also legends and farmers and vagabonds and poets.

Poems. 1932. The reader who has his doubts about this "Celtic witchery" and wants to keep them, had better steer clear of this book

Commager, Henry S.   1902-

AMERICAN MIND; AN INTERPRETATION OF AMERICAN THOUGHT AND CHARACTER SINCE THE EIGHTIES. 1950. A series of critical essays on individual American writers and thinkers. (Supplements "Parrington," *q.v.*) "Extremely good."—*New York Herald Tribune.* "A rich and brilliant book."—A. M. Schlesinger, Jr., in *Nation.*

Commager, Henry S.   1902-   and **Nevins, Allan   1890-**   editors.
Both Americans, Commager is a historian and professor of history at Columbia, as is Nevins, who is also a member of the National Institute of Arts and Letters.

HERITAGE OF AMERICA. 1939. (IV) Collection of 252 original documents making plain what America is and has been about. Their range is from Leif Ericson to Franklin Roosevelt. These documents abound in human interest and are very readable.

SHORT HISTORY OF THE UNITED STATES. 1945. "Historians of the first rank have written a book for the layman, designed to meet the need for a compact narrative."—*Good Reading.*

Compton-Burnett, Ivy   1892-   English novelist. "Our English cousins across the sea have every reason to be proud of the writing of Ivy Compton-Burnett."—*Saturday Review of Literature.*

BULLIVANT AND THE LAMBS. 1948. Ironical novel of family life in England in the Nineties.

TWO WORLDS AND THEIR WAYS. 1949. The two worlds are those of home and school in England half a century ago. "This latest novel . . . is superior to *Bullivant and the Lambs*, if that is possible."—*Saturday Review of Literature.*

Comte, Auguste   1798-1857   French philosopher.

POSITIVE PHILOSOPHY. 1839-42. (I) Comte's positivism is an attempt to apply the methods and findings of science, not only to philosophy, but also to social science and even to religion, hoping thereby to achieve social reform. The doctrine of this socio-ethical religion is epitomized in the principle *vivre pour autrui*—to live for others.

Conant, James Bryant 1893- American chemist; President of Harvard, 1933-

ON UNDERSTANDING SCIENCE; AN HISTORICAL APPROACH. 1947. "A stimulating contribution to the difficult problem of how science can best be assimilated into the cultural pattern; deserves to be read widely by teachers and laymen alike."—*Chemical and Engineering News.*

Confucius 550-478 **B.C.** Chinese philosopher and formulator of maxims to govern conduct. He was one of the greatest men who ever lived for, like Jesus, Buddha, and Mohammed, he has influenced through centuries the lives of *billions* of his fellowmen. The scriptures of Confucianism are composed of the so-called *Nine Classics.* Of these, *The Book of Spring and Autumn* is the one most generally attributed to the Master. But it is the *Analects* which is probably the best known. This consists of the digested conversations of Confucius and is composed chiefly of his sayings; for example, "What you do not like when done to yourself do not do to others."

WISDOM OF CONFUCIUS; edited and translated with notes by Lin Yutang. 1943.

Congreve, William 1670-1729 English dramatist.

SELECTED WORKS. These plays reflect the manners of Restoration England like hard, polished, glittering mirrors; and very naughty manners they were. There is general agreement that *The Way of the World* is Congreve's best play. Swinburne called it "The unequaled and unapproached masterpiece of English comedy." *The Mourning Bride, The Old Bachelor,* and *The Double Dealer* have also been lavishly praised.

Connelly, Marc 1890- American playwright, much of whose writing has been in collaboration with George Kaufman. His most successful play, which won him a Pulitzer prize in 1930, is

GREEN PASTURES; a Fable Suggested by Roark Bradford's Southern sketches, *Ol' Man Adam an' His Chillun* (*q.v.*), 1929. (III) This play sets forth in seventeen scenes the plantation Negroes' conception of God's dealing with his foolish, troublesome creatures on earth.

Conrad, Joseph 1857-1924 English novelist. Born a Pole, Conrad was a grown man before he first heard English spoken. He followed the sea twenty years, became a British subject in 1884 and a Master Mariner in 1887. He was recognized during his last dozen years as a master also of English fiction and as perhaps the world's greatest teller of sea tales.

ALMAYER'S FOLLY. 1895. (I) Story of Malays, half-breeds, and decaying Europeans in Java, where the teeming, flamboyant tropical life both enchants and corrupts the hapless alien.

NIGGER OF THE *Narcissus*. 1898. (I) Tale of a voyage from Bombay to London, during which a giant Negro sailor, terror-stricken and unreconciled, lies dying of tuberculosis. His desperation, in one way or another, reacts upon the whole ship's company.

LORD JIM. 1900. (I) Story of the hero's lifelong efforts to atone for a moment's instinctive cowardice. Often considered the author's masterpiece.

YOUTH. 1902. (I and II) This book comprises three long short stories: *Youth, Heart of Darkness,* and *The End of the Tether.* All show Conrad at his best. Mencken hailed *Heart of Darkness* as "one of the most magnificent narratives, long or short, old or new, in the English language."

TYPHOON. 1902. (II) Another absorbing "long short," this time about a terrific storm in the China Sea, and what it did to a group of white sailormen aboard a British-built, Siamese-owned steamer.

NOSTROMO. 1904. (I and II) This story of a revolution in South America, says Cornelius Weygandt, first revealed Conrad as a novelist of the first rank. It has many of the qualities of an epic.

MIRROR OF THE SEA. 1906. (II) Word-pictures of the sea's romance and reality. Not fiction; just life as it was in the old windjammers.

PERSONAL RECORD. 1912. (II) *Some Reminiscences* is the title in England. The author succeeds admirably in revealing his own personality, first as Polish child and youth, then as British seaman and author.

CHANCE. 1914. (II) Rather gloomy story of a woman who is the helpless victim of untoward circumstances. At least one critic considers it surpassed only by *Lord Jim* and *Nostromo.*

VICTORY. 1915. (II) Tragic tale of the rescue of a girl from a world-wandering "ladies' orchestra." Considered one of his best books.

SHADOW-LINE. 1917. (II) Autobiographical; tells how the author, in charge of his first ship, crossed the shadow-line separating the youth from the man, when fever-stricken on an unlucky voyage.

ARROW OF GOLD. 1919. (II) Curious tale of love and Carlist intrigue during the attempt of the Seventies on the Spanish throne. Inspired by personal adventures of Conrad's youth.

THE RESCUE. 1920. (II) A South Sea story. Searchers for the magic of Conrad's earlier books will find it again in this one.

NOTES ON LIFE AND LETTERS. 1921. (II) Essays on James, Crane, Maupassant, Daudet, France, and Turgenev, as well as stories of the sea.

JOSEPH CONRAD, LIFE AND LETTERS; edited by G. J. Aubry. 2v. 1927. (III) The first 170 pages are straight biography of Conrad's early years. Thereafter the letters tell the story.

Cook, James 1728-79 British navigator and explorer.
VOYAGES. 3v. 1773-84 (I) The account of the first voyage was by Dr. Hawkesworth; that of the second, by Captain Cook himself; that of the third by Lieutenant King, mostly from Cook's notes.

Cooper, James Fenimore 1789-1851 American novelist in two kinds: tales of Indians and backwoodsmen, and tales of the sea.

THE LEATHERSTOCKING TALES, Cooper's best known books, are a series of five tales of frontier life. All have the same hero—Natty Bumppo, also known as Leatherstocking, Hawkeye, and Deerslayer. Listed by dates of publication the five titles are as follows; *The Pioneers* (1823) ; *Last of the Mohicans* (1826) ; *The Prairie* (1827) ; *The Pathfinder* (1840) ; and *The Deerslayer* (1841). Listed by dates of the events chronicled, their order is as follows: *The Deerslayer* (I) tells of the youthful Natty's first experience of Indian warfare; *The Pathfinder* (I) shows him as a young lover; *Last of the Mohicans* (I) presents him in the prime of life as a scout in the campaign against Fort William Henry in 1757. (This is generally regarded as the best book of the series.) *The Pioneers* shows Natty, as an old man, fleeing through the Alleghanies from advancing civilization; in *The Prairie,* Natty, as a still older man, continues this flight to the Western plains, where he dies.

THE SPY. 1821. (I) Westchester County, New York, is the scene of this tale of the Revolution, wherein the hero, Harvey Birch, a wandering peddler, acts as spy for the Americans.

THE PILOT. 1823. (I) Perhaps the best of Cooper's sea tales. Paul Jones and Long Tom Coffin are among the characters.

RED ROVER. 1827. (I) This tale of a noble-hearted pirate holds the reader's interest admirably, with its vivid descriptions of tempest and battle. The time is before the Revolution; the scene, mostly Newport, Rhode Island.

Copernicus, Nicolaus   1473-1543   German or Polish astronomer.

REVOLUTIONS OF THE HEAVENLY BODIES. 1543. (I) This book, first published in the author's original Latin version in the year of his death, overturned the Ptolemaic astronomy and won acceptance for his theory that the sun is the centre of our planetary system and that the earth and other planets revolve around it.

Corneille, Pierre   1606-84   French dramatist.

PLAYS. (I) Most moderns consider Corneille dry reading. His importance, though generally admitted, is mainly historical. As the father of French classical drama he initiated traditions of stage decorum and insisted on the unities of time, place, and action. Among his best tragedies are the following: *Médée* (1635); *The Cid* (1636-37), by some considered his masterpiece; *Cinna* and *Horace* (1640); *Polyeucte* (1642)—perhaps his best play. His finest comedy is said to be *Le Menteur* (The Liar) (1642).

Cortissoz, Royal, joint author *See* Isham, Samuel

Coster, Charles de   1827-79   Belgian writer.

TYL ULENSPIEGEL. 1868. The man so-called was a hero of German folklore. Carlyle said that "his tombstone still stands at Mollen, near Lübeck, where since 1350 his once nimble bones have been at rest." His story is an amusing picaresque romance that through the centuries, in several languages, has been many times retold. *Tyl Owlyglass* and *Howleglass* are English variants of the hero's name.

Couperus, Louis   1863-1923   Dutch novelist.

BOOK OF SMALL SOULS. 4v. 1914-18. (II) A series of four novels comprising a family chronicle: *Small Souls, Later Life, Twilight of the Souls,* and *Dr. Adriaan.* "These small souls are such stuff as life is made of.   Their creator neither values nor mocks them, but sets them forth for what they may be worth, with a smile of kindly irony."—*Nation*.

Covarrubias, Miguel   1902-   Caricaturist, painter, author. Born in Mexico and entirely self-taught; spent two years in China, Java, and Bali.

ISLAND OF BALI; WITH AN ALBUM OF PHOTOGRAPHS.   1937. (IV) A very beautiful book.   "The art and culture, the background and the daily life of the Balinese as seen through the sympathetic and understanding eyes of an artist."—*Book Review Digest*.

Coward, Noel   1899-   English dramatist, actor, and all-round man of the sophisticated theatre.

PLAY PARADE.   1933. "Omnibus of the chief plays by the leading master of sophistication."—*Good Reading*.

PRESENT INDICATIVE.   1937. Autobiography.   "Practically a treatise on amiability.   It is also swell."—*New York Times*.

Cowper, William   1731-1800   English poet. Innocent, pious, and confiding—and witty and humorous when in the mood—he lived in constant dread of everlasting punishment. His merry ballad of *John Gilpin* (I) is his best known poem, though his *Task* (I), a long poem in six books, better reflects the gentle, domestic, nature-loving characteristics of the author.

LETTERS.   (I) No mean critic himself, he corresponded with interesting people, and competent judges say that his letters are among the best in the English tongue.

Cozzens, James Gould   1903-   American novelist. Major in the Air Forces in World War II.

JUST AND UNJUST.   1942. (IV) Story of a three-day murder trial in a New England country town.   There is no hero, no heroine—just good objective characterization of not very remarkable people.   But critics praised it and it became a best-seller.

GUARD OF HONOR.   1948. Novel about three days in 1943 in an army air-base in Florida. Pulitzer prize, 1949. "Finest work so far of an absolutely first-rate American writer."—*Saturday Review of Literature*.

Crabbe, George   1754-1832   British poet. The favorite poet of Lord Byron, Sir Walter Scott, and Cardinal Newman.

POEMS. (I) His work is full of humanitarianism devoid of sentimentality. "The poet of the poor." His best known poem, *The Village,* is a satirical reply to Goldsmith's *Deserted Village.* Byron described him as "nature's sternest poet, yet her best."

Crane, Hart   1899-1932   American poet. He was too sensitive for the age into which he was born.

COLLECTED POEMS. 1933. His subject was man in the modern world, particularly America. It tortured him intolerably. "Out of his divided soul he attempted to precipitate in poetry his vision of an ideal America."

Crane, Stephen   1871-1900   American fictionist; a pioneer in American realism, whose reputation was well established before his death at twenty-nine.

MAGGIE: A GIRL OF THE STREETS. 1892. Sometimes accounted the first American novel of the naturalistic school.

RED BADGE OF COURAGE. 1895. Story of a raw recruit's ordeal by battle. Completely convincing, though when it was written the author himself had never been under fire.

Crankshaw, Edward   English journalist and historian.

RUSSIA AND THE RUSSIANS. 1948. Soviet behavior in the light of Russian history and geography. "It leaves on the reader's mind a confused but satisfying impression of what the Russians are like."—*Times* (London).

Craven, Thomas   1889-   American art critic.

TREASURY OF ART MASTERPIECES, FROM THE RENAISSANCE TO THE PRESENT DAY. 1939. (IV) Includes 144 new color plates, each with a page of comment. "The one American publication of its type that we should place at the top of its class. The editor's contributions add mightily to its popular value."—*Boston Transcript.*

STORY OF PAINTING. 1943. "From cave pictures to modern art."

Creasy, Sir Edward S.   1812-78   English historian.

FIFTEEN DECISIVE BATTLES OF THE WORLD. New edition, 1943. The original work described battles from Marathon to Waterloo. The new edition, by R. H. Murray, adds nine additional battles, the latest being Mukden (1905).

Creel, George   1876-   American journalist; Chairman, Public Information Committee, 1917-19.

REBEL AT LARGE; RECOLLECTIONS OF FIFTY CROWDED YEARS. 1947. "Highly entertaining first-hand history."—*New Yorker.*

Creighton, Donald Grant   1902-

DOMINION OF THE NORTH; A HISTORY OF CANADA. 1944. The best short history of our northern neighbor.

Croce, Benedetto   1866-   Italian philosopher, critic.

HISTORY AS THE STORY OF LIBERTY. 1941. "What must perplex the reader, as it has perplexed me, is how did Mussolini ever permit this truly noble book, hostile to him and his ilk, to get out of Italy."—John Cournos, in *New York Times.*

EUROPEAN LITERATURE IN THE NINETEENTH CENTURY. 1924. "The 26 writers discussed . . . are representative of Nineteenth Century literature but not necessarily representative of the mass."— *A.L.A. Catalog,* 1926.

Cromwell, Oliver   Letters and Speeches. *See* Carlyle, Thomas.

Cronin, Archibald Joseph   1896-   Scottish novelist and physician. Frankly a popular writer, but a good one who is always on the side of the angels.

HATTER'S CASTLE. 1931. Tragic story of lives broken by the mad egoism of the head of the family. Scene, the Scottish Lowlands.

STARS LOOK DOWN. 1935. (III) Long novel about the coal miners of northern England, written out of familiarity with the conditions described and with an effective use of plot intricacies which is quite Dickensian.

THE CITADEL. 1937. (IV) About the character development of a young Scottish doctor. "All who enjoy a good novel for its own sake will find it an engrossing, finely written story that needs no justification whatever."—*Saturday Review of Literature.*

Cross, Mrs. Mary Ann Evans *See* Eliot, George.

Cross, Wilbur L. 1862-1948 Grand old man of Yale—and Connecticut; editor of *Yale Review*; Chancellor of the American Academy of Arts and Letters.

CONNECTICUT YANKEE. 1943. (IV) Half of this autobiography is devoted to his long academic career at Yale, the rest to his eight years of stalwart wrestling, as Governor, with Connecticut politics.

Crothers, Rachel 1878- American author of social comedies, often dealing with current topics. John Golden, the producer, declared her in 1937 to be the "greatest woman playwright alive."

SUSAN AND GOD. 1938. Inspired—or instigated—by Buchmanism.

Crothers, Samuel M. 1857-1927 He and Agnes Repplier were the favorite American essayists of their day.

GENTLE READER. 1903. (I and II) His first and perhaps his best book of essays.

DAME SCHOOL OF EXPERIENCE. 1920. (II) Common sense with a dash of humor is the basis for this delectable dish.

AMONG FRIENDS. 1910. (II) Wit and wisdom are combined in these eleven engaging essays. (One deals with the Hundred Worst Books.)

Crouse, Russel 1893- **and Lindsay, Howard** 1880- Collaborating American playwrights. Crouse is also a producer and Lindsay, an actor.

STATE OF THE UNION. 1945. Won the Pulitzer prize in 1946.

LIFE WITH FATHER. 1939. Phenomenally successful on the stage. Founded on the book by Clarence Day.

Crow, John Armstrong   1906-   American college professor; author of many books on Spanish-American life, letters, and history.

EPIC OF LATIN AMERICA.   1946.   "Brilliant and broad-scale ethnic, cultural, economic, and political history of the countries to the south."— *New Yorker.*

Crum, Bartley C.   1900-   American journalist, radio executive. Lawyer.

BEHIND THE SILKEN CURTAIN; A PERSONAL ACCOUNT.   1947. Anglo-American diplomacy in Palestine and the Middle East. "Tells an interesting story and tells it extremely well."—*Saturday Review of Literature.*

Cummings, B. F.   *See* Barbellion, W. N. P., pseudonym.

Cummings, Edward Estlin   1894-   American writer and painter. His poetry has been handicapped by obscurantism, typified by his insistence upon typographical eccentricity.

ENORMOUS ROOM.   1922.   Describes his imprisonment (1917-18) in a French military concentration camp to which he was sent on a false charge of treason.

COLLECTED POEMS.   1938.   (IV)   "Here are collected some of the finest lyric poems of our day. . . . This is the poetry of a man of complete artistic integrity."—*Saturday Review of Literature.*

Cunliffe, John William   1865-1946   Anglo-American scholar in English literature.

MODERN ENGLISH PLAYWRIGHTS; A SHORT HISTORY OF THE ENGLISH DRAMA FROM 1825.   1927.   (III)   Emphasizes the Twentieth Century dramatists.

Curie, Eve   1904-   French author, war correspondent, musician. Daughter of Pierre and Marie Curie, discoverers of radium.

MADAME CURIE, A BIOGRAPHY.   1937.   (IV)   "A book so moving, so finished, so profoundly affecting that one comes to think of Mme. Curie's life as a symphony—by Beethoven, perhaps, or by Sibelius."—*New York Times.*

JOURNEY AMONG WARRIORS.   1943.   (IV)   Miss Curie visited the war fronts in Africa, the Near East, Russia, Iran, China and

India. "Never before has the whole panorama of the world at war been so honestly, so skillfully and so beautifully presented."—W. L. White, in *New York Times*.

Curti, Merle   1897-   He has been professor of history at many American colleges.

GROWTH OF AMERICAN THOUGHT. 1943. (IV) Social history of American thought from Jamestown to Pearl Harbor. Won the Pulitzer prize in 1944.

Cushing, Harvey   1869-1939   American surgeon and neurologist.

LIFE OF SIR WILLIAM OSLER. 2v. 1925. The worthy record of significant achievement, in Canadian, American, and British medical history, of a great doctor, endowed with a most engaging personality.

D., H. *See* Doolittle, Hilda.

Dalton, John   1766-1844   English chemist and physicist. A poor weaver's son, he was largely self-taught.

NEW SYSTEM OF CHEMICAL PHILOSOPHY. 1810. "He perfected about 1804 the atomic theory which he later propounded" in this work, which appears in Unesco's tentative list of "Representative English Classics Worthy of Translation."

Damon, Samuel Foster   1893-   American man of letters.

AMY LOWELL, A CHRONICLE; WITH EXTRACTS FROM HER CORRESPONDENCE. 1935. (III) Written by her close friend, this ample narrative promotes the reader's intimate acquaintance with the sturdy personality who led the movement for the New Poetry from 1910 to 1925.

Dana, Richard Henry   1815-82   American author and lawyer.

TWO YEARS BEFORE THE MAST. 1840. (I) Story of a voyage around Cape Horn before the days of steam. It has been a classic of the sea for more than a century and will doubtless be perused by many armchair mariners a hundred years hence.

Daniels, Jonathan   1902-   American journalist and author; son of Josephus Daniels, President Wilson's Secretary of War.

SOUTHERNER DISCOVERS THE SOUTH. 1938. (IV) "The best book on the modern South that has yet been written."—*New York Herald Tribune*.

Southerner Discovers New England. 1940. (IV) "Mr. Daniels is the best of teachers. . . . I know far more about New England than I did two days ago, even after fifty years' acquaintance."—Mary Ellen Chase.

Dante Alighieri   1265-1321   Italian poet.

Divine Comedy. Written 1300-18. (I) An epic poem which describes the pilgrimage of the soul of man, in three parts: *Inferno, Purgatorio, Paradiso.* It has been described as being "at once a vision of the other world, an allegory of the Christian life, a spiritual autobiography, and a cyclopedic embodiment of all the knowledge of its day." Without doubt it is the greatest literary production of the Middle Ages. There have been many English translations. Still among the best are the metrical version by Longfellow and the one in prose by Charles Eliot Norton.

Vita Nuova. Written about 1291. (I) This work in prose, lyric poems and sonnets celebrates the poet's spiritual love for the lady Beatrice. It found an almost perfect translator in Dante Gabriel Rossetti.

Dark, Eleanor   1901-   Australian novelist.

Timeless Land. 1941. (IV) Australia in fiction—the early days of the colony at Sydney (1787-92), with special attention to describing the reactions of the aborigines. "A rare, beautiful book, rich with authentic history, and the best of fiction."—*Nation.*

Darrow, Clarence S.   1857-1938   American trial lawyer. He fought many legal battles against monopolies and bigots and in defense of the underdog.

Story of My Life. 1932. (III) The sad story of a compassionate cynic, with reflections on crime, criminals, punishments, life, and the world to come.

Darwin, Charles   1809-82   English naturalist, originator of the Darwinian theory of evolution.

Voyage of the *Beagle.* 1845. (I) Report of a trip around the world that is at once an interesting travel book and a scientific document of great historic significance. "Forever interesting as the unrecognized herald of the doctrine of evolution."—*Nation.*

On the Origin of Species by Means of Natural Selection. 1859. (I) Its main thesis has won practically universal acceptance and has influenced every field of thought, though today's scientists question some of the details—for example, the argument for the survival of the fittest and the inheritance of acquired characteristics.

Descent of Man. 1871. (I) Expounds the theory of man's purely animal origin—that man is descended from apelike animals, though not from apes, as Mr. Bryan and his fundamentalist fellows misconceived the doctrine.

Daudet, Alphonse   1840-97   "The French Dickens." "A delightful story-teller as well as the gentlest of satirists and the most genial of humorists."

Tartarin of Tarascon. 1872. (I) The first of the pleasing burlesques of his bragging brother-Provençals. It was followed by *Tartarin in the Alps* (1885), and *Port Tarascon* (1890). Tartarin belongs to the beguiling race of innocent frauds, like Mr. Pickwick and Don Quixote. Among Daudet's novels of Parisian life the more successful are

Fromont Jr. and Risler Sr. 1874. Regarded by some critics as his best book.

Jack. 1876. The tragic life of an unwanted stepson.

Sapho. 1884. A tale of Parisian gallantry.

Davenport, Marcia   1903-   American novelist and musical critic; daughter of Alma Gluck; former wife of Russell W. Davenport.

Valley of Decision. 1942. (IV) Story of five generations of a Pittsburgh mine-owning family; "as enjoyable as it is distinguished."

Davenport, Russell W.   1899-   American editor and poet; husband of Marcia Davenport.

My Country: a Poem of America. 1944. (IV) This long patriotic poem is "the song of the internationalist who knows that if he is not bold, not generous, not committed to the brotherhood of man, then . . . his own roof will give way, and there will be no more kindly dreaming beside the heap of rubble that was once his fireplace. . . . An emotion that makes the pulses beat like drums and the eyes grow misty may not be unmanly—it may be the strongest, the most practical thing in the world."—R. L. Duffus, in *New York Times*.

Davies, William Henry   1871-1940   British poet.

AUTOBIOGRAPHY OF A SUPER-TRAMP. 1908. The naïveté of this account of rough-and-tumble adventures and escapades gives this book a disarming charm. Here is prose that is excellent, largely because it is rough, simple, and direct.

COLLECTED POEMS; with introduction by Sir Osbert Sitwell. 1946. (II) "There are those who think him the most dependable poet in England."—Mark Van Doren.

Davis, Harold Lenoir   1896-   American novelist, born in Oregon; owns a cattle ranch.

HONEY IN THE HORN. 1935. (III) Story of pioneers on our last frontier—Oregon in the homesteading days of 1906 to 1908. A robust, uproarious man's story. Won the biennial Harper prize for fiction, as well as the Pulitzer prize, 1936.

Davis, Owen   1874-   American playwright; author of popular melodramas, like *Nellie the Beautiful Cloak Model*; but also member of the National Institute of Arts and Letters.

ICEBOUND. 1922. Serious play about a Maine family. The hero explains that they are "half-froze" before they are born. They need to be "mean and hard so that they can live the mean hard life they have to live on a farm that is frozen half the year." Yet the play has a happy ending.

Davis, Richard Harding   1864-1916   American war correspondent and author. In the Gay Nineties he was the literary idol of American youth. His reputation is not what it was. Still, he wrote excellent short stories, and it is interesting to read what grandmother in her naïveté so greatly admired.

VAN BIBBER AND OTHERS. 1890. The inimitable Van Bibber is ever "a charming fellow, combining the exquisiteness of the aristocrat with the sterling virtues of the American people."

GALLEGHER AND OTHER STORIES. 1891. Many of the tales recount further adventures of Van Bibber, Admirable Crichton of old Fifth Avenue.

Davis, William Stearns   1877-1930   American historical novelist and teacher of history, whose books are both readable and painlessly instructive.

LIFE ON A MEDIAEVAL BARONY.   1923.   A favorite prescription of instructors in European history.

Day, Clarence   1874-1935   American humorist. His most amusing books were written during his last years when he had long been crippled by arthritis.

CLARENCE DAY OMNIBUS.   1945.   Besides other good things this book contains the matchless *Life with Father* (1935) and *Life with Mother* (1937)—humorous sketches of family life in the New York of the brownstone era, under the benevolent despotism of a gusty and explosive father, tempered by the soft influence of a gently Victorian mother.

Deane, J. R.   1896-   American major-general, retired; headed American military mission to Moscow, 1943-45.

STRANGE ALLIANCE; the story of our efforts at wartime cooperation with Russia.   1947.   "Important documentation on the most important problem facing the United States and the world."

Defoe, Daniel   1661-1731   British novelist and pamphleteer.

ROBINSON CRUSOE.   1719.   (I)   Grandfather of all the wrecked-on-a-desert-island stories.   This one has delighted successive generations of young people for more than two centuries.

JOURNAL OF THE PLAGUE YEAR.   1722.   (I)   This gruesome book is a striking example of Defoe's extraordinary ability to make fiction sound like fact.   Reading it, one keeps forgetting it is not the authentic, contemporary document it purports to be.

MEMOIRS OF A CAVALIER.   1720.   (I)   Historical romance of the English Civil War.   Lord Chatham was completely fooled by it.   Saintsbury described it as "one of the most vivid and apparently genuine military histories ever printed."

CAPTAIN SINGLETON.   1720.   (I)   "Bloodcurdling but convincing narrative of piracy."—*Good Reading.*

MOLL FLANDERS.   1722.   (I)   Novel (in the form of an autobiography) of low life in London and Virginia in the early Eighteenth Century.

Dekker, Thomas 1570(?)-1641(?) English dramatist and pamphleteer. He collaborated often with fellow playwrights, one of whom was Jonson, with whom he later had a pen-and-ink quarrel.

PLAYS. Among his best are *Shoemaker's Holiday* (1600) (I), a frolicsome picture of London life in that day; *Satiromastix* (1602) (I), a good-humored reply to Jonson's merciless attack on *Poetaster*; and *Fortunatus* (1600) (I), about the unhappy fate of the man with an inexhaustible purse.

GULL'S HORNBOOK. (1609) (I) Dekker's best known work. A primer of etiquette for rich youths from the country who come to town to have a good time and lose their money.

De Kruif, Paul 1890- American scientist and popularizer of scientific subjects.

MICROBE HUNTERS. 1926. (III) Dramatic account of the achievements of bacteriologists.

Delacroix, Eugène 1799-1863 French painter; leader of the romantic school.

JOURNALS; illustrated with his paintings and drawings. 1937. (IV) From 1822 to 1863 Delacroix told the truth as man and artist. It makes delightful and instructive reading.

De la Mare, Walter 1873- English poet. "From 'faery lands forlorn' comes Walter De la Mare, singing of beauty and of grief." —Agnes Repplier.

COLLECTED POEMS. 2v. 1941. (II) Especially *The Listeners* and other mystical verse; and his incomparable poetry for children, like *Peacock Pie* and *A Child's Day*.

MEMOIRS OF A MIDGET. 1922. (II) A long, modern fairy tale for adults that is poetic, dramatic, meditative, poignant. And it is also a triumph in the art of characterization.

Deland, Margaret 1857-1945 American novelist and short story writer, whose locus is usually "Old Chester," Pennsylvania.

JOHN WARD, PREACHER. 1888. Deals with the conflict between a Calvinist husband and an agnostic wife.

DR. LAVENDAR'S PEOPLE. 1903. (II) More stories of Old Chester. Dr. Lavendar, a wise and kindly old clergyman, has been called "one of the few living figures in American fiction."

AWAKENING OF HELENA RICHIE. 1906. (II) Penetrated, as it is, with an inward and spiritual grace, many consider this the author's best book. Its text? A little child shall lead them.

De La Roche, Mazo   1885-   Canadian novelist of mixed English, Irish, and French stock. No books have come to the United States from its northern neighbor that can equal in popularity her many-volumed saga about the vigorous Whiteoak family, whose many members countless Americans have come to know very well indeed.

JALNA. 1927. (III) This first book of the series that now runs to about a dozen volumes won *The Atlantic's* ten thousand dollar prize. It was followed by *Whiteoaks of Jalna* (1929), *Finch's Fortune* (1931), *Master of Jalna* (1933), *Young Renny* (1935), *Whiteoak Harvest* (1936), *Whiteoak Heritage* (1940), *Wakefield's Course* (1941), *Building of Jalna* (1944), *Return to Jalna* (1946), *Mary Wakefield* (1949), *Rennie's Daughter* (1951).

Deledda, Grazia   1872-1936   Italian novelist.

THE MOTHER. 1920. Poignant novel of love, religion and renunciation during two days in a Sardinian village. Awarded Nobel prize for literature in 1926.

Dell, Floyd   1887-   American journalist and novelist, who in the early jazz age held what were then considered extremely advanced opinions.

MOON-CALF. 1920. (II) The hero is one of the Lost Generation who suffered and burned the candle at both ends during the years of disillusionment that followed World War I.

BRIARY BUSH. 1921. (II) This sequel to *The Moon-Calf,* says Carl Van Doren, is less varied and more profound than its predecessor. The two books together make up a full-length portrait of the American youth of the period.

De Morgan, William   1839-1917   This English potter, inventor, and illustrator began writing novels at sixty-five, to the delight of thousands of readers.

JOSEPH VANCE. 1906. (II) Here are 300,000 words; but, said *The Dial*, "the writer's style is so enjoyable that it makes garrulity a virtue and gives point to the most pointless digressions."

ALICE-FOR-SHORT. 1907. (II) Characteristically faulty and delightful story of a London waif, adopted into a rich, middle-class English family. With eager interest and sympathy we watch her development and the progress of her love affairs, puzzling meanwhile over "the secret of her birth."

SOMEHOW GOOD. 1908. (II) There is garrulity in it and unabashed Victorian feeling; but both are pleasing because of the author's rich, warm-hearted humor.

Demosthenes   384-322 B.C.   Greatest of the Greek orators.

ORATIONS; especially the three *Philippics* against the encroachments of Philip of Macedon; *On the Peace*; and *On the Crown*.   (I)

De Quincey, Thomas   1785-1859   English essayist and stylist; a friend and for a time a neighbor of Wordsworth and Coleridge in the Lake Country.

CONFESSIONS OF AN ENGLISH OPIUM EATER. 1822. (I) His most famous book. The story of his addiction to the drug, told in brilliant and beautiful prose.

ESSAYS. (I) Among the best of these may be noted *The English Mail-Coach, Murder Considered as One of the Fine Arts* and *Joan of Arc*.

Derounian, Arthur   *See* Carlson, John Roy (pseudonym).

Descartes, René   1596-1650   French philosopher and mathematician; founder of the Cartesian philosophy.

DISCOURSE ON THE METHOD OF RIGHTLY CONDUCTING THE REASON AND SEEKING THE TRUTH IN THE SCIENCES. 1657. (I) Wherein "mathematical method becomes the key to rationalistic truth."

Deutscher, Isaac   1907-   Born in Poland, he went to London in 1939 and became a European correspondent for English journals.

STALIN, A POLITICAL BIOGRAPHY. 1949. "Fascinating treatment of . . . the success story of the Twentieth Century."—*New Yorker*. "This lucid, massive, and highly readable book is bound to appeal to a wide audience. . . . Students of government in particular will find it very stimulating and profitable reading."—*American Political Science Review.*

De Voto, Bernard 1897- American author, editor and teacher.

MARK TWAIN'S AMERICA. 1932. (III) Surveying Mark Twain's early life and environment, the author concludes, first, that Mark was never a frustrate; and, second, that he was greatly indebted to the frontier for the stimulation and development of his genius. (Cf. *The Ordeal of Mark Twain,* by Van Wyck Brooks.)

YEAR OF DECISION, 1846. 1943. (IV) The true story of "some people who went west in 1846"—the year that saw the culmination of the whole westward migration from the Atlantic to the Pacific. "De Voto's best book to date. And that makes it good enough to become a part of the permanent literature of the nation." —*Saturday Review of Literature.*

ACROSS THE WIDE MISSOURI. 1947. About the Rocky Mountain fur trade of the Thirties. Well illustrated. "Some one perceived that Mr. De Voto's knowledge of the mountain men and Mrs. Porter's plan for an album of Miller pictures could be admirably combined, and this book is the result."—*New York Herald Tribune.*

Dewey, John 1859-1952 American philosopher, psychologist and educator. Professor M. R. Cohen called Dewey the most influential philosopher that America has produced. He is the father of the Progressive School and co-leader with William James of the Pragmatic movement.

HOW WE THINK. 1909 and 1933. (II) "The best book on the subject."—*A.L.A. Catalog,* 1926.

DEMOCRACY AND EDUCATION. 1916. (II) "The Twenty-first Century will study three great stages in educational theory: Plato, Rousseau, and Dewey."—*The Dial.*

RECONSTRUCTION IN PHILOSOPHY. 1920. (II) "Although the name *pragmatism* scarcely occurs in its pages, the book is the most comprehensive and enlightening pragmatic document that has yet appeared."—*Nation.*

HUMAN NATURE AND CONDUCT. 1922. (II) Discusses the shares of habit, impulse and intelligence in determining conduct. Inspirational in tone—graceful in style.

EXPERIENCE AND NATURE. 1925. "Here is a philosophy as soundly American as that of Emerson, Thoreau, Whitman, or William James."—R. L. Duffus, in *New York Times*.

ART AS EXPERIENCE. 1934. "May be taken as a summary of what Mr. Dewey has written within the last thirty years."—H. Gregory, in *New York Herald Tribune*.

LOGIC, THE THEORY OF INQUIRY. 1938. "A charter for the liberal intelligence in a time when escape and fanaticism are in the saddle."—Irwin Edman, in *New York Herald Tribune*.

INTELLIGENCE IN THE MODERN WORLD. 1939. The author speaks here as the typical American advocate of pragmatic democracy.

FREEDOM AND CULTURE. 1939. (IV) "It plumbs the fundamentals of the problem of democracy."—*New York Times*.

Dickens, Charles   1812-70   English novelist. With all his faults, Dickens is probably the greatest novelist the world has seen, though the present generation must approach him fully realizing that the world and the novel with it have greatly changed since his day. . . . "Dickens is too sentimental." "Dickens is too melodramatic." Of course. Yet his books, not only have done more good, but have also given more wholesome pleasure to minds of all sorts, from the highest to the lowest, than those of any other writer who ever lived. With the exercise of a bit of good will the modern generation too can share this largess.

Let us begin by looking first at his three best books.

DAVID COPPERFIELD. 1850. (I) He who would know and love Dickens should begin with this autobiographical novel. It is freer from defects than any other of his books. "Dickens's masterpiece as a novel."—Andrew Lang. "Dickens says in his preface that David Copperfield was his 'favorite child,' and I don't wonder, for it is amazingly well done."—J. R. Lowell. "What treasuries of gaiety, invention, life, are in that book! What alertness and resource! What a soul of good-nature and kindness governing the whole!"—Matthew Arnold.

PICKWICK PAPERS. 1837. (I) "The glory of Charles Dickens will always be in his *Pickwick*, his first, his best, his inimitable triumph."—Frederic Harrison. "*Pickwick* is scarcely surpassable in humor."—Harriet Martineau. "As a child I shied away from this glorious book for years, just because its title had a dry, *documentary* sound—though of course that word, as we know it, was yet to be invented."—A. D. Dickinson.

TALE OF TWO CITIES. 1859. (I) A novel of the French Revolution, founded upon Carlyle's dramatic history. *"A Tale of Two Cities,* one of his shorter novels, and the one least thought of by the public of his own day, is the work that will assure him an enduring fame. . . . Almost a peerless book in modern literature!"—Richard Grant White.

OLIVER TWIST. 1838. (I) Because "Fagin the Jew" is one—but only one—of the villains in this crime-story, Dickens has been accused of anti-Semitism. The book did a great deal to bring about a much needed revision of the English Poor Laws.

NICHOLAS NICKLEBY. 1839. (I) In this book Dickens launched a crusade against cheap boarding-schools where helpless and unwanted youths were starved and exploited. It is not one of his best, but readers will never forget Dotheboys Hall, Smike, The Infant Phenomenon, and Mrs. Nickleby, the wooden hero's silly mother.

BARNABY RUDGE. 1841. (I) This plot-ridden story of the "No Popery" riots (1780) of Lord George Gordon is the author's first try at historical fiction. While not particularly successful, it achieves a certain atmosphere and one recalls with pleasure Barnaby and his raven, the brutish Maypole Hugh, the Dresden shepherdess (Dolly Varden), and the villainous Mr. Chester, a character drawn from the worldly Lord Chesterfield of the "Letters."

OLD CURIOSITY SHOP. 1841. (I) In this story of Little Nell Dickens slumps from pathos to maudlin bathos, yet Howells finds an excuse for this defection: "When all is said against the lapses of taste and truth . . . there is in all a sense of the dignity in common and humble lives, which is the most precious quality of literature. . . . It is this quality in Dickens which Tolstoi prizes and accepts as proof of his greatest art."

CHRISTMAS CAROL. 1843. (I) "The world laughed and cried over it, and Scrooge and Scrooge's nephew, and Old Fezziwig, and Bob Cratchit, and Tiny Tim, became household words in a million homes." These words were written long ago, but they are still true today.

CRICKET ON THE HEARTH. 1845. (I) A. W. Ward, a biographer of Dickens, considered this the best of his Christmas books and declares that it is "as tender and delicate a domestic idyl as any literature can boast."

DOMBEY AND SON. 1848. (I) This is another of the master's
tear-jerkers. This time it is little Paul who is done to death, and
soft-hearted Thackeray was so moved that he exclaimed, "There's no
writing against such power as this—one has no chance! Read that
chapter describing young Paul's death: it is unsurpassed—it is stu-
pendous!"

BLEAK HOUSE. 1853. (I) Long and plot-ridden. We become
as weary as did the litigants in the great Chancery suit of Jarndyce and
Jarndyce. Yet one wishes to read it to the end. Note his caricatures
of two friends: Walter Savage Landor as Lawrence Boythorn, and
Leigh Hunt as Harold Skimpole.

HARD TIMES. 1854. "He is entirely right in his main drift and
purpose in every book he has written; and all of them, but especially
Hard Times, should be studied with close and earnest care by persons
interested in social questions."—John Ruskin. From a literary point
of view, the least admirable of his books.

LITTLE DORRIT. 1857. (I) Critics find this book oppressively
gloomy, yet there are those who love it for its pictures of the Old
Marshalsea prison for debtors, the Circumlocution Office, and the
explosive "Mr. F's Aunt."

GREAT EXPECTATIONS. 1861. (I) A favorite with many Dick-
ensians. Miss Havisham and her strange trappings may be impossible
but one remembers them. And what a grand moving picture they
made!

OUR MUTUAL FRIEND. 1865. (I) Here again we are wearied
by a clumsy, overelaborate plot and by a group of incredible "society"
people. But the author makes ample amends with his humbler folk—
the dear Boffins, Jenny Wren, and Riah, the *good* Jew through whom
canny Dickens apologized belatedly for the villainous Fagin of *Oliver
Twist.*

MYSTERY OF EDWIN DROOD. 1870. The author died when half
way through this murder story. George Gissing thought it "would
probably have been his best constructed book. . . . The story hangs
well together, showing a care in the contrivance of detail which is
more than commonly justified by the result."

Dickinson, Emily 1830-86 American poet. She lived a life
of almost conventual seclusion in the family mansion at Amherst,
Massachusetts, and but two of her poems were printed in her

lifetime. But her importance in the history of American literature has increased steadily during the first half of this century. (See also Glaspell, Susan—*Alison's House.*)

POEMS. 1937. "Here the humbly familiar and the cosmic unite to form lyrics of explosive power and of a strange and startling loveliness."—*Good Reading.* (Contains all the poems published before 1937.)

LIFE AND LETTERS; edited by M. G. D. Bianchi. 1924. (II) Herein an elusive personality is strikingly, if intermittently, revealed. Her letters are "as startlingly original in thought and image and as condensed in expression as her poems."

BOLTS OF MELODY. 1945. Hitherto unpublished poems.

Dickinson, G. Lowes   1862-1932   English essayist. "A gentleman and a scholar and a bachelor to the end."

GREEK VIEW OF LIFE. 3rd edition. 1906. "Lucid in presentation; fresh and penetrating in its criticisms."—*Spectator.*

LETTERS FROM A CHINESE OFFICIAL. 1903. (II) This Eastern view of Western civilization is written in the author's golden prose and "may be accepted as a faithful representation of the point of view which it pretends to give at first hand."

MODERN SYMPOSIUM. 1905. (II) A group of fictitious philosophers presents, severally, their liberal, socialist, anarchist, commercial, and Quaker points of view. "An admirable means of looking back over the wide tracts through which Nineteenth-Century minds have wandered."

Dickinson, Thomas Herbert   1877-   American student of the drama.

OUTLINE OF CONTEMPORARY DRAMA. 1927. (III) Survey of the drama in Europe and America since 1800, against a well-wrought background of the sources whence it sprang.

Diderot, Denis   1713-84 French encyclopedist and philosopher, editor, with others, of the

ENCYCLOPAEDIA OF ARTS AND SCIENCES. 35v. 1751-65. An epoch-making repository of scientific inquiry and secular knowledge as it existed two centuries ago. It was also in fact a veritable explosion of the ideas for freedom and humanitarian progress which heralded the French Revolution that followed a quarter-century later.

Dimnet, Ernest   1869-   French ecclesiastic and man of letters; interested in Anglo-American life and culture.

ART OF THINKING. 1929. (III) Wise, witty and urbane treatise, offering many practical suggestions—a book to be read slowly and of course thoughtfully. A best-seller in the United States.

WHAT WE LIVE BY. 1932. (III) Essays in persuasive advocacy of the good life—devotion to the true and the beautiful.

Dinesen, Isak (Baroness Karen Blixen)   1885-   Danish writer.

SEVEN GOTHIC TALES. 1934. "A work of the imagination, very subtle and graceful; a rare and curious book, it will be white magic to many and mere mummery to others."—*New York Times.*

Disraeli, Benjamin (Earl of Beaconsfield)   1804-81   British statesman and novelist; alternated with Gladstone as Queen Victoria's prime minister; son of Isaac D'Israeli (*q.v.*).

VIVIAN GREY. 1826-27. Published anonymously, its clever cynicism became the talk of London. "With all its youthful faults *Vivian Grey* gives one a greater impression of purely intellectual brilliance than anything else he ever wrote or spoke."—James Bryce.

CONINGSBY. 1844. (I) "Much more than a novel; a political manifesto with a serious practical aim, to furnish a programme for a new Conservative party."—E. A. Baker.

LOTHAIR. 1870. (I) "Premiers not uncommonly write sad stuff; and we should be thankful if the stuff be amusing. But the mature thoughts on life of one who has governed an empire on which the sun never sets, have an inner meaning to the thoughtful mind." —Frederic Harrison.

D'Israeli, Isaac   1766-1848   British bookworm; descended from a family of Spanish Jews; father of Benjamin Disraeli.

CURIOSITIES OF LITERATURE. 6v. 1791-1834. A treasury of curious literary and historical information—an entertaining assemblage of the little known.

AMENITIES OF LITERATURE. 3v. 1841. A repository of much curious book gossip and authors' lore.

Dobson, Austin 1840-1921 English author of prose and verse; specialist in Eighteenth-Century life and literature.

SELECTED POEMS. Experiments in many quaint forms of verse used by poets of an older day. (Published in *World's Classics* series.)

EIGHTEENTH CENTURY VIGNETTES. 3v. 1892-96. Charming essays on many subjects in his chosen field.

Dodd, William E. 1869-1940 American publicist; ambassador to Berlin, 1933-37.

AMBASSADOR DODD'S DIARY, 1933-38. 1941. (IV) No study of World War II can afford to neglect these daily notes of the gathering storm.

Dodgson, C. L. *See* Carroll, Lewis (pseudonym).

Donald, David 1920- American teacher of history.

LINCOLN'S HERNDON. 1948. "A Lincoln book of first importance." "Scholarly biography of William Herndon, the friend, law partner and biographer of Abraham Lincoln."—*Book Review Digest.*

Donne, John 1573-1631 British poet and clergyman; "one of the four literary titans of Seventeenth-Century England"; greatest of the "metaphysical poets."

COMPLETE POETRY AND SELECTED PROSE. (Nonesuch Press.) His verse, which deals often with human nature, love, and spiritual struggle, is strikingly modern in thought and feeling. This century has witnessed a remarkable revival of interest in Donne's work. T. S. Eliot has publicized it. Hart Crane wrote under its influence. Hemingway borrowed a phrase from him to name *For Whom the Bell Tolls.*

Doolittle, Hilda (H.D.) 1886- American poet, who has lived mostly abroad; the most consistent of the Imagists.

COLLECTED POEMS. 1925. "She makes pure imagery carry the burden of precipitating intense emotion," and writes generally under a strong classical influence.

Dorsey, George A. 1868-1931 American anthropologist and "popularizer."

WHY WE BEHAVE LIKE HUMAN BEINGS. 1925. (II) A book on the natural history of man. He has collected the results of recent research in science and psychology and has tried to make them tell "a complete and up-to-date story" about the human machine.

Dos Passos, John 1896- "One of the most original and important of Twentieth Century American novelists." He has long cherished a lively and sympathetic interest in Russia, the common soldier, and the masses, but has lost faith in the Communist program. Member, National Institute of Arts and Letters.

THREE SOLDIERS. 1921. (II) This brilliant but unpleasant novel, presenting the seamy side of experiences with the American Expeditionary Force in World War I, is an impressive indictment of militarism. It evoked wide and bitter discussion.

MANHATTAN TRANSFER. 1925. (II) Upton Sinclair called this picture of sharp contrasts in metropolitan life "a novel of the very first rate importance, that may be the foundation of a new school of novel-writing."

U. S. A. 1937. A trilogy consisting of *The 42nd Parallel* (1930), *Nineteen Nineteen* (1931) (III), and *The Big Money* (1936) (IV). The three titles display a cross-section of American life from 1900 through the boom of the Twenties, "and embody original but effective methods in the technique of the novel."

STATE OF THE NATION. 1944. (IV) Not a novel. An objective, first-hand report on the United States during World War II, with special attention to labor-management relations. Some readers will be annoyed by the author's characteristic mannerisms.

Dostoievski, Feodor 1821-81 Russian novelist. He became active in the revolutionary movement of his day, was arrested, condemned to death, and was actually standing before a firing-squad when his sentence was commuted to hard labor in the Siberian salt mines.

CRIME AND PUNISHMENT. 1866. (I) This sordid story of abnormal psychology is usually regarded as his masterpiece. The hero—a half starved, despairing student—murdered an old woman for her money. But the book closes with hope for the regeneration of a repentant sinner.

BROTHERS KARAMAZOV. 1879-80. (I) Story of four brothers, one of whom—epileptic, illegitimate, and unacknowledged—kills their father. Hugh Walpole considered this book "the greatest novel the world has yet seen," and Arnold Bennett confirmed this judgment.

THE IDIOT. 1868-69. (I) Story of an epileptic Russian nobleman who is driven mad by the events which follow his contact with the debased and criminal world of St. Petersburg.

HOUSE OF THE DEAD. 1861. Account of the author's four miserable years of imprisonment in Siberia.

LETTERS (SELECTED). 1915. (I) These reveal his lifelong struggle with poverty, no less than his love for Russia and belief in her high mission which he formulates as follows: "The inmost essence and ultimate destiny of the Russian nation is to reveal to the world her own Russian Christ."

DIARY OF A WRITER. 2v. 1949. First complete English translation of a major work which was first published 1873-81. Contains politics, short stories, criticism, etc. "As a document of Russia's always uneasy relations with the outside world and itself, the *Diary* is invaluable; as a literary performance, it is often highly exasperating, yet finally overwhelming in its personal force."—A. Kazin, in *New Yorker*.

Doughty, Charles M. 1843-1926 British traveler and author.

TRAVELS IN ARABIA DESERTA. 1888. Sympathetic description of life among the Bedouins; written mostly in the archaic English of Chaucerian or Elizabethan times, liberally laced with Arabic. This is one of those books of which most literate persons are respectfully cognizant, but few of them have read.

Douglas, Henry K. 1840-1903 Aide-de-camp to General Jackson of the Confederate Army.

I RODE WITH STONEWALL. 1940. (IV) A book of rare quality —intimate, frank, and discerning. Stonewall Jackson appears human, likable, and understanding.

Douglas, Lloyd C. 1877-1950 American clergyman and author of best-selling religious historical novels.

THE ROBE. 1942. The centurion who superintended the crucifixion of Jesus describes the dawn and early days of Christianity as he witnessed them.

Douglas, Norman 1868-1952 British novelist, naturalist, traveler.

SOUTH WIND. 1917. "A playfully cynical novel, full of 'noble liars but excellent people' on Nepenthe[Capri ?], an imaginary Mediterranean island."—*Good Reading*.

OLD CALABRIA. 1915-28. Historical and artistic comment on a little known region of southern Italy. The style is delightfully informal. A minor classic.

Douglas, William O. 1898- American jurist; Associate Justice, Supreme Court, 1939-.

OF MEN AND MOUNTAINS. 1950. Autobiography. "A highly interesting and rewarding book, for its clear and honest picturing both of our northwestern mountains and its notable author."—*New York Times*.

Doyle, Sir Arthur Conan 1859-1930 British fictionist, spiritualist, physician.

MICAH CLARKE. 1889. (I) Spirited story of Monmouth's Rebellion, in the days of James II.

WHITE COMPANY. 1891. (I) Historical romance of the Fourteenth Century: gallant fighting under the Black Prince.

SIR NIGEL. 1906. Earlier adventures of the warriors who appeared in *The White Company*.

SHERLOCK HOLMES STORIES. (I and II) Holmes, the redoubtable amateur detective, wearied his creator till he killed him; but so phenomenally popular was he that Doyle was forced to bring him back to life. Holmes's first adventure was *A Study in Scarlet* (1887). His career continued through at least eight other books to *The Case Book of Sherlock Holmes*, which appeared thirty years later. He is said to be the most widely known fictional character in the world.

Dreiser, Theodore 1871-1945 American novelist in the tradition of naturalism; brother of Paul Dresser (*sic*), popular songwriter. Critical reaction to Dreiser has been extraordinary. He has been hailed as "The Grand Old Man of Realism"; "the greatest novelist in America"; and "the Caliban of contemporary fiction." John T. Winterich asks, "Which is he, the greatest American novelist of his time or a ponderous numskull who exudes words?" while Edmund Wilson says, "Dreiser commands our respect; but he writes so badly that it is almost impossible to read him and, for this reason, I have difficulty in believing in his literary permanence." And Mencken, *one of Dreiser's champions*, said that he could dispute "for the title of the vulgarest voice yet heard in American literature"; but also stated that "most literate foreigners, asked to name the principal novelist in practice today, would nominate Theodore Dreiser."

SISTER CARRIE. 1900. (I) With the help of her lovers the heroine wins spectacular fame on the stage. (This novel was suppressed by a timid publisher after being accepted for publication.)

JENNIE GERHARDT. 1911. (II) A tale of two immigrant families, Irish and German. Jennie is a sweet girl, piously reared, who comes to grief and punishment, she knows not why.

THE FINANCIER. 1912. (II) This is the first book in the trilogy about "Cowperwood." The scene is Philadelphia, about 1870. Carl Van Doren said that it is "as considerable an epic as American business has to show." (Revised edition, 1927.)

THE TITAN. 1914. (I and II) Sequel to *The Financier*. "Ponderous but impressive biography of a business pirate."—*Good Reading*.

THE STOIC. 1947. Concludes the Cowperwood "trilogy of desire," which was built upon the lusts for power and for women.

THE GENIUS. 1915. (II) Artist-hero forsakes his art for easy success in journalism and in the pursuit of women. Amorous adventure in 330,000 words.

AMERICAN TRAGEDY. 2v. 1925. (II) Founded on an actual murder case of the period. "Clyde Griffith is condemned to the electric chair for drowning the girl he had seduced. Dreiser condemns the social system that made Griffith what he was."—*Good Reading*. The *London Spectator* called this book "the finest work of fiction yet produced in the United States." Said *The Saturday Review*, "it is tremendous." John Macy described it as "the Mount Everest of American fiction," and declared it "one of the high hills of all the fiction in the world."

GALLERY OF WOMEN. 2v. 1928. (III) Collection of honest, earnest, wordy, humorless novelettes about women—no, *females*, by a sympathetic but indelicate male.

Drinkwater, John 1882-1937 English poet, dramatist, and critic.

ABRAHAM LINCOLN. 1918, (II) Play based upon Lord Charnwood's excellent biography. It was very successful both in England and in the United States, despite the astonishing eccentricities of its American idiom and local color.

Dryden, John 1631-1700 (I) "The greatest craftsman in English letters"; "the father of English criticism"; and the leader of the second rank of English poets.

Works. 1659-97. (I) The following titles are especially noteworthy: *Absalom and Achitophel* (satire in verse on the Popish Plot of 1681); *Alexander's Feast* (on the power of music—his finest poem); *All for Love* (his most successful play—an imitation of Shakespeare's *Antony and Cleopatra*); *Fables* (versified paraphrases of tales by Chaucer and Boccaccio); *The Hind and the Panther* (written, as a recent convert, in defense of the Catholic Church); and his famous Prefaces.

Du Bois, W. E. Burghardt 1868- American scholar and author. Born in Massachusetts, of mixed ancestry, Dutch, French and African. The author of many books on the Negro race, he has been a leader in the movement for its advancement and has also been prominent in left-wing politics.

Black Reconstruction . . . The Part Which Black Folk Played in the Attempt to Reconstruct Democracy in America, 1860-1880. 1935. (III) Controversial book on the Civil War and its aftermath, written with eloquence and earnestness, and based upon scholarship and careful documentation.

Dubos, René J. 1901- American bacteriologist; born in France; came to the United States in 1927; Member, Rockefeller Institute for Medical Research.

Pasteur, Free Lance of Science. 1950. "Excellent study of Pasteur the man, his methods, strengths, weaknesses, and fate; and in addition, a brilliant cross-section of scientific progress in action."— *United States Quarterly Booklist.*

Dudevant, Mme *See* Sand, George (pseudonym).

Duguid, Julian 1902- British author and explorer.

Green Hell; Adventures in the Mysterious Jungles of Eastern Bolivia. 1931. (III) Spirited narrative of danger and hardship by a writer with a gift for making those who read him share the thrills he has experienced.

Duhamel, Georges 1884- French novelist and physician; member, French Academy.

CIVILIZATION (1914-17). 1919. (II) Stories enriched with sympathy, humor and irony, inspired by the author's work as a surgeon in French war hospitals. Won the Prix Goncourt in 1918.

PASQUIER CHRONICLES. 5 pts. 1938. IV. A wonderful picture of French life and character—much more enlightening than the average tour of France. "'These are men and women—hear them quarrel, watch them eat, see how touchingly ridiculous a good man can be." —*New York Herald Tribune.*

Dumas, Alexandre 1802-70 French master of the romantic historical novel.

COUNT OF MONTE CRISTO. 1844. (I) Hero is a gallant young sailor of Marseilles who, falsely accused of political intrigue, is imprisoned for years in the Chateau d'If. Escaping at last, he digs up the fabulous treasure of which another prisoner has told him and becomes a powerful and mysterious figure in France, who devotes himself to a fearful revenge upon his enemies.

THREE MUSKETEERS. 1844. (I)

TWENTY YEARS AFTER. 1845. (I)

VICOMTE DE BRAGELONNE. 1848-50 (I)

The three titles above form the trilogy which recounts the adventures of the dashing young Gascon swordsman, D'Artagnan, from his arrival in Paris in 1625, with three crowns in his pocket, till his death forty years later, by which time he has become Marshal of France.

FORTY-FIVE GUARDSMEN. 1848. (I) This is the third and best of a series known as the Valois romances. The scene is Paris in the winter of 1585-86, during the time of Henri III and the ambitious queen-mother, Catherine de Medici. The story of political intrigue unfolds with fine dramatic effect.

Dumas, Alexandre 1824-95 French dramatist; son of Alexandre Dumas, 1802-70.

CAMILLE (La Dame aux Camélias, 1852), a sentimental play, first written as a novel, about a beautiful courtesan. It has been a perennial success on both the French and American stages. Verdi's opera *La Traviata* (1853) is founded on the same story.

Du Maurier, Daphne (Mrs. F. A. M. Browning) 1907- British novelist.

REBECCA. 1938. (IV) An absorbing story. Its drama lapses now and then into melodrama, as happened in another fine tale of a second marriage, called *Jane Eyre*. The critics have often brought up the Brontës in discussing this book.

Du Maurier, George 1834-96 English novelist and illustrator; father of Sir Gerald Du Maurier, actor; grandfather of Daphne Du Maurier, novelist.

TRILBY. 1894. (I) Charming story of Bohemian life in Paris a century ago. The wealth of illustration by the author's able hand helped greatly to build its enormous success.

PETER IBBETSON. 1892. (I)

THE MARTIAN. 1897. (I) Even as hypnotism played an important part in *Trilby*, supernaturalism and the life of dreams are prominent in the less popular but more intellectual novels, *Peter Ibbetson* and *The Martian*.

Dunbar, Paul Laurence 1872-1906 American Negro poet.

COMPLETE POEMS. 1913. Neither controversial nor obscure, Dunbar was content to express the emotions and folkways of his race with sympathy, tenderness, and at times with a sense of humor that is very appealing.

Dunne, Finley Peter 1867-1936 American humorist; creator of Martin Dooley, Irish-American saloon-keeper of Archey Road, Chicago.

MR. DOOLEY AT HIS BEST. 1938. His best was very good indeed. Historians will neglect at their peril his sometimes genial, sometimes pungent—but always humorous—comments on the American scene in the century's first two decades.

Dunsany, Lord (E. J. M. D. Plunkett) 1878- Irish dramatist and romancer. One of the most original of modern authors, he is drawn to themes uncanny, oriental, mystical, or horrible. But there is poetry in them too, and beauty.

BOOK OF WONDER. 1912. (II) "Fanciful tales, charmingly told."—*A.L.A. Catalog*, 1926.

DREAMER'S TALES. 1917. (II) Tales fascinating for their melodious diction, in a mood melancholy or macabre.

PLAYS OF GODS AND MEN. 1917. (II) "Highly imaginative plays which create a world of their own—a remote and unreal region in which men are pictured in stirring conflict with the gods."—*A.L.A. Catalog*, 1926.

FIVE PLAYS. 1924. (II) Includes much of his best and most characteristic writing, notably *The Glittering Gate.*

Durant, Will 1885- American author; studied for the priesthood; later gave himself to socialism, adult education, the labor movement, and finally to history.

STORY OF PHILOSOPHY; THE LIVES AND OPINIONS OF THE GREATEST PHILOSOPHERS. 1926. (III) Addressed to the average man, who responded with such enthusiasm that more than half a million copies were sold within a few years.

OUR ORIENTAL HERITAGE. 1935. (Vol. 1 of his *Story of Civilization.*)

STORY OF GREECE. 1939. (IV) "Eminently suited to the needs and tastes of one who comes almost virgin-minded to the great feast of Greek life and literature."—*New York Times.* (Vol. 2 of his *Story of Civilization.*)

CAESAR AND CHRIST, A HISTORY OF ROMAN CIVILIZATION AND OF CHRISTIANITY FROM THE BEGINNING TO A.D. 325. 1944. (IV) "Merits a place of honor in a world that has enjoyed Gibbon, Mommsen, and Ferrero. . . . Scholarly research has rarely been transfused into such a lively, yet stimulating and accurate history." —*Saturday Review of Literature.* (Vol. 3 of his *Story of Civilization.*)

AGE OF FAITH. 1950. History of medieval civilization from Constantine to Dante (325-1300). "A magnificent feat of popularization." (Vol. 4 of his *Story of Civilization.*)

Duranty, Walter 1884- Anglo-American journalist; special correspondent in Russia for the *New York Times.*

DURANTY REPORTS RUSSIA. 1934. (III) Impartial account of events in Russia during the years 1922-33, from the daily reports of an eye-witness trained to see and to tell what he sees. One of the best among the thousands of books that Russia has evoked in recent years.

I WRITE AS I PLEASE. 1935. (III) The book reads as the good talk of a brilliant man sounds. That is how he writes as he pleases. The discourse is of himself, of Russia and the life he led there, 1921-35. And one enjoys the revelation of a personality no less than the descriptions of a trained observer and reporter.

Duruy, Victor 1811-94 French historian.

HISTORY OF FRANCE. New edition, revised and continued to 1919. 1920. Good standard history, by an eminent historian.

Duun, Olav 1876-1939 Norwegian novelist; once called "the greatest living exponent of the peasant mind."

PEOPLE OF JUVIK. 6v. 1918-23. Series of novels dealing with four generations of a family of peasant landowners.

Eastman, Max 1883- American radical and man of letters. Founded *The Masses* and, on its suppression, in 1917, *The Liberator*. In recent years his social opinions have become less extreme.

ENJOYMENT OF POETRY. 1913. Probably his best known book.

LITERARY MIND; ITS PLACE IN AN AGE OF SCIENCE. 1931. (III) Gentle Lady Letters, he seems to say, is in retreat before the bullying advance of Science. This book contains his *Cult of Unintelligibility*, a blast at modern poetry.

ARTISTS IN UNIFORM; A STUDY OF LITERATURE AND BUREAUCRACY. 1934. A vigorous attack on the regimentation of writers and artists in Soviet Russia.

ENJOYMENT OF LAUGHTER. 1936. A study of the psychology of humor. His most popular book since *The Enjoyment of Poetry*.

Echegaray, José 1832-1916 Spanish dramatist, poet, statesman. Awarded Nobel prize for literature in 1904.

GREAT GALEOTO. *c.* 1912. Produced in America with title *The World and His Wife*, and in England as *Calumny*, which is the play's subject.

Eddas. 9th to 13th Centuries. Two ancient collections of Icelandic mythology.
   1. The Elder or Poetic Edda of Saemund; 9th to 12th centuries.
   2. The Younger or Prose Edda of Snorri; 12th century.

(See *Corpus Poeticum Boreale* and R. B. Anderson's *Norse Mythology*; and see also *Heimskringla*, on page 157 of this book.)

Eddy, Mary Baker G.   1821-1910   Founder of the Church of Christ, Scientist (1879) ; born in New Hampshire.

SCIENCE AND HEALTH, WITH KEY TO THE SCRIPTURES. 1875. Book of devotion which formulates the basic principles of Christian Science, such as belief in the unreality of evil and in the power of Truth over all disease and unhappiness. An important book for Americans to know about, as it is one of the two "Bibles" written in the United States.

Edgeworth, Maria   1767-1849   English novelist and educator who lived chiefly in Ireland.

CASTLE RACKRENT. 1800. (I) Tale describing the wild lives and manners of the Irish landed gentry of the author's day.

THE ABSENTEE. 1812. (I) Lord Clonbrony is persuaded by his wife to leave his Irish estates and enter fashionable London society.

Edmonds, Walter D.   1903-   American novelist who writes good tales, generally of the Mohawk country in Revolutionary days.

DRUMS ALONG THE MOHAWK. 1936. (IV) "A novel without dull moments, of drama, poetry and understanding."—R. L. Duffus.

Eggleston, Edward   1837-1902   American author and Methodist minister.

HOOSIER SCHOOLMASTER. 1871. (I) Good story of rough and homely pioneer-life in Indiana a century ago.

Ehrenburg, Ilya   1891-   Russian Communist novelist, journalist, and propagandist.

OUT OF CHAOS. 1934. "This pro-Soviet . . . Russian novelist maintains a clearer perspective than do most of the Bolshevik novelists writing from the inside. . . . This is a rich novel."—*New York Herald Tribune.*

THE STORM. 1949. Propaganda novel of World War II; won Stalin prize in 1948. "Should be read for . . . its study of Russian temperament and credulity, and for a few memorable French and Russian characters."—Harrison Smith, in *Saturday Review of Literature.*

Ehrlich, Leonard   1905-   American novelist.

GOD'S ANGRY MAN. 1932. (III) Broadly, this book is a historical novel of the Abolition movement; specifically, it is a fictionalized biography of John Brown of Ossawatomie.

Einstein, Albert   1879-   German-born American theoretical physicist.

RELATIVITY. 1920. (II) In this exposition of his epoch-making theory the author has tried to write so as to be understood by readers unversed in the higher mathematics.

Einstein, Albert   and Infeld, Leopold   1898-   Polish physicist.

EVOLUTION OF PHYSICS: THE GROWTH OF IDEAS FROM EARLY CONCEPTS TO RELATIVITY AND QUANTA. 1938. (IV) "Remarkably lucid exposition of the attempt of the human mind to find a connection between the world of ideas and the world of phenomena." —*Good Reading.*

Eisenhower, Dwight D.   1890-   Commander of the Allied Armies of the West in World War II; President, Columbia University, 1948-52; elected President of the United States in 1952.

CRUSADE IN EUROPE. 1948. "Account of the war in Western Europe. . . . The General's account of his mission, addressed to the American public; it is military history written by a professional soldier, who has himself had a soldier's life, culminating in supreme command."—Crane Brinton, in *Saturday Review of Literature.*

Elia, pseudonym *See* Lamb, Charles.

Eliot, George (Mrs. Mary Ann Evans Cross)   1819-80   English novelist. "George Eliot was always, from first to last, a philosopher and moralist."—Wilbur L. Cross. "Her people are all real people. You have seen such people, or you feel you might have seen such—so utterly different from the forced wit and vulgarity of so many characters of Dickens."—E. A. Freeman. "Such wealth and depth of thoughtful and fruitful humor, of vital and various intelligence, no woman has ever shown—no woman perhaps has ever shown a tithe of it."—A. C. Swinburne.

SCENES FROM CLERICAL LIFE. 1857. (I) Three long short stories. From reading them, Dickens guessed their author's secret. Writing "Mr. Eliot" soon after their publication, he says, "I have observed what seemed to me such womanly touches in these moving fictions, that the assurance on the title-page is insufficient to satisfy me even now. If they originated with no woman, I believe that no man ever before had the art of making himself mentally so like a woman."

ADAM BEDE. 1859. (I) The sterling character of the hero was drawn from that of the author's father, George Evans. Sidney Lanier said that this book placed its author "decisively at the head of English novel-writers, with only Dickens for second, even."

MILL ON THE FLOSS. 1860. (I) George Saintsbury said: "I suppose it is her best book"; and A. C. Swinburne called it "the highest and the purest and the fullest example of her matchless powers."

SILAS MARNER. 1861. (I) "Holds a higher place than any other of the author's works. It is more nearly a masterpiece."— Henry James.

Apropos of the above three titles, *Good Reading* remarks that "George Eliot's charming humor and attractive portrayal of idyllic country scenes contrast sharply with her somber studies of soul struggle and retribution."

ROMOLA. 1863. (I) Study of moral deterioration, against vivid background of Florence in the days of the Medici and Savonarola.

MIDDLEMARCH. 1871-72. (I) "Perhaps the writer's fullest expression of her philosophy of life."—W. C. Brownell. "One of her works . . . must always be the guide of those who would know the provincial England of her day. *Middlemarch* is nature itself. If merit is to be judged by perfection of execution, this depressing work sets George Eliot higher than the mingled pathos and humor of *Adam Bede* and *The Mill on the Floss*, or the dignity of *Romola.*" —Richard Garnett.

Eliot, George Fielding 1894- Anglo-American military expert.

RAMPARTS WE WATCH. 1938. (IV) A study of the problems of our national defenses, written in expectation of World War II. It is interesting to read, *after the fact*, an exposition written before the fact.

Eliot, Thomas Stearns 1888- Expatriate American poet. Long resident in England and married to an Englishwoman, in the late Twenties he became a British subject and announced himself "an

Anglo-Catholic in religion, a classicist in literature and a royalist in politics." *Good Reading* describes him as a "subtle, nonconforming poet, who grows in significance and stature with the passing years."

SELECTED ESSAYS: 1917-1922. 1932. (III) The author's own choice from the bulk of his literary criticism, chiefly of English poetry. Probably no judgments of greater authority have been handed down during this generation.

MURDER IN THE CATHEDRAL. 1935. (III) Drama in verse, dealing with the last weeks of Thomas à Becket (1118-70) and culminating in his violent death at the cathedral altar. While by no means simple, this play is less obscure than much of Eliot's poetry.

COLLECTED POEMS, 1909-1935. 1936. (IV) Includes *The Waste Land*, 1922, wail of the "lost generation"—an important landmark in latter-day literature. "Gives a birdseye view of Mr. Eliot's poetic progress."—*New Statesman.* "A body of verse that . . . has a technical eloquence equaled by the fewest of his contemporaries. His accomplishment may be measured by the very violence of the reaction against him."—Babette Deutsch, in *New York Herald Tribune.*

IDEA OF A CHRISTIAN SOCIETY. 1939. "It is bound to exercise a lasting influence upon all future investigations regarding the nature and function of the social order."—*Spectator.*

FOUR QUARTETS. 1943. (IV) Some critics consider these religious poems his best work. "You do not read great poetry unprepared, ignorant or carelessly. Mr. Eliot's poetry is exacting: it has the right to be."—*Commonweal.*

NOTES TOWARDS THE DEFINITION OF CULTURE. 1949. "Interesting and provocative little work . . . by an intellectual, and for intellectuals."—*Kirkus.* "A sermon once again on the idea of a Christian society."—*New York Times.*

COCKTAIL PARTY. 1950. "The way he can put the English language through hoops is always something to see."—*New Yorker.* "Most will agree that the play is fascinating to read as well as to see on the stage. . . . It introduces a new note into writing for the contemporary theatre."—J. W. Krutch, in *New York Herald Tribune.*

Ellis, Havelock   1859-1940   English psychologist and literary critic; best known for his *Psychology of Sex* (1900-1910), a monumental work in 6 volumes, for specialists.

DANCE OF LIFE. 1908. (II) About life as an art. Essays on dancing, thinking, writing, religion, and morals.

Elyot, Sir Thomas   *c*. 1490-1546   British scholar and diplomat.

BOKE NAMED THE GOVERNOUR. 1531. One of the earliest treatises in English on education, this book gives directions for training a youth who is destined to become a ruler.

Emerson, Ralph Waldo   1803-82   American essayist, poet and philosopher. "One of the few men of genius that our age has produced. There needs no better proof of it than his masculine faculty for fecundating other minds."—James Russell Lowell. "In all his writings and speakings the great man shines through and eclipses the great writer. The flavor of character shines through and dominates the pages."—John Burroughs.

NATURE. 1836. (1) *The Cambridge History of American Literature,* polysyllabically, calls this first volume in the Emersonian canon "the philosophical constitution of Transcendentalism."

ESSAYS. 2v. 1841-44. (1) Paul Elmer More considered these the "most characteristic and influential of his books."

REPRESENTATIVE MEN. 1850. (I) Studies of Plato, Swedenborg, Montaigne, Shakespeare, Napoleon, and Goethe.

POEMS. 1847. (I) They have been described as "intellectual, gnomic, and metaphysical." "Emerson for his sweet vital-tasting melody, rhymed philosophy, and poems as amber-clear as the honey of the wild bee he loves to sing."—Walt Whitman.

ENGLISH TRAITS. 1856. (I) "Probably the most masterly and startling analysis of a people which has ever been offered; unsurpassed too in brilliance and penetration of statement."—George Parsons Lathrop.

CONDUCT OF LIFE. 1860. (I) Based on lectures delivered in 1851.

SOCIETY AND SOLITUDE. 1870. (I) Based on lectures delivered from 1858 on.

Among the most admired single essays of Emerson may be mentioned *The American Scholar, Compensation, Friendship, The Oversoul, Nature, The Poet, Love,* and *Man the Reformer.*

LETTERS, 1813-1881. 6v. 1939. (IV) "These letters are from a Nineteenth-Century mind who presumably rivals Lincoln as one of the seminal minds of the age. . . . More abundantly than the formal *Essays* or the *Journals* this encyclopedic edition of Emerson's *Letters* fills interstices in his outer and, to a lesser extent, his inner life."—*Yale Review.*

Engels, Friedrich, joint author   *See* Marx, Karl.

Epictetus   *c.* **60-120**   Greek Stoic philosopher who taught in Rome.

MORAL DISCOURSES. (I)   Collected by his pupil, Arrian. The gist of his doctrine is to desire nothing but freedom and contentment; happiness depends upon our own wills, which even Zeus cannot break.

Erasmus, Desiderius   1465-1536   Dutch satirist, and classical and theological scholar; called the Voltaire of the Renaissance. His best service to theology was his edition (1516) of the New Testament in Greek, with Latin translation.

PRAISE OF FOLLY. 1509. (I)   Satire on clerical abuses and human foolishness.

COLLOQUIES. 1516. (I)   A book of caustic dialogs which was the best-seller of the Sixteenth and Seventeenth Centuries. For the most part, like its predecessor, this book is devoted to a castigation of the vices of both priests and laymen.

Erckmann, Émile   1822-99   and **Chatrian, Alexandre   1826-90** These authors, both born in Lorraine, collaborated on many historical novels and some plays.

THE CONSCRIPT. 1864. (I)   Adventures of a   peasant-hero, forced into the bloody struggle of the Napoleonic Wars.

FRIEND FRITZ. 1864. (I)   Tale of Alsatian village life; perhaps their best book.

Erskine, John 1879-1951 American professor, poet, novelist, musician; member, National Institute of Arts and Letters.

PRIVATE LIFE OF HELEN OF TROY. 1925. (II) This story of Helen's life after the Trojan escapade is made amusing by flashing epigram and sparkling dialog.

DELIGHT OF GREAT BOOKS. 1928. (III) Critical interpretations which introduce the reader to about a dozen great books and great writers of English literature.

MY LIFE AS A TEACHER. 1948. He opens the door to a delightful kind of self-education in all things that make life fine and enjoyable.

Ervine, St. John 1883- Irish dramatist and novelist.

JANE CLEGG. 1913. (II) This play depicts a fine woman's struggle for the sake of the children, with an inferior husband.

JOHN FERGUSON. 1914. (II) A freak of chance—failure to post a letter—brings overwhelming ruin in this Irish tragedy.

ALICE AND A FAMILY. 1915. (II) Humorous story of how a capable Cockney woman bullied a group of shiftless Londoners into industry and consequent prosperity.

Eucken, Rudolf C. 1846-1926 German philosopher who emphasized the spiritual rather than the physical and biological aspects of man, and upheld the Christian point of view. Won Nobel prize in 1908.

CHRISTIANITY AND THE NEW IDEALISM. 1907. (II) Discussion of the spirit of Christianity, urging the need for its regeneration.

PROBLEM OF HUMAN LIFE AS VIEWED BY THE GREAT THINKERS. 1909. Revised edition. 1914. (II) Introduction to the history and criticism of philosophy. Author was convinced that human destinies are ruled by spiritual necessities.

Euripides. 480-406 B.C. The last of the three great authors of Greek tragedy. He is more modern and realistic than Æschylus and Sophocles, and he wrote of men rather than of gods and demigods.

WORKS. (The Everyman's Library edition, 2 vol., is satisfactory.) Of about 90 plays written by him 18 survive, and of these the favorites are perhaps *Alcestis* (illustrating woman's devotion),

Hippolytus (on the illicit love of Phaedra), *Bacchae* (glorification of Bacchus), *Medea* (the sorceress who killed her sons), *Andromache* (devoted wife of Hector), *Iphigenia* (whom her father, Agamemnon, vowed to sacrifice), *Hecuba* (sorrowing mother of Hector), *Electra*, *Orestes*, and *The Trojan Women*.

Evelyn, John   1620-1706   British diarist and scholar.

DIARY. (I)   Covers the years 1641-95, while Pepys, his less exemplary but more interesting rival, recorded events of 1660-69 only.

SYLVA, OR A DISCOURSE ON FOREST TREES.   1664.   The first English work on forestry.

Everyman.   English morality play of the Fifteenth Century. These plays were quaint precursors of the noble drama of the Elizabethan Age. *Everyman* is symbolic of humanity. The characters with whom he has to deal are personified vices and virtues. (Everyman's Library.)

"F. P. A."   *See* Adams, Franklin Pierce.

Fabre, Jean-Henri   1823-1915   French entomologist. Maeterlinck called him "the insects' Homer." He was an unusual personality: at once peasant, man of letters, and scientist.

SOCIAL LIFE IN THE INSECT WORLD.   1912.   (II)   "One of the most captivating books of our generation."—*Athenaeum.*

LIFE AND LOVE OF THE INSECT.   1912.   (II)   Lively descriptions of the habits of beetles, etc.

LIFE OF THE SPIDER.   1913.   (II)   All his books are readable, but this has been called the best of them.

Fairbank, John King   1907-   In China he studied the impact of western imperialism on oriental society.

THE UNITED STATES AND CHINA.   1948.   "Will assist the American public—and American policy-makers if they will read it—to understand the realities of our contest with communism for the favor of the Chinese people."—*Political Science Quarterly.*

Falkner, J. M.   English author.

MOONFLEET. 1893. This tiptop adventure story of England in the Eighteenth Century is little known in the United States. It appeals strongly to most men and boys, and has been often compared to *Treasure Island* and *Kidnapped*.

Falkner, William   *See* Faulkner, William.

Faraday, Michael   1791-1867   English chemist and physicist. "He was a Shakespeare of research," the story of whose work—especially with electricity—has permanent interest.

EXPERIMENTAL RESEARCHES IN ELECTRICITY. 3v. 1839-55. A monumental work, both in the history and literature of science. "In masterly clearness of exposition . . . Faraday was as remarkable as he was in intellectual power and in discoveries."

Farigoule, Louis   *See* Romains, Jules (pseudonym).

Farnol, Jeffery   1878-1952   English author of blamelessly romantic costume novels.

BROAD HIGHWAY. 1911. (II) Romance *in excelsis*. The Eighteenth Century lives again—robustly—in this high-colored tale of the English countryside.

Farquhar, George   1678-1707   British dramatist of the Restoration period.

BEAUX' STRATAGEM. 1707. A witty comedy and the author's masterpiece; written during the progress of what he knew to be a fatal illness.

Farrell, James T.   1904-   Prolific American novelist who usually writes in the tradition of naturalism, combined with a strain of the stream-of-consciousness technique. He says, "We don't need censorship here. American authors do not try to tell enough of the truth to invite censorship."

STUDS LONIGAN. 3v. 1932-35. Trilogy composed of *Young Lonigan, Young Manhood of Studs Lonigan*, and *Judgment Day*. It paints a grim picture of the sordid life of young Irish Catholics in the Chicago slums.

Faulkner, William 1897-   American fictionist of Mississippi, whose preoccupation with both genteel and proletarian degeneracy has not prevented his slow and steady rise to an eminence of critical acclaim that is unequaled by any American contemporary. "The South, as Faulkner depicts it, is the abode, not of gentility and elegance, but of degeneracy and morbidity. . . . This is the nightmarish world of a horribly wise and tormented child. . . . Faulkner writes like a man possessed of devils."—F. B. Millett. In 1951 Faulkner was awarded the Nobel Prize for literature.

THE SOUND AND THE FURY. 1929. An idiot son observes the decay of an aristocratic Southern family.

AS I LAY DYING. 1930. A poor-white mother dies and is buried by her brood.

SANCTUARY. 1930. (III) Concerned to a great extent with murder and lynching.

THE UNVANQUISHED. 1938. (IV) Normal story of the Sartoris family during Civil War and Reconstruction.

WILD PALMS. 1939. (IV) "After a while this bestiality becomes merely ludicrous."—Clifton Fadiman, in *New Yorker*. "It is very good Faulkner."—P. M. Jack, in *New York Times*.

THE HAMLET. 1940. (IV) "For extremely limited library purchase because of its abnormalities and its tortured style."—*Library Journal*.

INTRUDER IN THE DUST. 1948. A brilliant story of morality and murder. "An important book in a major literary career."—*Library Journal*. "The mood is an unusual one for Faulkner. Hate, violence and degradation are in the background."—Edward Weeks, in *Atlantic*. "It is not easy reading. But the reward is worth the trouble."—*Time*.

COLLECTED STORIES. 1950. A collection of 42 short stories; it won the Nobel prize. "There is not a story in this book which does not have elements of great fiction."—*Chicago Tribune*. "These *Collected Stories* certainly strengthen the case of those critics who have steadily maintained that Faulkner is the greatest living American writer."—*Atlantic*. "William Faulkner is beginning to emerge rather clearly as the most considerable Twentieth Century American writer of short fiction; the present volume is a publishing event of real significance."—*Saturday Review of Literature*.

Faure, Élie   1873-1937   French art critic.

History of Art. 4v. 1923-30 (II) In this history he "reconstructs the life of the people and shows their art as an expression of their life."

Faÿ, Bernard   1893-   French scholar, specializing in American history and biography. Served in French army in World War I; collaborated with Germans in World War II.

Franklin, the Apostle of Modern Times. 1929. (III) Readable and scholarly. One of the best recent biographies of Franklin.

George Washington, Republican Aristocrat. 1931. (III) Shrewd and witty interpretation of Washington as the lonely, landholding aristocrat who made our democracy possible.

Fay, Sidney Bradshaw   1876-   American professor of history.

Origins of the World War. 2v. 1928. (III) Why World War I happened. Scholarly and well documented; clearly written and interesting. Revised edition in one volume appeared in 1930.

The Federalist; a Commentary on the Constitution of the United States. First published in newspapers, (1788). (I) Alexander Hamilton wrote most of these eighty five papers, but a few are by James Madison or John Jay. In them the Constitution is defended as well as expounded. Brander Matthews described them as "perhaps the ablest political essays in the English language." There are excellent editions by H. C. Lodge (1891) and by P. L. Ford (1898).

Federova, Nina, pseudonym (Antonina Riasanovsky)   1895-   Russian-born writer, now a citizen of the United States.

The Family. 1940. (IV) Story of a group of White Russians in China in 1937, before and during the Japanese invasion. Won *The Atlantic's* ten-thousand-dollar prize.

Feis, Herbert   1893-   American economist.

Spanish Story. 1948. About Franco and World War II. Authoritative account of how the United States and Britain kept Spain passably neutral.

Fénelon, François de　1651-1715　French ecclesiastic and author.

ADVENTURES OF TELEMACHUS. 1699. (I) A masterpiece of French classic prose, this didactic romance was designed to instruct the author's pupil, grandson of Louis XIV, in the conduct of life and the responsibilities of absolute government. It describes the adventures of the son of Ulysses in search of his father.

Ferber, Edna　1887-　American fictionist and playwright; member, National Institute of Arts and Letters.

So BIG. 1924. (II) The stout-hearted heroine made a good life and a career of truck farming. Won Pulitzer prize in 1925.

SHOW BOAT. 1926. (III) A melodramatic story of the Mississippi that, between covers and on stage and screen, delighted millions with its lively presentation of a picturesque if shoddy phase of American life.

CIMARRON. 1930. (III) Gorgeous tale of Oklahoma, from the "Boomers" of 1889 to the Oil Boom of recent years.

PECULIAR TREASURE. 1939. (IV) Good-humored and entertaining autobiography. America has been good to her. She is aware of this and says frankly that she loves the United States and its institutions.

Ferrero, Guglielmo　1872-1942　Italian historian and sociologist.

GREATNESS AND DECLINE OF ROME. 9v. 1902-08. (I and II) This is history written boldly in the bright light of current events, rather than cautiously in the twilight of archaeological tradition.

Feuchtwanger, Lion　1884-　German novelist and dramatist. His books were suppressed in Germany during World War I, and under the Nazis he went into exile.

POWER. 1926. (III) Historical romance of an ambitious Jew's rise and fall at the court of Wurtemburg in the Eighteenth Century. (Published in English also as *Jud Süss*, its German title.)

THE OPPERMANNS. 1934. (III) Novel about a Jewish family in Berlin during Hitler's rise to power. The author writes always with a restraint which increases the book's impressiveness.

Field, Eugene   1850-95   American poet, humorist, and book-lover; with a personality sentimental, child-loving, pleasantly book-ish and irresponsible.   (He called himself "the good knight *sans peur et sans monnaie.*")

Works; especially *Little Book of Profitable Tales, With Trumpet and Drum* (verses for and about children), and *Love Affairs of a Bibliomaniac* (essays).

Field, Rachel Lyman (Mrs. Arthur Pederson) 1894-1942 American novelist.

Time out of Mind.   1935.   (III)   An old-fashioned sentimen-tal romance—but a good one—about three generations of a Maine shipbuilding family.

All This and Heaven Too.   1938.   (IV)   Novel based on curious events in the author's own family history. She was the great-niece of her heroine, defendant in a murder trial which was a *cause celèbre* in Paris in 1847.

Fielding, Henry   1707-54   English novelist.

Joseph Andrews.   1742.   (I)   Hero of this satirical novel is a handsome but disconcertingly chaste footman, brother of Richard-son's fatiguing heroine, Pamela, who was also virtuous and pursued.

Jonathan Wild.   1743.   Fielding here follows Defoe in writing a novel about the career of Wild, an actual criminal who was hanged at Tyburn.

Tom Jones.   1749.   (I)   Fielding's masterpiece.   As the first English novel in which character is stressed as strongly as inci-dent, this book is an important landmark in English literature.

Amelia.   1751.   (I)   It was a softened, chastened Fielding who wrote this book.   The heroine, drawn from his own wife, is a model of patient, long-suffering, conjugal affection.

Firdausi.   940(?)-1020(?)   Persian epic poet.

Shah Namah, or the Book of Kings, is the great epic of Persia, and has been called one of the six great epics of the world.   Rus-tum, the hero, is so redoubtable that as a babe he required the services of ten wet nurses.

Fischer, John 1910- American editor, foreign correspondent, government official.

WHY THEY BEHAVE LIKE RUSSIANS. 1947. (*The Scared Men in the Kremlin* is the British title.) "This book will go unusually far to help Americans understand the Russians."—*Christian Science Monitor.* "Deserves and should have the widest popular reading by all Americans concerned with their country's foreign policy."—F. R. Dulles, in *New York Herald Tribune.*

Fischer, Louis 1896- American foreign correspondent.

GANDHI AND STALIN: TWO SIGNS AT THE WORLD'S CROSSROADS. 1947. "An old hand at the Russian problem . . . has here written a competent, dogmatic book that states the facts, analyzes them soundly, and sets down a program."—Brooks Atkinson, in *Saturday Review of Literature.*

LIFE OF MAHATMA GANDHI. 1950. "Long affectionate biography, based on a variety of sources . . . and personal interviews."—*Book Review Digest.* "Louis Fischer, who knew Gandhi as intimately as any American, has undertaken to show us how greatness took hold of this little man and made of him one of the world's most striking personalities."

Fisher, Dorothy Canfield 1879- American novelist. Member, National Institute of Arts and Letters. Since before the World Wars hers has been a sane and wholesome influence in American life and letters.

MONTESSORI MOTHER. 1912. (II) This venture into the pedagogical field by Mrs. Fisher, the matron, met with such success that it has been translated into at least five foreign tongues.

THE BENT TWIG. 1915. (II) Story of a good mother's influence on a daughter's life.

BRIMMING CUP. 1921. (II) "Genuinely first class achievement. . . . The heart searchings of a nice *talented* woman absorbed in family cares."—*Saturday Review of Literature.*

ROUGH HEWN. 1922. (II) About the earlier life of the principal characters in *The Brimming Cup.* "Mrs. Fisher has never written with a surer wisdom, or a defter touch."—John Farrar.

HER SON'S WIFE. 1926. (III) Who can write about the old New England stock like Mrs. Fisher? Her books are as native, as wholesome, as fragrant as birch beer; but they have a deal more body. This is one of the best of them.

DEEPENING STREAM. 1930. (III) The critics are agreed that this is one of her most satisfactory novels. That means that it is distinctly worth while.

SEASONED TIMBER. 1939. (IV) This novel is about a Vermont academy. "Miss Canfield has finely brought her New England skilfully and inevitably into the current of a changing time." —*Saturday Review of Literature.*

Fisher, Dorothy Canfield, translator *See* Papini, Giovanni.

Fisher, Vardis 1895- American novelist; born in Idaho, of old Mormon stock.

CHILDREN OF GOD. 1939. (IV) A novel which tells the tale of the first fifty years of Mormonism. "One of the most extraordinarily interesting stories I have ever read."—Clifton Fadiman.

Fiske, John 1842-1901 American philosopher and historian.

DESTINY OF MAN. 1884. (I) Explains the general theory of evolution and reconciles the spirit and teachings of science with those of the New Testament.

CRITICAL PERIOD OF AMERICAN HISTORY, 1783-89. 1888. (I) Compact, readable study of the years of constitution making.

BEGINNINGS OF NEW ENGLAND. 1889. "Fortunately," he tells us, "we can learn something from the stumblings of our forefathers."

AMERICAN REVOLUTION. 1891. (Richly illustrated edition, 1896.) (I) "Exhibits a delightful vivacity, and dramatic skill in the portrait of Washington as the central figure of the American revolt."

FitzGerald, Edward 1809-83 English translator and poet. "A scholar and a gentleman."—James Russell Lowell. "An eccentric man of genius who took more pains to avoid fame than others do to seek it."—William Aldis Wright.

LETTERS. 1889-1902. Edmund Gosse declared him to be "one of the most pungent, individual and picturesque of English letter-writers." In this field he deserves to rank with Gray and Cowper, Walpole and even Lamb.

(*See also* Omar Khayyam.)

Fitzgerald, F. Scott   1896-1940   American fictionist. He spoke for the Jazz Age after World War I—and depicted its disillusion, confusion, and eventual tragedy.

THIS SIDE OF PARADISE. 1920. The book which made Fitzgerald. Its sad picture of the times, "Flaming Youth," became the rage and was widely imitated.

TENDER IS THE NIGHT. 1934. Depressing picture of wealthy, sophisticated Americans sadly trying to have a good time on the French Riviera.

THE LAST TYCOON, AN UNFINISHED NOVEL, TOGETHER WITH THE GREAT GATSBY AND SELECTED STORIES. 1941. (IV) The unfinished novel is a striking story about Hollywood. *The Great Gatsby*, here reprinted, is a short novel about life, fast and furious, on Long Island in the days of Prohibition; it is generally considered his masterpiece. *The Nation* said that this volume presents the best of Fitzgerald.

CRACK-UP, WITH OTHER UNCOLLECTED PIECES, NOTEBOOKS AND UNPUBLISHED LETTERS; edited by Edmund Wilson. 1945. (IV) "The perfect tribute to his life and work, for it is incomplete, romantic, full of verve and promise, full of love, yet somehow tragically unsatisfying."—*Book Week*.

Flaubert, Gustave   1821-80   French novelist, by turns realist and romanticist.

MADAME BOVARY. 1857. (I) A miracle of scientific realism, this study of the disintegration of a romantic woman's character, is both the author's masterpiece and his first book. He spent eight years of painfully hard labor writing it.

SALAMMBÔ. 1862. (I) Gorgeous historical romance of old Carthage. Erudite in the extreme, it is also overelaborate. All the details, whether important or not, are painted with equal care and splendor. In short, the author seems to have done his best to fabricate a technicolor movie a century ahead of time.

SENTIMENTAL EDUCATION. 1869. (I) Melancholy and satirical picture of Parisian life and character among the dilettantes, intellectuals, and politicians at the time of the Revolution of 1848.

Flavin, Martin 1883- American playwright (1923-37) and, later, novelist.

JOURNEY IN THE DARK. 1943. (IV) This story won both the Harper and the Pulitzer prizes. "He has taken a superficially uninteresting man and made him interesting. . . . No mean achievement. He has also made a plain Middle Western business man a symbol of all these United States."—*New York Times.*

Flecker, James Elroy 1884-1915 English poet.

COLLECTED POEMS. 1916. (II) "His ideal in poetry was the jeweled phrase, the gem-like verse, the exquisitely chiseled stanza."

Fleming, Peter 1907- British journalist and traveler.

BRAZILIAN ADVENTURE. 1934. (III) Partly satirical, wholly entertaining account of travel and adventure with an expedition to the unexplored regions of central Brazil.

Fletcher, John, joint author *See* Beaumont, Francis and Fletcher, John.

Flexner, Simon 1863-1946 **and Flexner, James Thomas** 1907- Medical scholars and teachers; father and son.

WILLIAM HENRY WELCH AND THE HEROIC AGE OF AMERICAN MEDICINE. 1941. (IV) "The best history we have read of the birth of medical science in the United States. The Flexners, father and son, have made a worthy contribution to the biography of their time."—*Commonweal.*

Flynn, Edward Joseph 1891- American politician; Democratic party boss of the Borough of the Bronx, New York City.

YOU'RE THE BOSS. 1947. An autobiography. "Clearly destined to become a small political classic."—A. M. Schlesinger, Jr., in *Nation.* "Probably the frankest and most candid exposition of the rules and gimmicks of practical politics to come from the pen of an urban political leader. . . . This apologia for bosses and machines . . . is so complete that one wonders if the author realizes the extent of his own self-revelation."—*American Political Science Review.*

Foerster, Norman   1887-   American critic and professor of English.

AMERICAN CRITICISM; A STUDY IN LITERARY THEORY FROM POE TO THE PRESENT. 1928. (III)   Consideration of the literary theories of Poe, Emerson, Lowell, and Whitman.

TOWARDS STANDARDS. 1930.   Study of current literary problems "from the specifically Humanistic point of view."

Fogazzaro, Antonio   1842-1911   Italian novelist, representative of the liberal Catholic movement in Italian literature.   In his trilogy about the Maironi family his aim is to present in fiction a movement to reconcile Roman Catholicism with modern science, and incidentally to encourage reform in the Church.   The trilogy consists of *The Patriot* (1895), *The Sinner* (1901)   (II),   and *The Saint* (1905)   (II).

Forbes, Esther   1894-   American author who specializes in vivid and convincing re-creations of the life of colonial New England.

PARADISE. 1937.   (IV)   Story of a Massachusetts family who settled in 1639 on an estate twenty miles inland from Boston.   The story ends with an exciting picture of King Philip's War.

PAUL REVERE AND THE WORLD HE LIVED IN. 1942.   (IV)   Won the Pulitzer prize.   "Her biography of Paul Revere takes at once a high and lasting place in American literature."—Carl Van Doren, in *New York Herald Tribune.*

RUNNING OF THE TIDE. 1948.   Novel about Salem, Massachusetts, from 1795 till after the War of 1812.   "I know no chronicle of a New England town that is better . . . nor any Salem novel to be compared with it since Hawthorne."—Carl Van Doren, in *New York Herald Tribune.*

Ford, Ford Madox (originally Ford Madox Hueffer)   1873-1939   English novelist and critic; nephew of William Rossetti.

PARADE'S END. 1950.   Four out-of-print novels are now brought together in this one volume.   They are *Some Do Not* (1924), *No More Parades* (1925), *A Man Could Stand Up* (1926), and *The Last Post* (1926).

"This novel, so curiously neglected for a quarter of a century, now emerges as one of the few real masterpieces of fiction that have been produced during our era."—Lloyd Morris, in *New York Herald Tribune*. It tells the story of an English gentleman before, during and after World War I.

Ford, John   1586-1640(?)   English dramatist; last of the great Elizabethans.

BROKEN HEART. 1633. "I do not know where to find, in any play, a climax so grand, so solemn, and so surprising as this."— Charles Lamb.

PERKIN WARBECK. 1634. "It is indeed the best specimen of the historical drama to be found out of Shakespeare."—Hartley Coleridge.

Ford, Paul Leicester   1865-1902   American novelist, historian, biographer.

HONORABLE PETER STIRLING. 1894. (I) Story of New York City politics half a century ago. The hero's personality, character, and career are supposed to have been suggested by those of Grover Cleveland.

JANICE MEREDITH. 1899. (I) Romance of the American Revolution. Historically above reproach and very popular.

Forester, Cecil Scott   1899-   English novelist.

CAPTAIN HORATIO HORNBLOWER. 1937. "Three-decker yarn about a first-class sailing man in fights and frolics."—*Good Reading*.

SKY AND THE FOREST. 1948. A story of primitive Africans and Arab slavers.

Forster, Edward Morgan   1879-   English novelist and critic.

PASSAGE TO INDIA. 1924. (II) Sad story about the lack of mutual sympathy and understanding between cultured Indians and the British official class a quarter-century ago. "This book is beautiful and ironic and clear as divining crystal."—Elinor Wylie.

ASPECTS OF THE NOVEL. 1927. Developed from a series of lectures delivered at Cambridge University.

ABINGER HARVEST. 1936 and 1947. Selected critical essays. "They are keen, provocative, entertaining, learned—and whatever else good essays should be."—*Christian Century*.

Room with a View.   1908, 1923, 1943.   Subtle, witty, and ironic romance of a conventionally-minded English girl in Italy.

Forster, John   1812-76   English biographer.

Life of Charles Dickens.   1872-74.   (I)   This is not the only good life of Dickens but it is the earliest one and the only one written by an intimate friend.

Fosdick, Harry Emerson   1878-   American clergyman and publicist.

Christianity and Progress.   1922.   (II)   "Interpretation of Christianity as a dynamic religion, capable of using its magnificent inheritance for the making of a better world."—*Journal of Religion.*

Guide to Understanding the Bible.   1938.   "Tracing the development of concepts of God, man, right and wrong, suffering and immortality."—*Good Reading.*

On Being a Real Person.   1943.   (IV)   Consideration of human problems, the adequate solution of which makes possible the well-organized life.   "One of the most helpful books in this field I have ever read."—E. H. Johnson, in *Survey Graphic.*

Fowler, Gene   1890-   American journalist, playwright, biographer.

Good Night, Sweet Prince.   1944.   *Saturday Review of Literature* reviewer calls this life of John Barrymore "a tasteful, affectionate and impeccably accurate book. . . . To read it is to know the rare and tragic man that was John Barrymore."

Beau James.   1949.   Life and times of Jimmy Walker, Mayor and favorite playboy of New York in the Twenties, long a famous figure in the night-life of the city.   "Packed with good anecdotes, Broadway lore, and samples of Walker's quick wit and gift for repartee."—C. J. Rolo, in *Atlantic.*   "It is moving, it is funny, and somehow it is as sad as clods falling on a coffin."—*New York Herald Tribune.*

Fox, George   1624-91   English founder of the Society of Friends.

Journal.   1694.   "One of the most remarkable and revealing of religious autobiographies."—Keller.   "Beneath the simplicity of the man . . . lay the complexities of the mystic, with the strength of a martyr."—*English Library.*

Fox, John 1863-1919 American popular novelist. His romances were wholesome and flavored with his lively appreciation of the sylvan beauty of the Southern highlands.

LITTLE SHEPHERD OF KINGDOM COME. 1903. (II) Love story of a Kentucky mountain boy during the Civil War.

TRAIL OF THE LONESOME PINE. 1908. (II) This love story is dashed with melodrama. In the background are an industrial boom and an old-time Kentucky feud.

Foxe, John 1516-87 English martyrologist.

ACTES AND MONUMENTS. 1563. Generally known as *Foxe's Book of Martyrs,* this history of religious persecution from the days of St. Stephen to those of Bloody Mary is a curiosity of literature. A century ago a large edition, with crude, well-worn, but terrifying woodcuts, lay on the parlor table of every well-conducted Protestant grandfather. It was a grand book to shudder over on a rainy Sunday afternoon, but it was not wise to study it just before going to bed.

France, Anatole 1844-1924 French novelist and satirist; "true son of Voltaire."

CRIME OF SYLVESTRE BONNARD. 1881. (I) Delightful and perfectly innocuous story of an old French scholar.

THAÏS. 1890. Egyptian love story of a beautiful pagan and an early Christian ascetic.

AT THE SIGN OF THE REINE PÉDAUQUE. 1893. Novel about the irreverent but philosophical Abbé Coignard, one of France's best characters.

PENGUIN ISLAND. 1908. (I and II) "Ironical history of the human race . . . destructive in its mockery."—E. A. Baker.

GODS ARE ATHIRST. 1912. (II) Novel of the French Revolution—"a masterpiece of sardonic humor."

MAN WHO MARRIED A DUMB WIFE. 1915. (II) Diverting farce in the medieval manner. Full of broad comedy, robust humor, and verbal prestidigitation.

ON LIFE AND LETTERS. 4v. 1911-24. (II) Very readable essays in his characteristic style.

Francis of Assisi, Saint   1182-1226

LITTLE FLOWERS.   Collection of miracles and legends, attributed to the most Christlike of the saints.

Franklin, Benjamin   1706-90   American statesman, diplomat, author, scientist, craftsman, and inventor.

AUTOBIOGRAPHY.   (I)   Tells the story of his life from 1707 to 1757. "Not only remains one of the most widely known and readable books in our language but [often translated] has had the distinction of enriching the literature of nearly every other."—John Bigelow.

Frazer, Sir James George   1854-1941   British anthropologist.

GOLDEN BOUGH.   3rd edition   12v.   1911-15.   World-renowned work on anthropology and comparative folklore, mythology and primitive religion—magic, totems, taboos, fetishes, etc.

Frazier, Edward Franklin   1894-   American sociologist since 1920; he has specialized in the Negro problem.

NEGRO IN THE UNITED STATES.   1949.   A scholarly summing up of his history and sociology. "It would seem to be the definitive work on its subject . . . almost in the class of required homework for anyone who would pretend to speak with authority on the not yet completely emancipated tenth of our population."—*New Yorker.*

Freeman, Douglas Southall   1886-   "Our most eminent biographer and ablest military historian."—Allan Nevins.

ROBERT E. LEE; A BIOGRAPHY.   4v.   1934-35.   (III)   Biography of the old school: the fruit of a Southern scholar's twenty years of patient toil. Won the Pulitzer prize for biography in 1934.

LEE'S LIEUTENANTS.   3v.   1942-44.   "The standard of scholarship and literary craftsmanship . . . will not disappoint the many admirers of Dr. Freeman's *Robert E. Lee.* As a writer of military biography Freeman has few equals."—*Yale Review.*

GEORGE WASHINGTON; A BIOGRAPHY.   Vols. 1 and 2 (of six vols.)   1948.   "From it emerges a great figure, for the first time thoroughly, clearly and faithfully delineated."—L. H. Butterfield, in *Saturday Review of Literature.* (Vols. 3 and 4 were issued in 1951.)

Freeman, Edward Augustus 1823-92 British historian.

HISTORY OF THE NORMAN CONQUEST. 6v. 1867-79 (I) The chief authority for the period. C. K. Adams called it "one of the greatest monuments of English historical scholarship."

Freeman, Mrs. Mary E. Wilkins 1862-1930 American fictionist. Mrs. Freeman has written remarkable stories about New England life. Her heroines are often neither pretty nor clever, nor rich; sometimes they are not even young. Their lives appear to be as barren as the rocky hills about them. Nevertheless this author contrives not only to find in them hidden beauty and human interest, but also to make these qualities manifest to her readers.

HUMBLE ROMANCE, AND OTHER STORIES. 1887. (I)

NEW ENGLAND NUN, AND OTHER STORIES. 1891. (I) The two titles named above are among her earlier and more characteristic books of short stories. Among her novels the following title is in many ways a good example.

JEROME, A POOR MAN. 1897. (I) A study of character, developed by struggle, as the boy becomes the man.

Frenssen, Gustav 1863- German novelist.

JÖRN UHL. 1905. (II) Somber, yet hopeful, sincere and wholesome story of Germany before the Wars. Full of poetic feeling.

Freud, Sigmund 1856-1939 Austrian psychologist and founder of psychoanalysis who emphasized thwarted sex as the cause of psychic disorders. Most of his colleagues now admit that there are other momentous factors in human relationships.

BASIC WRITINGS. 1938. (Modern Library Giants) "Collection of the essential theories of one of the most influential modern psychologists."—Good Reading.

Froissart, Jean 1337-1410 French historian and poet.

CHRONICLES. 1523. (First English translation). (I) Contemporary record of the history, character, and manners of the Fourteenth Century in Europe—the fighting, feasting, and pageantry of feudal times.

Frost, Robert 1875- American poet, college-professor-at-large, and farmer. Winner of the Pulitzer prize for poetry in 1924, 1931, 1937, and 1943. Member, American Academy of Arts and Sciences.

COMPLETE POEMS. 1949. (II) Includes the contents of ten books from *A Boy's Will* (1913) to *A Masque of Mercy* (1947). "At his best he is in the tradition of Hesiod and, to a different degree, of Theocritus and Virgil, as well as the English Georgians." —David Daiches, in *New York Times*.

Froude, James Anthony 1818-94 English biographer and historian.

SHORT STUDIES ON GREAT SUBJECTS. 2v. 1877-82. (I) "The peculiar charm of Froude . . . lies in his picturesque and almost romantic manner, making past events and persons live once more and move across his pages."—Keller.

CAESAR, A SKETCH. 1879. (I) Outline picture of Roman life and conditions in Caesar's time, while the Roman republic was being converted into a military empire.

Fry, Christopher 1907- English playwright.

LADY'S NOT FOR BURNING. 1950. "Unquestionably, this is a work of genius."—*Catholic World*. "A medieval comedy rich in character-drawing, killingly funny even in the library, and shot with brilliant poetry."—*Chicago Sun*.

Fry, Roger 1866-1934 British art critic.

VISION AND DESIGN. 1920.

TRANSFORMATIONS. 1926. "These two books have helped many who like sculpture and pictorial art to look at the masters and at the work of modern artists with understanding and critical appreciation."—*English Library*.

Fuller, Thomas 1608-61 English historian and divine; chaplain to Charles II.

WORTHIES OF ENGLAND. 1662. Part biographical, part topographical. The bedside companion of many generations of readers. "A fascinating storehouse of gossiping anecdote and quaintness; a most delightful medley . . . presenting entertainment as varied as it is inexhaustible."

Gaboriau, Émile   1835-73   French writer of detective stories.
FILE No. 113   (1867)   (I)   and   M. LECOQ (1869)   (I)   are classics in this genre. Chronologically they stand between Poe and Conan Doyle.

Gairdner, J., editor   *See* Paston Letters.

Gaither, Mrs. Frances (Rice)   1889-   American writer; born in Tennessee.

DOUBLE MUSCADINE. 1949. Novel of Mississippi in the 1850's. The trial of a Negro maid for murder. "A novel of unmistakable distinction."—*New York Times.* "An extremely interesting and worthwhile novel."—*Catholic World.*

Galdós, Benito Pérez   *See* Pérez Galdós, Benito.

Gale, Zona   1874-1938   American novelist who has painted true yet kindly pictures of the small towns of Wisconsin and their peoples.

FRIENDSHIP VILLAGE. 1908. (II) "Neighborly friendships and the pathos and humor of quiet lives."

BIRTH. 1918. (II) Tragic story of father and son in a Wisconsin village.

MISS LULU BETT. 1920. (II) The family drudge—a wistful old maid—wins her freedom through an apparently tragic experience. Dramatized, this appealing story won a Pulitzer prize in 1921.

Galsworthy, John   1867-1933   English novelist, dramatist, and gentleman. In the unhappy years after World War II he was almost forgotten; but after thirty years Professor J. W. Cunliffe's summation remains perfectly true: "No critic has revealed the shortcomings of his class with greater fearlessness; no social observer has set forth the wrongs and sufferings of the down-trodden with deeper sympathy. . . . It will be long . . . before a generation will arise which has no need of the message of consideration and human kindness which Galsworthy has conveyed with so much subtlety and artistic charm." His day now seems gone; but if civilization survives, after the dust settles, he will return again to favor.

COUNTRY HOUSE. 1907. (I and II) This novel is a social satire directed against the conservatism and complacency of the British county families before World War I.

FRATERNITY. 1909. (I and II) This early masterpiece is an ironical story in which the author demonstrates with a pain-twisted smile the impossibility of real fraternity between class and class in England before the World Wars.

SILVER BOX. 1906. (II) A play in which is discussed the problem of whether or not there was one law for the rich and another for the poor, in pre-war England.

STRIFE. 1909. (I and II) A play considering with moderation, but also with relentless intelligence, the struggle between capital and labor.

JUSTICE. 1910. (I and II) Realistic and impartial play dealing with English criminal law and the prison system.

LOYALTIES. 1922. (II) In this fine play a purse of money disappears at a house-party and evokes dramatically the loyalties due to class, race, family, and profession.

FORSYTE SAGA. 1922. (II) Contemporary critics agreed that when published this was Galsworthy's master-work. Probably he never surpassed this trilogy-plus, composed of three novels (*Man of Property, In Chancery,* and *To Let*) and two short stories (*Indian Summer of a Forsyte* and *The Awakening*) which link the novels together. A member of this famous family tells us that "The Forsytes are middlemen, the commercials, the pillars of society, the cornerstones of convention. . . . They possess . . . the power of never being able to give themselves up to anything soul and body, and the sense of property."

MODERN COMEDY. 1929. (III) Composed of *The White Monkey, The Silver Spoon,* and *Swan Song,* this is another trilogy which concludes the history of the older Forsytes. It is but little inferior in fascination to the earlier group. For readers who have developed an insatiable appetite for Forsytes, their descendants and connections, there is yet another trilogy:

END OF THE CHAPTER. 1934. (III) This is made up of *Maid in Waiting, Flowering Wilderness,* and *One More River.* And so a long chapter came at last to an end. It proved to be the *last* chapter, for Galsworthy died in 1933.

CARAVAN. 1925. (II) Fifty-six of his best short stories, written 1900 to 1923.

Gardner, Helen   American teacher of art history.

ART THROUGH THE AGES: AN INTRODUCTION TO ITS HISTORY AND SIGNIFICANCE. 1948. (III) All inclusive. Nine hundred illustrations. Excellent for the general reader's reference shelves.

Gardner, Percy   1846-1937   British archaeologist.

PRINCIPLES OF GREEK ART. 1914. (II) Revision of his earlier *Grammar of Greek Art.* Simple, yet scholarly.

Garland, Hamlin   1860-1940   American fictionist and biographer, whose books are of the West, as the toilsome farmer-pioneers knew it. Member, American Academy of Arts and Letters.

MAIN TRAVELLED ROADS. 1890. (I) Realistic stories of the hard-worked farmer in the Mississippi Valley.

SON OF THE MIDDLE BORDER. 1917. (I and II) Mencken called this autobiographic narrative the best of all his books and Howells considered that as autobiography, it ranked "with the very greatest of that kind in literature."

DAUGHTER OF THE MIDDLE BORDER. 1921. (II) More autobiography. As the "Son" is about his life as the son of a pioneer, this book deals with his later years as husband, father, and author.

Garnett, David   1892-   English novelist.

LADY INTO FOX. 1922. The young wife, by some mischance, was changed into a fox while walking in the woods with her husband. Life became queer for both of them until at the end, pursued by the hounds, she died in his arms. Won the Hawthornden prize and the James Tait Black Memorial prize.

Gaskell, Mrs. Elizabeth   1810-65   British novelist and biographer.

CRANFORD. 1853. (I) Humorous yet pathetic story, which describes the social life of genteel spinsters and widows in an English country town a century ago.

LIFE OF CHARLOTTE BRONTË. 1857. (I) A very good biography, written by a friend and contemporary. Clement K. Shorter, himself a Brontë specialist, said that it deserves to stand with Boswell's *Johnson* and Lockhart's *Scott.*

Gautier, Théophile   1811-72   French novelist and poet.

MLLE. DE MAUPIN. 1835. (I) Pagan glorification of beauty and love and abnormality. Brilliantly written, but not for *les jeunes filles.*

ROMANCE OF A MUMMY. 1856. A remarkable *tour de force.* The romance is trite enough, but its background is embroidered with all the gorgeous details of the "manners and customs of the ancient Egyptians" that were to be found in the archaeologists' books of Gautier's day.

CAPTAIN FRACASSE. 1863. (I) Picaresque romance describing the adventures of a band of strolling players (including Molière) in Paris and the French provinces, in the time of Louis XIII.

Gay, John   1685-1732   English poet and playwright.

TRIVIA, OR THE ART OF WALKING THE STREETS OF LONDON. 1716. Long poem: a panorama of English street life in the Eighteenth Century.

BEGGAR'S OPERA. 1728. This versified burlesque of polite society might be called the first musical comedy, wherein the riffraff of the street sing ballads of false sentiment.

Gébler, Ernest   1915-   Of Czech and Irish ancestry, he has never been in the United States.

THE PLYMOUTH ADVENTURE. 1950. A chronicle novel about the voyage of the *Mayflower* and the first winter in Plymouth; based on letters, journals, histories and biographies. "The *Mayflower* story stripped of its stultifying conventions . . . a living chronicle of living men and women."—*Christian Science Monitor.*

Geismar, Maxwell David   1909-   American literary scholar; critic of American literature.

LAST OF THE PROVINCIALS: THE AMERICAN NOVEL. 1915-25: Lewis, Cather, Anderson, Fitzgerald. 1947.

Geoffrey of Monmouth   1100(?)-1154   English chronicler.

HISTORIES OF THE KINGS OF BRITAIN. About 1147. Legendary history of the English. Its stories of King Arthur, King Lear, Brutus, and others became of great literary importance when passed on, through Holinshed, to Shakespeare and other poets.

George, Henry   1839-97   American economist.

PROGRESS AND POVERTY. 1879. In which he develops and urges his theory of economic reform by means of a "single tax" on land, as the source of all wealth.

Géraud, André   *See* Pertinax (pseudonym).

Gerould, Mrs. Katharine Fullerton   1879-1944   American fictionist and essayist. Conservative and intellectual, a trifle cold-blooded and snobbish sometimes, she was of the austere company of craftsmen like Henry James and Mrs. Wharton.

VAIN OBLATIONS. 1914. (II) Short stories which "plumb the depths of human horror."

GREAT TRADITION. 1915. (II) Short stories of married life.

MODES AND MORALS. 1919. (II) Essays—charming, clever, wise, and witty—on behalf of conservatism.

Geyl, Pieter   1887-   Professor of history at the University of Utrecht.

NAPOLEON: FOR AND AGAINST. 1947. "Not a new life of Napoleon, but a survey of the French historians on that inexhaustible, entrancing theme."—A. Guérard, in *New York Herald Tribune*. "While it may prove too complex for the general reader, it deserves to take its place as the best single volume on Napoleon."—*American Historical Review*.

Gibbon, Edward   1737-94   English historian; "the greatest of modern historians."

DECLINE AND FALL OF THE ROMAN EMPIRE. 1776-88. (I) "The greatest historical work ever written."—C. K. Adams. "The most perfect historical composition that exists in any language." —Frederic Harrison. "Thorough and accurate treatment of the period 180-641; swifter and more prejudiced for the period 641-1453."—*Good Reading*.

AUTOBIOGRAPHY. 1796. (I) Deserves to stand on the shelf reserved for the world's best autobiographies. It is largely the story of the conception, gestation, and writing of his great history.

Gibson, W. W.   1878-   English poet; "one of labor's strongest voices."

COLLECTED POEMS, 1905-25. 1926. (II) "Most of them deal with commonplaces of daily life, but with sympathy, tenderness and often lyrical quality. Others are true idylls."—*Best Books*, 1917.

Gide, André   1869-1951   French novelist, critic, autobiographer, and diarist.

COUNTERFEITERS. 1925 and 1947. His most famous novel. "In this episodic, subtle, intellectually wide-ranging novel the relationships of adolescents to their elders are unblushingly explored." —*Good Reading*.

STRAIT IS THE GATE. 1924. "Struggle between sacred and profane love on the part of two young French Protestants who love each other fervently. The spirit of the story harks back to the 'otherworldliness' of the Middle Ages."—Cleveland Public Library.

JOURNALS, 1889-1939. 3v. 1947-49. "What makes the *Journals* more than a brilliant literary memoir is Gide's record of the inner personality; of his restlessness, scruples, prayers, resolutions."—*New Republic*.

Gilbert, Sir William S.   1836-1911   British humorist, dramatist, and poet; collaborator with Sir Arthur Sullivan in the Savoy operettas. "His foe was folly and his weapon wit."

BAB BALLADS. *c.* 1869. Gems of genial satire, wit, and whimsicality.

OPERETTAS. They contain "the cleverest and wittiest satirical verse in English" and were first produced between 1875 and 1896. Collected editions have been published in Modern Library Giants and in the Modern Readers Series.

Gilbreth, Frank Bunker   1911-   and **Carey, Ernestine Moller Gilbreth**   1908-   Two of the twelve children of the industrial engineer who invented time-and-motion studies.

CHEAPER BY THE DOZEN. 1949. Amusing picture of life as it was lived in a copious suburban family. "It is sound Americana." —J. T. Winterich, in *Saturday Review of Literature*.

Gill, Brendan   1914-   American fictionist; "master of the *New Yorker* short story, this is his first novel."

TROUBLE OF ONE HOUSE. 1950. "A deeply moving work and one of the highest integrity."—R. H. Rovere, in *New Yorker*. "Character study of a woman who called forth either love or hate in everyone who knew her well."—*Book Review Digest*.

Giono, Jean   1895-   French novelist; "a great prose poet of nature, as pagan as a faun."

SONG OF THE WORLD. 1937. "Distinguished earthy novel, vigorously realistic and yet symbolic in its portrayal of different kinds of love. Glorifies the natural life of primitive people."—*Booklist*.

Gissing, George   1857-1903   British man of letters.

PRIVATE PAPERS OF HENRY RYECROFT. 1903. (I and II) A novelist's notebook. Semi-autobiographic comments on literature and society; "the mellowest, kindest and most human fruit of Gissing's pen."

NEW GRUB STREET; A NOVEL. 1891. (I) Pessimistic study of the life of a writer in London sixty years ago.

BY THE IONIAN SEA, NOTES OF A RAMBLE IN SOUTHERN ITALY. 1901. (II) Written in Gissing's least unhappy sunset years. "A honey-toned thing, this study of Greek Italy, mellow as old marble lying warm in the sun."—Cornelius Weygandt.

Glasgow, Ellen   1874-1945   American novelist whose books are realistic and sometimes satiric studies of social change and contrasting social classes in the South, and particularly Virginia. Member, American Academy of Arts and Letters.

THE DELIVERANCE. 1904. (II) Life on a Virginia plantation after the Civil War. Class pride, revenge, and love are the driving powers.

ROMANCE OF A PLAIN MAN. 1909. (II) Virginia aristocracy tries to ostracize a self-made man. He tells the story of his career in Richmond after the Civil War.

VIRGINIA. 1913. (II) "The most thorough and the most pathetic picture extant of the American woman as Victorianism conceived and shaped and misfitted her."—Carl Van Doren.

BARREN GROUND. 1925. (II) "The best of many excellent books by Ellen Glasgow."—James Branch Cabell. "One of the best novels of this generation."—Edmund Fitzgerald.

ROMANTIC COMEDIANS. 1926. (III) The wise author tells with cool and kindly amusement what happened when December married May.

THEY STOOPED TO FOLLY; A COMEDY OF MORALS. 1929. (III) Theme is the revolution during one lifetime of the moral code governing feminine conduct. Wise, witty, sparkling with epigrams, this is perhaps the author's masterpiece.

SHELTERED LIFE. 1932. (III) Tragic story of the weakness of human nature. One of the best books of this fine literary craftsman.

VEIN OF IRON. 1935. (III) A grave, strong, true novel about the fifth generation (1900-1932) of a stalwart Virginia family of Scotch Presbyterians.

IN THIS OUR LIFE. 1941. (IV) This "most distinguished novel of the year," which won the Pulitzer prize for fiction, recognizes the chasm which separates the generations while describing the manifestations of kinship among decayed aristocrats in a Southern city.

CERTAIN MEASURE: AN INTERPRETATION OF PROSE FICTION. 1943. (IV) Essays which served as prefaces to the Virginia Edition of her novels. They present a picture of Southern manners from 1850 to 1939 and enable one to perceive, understand and admire Miss Glasgow's growth in craftsmanship through the years.

Glaspell, Susan (Mrs. George Cram Cook) 1882-1948 American playwright and fictionist. A founder and moving spirit of the Provincetown Players, with whom she served as actor, author, and producer.

PLAYS. 1920. (II) Includes eight plays. One, *Trifles*, has been called the best American one-act play.

ALISON'S HOUSE. 1931. Based upon the life of Emily Dickinson, this play received the Pulitzer prize for the season 1930-31.

AMBROSE HOLT AND FAMILY. 1931. (III) Realistic novel about modern family life. Heroine is beautiful but not at all "dumb," though her clever husband is slow to find this out.

Godwin, William 1756-1836 English philosophical anarchist and novelist. Father-in-law of Shelley and father of the author of *Frankenstein*.

ADVENTURES OF CALEB WILLIAMS. 1794. (I) A powerful, "gripping," murder-mystery, written more than a century and a half ago. A literary curiosity.

Goethe, Johann Wolfgang von 1749-1832 German poet, dramatist, novelist, philosopher, statesman.

GOETZ VON BERLICHINGEN. 1773. The tragedy which established Goethe's fame as a dramatic poet. Based on the autobiography of a Sixteenth Century knight.

SORROWS OF YOUNG WERTHER. 1774. The sentimental hero of this novel, who was really Goethe himself, commits suicide because of "the pangs of disprized love." The story set a host of lovesick swains to posturing, but it is a bit hard to take seriously in this day and age.

WILHELM MEISTER'S APPRENTICESHIP. 1777-96. (I) Rambling romance describing the career of a weak-willed young German artist, who gradually achieves self-control. "A richly colored picture of the life of Goethe's time."

EGMONT. 1788. (I) Historical tragedy founded on the career of Count Egmont, Flemish soldier-patriot, who was executed because of his opposition to Philip II of Spain.

FAUST. 1790-1833. (I) This play—the author's masterpiece —ranks as one of the greatest products of human genius. It is the poetical expression of modern man seeking the answer to the question which eternally besets him: What is the purpose of life?

HERMANN AND DOROTHEA. 1797. (I) The finest example of Goethe's narrative verse: an idyllic pastoral in 2000 hexameters.

POETRY AND TRUTH. 1811-14. (I) Unfinished autobiography, written in old age. It reaches only 1775, but is interesting as an old superman's picture of his youth.

CONVERSATIONS WITH ECKERMANN. 1836-48. Eckermann was Goethe's friend, helper and literary executor. After the master's death he compiled these records of his "table-talk."

Gogol, Nikolai Vasilievich   1809-52   Russian novelist and dramatist; the father of Russian realism.

INSPECTOR GENERAL. 1836. This play is a satire on the pettiness and corruption of the government officials.

DEAD SOULS. 1842. Novel about the old days of Russian serfdom. A satirical picture of the landowning class.

TARAS BULBA. 1842. Historical novel about the struggle of the Cossacks in the Sixteenth Century with the Catholic Poles and the Mohammedan Tartars. The first great Russian novel.

Golding, Arthur, translator   *See* Ovid.

Goldoni, Carlo   1707-93   Italian dramatist. Writing in the spontaneous style of Molière, he overthrew the old conventionalized *Commedia dell' arte* of Italy.

MASTER OF THE INN. 1752. One of his best comedies, few of which have been translated.

MEMOIRS. 1877. Sprightly picture of life in the Eighteenth Century, as lived by actors and playwrights in Italy and France.

Goldsmith, Oliver   1728-74   English poet, novelist, dramatist and all-round man of letters. As Coleridge put it, Goldsmith did everything happily.

CITIZEN OF THE WORLD. 1762. Diverting essays, supposedly written by a Chinese philosopher; full of sprightly comment on the life and manners of the time.

THE TRAVELLER. 1764. (I) "The best poem since the death of Pope"; highly praised by Samuel Johnson.

DESERTED VILLAGE. 1770. (I) One of the most charming of long English descriptive poems.

SHE STOOPS TO CONQUER. 1773. (I) Sprightly comedy of Eighteenth Century manners; often revived on the modern stage.

VICAR OF WAKEFIELD. 1776. (I) The first blameless English novel—a simple idyll, devoid of coarseness but full of genial humor and good character-drawing that compensate for the ample measure of moralizing.

Goncharov, Ivan Aleksandrovich   1812-91   Russian novelist.

OBLOMOV. 1858. The hero, for whom the book is named, has a generous heart and a keen intellect, but is incapable of decision or action. He dreams away his life, despite the efforts of his friends to rouse him. This ineffectual type is, or was, not uncommon in Russia. "Oblomovism" has come to be the designation in Russian literature for this affliction.

Goodrich, Marcus   1897-   American novelist; saw service in Army, Navy, and Air Force (1914-20), and in the Navy in World War II.

DELILAH. 1941. (IV) Story of an American destroyer during the six months before the United States entered World War I. "One of the most powerful and symbolic sea stories since *Moby Dick.*"

Goodspeed, Edgar Johnson   1871-   American biblical scholar.

STORY OF THE BIBLE. 1936. "Very readable, authentic account of the manuscripts that form the Bible."—*Good Reading.*

HOW TO READ THE BIBLE. 1946. "The perfect 'reader's guide' to the Bible."—J. H. Holmes. "The minister could have no more valuable reference book."

LIFE OF JESUS. 1950. "Combines literary charm, critical integrity, and true religious fervor. Dr. Goodspeed has given us the book for which we have been waiting."—*Chicago Tribune.* "A mature product of biblical and historical scholarship which is also a help to faith."—*Christian Century.*

Gordon, R. K., editor   *See* Anglo-Saxon Poetry.

Gorki, Maxim (A. M. Pieshkov)   1868-1936   Russian fictionist, dramatist, revolutionary; greatly honored in the U.S.S.R.

MOTHER. 1905. (II) "Story of a peasant woman whose soul is awakened through devotion to her revolutionary son."—*A.L.A. Catalog,* 1926.

MY CHILDHOOD. 1915. (II) Painful story of his own childhood, to the age of eight.

LOWER DEPTHS. 1923. Gorki's most famous play: produced in both London and New York.

THE BYSTANDER. 1930. Historical fiction that conveys the restless spirit of pre-war Russia. Story ends with the coronation of the last czar.

BOOK OF SHORT STORIES. 1939. Excellent representative selection.

Gosse, Sir Edmund　1849-1928　British all-round man of letters.

FATHER AND SON. 1907. (II) This autobiographic record of a Calvinistic Victorian father's mistaken treatment of his son is the one *great* book written by this prolific bookman. It has been crowned by the French Academy.

Goudge, Elizabeth　1900-　British novelist, with a churchly background.

GREEN DOLPHIN STREET. 1944. (IV) Historical novel (1830) of New Zealand and the Channel Islands. Won an "M.G.M." award. "It is the New Zealand scenes in the early years of British colonization which are the making of this novel."—*Times* (London).

Graham, Gwethalyn　1913-　Canadian prize-winning novelist.

EARTH AND HIGH HEAVEN. 1944. (IV) Story of the love of Jew and Gentile. "Vivid glimpses of social and professional life in Montreal. Characterizations are lively and convincing, the portrait of the sensitive hero being especially well done."—*Spectator*.

Grahame, Kenneth　1859-1932　English author of charming fantasies for children, which are also much enjoyed by adults.

GOLDEN AGE. 1895. Book about five children playing and learning in the English countryside in the happy days before World Wars were dreamed of.

DREAM DAYS. 1898. Continues *Golden Age*. Written with equal charm and truth.

WIND IN THE WILLOWS. 1908. (II) About Mr. Toad, Mr. Rat, and Mr. Mole, and their strange, surprising adventures with the other creatures who were neighbors in their riverside life.

Grant, Ulysses Simpson　1822-85　Civil War General and President of the United States.

PERSONAL MEMOIRS. 2v. 1885-86. (I) Written during his painful last illness, to provide for his wife and family. Honest, straightforward, simple as the man himself, they commanded a large sale. Mark Twain was the promoter and always helpful publisher.

Granville-Barker, H. G. 1877-1946 English playwright, producer, actor.

MADRAS HOUSE. 1910. (II) Clever play studying the woman problem as presented in the life of a department store.

PREFACES TO SHAKESPEARE. Vols. I and II. 1947. Ten plays and their staging are fully described. Not for Shakespeare or drama neophytes.

Graves, Robert 1895- English poet and novelist.

I, CLAUDIUS. 1934. (III) Historical novel: Rome in the early days of the Empire. The approach is psychological. Augustus, Tiberius, Messalina, Agrippina, as well as Claudius, are prominent characters.

Gray, Thomas 1716-71 English poet.

POEMS. (I) Famed for a few superlatively fine gems. The *Elegy* is unsurpassed in the English language.

LETTERS. 1775. (I) Gray has been praised almost as highly for his letters as for his poems. Leigh Hunt called him "the best letter-writer in the language."

Grayson, David pseudonym *See* Baker, Ray Stannard.

Green, Henry 1905- English novelist, engineer, and businessman.

LOVING. 1949. "Love story of two English servants, employed in an Irish castle at the beginning of World War II."—*Book Review Digest.* "In my accounting, *Loving* is one of the top literary dividends of 1949."—C. J. Rolo, in *Atlantic.* "The richest and most entrancing novel that has come out of England since Virginia Woolf's *Between the Acts.*"—*Nation.*

Green, John Richard 1837-83 English historian.

SHORT HISTORY OF THE ENGLISH PEOPLE. 1874. (I) A *popular* history in more senses than one. The emphasis is on the people's development, rather than the doings of courts and kings. It has almost certainly been read by more people than any other history of England.

Green, Paul Eliot   1894-   American playwright.

IN ABRAHAM'S BOSOM.   1926.   This play of Negro life in the South won the Pulitzer prize in 1927.

HOUSE OF CONNELLY.   1931.   Study of "new and old cultural values in the lives of whites in the new South."

Greene, Graham   1904-   English author of psychological novels.

HEART OF THE MATTER.   1948.   Novel of West Africa: about sin and the conscience.   "A powerful, deep-striking novel, with the surface calm of a summer river, and underneath the swift, drowning melancholy of a spirit lost in the darkness of the flesh." —*New York Herald Tribune.*

Greenough, J. B.   1833-1901   American scholar.

WORDS AND THEIR WAYS IN ENGLISH SPEECH.   1901 and 1945. (Written with George Lyman Kittredge.)

Greenslet, Ferris   1875-   American author, editor, and sportsman.   Member, National Institute of Arts and Letters.

UNDER THE BRIDGE.   1943.   (IV)   Autobiography.   "His world lacked many things ours has, but it seems, as ours does not, to have been largely populated by mature people."—Clifton Fadiman.   "Life can be good, and fun, and satisfying.   That is the welcome testimony of Ferris Greenslet."—*Springfield Republican.*

THE LOWELLS AND THEIR SEVEN WORLDS.   1946.   History of the famous Massachusetts family through seven generations. "Skillfully arranged, informative, entertaining, discreetly revealing and judicious."—*New Republic.*   "Success does not invariably spring from the thin soil of poverty."—E. Sedgwick, in *Saturday Review of Literature.*

Gregory, Augusta (Lady Gregory)   1852-1932   Irish playwright and producer; the leading figure in the Irish theatre movement.

SEVEN SHORT PLAYS.   1907.   (II)   "Simple incidents of Irish life, humorous and pathetic."   (Includes *Rising of the Moon* and *Spreading the News.*)

CUCHULAIN OF MUIRTHEMNE.   1902.   (II)   Old Irish tales of great interest and literary merit, told in the Anglo-Irish idiom.

Grew, Joseph Clark   1880-   American diplomat.

TEN YEARS IN JAPAN. 1944. (IV) An important contribution to the literature of World War II, and very interesting reading. "It answers very definitely the important question—Why did Japan attack us?"

Grey of Falloden, Viscount (Sir Edward Grey)   1862-1933   British statesman, patriot, gentleman.

TWENTY-FIVE YEARS, 1892-1916. 1925. Account of his quarter-century of service in the Foreign Office. It ended two years after the fateful night when, from his window in Downing Street, he watched the lights of Europe going out one by one.

Grey, Zane   1875-1939   Author of dozens of "Westerns." He was the favorite author of the A.E.F. in World War I, and between 1914 and 1926 was probably the most popular American writer, at any rate among men. The local color of his stories is authentic, acquired at first hand.

RIDERS OF THE PURPLE SAGE. 1912. (II) Melodramatic romance of Utah and the Mormons; one of his best stories. In the same class are *Heritage of the Desert* (1910), *Lone Star Ranger* (1915), and *The U.P. Trail* (1918).

Grimm, Jakob   **(1785-1863)**   and **Grimm, Wilhelm**   **(1786-1859)** German folklorists and philologists.

HOUSEHOLD TALES. 1812-15. (I) Fairy tales that have long been recognized as children's classics, despite their occasional grisliness.

Grimmelshausen, H. J. C. von   1625-76   German teller of tales.

ADVENTUROUS SIMPLICISSIMUS. 1669. A picaresque romance that has been described as the single German prose classic of the Seventeenth Century. It is a medley of adventure and observation of life and society during the Thirty Years' War, and is based largely on the author's own experiences.

Grotius, Hugo   1583-1645   Dutch jurist, theologian, man of letters.

DE JURE BELLI ET PACIS. 1625. (English translation by Whewell: *Law of War and Peace*, 3v., 1853.) One of the most permanently important of books—the cornerstone of modern international law.

Guareschi, Giovanni   1908-   Italian novelist, who has been described as an Italian approximation of Saroyan.

LITTLE WORLD OF DON CAMILLO. 1950. Humorous short stories about an impulsive village priest and his friendly enemy, the Communist mayor. "This little gem in the field of clarity-amid-confusion."—Thomas Sugrue, in *Saturday Review of Literature.*

Guedalla, Philip   1889-1944   English biographer and historian; often compared with Lytton Strachey as a revivifier of biography and history.

SECOND EMPIRE. 1922. (II) Brilliant picture of France under Napoleon III (1852-70). His narrative is as vivid as that of an eye-witness.

WELLINGTON. 1931. (III) "Deft analysis of Napoleon's calmly competent Nemesis."—*Good Reading.*

Guest, Charlotte (Lady Guest)   *See* Mabinogion.

Guizot, F. P. G.   1787-1874   French historian and statesman.

HISTORY OF CIVILIZATION IN EUROPE. 1828-30. (New English edition, with notes, 1896.) (I) Still regarded as both an excellent and a readable book in its field.

Gulbranssen, Trygve   1894-   Norwegian novelist.

BEYOND SING THE WOODS. 1936. Story of the hardy, hill-dwelling Björndal family and their emergence into the fertile plain where life became in some ways easier.

Gunther, John   1901-   American author, foreign correspondent, radio commentator on foreign affairs. Best known for his famous surveys "Inside" various quarters of the globe.

INSIDE EUROPE. 1936. (Numerous revised editions, 1937-40.) (IV) Survey of leaders and conditions in various countries just before World War II.

INSIDE ASIA. 1939. (Revised edition, 1942.) (IV) Political survey of half the world's populations, with lively comment on issues and personalities.

INSIDE LATIN AMERICA. 1941. (IV) A superb reporter presents material purposefully gathered on a plane trip through twenty countries.

INSIDE U.S.A. 1947. Highly readable political and geographic guide to the United States in 979 pages. "It is impossible to describe all the excellences of this book. Mr. Gunther has tried to report everything of importance in the United States, to explain its meaning, to describe the men and women who run the country." —*Christian Science Monitor.*

DEATH BE NOT PROUD. 1949. Biographical sketch of his brave young son who died in 1947 at the age of seventeen. "A heartbreaking tale, beautifully written."—*New Yorker.* "Gunther never wrote so good a book."—*Time.* "The keynote of this book is not horror and suffering but bravery, strength and cheerfulness." —Walter Duranty, in *New York Herald Tribune.*

ROOSEVELT IN RETROSPECT. 1950. "With his customary acute eye for engaging detail, pertinent anecdote, and illuminating sidelight, John Gunther has put together a fascinating picture and appraisal of F.D.R."—*Saturday Review of Literature.*

Guthrie, Alfred B. 1901- American novelist.

BIG SKY. 1947. Tale of adventure with the first white hunters in the West, 1830-43. A first novel, "pungent as hickory smoke." "This book which succeeds so beautifully in evoking a time, a land, and a people, ought to have a long, long life."—Bruce Lancaster, in *Atlantic.*

WAY WEST. 1949. Story of an emigrant trek in the 1840's from Independence, Missouri, to Oregon. Awarded the Pulitzer prize for fiction. "Joins a thorough knowledge of historical fact to a great talent for presenting his characters as individuals and as members of a community, rather than as stereotyped actors in the drama of western settlement."—*United States Quarterly Booklist.*

H. D. *See* Doolittle, Hilda.

Hacker, Louis Morton 1899- American historian, economist.

TRIUMPH OF AMERICAN CAPITALISM. 1940 and 1947. (IV) An economic history of the United States to 1900. "Remarkable . . . interpretative study . . . of the many trends in the economic growth of the nation."—Allan Nevins. "Readable, scholarly, freshly documented book."—*New Yorker.*

Hackett, Francis   1883-   Irish-American man of letters.

HENRY THE EIGHTH. 1929. (III) At once a scholarly book and an exciting one. Its baleful subject is not toned down in the least but glows lurid in the light of the author's Celtic imagination.

I CHOSE DENMARK. 1940. (IV) The author tells why he chose to live in his wife's homeland. He liked the country, its wholesome people and the clean, conservative socialism that was working so well before the Nazis came.

Hagedorn, Hermann   1882-   American novelist, poet, and biographer.

EDWIN ARLINGTON ROBINSON. 1938. (IV) Convincing and readable. "If the book is not the final word on Robinson, it is in all probability the standard life which future biographers must always use."—*Boston Transcript.*

Haggard, Sir H. Rider   1856-1925   English agricultural economist and author of sensational tales of adventure, generally in a very primitive Africa.

KING SOLOMON'S MINES. 1885. "His most successful adventure story."

SHE. 1887. In which mystery and magic are blended with thrilling adventure.

Hahn, Emily (Mrs. Charles Boxer)   1905-   American author who has spent many years in China (1935-41) and other foreign countries.

SOONG SISTERS. 1941. (IV) Lively book about a famous Chinese trio of sisters: Mme. Sun Yat-sen, Mme. Chiang Kai-shek, and Mme. Kung Hsiang-hsi.

Haines, William Wister   1908-   American writer and soldier; in the Air Force, 1942-45.

COMMAND DECISION. 1947. Novel about the ordeal of an American brigadier who commanded a unit of bombers in World War II. "Immensely readable and unflagging in its excitement." —*New York Herald Tribune.*

Hakluyt, Richard 1552-1616 British geographer, and editor and compiler of explorers' journals.

PRINCIPAL NAVIGATIONS, VOYAGES, TRAFFIQUES, AND DISCOVERIES OF THE ENGLISH NATION. 1589. (I) Thrilling and fascinating record—"the prose epic of the English." There have been several modern editions, one in *Everyman's Library.*

Hale, Edward Everett 1822-1909 American author and clergyman.

MAN WITHOUT A COUNTRY. 1863. (I) This long short story, a classic of American patriotism, did much to encourage the spirit of loyalty to the Union during the Civil War.

Halévy, Ludovic 1834-1908 French fictionist and dramatist. Member, French Academy.

ABBÉ CONSTANTIN. 1882. (I) Idyllic story of a gentle village priest. "It sparkles with light and graceful epigrams" and has long been a favorite with teachers of young people who are beginning to read French.

Hall, G. Stanley 1846-1924 American psychologist and educator; first president of Clark University.

ADOLESCENCE. 2v. 1904. (II) The psychology of adolescence and its relations to physiology, anthropology, sociology, sex, crime, religion, and education. The author supplemented this important and monumental work by an abridgment, *Youth,* 1907, which the general reader may find better suited to his needs.

Hall, James Norman, joint author *See* Nordhoff, Charles Bernard.

Halper, Albert 1904- American writer of proletarian fiction.

UNION SQUARE. 1933. Naturalistic picture of frustrated radicals and their manner of life in the New York slum area about Fourteenth Street.

Halsey, Margaret (Mrs. M. R. Stern) 1910- American author, interested in international and interracial prejudices in social relations.

WITH MALICE TOWARDS SOME. 1938. (IV) "Definitive work on the British art of annoying Americans."—*Forum.* "Her vivacious jesting should be thoroughly enjoyed, her criticisms not at all resented."—*Times* (London).

COLOR BLIND; A WHITE WOMAN LOOKS AT THE NEGRO. 1946.
"How social equality between the races actually worked at the
'Stage Door Canteen.'"   "Certainly the most readable book ever
written about the color problem."—*Christian Century.*

Hamilton, Alexander   1757-1804   *See* Federalist.

Hamsun, Knut   1859-1952   Norwegian novelist; won Nobel
prize for literature in 1920.

HUNGER. 1899. (I and II) Grimly realistic story of a young
writer who lives long on the verge of starvation.

GROWTH OF THE SOIL. 2v. 1920. (I and II) Exceedingly
fine, strong, grim novel. Stark, primitive living, transmuted into
vivid drama.

CHILDREN OF THE AGE. 1924. "Picture of the almost feudal
conditions persisting in rural Norway in the latter half of the
last century."—E. A. Baker.

Hanford, James Holly   1882-   American professor of English
literature; a Milton specialist.

JOHN MILTON, ENGLISHMAN. 1949. "A penetrating and revealing biographical portrait."—*Saturday Review of Literature.*
"Skilfully weaves together Milton's life and works, prose and verse,
in a way that sets off both, but never one at the expense of the
other."—*United States Quarterly Booklist.*

Hardy, Thomas   1840-1928   In his later years this last of the
great Victorian novelists became also a great but little read poet,
whose ashes are enshrined in the Poets' Corner, Westminster
Abbey. Realist and fatalist, Hardy "presents scenes of strange
beauty and symbolic significance, as a dramatic background for
man's futile struggle in an unfriendly universe." Among his novels
the following nine titles, listed chronologically, are probably the
most important.

FAR FROM THE MADDING CROWD. 1874. (I) "You have to turn
back to Shakespeare for any tale of peasants and clowns and
shepherds to compare with the conversations in this novel, so
racy are they of the soil, and yet so touched with the finest art."
—C. D. Warner.

RETURN OF THE NATIVE. 1878. (I) One of Hardy's best. "Story of joy, sorrow and tragedy against the sombre background of Egdon Heath, silent, watchful, inscrutable."—*Good Reading.*

TRUMPET MAJOR. 1880. Genial and happy love story in the days of Napoleon's threatened invasion of England's south coast.

MAYOR OF CASTERBRIDGE. 1886. Egotism and obstinacy compass inevitably the ruin of an impetuous, domineering tradesman.

WESSEX TALES. 1888. Contains eight of perhaps the best of Hardy's short stories. His "Wessex" is Dorsetshire.

TESS OF THE D'URBERVILLES. 1891. (I) This poignant tragedy of a betrayed woman is the most famous and probably the best of Hardy's novels.

LIFE'S LITTLE IRONIES. 1894. The author calls this "a set of tales with some colloquial sketches . . . a few crusted characters."

JUDE THE OBSCURE. 1896. (I) Sombre and painful story of a peasant scholar's foiled ambition; but it is one of Hardy's most powerful books.

THE DYNASTS. 1904-08. (II) A monumental epic, in drama form, of the Napoleonic Wars. There are 3 parts—19 acts— 130 scenes. "The grandest poetic structure planned and raised in England in our time."—Sir A. T. Quiller-Couch. "One of the most ambitious and . . . successful literary ventures ever undertaken by an ancient or a modern man."—Carl Van Doren.

COLLECTED POEMS. 1926. "It is impossible not to find in them the strong, sad sincerity, occasional bitterness, and tragic recognition of life's futility that form a kind of ground bass to the novels."—*Doubleday's Encyclopedia.*

Hardy, Mrs. Thomas (Florence Emily Dugdale Hardy) d. 1937 Formerly the novelist's secretary. He married her at seventy-four.

EARLY LIFE OF THOMAS HARDY, 1840-91. 1928. (III) Straightforward narrative of a great man's first half-century. "Compiled largely from contemporary notes, letters, diaries and biographical memoranda, as well as from oral information extending over many years."

Hargrove, Marion   1919-   American journalist.

SEE HERE, PRIVATE HARGROVE.   1942.   (IV)   This book of skits about the rookie of World War II was "the laughing sensation of the war"—fit to rank with *Dere Mabel*, its predecessor in World War I. Two million copies of Hargrove's book were sold in the first year after publication.

Harrington, James   1611-77   English political writer. Though a republican, he attended Charles I to the scaffold.

COMMONWEALTH OF OCEANA.   1656.   In this political treatise, which is also a semi-romance, he maintains that property, especially landed property, is the prime basis of power.

Harris, Frank   1856-1931   Irish-American-English   journalist, critic, biographer; long resident in London.

CONTEMPORARY PORTRAITS.   4v.   1914-23.   (II)   A   first-rate critic of his time. . . . His sometimes uninhibited opinions of his contemporaries are certain to affect the views of posterity.

Harris, Joel Chandler   1848-1908   American author, best known for his quaintly humorous tales in Negro dialect—authentic folklore of the American South—carefully set down from his own childhood memories of what he had been told by Negroes of the doings of Brer Fox, Brer Rabbit, and the other animals.

UNCLE REMUS, HIS SONGS AND HIS SAYINGS.   1880.   (I)

NIGHTS WITH UNCLE REMUS.   1883.   (I)

UNCLE REMUS AND HIS FRIENDS.   1892.   (I)

Hart, James David   1911-   Author, *The Oxford Companion to American Literature.*

THE POPULAR BOOK; A HISTORY OF AMERICA'S LITERARY TASTE. 1950.   "Probably the most complete survey ever made of American best-sellers. . . ."   "Lively and gossipy . . . for the general reader."

Hart, Moss, joint author   *See* Kaufman, George S.

Harte, Bret   1839-1902   American author, once extremely popu- lar both at home and abroad, for his tales and poems (often in dialect) of the Far West in Gold Rush days.

BRET HARTE'S STORIES OF THE OLD WEST.   1940.   (I)   This collection contains practically all of the old favorites originally published between 1868 and 1875.

POEMS. 1871. Verses humorous and tender—greatly enjoyed by our grandfathers.

Harvard University

GENERAL EDUCATION IN A FREE SOCIETY. 1945. (IV) This outstanding report "reveals the shortcomings of secondary education and recommends repair in the first two years of college."

Hasek, Jaroslav   1883-1923   Czech fictionist.

GOOD SOLDIER: SCHWEIK. 4v. 1930. Satiric novel on war, and particularly on World War I. It has been honored by comparison with Rabelais and Cervantes.

Hauptmann, Gerhart   1862-1946   German dramatist and novelist; awarded the Nobel prize in 1912.

THE WEAVERS. 1892. (I) Play presenting the struggle between capital and labor.

SUNKEN BELL. 1896. (I) Romantic fairy-play of mountain nymph, woodsprite, and frog-king.

FOOL IN CHRIST. 1910. (I and II) This novel is a moving re-statement of the lost meaning of the Christian mystery—the mystic mingling of human and divine—in the terms of contemporary life and characters.

ATLANTIS. 1912. (II) Love story of a German doctor and a depraved Swedish dancer. Much of the action takes place on an Atlantic liner which is wrecked on a mountain peak of what may have been the lost continent of Atlantis.

Hawes, Charles Boardman   1889-1923   American author of swashbuckling sea-tales, which are enjoyed by old and young. Perhaps his best is

THE MUTINEERS. 1920. (II) This yarn about a voyage out of Salem is a good one indeed. It lacks no element of the ideal sea story.

Hawkins, Sir Anthony Hope (Anthony Hope, pseudonym)   1863-1933   British novelist.

PRISONER OF ZENDA. 1894. Very successful romantic novel of modern love and intrigue in an old-world setting—the royal palace of an imaginary Balkan kingdom.

RUPERT OF HENTZAU. 1898. The equally successful sequel of the above. (Both books are "naturals for the movies," though written when the cinema was in swaddling clothes.)

Hawthorne, Nathaniel   1806-64   American fictionist.
"The greatest genius whom America has yet produced."— Henry Cabot Lodge. "He was a great writer—the greatest writer of prose fiction whom America has produced."—Andrew Lang. "In psychological insight he is unrivaled among the men of our times."—J. A. Symonds.

TWICE-TOLD TALES. 2v. 1837 and 1842. (I) Tales of pre-Revolutionary times, several involving supernatural incidents. Poe declared that "they belong to the highest region of Art—an Art subservient to genius of a very lofty order."

MOSSES FROM AN OLD MANSE. 2v. 1846. (I) Collection of tales and sketches—mystical, fanciful, allegorical.

SCARLET LETTER. 1850. (I) Many critics have considered this the prime classic of American fiction. W. C. Brownell called it "the New England Faust—the Puritan Faust"; and said, "Essentially the book is a story of concealment. Its psychology is that of the concealment of sin amid circumstances that make a sin of concealment itself."

HOUSE OF THE SEVEN GABLES. 1851. (I) Its grim motif is the sins of the fathers. The author thought it a better book than *The Scarlet Letter* and Henry James spoke of it as "the closest approach we are likely to have to the great work of fiction, so often called for, that is to do us nationally most honor and most good."

BLITHEDALE ROMANCE. 1852. (I) A story greatly admired by some critics, though it is read today chiefly by students of American literary history for its disguised picture of Brook Farm, the Transcendentalists' experiment in a communistic Utopia.

MARBLE FAUN. 1860. (I) Tale of American artists in Rome and of an only half-human, native-born son of Pan who, through sin and consequent suffering, wins a soul.

THE WONDER BOOK. 1852. (I) and

TANGLEWOOD TALES. 1853. (I) are stories from Grecian mythology, charmingly retold for girls and boys.

Hay, Ian (Sir John Hay Beith) 1876-1952 British war correspondent and novelist.

FIRST HUNDRED THOUSAND. 1915. (II) This book of sketches of "Kitchener's contemptible little army" is one of the war books of World War I that may be read with pleasure and profit by the veterans of World War II and their contemporaries.

Hay, John 1838-1905 American author and statesman; secretary and biographer of Abraham Lincoln.

PIKE COUNTY BALLADS. 1871. Frontier poems in dialect. (Includes *Jim Bludso, Little Breeches*, etc.)

CASTILIAN DAYS. 1871. As the author was both shrewd observer and poet, there is still good reading in these pages which picture so vividly the life of old Spain.

Haydon, Benjamin R. 1786-1846 British historical painter and author.

AUTOBIOGRAPHY AND JOURNALS. 1853. "He was a great writer, whereas he lived and died thinking himself a great painter. Through the absorbing pages of his journal flash all the famous writers of his age."—*English Library*.

Hayek, Friedrich August von 1899- Vienna-born British subject; teacher of economics in London and the United States.

ROAD TO SERFDOM. 1944. (IV) A rebuttal of socialism. After a first hand acquaintance with totalitarianism the author prefers freedom to economic security. TVA is no doubt a good thing, he would say, but it is fatally easy to get too much of many a good thing.

Hayes, Alfred 1911- American novelist and poet.

GIRL ON THE VIA FLAMINIA. 1949. Novel of World War II's last year: an American GI and a Roman girl—"the clash of victor and victim."

Hazlitt, William 1778-1830 (I) "Greatest of English essayists and critics."—*English Library*. "There is no greater critic than Hazlitt. . . . He is the critics' critic, as Spenser is the poets' poet."—George Saintsbury. He was a difficult man and, one would think, a most unhappy one. Yet his last words were, "Well, I've had a happy life!" His most successful books are probably the following:

CHARACTERS OF SHAKESPEARE'S PLAYS. 1817-18.

LECTURES ON THE ENGLISH POETS. 1818. (I)

LECTURES ON THE ENGLISH COMIC WRITERS. 1819. (I)

DRAMATIC LITERATURE OF THE AGE OF ELIZABETH. 1822.

TABLE TALK. 1821-24. There are several modern editions of selections from Hazlitt's works. *Selected Essays*—a Nonesuch Omnibus—is a good one.

Hearn, Lafcadio 1850-1904 A wandering writer of Anglo-Irish-Greek parentage, who ended his life a Buddhist and a citizen of Japan.

GLIMPSES OF UNFAMILIAR JAPAN. 1894. (I) He steeped himself in the art, myth, tradition, and philosophy of his adopted country.

GLEANINGS IN BUDDHA FIELDS. 1897. (I) Among subjects lovingly studied are Japanese art and folksong, Shintoism, Buddhism, nirvana, pre-existence, and rebirth.

JAPAN—AN ATTEMPT AT APPRECIATION. 1904. (I) "Exposition of the religion and social institutions of the country, laying great emphasis on the former, as the spring of all Japanese art, ethics and government."—Keller.

Hecht, Selig 1892-1947 Professor of biophysics at Columbia University.

EXPLAINING THE ATOM. 1947. "A first class job of popularization—clear, unpretentious, written at the right pace, free of condescension, and written without metaphysics."—*New Republic*.

Hegel, G. W. F. 1770-1831 German philosopher of classic intellectual idealism.

SELECTED WRITINGS. (Modern Students' Library.) "By his support of existing Prussian institutions Hegel obtained great political and social influence. . . . The individual is of no value by himself. . . . The state must protect the individual . . .

but not so as to interfere with progress. . . . Constitutional monarchy is the best form of government. . . . War is indispensable to progress; might is right, the weaker state is inferior to and absorbed in the stronger."—*Doubleday's Encyclopedia.* "Hegel's system as a whole is hard to understand. It has been said that all the books dealing with the secret of Hegel have managed to keep it."—*Reader's Encyclopedia.*

Heggen, Thomas   1919-49   American navy lieutenant in World War II.

MISTER ROBERTS. 1946. An amusing, rowdy first novel about life aboard a cargo ship during World War II. "The corroding effects of apathy and boredom on men who, in battle, might have been heroes."—*New Yorker.*

Heimskringla. (I) Sagas of the Norse kings; written and compiled in the Twelfth Century, probably by Snorri Sturluson. A collection of Scandinavian poetry and mythology. (Everyman's Library, 2v.)

Heine, Heinrich   1799-1856   German-Jewish poet. He became a Parisian expatriate and a Christian.

POEMS; TRANSLATED BY LOUIS UNTERMEYER. 1917. (I) They have placed their author "among the most illustrious poets in the world's literature."

PICTURES OF TRAVEL; TRANSLATED BY CHARLES G. LELAND. 1855. (I) Quaintly old-fashioned, naturally; but still to be counted among the most charming of travel books.

Heine, Heinrich   *See also* Untermeyer, Louis.

Heiser, Victor G.   1873-   American physician and expert on public health.

AMERICAN DOCTOR'S ODYSSEY; ADVENTURES IN FORTY-FIVE COUNTRIES. 1936. (IV) "Once in a very long time there comes a book, so wholly remarkable, so alluring, so wide and deep in its appeal, that one wants to rush to an international broadcasting station to shout, 'Read it!' This is such a book."—*New York Herald Tribune.*

Hemingway, Ernest 1898- American novelist; much imitated leader of the post-war "hard-boiled" school.

SUN ALSO RISES. 1926. American wastrels in Paris and Spain, drowning in debauchery their disillusionment after "victory" in World War I.

FAREWELL TO ARMS. 1929. (III) Story of tragic love against the background of World War I. Modernly frank in expression; laconic; boringly realistic in dialog. The hard-boiled crust is thin in places and breaks now and then to reveal depths of shame-faced tenderness.

DEATH IN THE AFTERNOON. 1932. Essays glorifying the art, ritual, and supposedly virile sport of bull-fighting.

FIFTH COLUMN, AND THE FIRST FORTY-NINE STORIES. 1938. (IV) *The Fifth Column* is hardly a great play, but bound with it are forty-nine short stories of which Clifton Fadiman says, "I don't see how you can go through this book without being convinced that Hemingway is the best short story writer now using English."

FOR WHOM THE BELL TOLLS. 1940. (IV) Story of an American volunteer in the Spanish Civil War—four days of love and danger ending in death. "Ernest Hemingway is an artist and his new novel is a rare and beautiful piece of work."—R. E. Sherwood, in *Atlantic*. "This is the best book Ernest Hemingway has written, the fullest, the deepest, the truest. It will, I think, be one of the major novels in American literature."—J. D. Adams, in *New York Times*.

Hémon, Louis 1880-1913 French-Canadian novelist.

MARIE CHAPDELAINE. 1921. (II) Charming story of farm life in Quebec. Lavishly praised by critics as "a work of pure genius," as having "the supreme simplicity of a master work," etc.

Hendrick, Burton J. 1871-1949 Journalist, historian, biographer; thrice a Pulitzer prize-winner; member, National Institute of Arts and Letters.

LIFE AND LETTERS OF WALTER H. PAGE. 3v. 1922-25. (II) Page was the American ambassador in London during World War I. "A book of great distinction . . . an invaluable contribution to history."—E. A. Alderman.

BULWARK OF THE REPUBLIC: A BIOGRAPHY OF THE CONSTITUTION. 1937. (IV) "It moves with breathless rapidity; it is studded with brilliant character sketches of jurists and statesmen; and it exploits to the fullest the dramatic possibilities of doubt and struggle."—H. S. Commager.

STATESMEN OF THE LOST CAUSE: JEFFERSON DAVIS AND HIS CABINET. 1939. (IV) "The book as a whole is a splendidly executed succession of fascinating studies."—Douglas Southall Freeman.

LINCOLN'S WAR CABINET. 1946. "A magnificent book. It has color, drama, detail and conflict. It is scholarly without being dull or pedantic. The characterizations and descriptions are superb."—*Christian Science Monitor.*

Henley, William E. 1849-1903 English poet.

POEMS. 1898. (I) Noted for vigor and the vivid realism of the impressionistic sketches called *In a Hospital. Invictus* is his most famous poem.

Henry, O., (pseudonym of William Sydney Porter) 1862-1910 A fabulously successful American practitioner of the art or craft of short-story writing. He was dubbed by the critics, variously, as the American Gogol, Kipling, Maupassant, Fielding, and Boccaccio; also, condescendingly, as "The Little Shopgirls' Knight." H. L. Mencken's disdainful allusion to "O. Henry, with his smoke-room and variety-show smartness," was—considering the source—uncalled for. John Macy was kinder: "a man of real talent and excellent humor, a born story-teller, but deficient in point of style, too journalistic." The stories were published in ten or more separately titled volumes, between 1904 and 1917. The most famous of these was *The Four Million* (1906). This collection included *The Gift of the Magi,* his most generally admired story. Inclusive and select collections of the tales are:

COMPLETE O. HENRY. 1937. (Garden City Publishing Company.)

BEST SHORT STORIES OF O. HENRY. 1945. (Modern Library.)

Herbert, A. P. 1890- English humorist and Member of Parliament.

WATER GIPSIES. 1930. (III) Genial, amusing, understanding tale of a beautiful 'ousemaid and others on the London waterfront. The book would have a decidedly old-fashioned, Dickensy flavor, if it were not so completely unsentimental.

Herbert, George   1593-1633   English author of religious poetry; brother of Lord Herbert of Cherbury.

THE TEMPLE. 1633. "So much piety was never married to so much wit."—R. W. Emerson. "I find more substantial comfort now in pious George Herbert's *Temple*, which I used to read to amuse myself with his quaintness, in short, only to laugh at, than in all the poetry since the poems of Milton."—S. T. Coleridge.

Herbert of Cherbury, Lord (Edward Herbert)   1583-1648   English deist, metaphysician, coxcomb, and autobiographer.

AUTOBIOGRAPHY. 1764. "One of the most curious works of the kind that has ever issued from the press."—J. H. Jesse. "As you read you cannot help thinking . . . that Thackeray could not have done it better if he had been minded to portray a gentleman of the first James's time. . . . It is one of the most remarkable instances of self-portraiture in any language."—W. D. Howells.

Hergesheimer, Joseph   1880-   American novelist, greatly interested in regional antiquarianism and obsessed with the details of interior decoration. But withal a fine stylist.

THREE BLACK PENNIES. 1917. (I and II)   The lives of three generations of Pennsylvania iron-masters are presented in this novel—the prime favorite of many of the author's admirers.

JAVA HEAD. 1919. (I and II)   Presents a colorful spectacle of Salem in the 1840's, with clipper ships setting sail for, and returning from the Orient laden with aromatic cargoes.

LINDA CONDON. 1919. (II)   A book for those interested in intensive character study rather than in plot. Carl Van Doren considers it the author's masterpiece and calls it "nearly the most beautiful American novel since Hawthorne and Henry James."

BRIGHT SHAWL. 1922. (II)   Story of Cuba before the Spanish-American War. An idealistic young American joins the Cubans in their fight for freedom. John Farrar called this book an example of Hergesheimer's style at its best.

Herndon, William Henry 1818-91 Lincoln's law partner. He collected Lincolniana for thirty years.

THE HIDDEN LINCOLN, FROM THE LETTERS AND PAPERS OF THE AUTHOR; edited by Emanuel Hertz. 1938. (IV) "Notable contribution to the Lincoln bibliography. Must be considered by those studying Lincoln or Herndon hereafter from any angle."— *Nation.*

Herodotus 484-425(?) B.C. Greek historian and traveler; called The Father of History.

HISTORY. (I) Deals chiefly with the war between the Greeks and the Persians, with historical and descriptive digressions on Egypt and other neighboring countries.

Herrick, Robert 1591-1674 English poet.

POEMS. (I) "None of the English lyric poets has shown a more perfect sense of words and their musical efficiency, none has united so exquisitely a classic sense of form to that impulsive tunefulness which we have come to consider essentially English." —Ernest Rhys.

Herrick, Robert 1868-1938 American novelist and Chicago University professor; "chiefly interested in studying the struggle of decent human beings with the forces of a materialistic society." His novels, says Carl Van Doren, "are indispensable documents upon the first and second decades of the Twentieth Century."

COMMON LOT. 1904. (I) Story of a well-intentioned young Chicago architect who, hard-pressed, is tempted beyond his strength.

TOGETHER. 1908. (II) Fictional study of the institution of marriage in the United States.

CLARK'S FIELD. 1914. (II) This novel and *Together* are Carl Van Doren's favorites among Herrick's books. Both expose the "general soullessness of the pampered, over-protected American woman of the prosperous middle class."

Hersey, John 1914- American author, born in China; war correspondent; novelist.

BELL FOR ADANO. 1944. (IV) Story about the troubles of an American Military Government officer in Italy, during the occupation after World II. It won the Pulitzer prize for fiction in

1945. *The Atlantic* calls it "a study of what America can and cannot do in Europe. As such it is very interesting and very good. . . . Its credo—that government, whatever its professions, can only be as good as the men who govern."

HIROSHIMA. 1946. Superb reporting. The story of six survivors of the bomb. "Certainly one of the great classics of the war," says the *New Republic*. "The book speaks for itself and, in an unforgettable way, about humanity," says *New York Times*

THE WALL. 1950. Novel of the Warsaw ghetto during the German occupation of Poland. "It is the most complex and brilliant of John Hersey's books so far. It is the best novel I have read in 1950 and it may be the best novel of the year."— M. Geismar, in *Saturday Review of Literature*.

Hertz, Emanuel, editor   *See* Herndon, William Henry.

Hesiod   *See* Virgil.

Hesse, Hermann   1877-   German-Swiss poet and novelist.

STEPPENWOLF. 1929 and 1947. "Strange, introspective study of a man who regards himself as a dual personality . . . half man and half wolf of the steppes."

Hesseltine, William Best   1902-   American university professor of history.

LINCOLN AND THE WAR GOVERNORS. 1948. "History of the conflict between Abraham Lincoln and the governors of the various Northern states over the conduct of the Civil War."—*Book Review Digest*.

Hewlett, Maurice   1861-1823   English romantic novelist; "an interpreter of the more recondite phases of the life and thought of the Middle Ages, especially in Italy."

FOREST LOVERS. 1898. Prosper le Gai rides singing through the mysterious forest of Morgraunt, rescues a pathetic little maiden in distress and within the week weds her.

RICHARD YEA-AND-NAY. 1900. Historical romance of Richard Cœur de Lion and the Third Crusade. A glowing tapestry of chivalry's best days.

QUEEN'S QUAIR. 1904. (II) Enchanting portrait of ill-fated Mary Stuart against a background of Renaissance life and sentiment.

Heyerdahl, Thor 1914- Norwegian ethnologist.

KON-TIKI. 1950. True story of a modern sea-venture. "This is an enthralling book, and I don't think I can be very far off in calling it the most absorbing sea tale of our time."—Hamilton Basso, in *New Yorker*. "If you pick up this book in the morning, your day will be ruined. If you open it in the evening you'll get no sleep that night."—*Christian Century*.

Heyward, Du Bose 1885-1940 American novelist and dramatist.

PORGY. 1925. "Violence and devotion, squalor and pathos among the Negroes in Charleston's Catfish Row."—*Good Reading*.

MAMBA'S DAUGHTERS. 1929. (III) Fine story of black and white on old Charleston's waterfront.

PETER ASHLEY. 1932. (III) This story presents a glamorous picture of Charleston, its life and people, in the exciting days which preceded the bombardment of Fort Sumter.

Hichens, Robert 1864-1950 English novelist.

GREEN CARNATION. 1894. Satirical novel about the *fin de siècle* aesthetes in England, and especially about Oscar Wilde.

GARDEN OF ALLAH. 1905. (II) Subtly presented study of a struggle between religion and passion against a splendidly painted desert background.

Hicks, Granville 1901- American author with radical interests. He is no longer a Communist but has said that he is still a believer in socialism.

JOHN REED, THE MAKING OF A REVOLUTIONARY. 1936. (IV) (Written with John Stuart.) Born in a wealthy home in Portland, Oregon, Reed died of typhus in Russia, at thirty-three, and was buried in Moscow, beside the Kremlin. "Wrong-headed and socially dangerous as he may have been, there was one of the most brilliant minds, one of the most unselfish hearts, one of the spirits most devoted to the cause of suffering humanity that our time has seen. . . . It would be hard for anyone to write a dull book about John Reed."—*Christian Century.*

Hill, F. E., joint author   *See* Auslander, Joseph.

Hillyer, Robert   1895-   American poet in the tradition of conservative romanticism; Boylston Professor of Rhetoric at Harvard; fellow, American Academy of Arts and Sciences.

COLLECTED VERSE. 1933. Conservative poetry, written by one "saturated in the best traditions of English literature." Won the Pulitzer prize for poetry in 1934.

Hilton, James   1900-   English novelist.

LOST HORIZON. 1933. Novel which begins with an airplane journey to the mythical land of Shangri-La in the high Himalayas, where no one grew old. It won the Hawthornden prize.

GOOD-BYE, MR. CHIPS. 1934. (III) Charming, Dickensian novelette about a lovable schoolmaster. Sentimental, but saved by humor from being maudlin.

Hindus, Maurice   1891-   Russian-born American author of books on Russia.

HUMANITY UPROOTED. 1929. (III) Informative, well-written book about the Russian people and Bolshevism, and how they fit each other.

RED BREAD. 1931. (III) Pictures of the Russian peasant under the Five Year Plan—an impartial report on individuals as affected by collectivization.

Hitler, Adolf   1889-1945   Austrian-born, he served as a corporal in the German army in World War I; became Chancellor of Germany in 1932, and Reichsführer in 1934, after Hindenburg's death. He is believed to have killed himself (1945) in Berlin, to avoid capture by the Allies.

MEIN KAMPF. 1939. (IV) The Nazis' Bible. *Historically,* an important book. "Devoid of intellectual content or any pretense of rationality . . . *Mein Kampf* differs from most Holy Writ in that it is vicious, vulgar and violent."—*Nation.*

Hobart, A. T. 1882- American novelist, long resident in China.

OIL FOR THE LAMPS OF CHINA. 1933. (III) Novel describing the life and personal relationships of a pair of American commercial exiles in the struggling, unhappy, changing China of the 1920's.

Hobbes, Thomas 1588-1679 "Hobbes stands with Bacon and Berkeley at the head of English-speaking philosophers, and is . . . in acuteness of thought and originality of expression, perhaps the superior of both his companions."—George Saintsbury (1845-1933).

LEVIATHAN, OR THE MATTER, FORM AND POWER OF A COMMONWEALTH. 1651. (I) A landmark in the history of English political theory. It is a plea for monarchy but ascribes the monarch's power to the consent of the governed and so paved the way for Rousseau's theory of the social contract.

Hobson, Laura (Zametkin) American novelist.

GENTLEMEN'S AGREEMENT. 1947. Novel about anti-Semitism. Handles the issue with wisdom and contributes its mite toward combating . . . intolerance."—Christian Science Monitor.

Hoffman, Malvina 1887- American sculptor.

SCULPTURE INSIDE AND OUT. 1939. "Famous sculptor gives historical outline and explains technique."—Good Reading.

HEADS AND TALES. 1936. An autobiography. First word in title is an allusion to her commission to execute 101 racial types in bronze for the Field Museum.

Hofstadter, Richard 1916- Professor of history at Columbia University.

AMERICAN POLITICAL TRADITION AND THE MEN WHO MADE IT. 1948. Twelve biographical essays which illustrate the competitive individualism of the American tradition, from the Revolution to Franklin Roosevelt. "The essays are brilliantly written, with telling phrase and epithet, and analyze our public figures without the usual propensity for hero-worship."—Survey.

Hogben, Lancelot 1895- English author and university professor. Fellow, Royal Society.

MATHEMATICS FOR THE MILLION. 1937. (IV) This book emphasizes "for the million" the historical and social aspects of mathematics. "A book . . . to delight any amateur who wishes to see what mathematics is about, and what it can do for human beings."—*Saturday Review of Literature.*

Holinshed, Raphael   c. 1520-80   English historian.

CHRONICLES OF ENGLAND, SCOTLAND AND IRELAND. 1577. "Crude material afterward beaten out into those plaques of gold, which we call Shakespeare's Historic Plays."—Donald G. Mitchell. This first edition of "Holinshed" was probably the best-thumbed volume on Shakespeare's "Five Foot Shelf."

Holmes, Oliver Wendell   1809-94   American man of letters; Harvard professor of anatomy and physiology.

AUTOCRAT OF THE BREAKFAST TABLE. 1858. (I) "Full of alert wisdom, droll humor, and sound observation of life." This is his best book.

PROFESSOR AT THE BREAKFAST TABLE. 1860. (I) In the same happy vein as *The Autocrat,* and only slightly less enjoyable.

ELSIE VENNER. 1861. (I)

GUARDIAN ANGEL. 1867. (I) Dr. Holmes sometimes spoke of these two books as his "medicated novels." Modern reviewers would probably use the word *psychological* in describing them. The preface to the first warns the reader that "it depicts a human nature developing itself in conflict with characteristics impressed on it during the prenatal period." The second book has been succinctly described as "a psychological study of heredity and moral responsibility."

POEMS. The greater part of Dr. Holmes's verse was of the occasional, after-dinner variety which, no matter how genial and graceful, is not rewarding to succeeding generations. He has left us however, ten or a dozen poems which are or should be known to every American. These may be confidently sought in the anthologies. See, especially, *The Chambered Nautilus, The Last Leaf, Old Ironsides* and *The Deacon's Masterpiece* (better known as *The One-Hoss Shay*).

Holmes, Oliver Wendell   1841-1935   Son of "The Autocrat"; soldier of the Civil War; Associate Justice, United States Supreme Court, 1902-32; and Pollock; Sir Frederick   1845-1937   English jurist.

THE HOLMES-POLLOCK LETTERS: THEIR CORRESPONDENCE, 1874-1932; edited by M. A. De W. Howe. 2v. 1941. (IV) "This correspondence for nearly sixty years between two men of profound learning and highest culture is without parallel. . . ."—*New York Herald Tribune.* "Holmes is the more human and has the lighter touch. He relished frivolities that had little temptation for Pollock. Yet both swapped views on life's ultimates."—*Nation.*

Holt, Rackham, (pseudonym of Margaret Van Vechten Saunders Holt) 1899- American author.

GEORGE WASHINGTON CARVER. 1943. (IV) Life of Dr. Carver of Tennessee, pioneer of scientific agriculture, leader of his race, and revered citizen. "She has created a complete picture—the multiplicity of interests and the cheerful, kind, simple dignity of a great-hearted and great-minded man."—Scientific Book Club.

Holtby, Winifred 1898-1935 English novelist.

SOUTH RIDING. 1936. Published shortly after the author's untimely death, this fine story of the conflict between old and new elements in English provincial society has been called "her magnificent epitaph." It was awarded the James Tait Black prize in 1937.

Homer **Flourished about the Eleventh Century B.C.** A shadowy blind bard of Greece.

THE ILIAD (I) Epic poem in 24 parts, telling of the siege of Ilium, or Troy, by the Greeks. Famous translations are those by Chapman (1611), immortalized by Keats's sonnet; by Pope (1715-20), far more Popish than Homeric; by Bryant (1870) in blank verse; by Lang, Leaf and Myers (1901), in prose; by Samuel Butler (1916), in prose; and by A. T. Murray (1924-25), in prose. The last is in the Loeb Classical Library.

THE ODYSSEY (I) Recounts in 24 parts the adventures of Odysseus (Ulysses) on his leisurely, roundabout journey back home to Ithaca after the fall of Troy. The best known translations are those by Chapman (1614); by Pope (1725); by Bryant (1871); by Butcher and Lang (1879); by Butler (1900), in prose; by A. T. Murray (1919), in the Loeb Classical Library; and by T. E. Lawrence (1932). Samuel Butler devoted a whole volume to his persuasive argument that *The Odyssey* was written by a woman: *The Authoress of the Odyssey* (1897).

Hooker, Richard   1554(?)-1600   English scholar and theologian.

LAWS OF ECCLESIASTICAL POLITY. 1594-97. "A philosophical defense of episcopacy in general and the Church of England in particular."—*Good Reading.* "He is known beyond the circle of theology. His English style has given him a high place in English literature."—John Dryden. "A standard work. It is as much moral and political as theological. . . . On the whole it is the first monument of splendid literary prose that we possess."—Stopford A. Brooke. "Hooker is the first important philosophical and religious English writer . . . the first great writer of practical English prose."—Edmund Gosse.

Hooton, Earnest Albert   1887-   American anthropologist.

UP FROM THE APE. Revised edition, 1946. (III) Story of human evolution, told with sprightliness by a competent scholar for the intelligent layman, with descriptions of the chief branches of the human family.

Hoover, I. H. (Ike)   Chief Usher of the White House.

FORTY-TWO YEARS IN THE WHITE HOUSE. 1934. (III) Personal, intimate, but wholesome, gossip about ten Presidents, from Cleveland to Herbert Hoover.

Hope, Anthony, pseudonym   *See* Hawkins, Sir Anthony Hope.

Hopkins, Gerard Manley   1844-89   English poet. Converted to Catholicism at twenty-two, he became a Jesuit and a follower of Cardinal Manning.

POEMS. 1918. Published twenty-nine years after the author's death, this "tense and turbulent" verse has considerably influenced the work of many modern English and American poets.

LETTERS TO ROBERT BRIDGES. 2v. 1935.

FURTHER LETTERS. 1938. "These three volumes may take their place with those of Keats as the sensitive and absorbing letters of a poet who influenced the course of English poetry."—*English Library.*

Horace (Quintus Horatius Flaccus)   65-8 B.C.   Roman poet: the indulgent satirist of the Augustan era.

POEMS. In Latin poetry Horace ranks second only to Virgil. Countless admirers have translated this "prince of Roman lyricists" in whole or in part. There is as yet no definitive English version, but those by J. Conington and by Sir Theodore Martin have been favorably known for many years.

Horton, Philip 1911- American author.

HART CRANE, THE LIFE OF AN AMERICAN POET. 1937. (IV) This book is a critical appraisal as well as an excellent biography of an unhappy neurotic who wrote admirable poetry.

Hough, Emerson 1857-1923 American historical novelist and nature lover.

MISSISSIPPI BUBBLE. 1902. (II) John Law, the Scottish financial adventurer, is the hero of this stirring novel of old London and New France in the early days of the Eighteenth Century.

COVERED WAGON. 1922. (II) First-rate story of a wagon-train which brought two thousand emigrants from Missouri to Oregon in the year 1848.

House, Edward Mandell 1858-1938 President Wilson's friend and personal ambassador to the European powers, 1914-18.

INTIMATE PAPERS; ARRANGED AS A NARRATIVE BY CHARLES SEYMOUR. 4v. 1926-28 (III) Perhaps these are, for Americans, the most revealing and important memoirs engendered by World War I.

Household, Geoffrey 1903- English novelist, who is well acquainted with many foreign countries.

ROGUE MALE. 1939. (IV) As the *New York Times* reviewer says, "the reader feels . . . a breath-taking uninterrupted concentration" in this tale of an English sportsman's adventures during and after his attempt to shoot an unnamed European dictator.

Housman, A. E. 1859-1936 English poet and classical scholar.

COLLECTED POEMS. 1940. (IV) Includes *Shropshire Lad, Last Poems, More Last Poems,* and some additional poems and translations. Like Hardy's novels, Housman's exquisite lyrics voice the idea that all things end in frustration and disillusionment. But while we mourn at the sadness of their message we rejoice at the beauty of its telling.

Housman, Laurence, editor *See* Wordsworth, William.

Howard, Leland Ossian   1857-1950   American entomologist.

INSECT MENACE. 1931. (III) Fifty years' study has convinced the author that in insects, as carriers of disease and destroyers of food, mankind faces its most formidable enemy. This book is his plea for recognition of the facts and vigorous action upon them.

Howard, Sidney   1891-1939   American dramatist, airman, farmer. Member, American Academy of Arts and Letters.

THEY KNEW WHAT THEY WANTED. 1924. This play, both a popular and artistic success, won a Pulitzer prize.

SILVER CORD. 1927. Concerns the plight of two brothers dominated by an unscrupulous mother. It is considered "his most powerful independent production."

Howe, Edgar Watson   1854-1937   American novelist and country newspaper editor.

STORY OF A COUNTRY TOWN. 1883. (I) As the first example of frankly pessimistic realism in American fiction, this book is a landmark in the history of American literature.

Howe, Helen Huntington   1905-   Author and monologist; born in Boston, the daughter of M. A. De Wolfe Howe.

WE HAPPY FEW. 1946. Satirical novel about Harvard professors and their wives, before and during World War II. Bernard De Voto says that "the first half of her novel is as good as anything that has come out of New England in two generations."

Howe, M. A. De Wolfe, editor   *See* Holmes, Oliver Wendell 1841-1935; *also* Chapman, J. J.

Howells, William Dean   1837-1920   American man of letters; friend and mentor of Mark Twain; first president (1909-20) of the American Academy of Arts and Letters. Mr. Howells wrote excellent books of travel, poetry, criticism, and biography. He wrote several amusing farces, such as *The Mouse Trap* and *The Albany Depot.* But it is as a novelist that he will be longest remembered. The titles listed below are among the best of their period in the discreetly realistic school of which he was the acknowledged leader. "Howells produced in his fourscore books the most considerable transcript of American life yet made by one man."—Carl Van Doren.

THEIR WEDDING JOURNEY. 1872. (I) His first novel decorously discusses things seen, heard, and experienced by two Bostonians on their wedding trip to Canada and back.

A CHANCE ACQUAINTANCE. 1873. (I) Aristocrat from Boston meets an unsophisticated but charming girl from the West. They fall in love but she soon perceives that he is a bit ashamed of her. To his surprise and sorrow she sensibly and decisively refuses to marry him.

LADY OF THE AROOSTOOK. 1879. Love story of a New England girl in Venice. Her surface rusticity is compensated by innate refinement, and she proves able to hold her own with the fashionable sophisticates with whom she is thrown.

MODERN INSTANCE. 1882. (I) Story of the courtship and unhappy marriage of a passionately jealous Maine girl and the "smart" but unprincipled young man who edits her father's newspaper.

RISE OF SILAS LAPHAM. 1885. (I) Many critics consider this Howells' best book. "In aristocratic Boston, Silas Lapham, self-made man, sacrifices his wealth to rise above common trickery."—*Good Reading*.

HAZARD OF NEW FORTUNES. 1890. (I) Picture of life in New York sixty years ago, as lived by the editor and publisher of a popular magazine.

TRAVELLER FROM ALTRURIA. 1894. Like the previous title, this book is an example of the author's later phase, when he had become interested in America's social, political, and economic problems. "Altruria" is a picture of an imagined ideal commonwealth.

THE LEATHERWOOD GOD. 1916. (II) Some critics think that Mr. Howells never wrote a more important novel than this study of a frontier impostor who proclaims himself a god.

Hudson, William Henry 1841-1922 Naturalist and man of letters. Though born in Argentina of American parentage his mature years were spent in England and he is always thought of as an Englishman.

PURPLE LAND. 1885. (New edition, 1916.) Romance of an adventurous Englishman in what is now Uruguay, when the Nineteenth Century was young.

GREEN MANSIONS. 1904. (I and II) This is generally considered Mr. Hudson's greatest book. Described in *Good Reading* as "an exotic romance of the South American jungles: extraordinary for beautiful descriptive passages."

LITTLE BOY LOST. 1905. (II) A child's fantasy, with an Argentinian background; based on his own early experiences.

SHEPHERD'S LIFE. 1910. (II) Critics agree that this collection of charming sketches is one of Hudson's best books.

TALES OF THE PAMPAS. 1916. (II) Stories of South American adventure. (The same material is found in his *South American Sketches* and *El Ombu.*)

FAR AWAY AND LONG AGO. 1918. (I and II) History of the author's youth on the pampas. Its romantic charm is exceeded only in *Green Mansions.*

HIND IN RICHMOND PARK. 1923. (II) The essayist, rather than the naturalist, is uppermost in this book which is regarded as among the author's best.

Hueffer, Ford Madox   *See* Ford, Ford Madox.

Hughes, Langston   1902-   American Negro author, who has been awarded several prizes for creative writing. His poetry has been translated into six foreign languages.

WEARY BLUES. 1926. Poems using the characteristic rhythms of jazz and Negro folk music.

NOT WITHOUT LAUGHTER. 1930. (III) In this novel Sandy, son of a gay mulatto father and a hardworking Negro mother, grows up in the care of his grandmother in a small Kansas town.

Hughes, Richard   1900-   Welsh novelist and dramatist.

INNOCENT VOYAGE. 1929. Thrilling story—for adults—of children captured by West Indian pirates. Successfully dramatized. Awarded *Femina's Vie Heureuse* prize in 1931. (English title is *A High Wind in Jamaica.*)

Hughes, Rupert 1872- American biographer and popular novelist.

GEORGE WASHINGTON. 3v. 1926-30. (III) This biography was frowned upon by some as an attempt to smear a national hero. It is really a successful and praiseworthy effort to restore the breath of life and virile humanity to one who had become to many an insensate stone image.

Hughes, Thomas 1822-96 English author and reformer.

TOM BROWN'S SCHOOL DAYS. 1857. (I) This story for boys about life at Rugby a century ago under Dr. Thomas Arnold, is old-fashioned of course. But reading it helps one understand how England has been able to produce men like Winston Churchill.

Hugo, Victor 1902-85 French author: the most famous and influential figure in Nineteenth-Century French literature: leader of the Romanticists. "His excesses are the defects of his qualities." His poems are no longer read. Of his many plays only one has retained a moderate degree of popularity. This is

HERNANI. 1830. With this tragedy of a noble-hearted bandit the new romanticism triumphed and Hugo became the idol of Paris.

NOTRE DAME DE PARIS. 1831. (I) This story of medieval Paris was the first of his great romances. It is also known in English as *The Hunchback of Notre Dame.* The cathedral itself is the main character, but close behind come the animated-gargoyle bellringer and an innocent and beautiful gypsy dancer, who is supposed to be a witch.

LES MISÉRABLES. 1862. (I) A vast panorama of the victims of French society in the post-Napoleonic era. In more senses than one has this monumental, humanitarian novel been accounted one of the very greatest books ever written. It is usually published in five closely packed volumes.

TOILERS OF THE SEA. 1866. (I) A story of the sailors of the Channel Islands. With eloquence the eternal struggle is described between the will of man and the forces of nature.

THE MAN WHO LAUGHS. 1869. (I) Extraordinary picture of English life and institutions in the days of the Stuart kings. "Sheer sensation and sublimity, grotesque comedy and utter tragedy alternate in this strange work of fiction."

NINETY THREE. 1874. (I) Grandiose rhetorical romance of the French Revolution at high tide.

Hulbert, Archer Butler 1873-1933   American historical scholar.

FORTY-NINERS; THE CHRONICLE OF THE CALIFORNIA TRAIL. 1931. (III) From about two hundred journals of actual Forty-niners the author has assembled the diary of a fictitious pioneer along the two thousand miles of the California Trail from Independence, Missouri, to Hangtown, California.

Hull, Cordell 1871-   Secretary of State, 1933-44.

MEMOIRS. 2v. 1948. A good gray book by the good gray secretary. "One of the historic monuments of the present age"; interesting without being exciting.

Hume, David 1711-76   Scottish philosopher and historian.

ENQUIRY CONCERNING HUMAN UNDERSTANDING. 1748. (I) "A rational skeptic unmasks the assumptions of idealistic rationalism." —*Good Reading.*

Huneker, James 1860-1921   American critic of music, the drama, and the graphic arts.

ICONOCLASTS. 1905. (I and II) Studies of ten European dramatists from Ibsen to Shaw.

IVORY, APES AND PEACOCKS. 1915. (I and II) Brilliant essays, rendered provocative by the author's colorful personality.

STEEPLEJACK. 1920. (I and II) Reminiscences of the author's life, among the artists—graphic, musical, literary—of New York, London, and Paris.

Hunt, Leigh 1784-1859   English writer; an intimate of Shelley, Byron, Keats, and other famous authors of his day.

AUTOBIOGRAPHY. 3v. 1850-61. (I) "One of the most interesting books ever written."—James T. Fields. "Except it be Boswell's of Johnson, I do not know where we have such a picture of human life as in these three volumes."—Thomas Carlyle.

Hurst, Fannie 1889-   American novelist; "expert in the ways of metropolitan New York."

HUMORESQUE. 1919. (II) Eight vivid stories of Jewish life in a great city."—*A.L.A. Catalog, 1926.*

Hurtado de Mendoza, Diego 1503-75 Spanish author and diplomat; supposed author of

LAZARILLO DE TORMES. 1553. Sprightly but unfinished tale about a rogue who began life as guide to a blind beggar. As an early example of the picaresque romance, a landmark in the history of fiction.

Hutchinson, A. S. M. 1880- Popular English novelist, to whom sophisticated critics were often unkind. "Hutchinson's dialogue sparkles, hits, jumps, races—does practically everything that human talk should."—Heywood Broun.

IF WINTER COMES. 1921. (II) Story of an unlucky idealist who at long last gets his deserts. "Not only a thrilling tale, it is an important work of art. . . . Its author is a creative artist and a spiritual force."—W. L. Phelps.

Hutchinson, Ray Coryton 1907- English novelist.

FIRE AND THE WOOD. 1940. (IV) Exciting, dramatic love story of a young German-Jewish doctor in the years just before and after the Nazis' rise to power.

Huxley, Aldous 1894- English writer; grandson of Thomas Huxley.

POINT COUNTER POINT. 1928. (III) The disillusioned generation, after World War I, amuses itself in London hopelessly and scandalously, talking brilliantly the while. Thackeray's *Vanity Fair* up to date.

BRAVE NEW WORLD. 1932. Satiric novel describing a future mechanistic universe and a world robbed of beauty.

EYELESS IN GAZA. 1936. Beset by doubts and vacillations, an intelligent youth grows to manhood in a time of war and turmoil. Says J. D. Adams, in the *New York Times*, "In this book Aldous Huxley emerges a moralist, a believer in the efficacy of the spiritual life."

ENDS AND MEANS; AN INQUIRY INTO THE NATURE OF IDEALS AND INTO THE METHODS EMPLOYED FOR THEIR REALIZATION. 1937. (IV) "A complete statement of a philosophy of living."—H. S. Canby. "A remarkable volume in its own right, its interest is heightened by the extraordinary transformation it reveals in Mr. Huxley's mental attitude."—Henry Hazlitt, in *New York Times*.

AFTER MANY A SUMMER DIES THE SWAN. 1939. (IV) A weird tale, with involved philosophic and religious sidelines, of an American millionaire who wishes to keep on living indefinitely.

GREY EMINENCE: A STUDY IN RELIGION AND POLITICS. 1941. (IV) A life of Father Joseph, Cardinal Richelieu's mysterious aide. "Unfolds a convincing argument concerning the legitimate roles of politics, morals, and mysticism."—*Commonweal.*

TIME MUST HAVE A STOP. 1944. (IV) "The mixture in this novel of deplorable characters and homiletic essays is deliberately artificial, packed with wit, rarely dull. Its basic theme is the Huxleyan conviction that world reform must begin in the individual soul."—*Time.*

PERENNIAL PHILOSOPHY. 1945. "Seeks to record the ultimate reality envisioned by saints, philosophers, thinkers and seekers of every age and every clime."—Helen E. Haines.

Huxley, Julian 1897- English scientist; brother of Aldous Huxley; became Director-General of Unesco in 1946.

AFRICA VIEW. 1931. Book of travel which, says Helen Haines, is "of far-reaching importance in a dozen different spheres of knowledge."

ON LIVING IN A REVOLUTION. 1944. "His thought, as always, is clear, compressed and stimulating. Some lighter pieces, like that which explodes 'the social myth,' enliven the more serious argument." —*Manchester Guardian.*

Huxley, Julian, joint author *See* Wells, H. G.

Huxley, Thomas H. 1825-95 English biologist; exponent of Darwin's theory of evolution; President, Royal Society.

MAN'S PLACE IN NATURE. 1863. (I) "Classic of biological science that is as fresh and true today as it was in 1863."—*Good Reading.*

Ibáñez, Vicente Blasco- *See* Blasco-Ibáñez, Vicente.

Ibsen, Henrik 1828-1906 Norwegian playwright—the greatest dramatist of the Nineteenth Century. His best plays dealt with social problems and were spurs to social reform.

BRAND. 1866. Play, in verse. Its theme is "the danger and destructiveness of the idealist who would force others to live in accordance with his ideals."

PEER GYNT. 1867. (I) Ibsen's last play in verse. "It satirizes the idealist who constructs a world only for himself and shuts all others out of it."

EMPEROR AND GALILEAN. 1873. Enormously long tragedy, exhibiting Julian the Apostate in his vain effort to restore paganism after the world had begun to embrace Christianity.

A DOLL'S HOUSE. 1879. (I) The life-hungry and self-sacrificing wife finally walks out on the stodgy and inappreciative husband.

GHOSTS. 1881. (I) Herein dreadful tragedy is caused by the wife's resolve *not* to walk out, whatever the provocation.

ENEMY OF THE PEOPLE. 1882. (I) The dramatist was so called by those who were shocked by *A Doll's House* and *Ghosts*. This play pleads for the truth at whatever cost to him who tells it.

THE WILD DUCK. 1884. (I) Shaw declared this play a warning that "the truth-teller who cannot hold his tongue on occasion may do as much mischief as a whole university of trained liars."

ROSMERSHOLM. 1886. (I) In this play the Eternal triangle ends in triple tragedy, which is also a triumph of idealism!

HEDDA GABLER. 1890. (I) Hedda has beauty, education, and culture, but she is a stony-hearted monster of selfishness. The fear of scandal is the only check on her maleficence. In the end it drives her to suicide.

Ickes, Harold L. 1874-1952 New Dealer and reputedly cantankerous reformer; Secretary of the Interior in cabinets of Roosevelt and Truman, 1933-46.

AUTOBIOGRAPHY OF A CURMUDGEON. 1943. (IV) "Self-flagellation by a contemporary Jonathan Edwards."—*Yale Review.* "The chief value of Mr. Ickes' book resides in the picture it presents of city politics and politicians, both machine and reformist, over a considerable period of time."—*Commonweal.*

Ingersoll, Ralph 1900- American journalist; enlisted as private in World War II and was mustered out a lieutenant-colonel.

BATTLE IS THE PAY-OFF. 1943. (IV) Detailed description of a battle in World War II as it appeared to an intelligent American soldier who was a combatant in Tunisia. "War reporting at its best." —*Nation.*

TOP-SECRET. 1946. Scathing, controversial book about the inside history of World War II, especially planning the D-Day invasion.

Ingoldsby, Thomas, pseudonym   *See* Barham, R. H.

Iron, Ralph, pseudonym   *See* Schreiner, Olive.

Irvine, William

Universe of George Bernard Shaw. 1949. An intellectual
biography. "The most intelligent guide to Shaw's philosophy that I
have read."—Hesketh Pearson.

Irving, Washington   1783-1859   American man of letters who
has been called "The Father of American Literature"; American
ambassador to Spain, 1842-46.

Diedrich Knickerbocker's History of New York. 1809. Described by the author as "a *jeu d'esprit*; written in a serio-comic vein,
and treating local errors, follies and abuses with good-humored satire."

Sketch Book. 1819. (I)   Includes *Rip Van Winkle, Legend of
Sleepy Hollow*; and other sketches, which are mostly of English life.
"One of the ten or twelve choicest books produced by an American."—
C. F. Richardson, in 1887.

Bracebridge Hall. 1822. (I)   Charming picture of the country
squire and his satellites in the England of a century and more ago.

History of Columbus. 3v. 1828. (I)   "An excellent piece of
historical work, as well as a literary production which it would be
superfluous to praise."—J. F. Jameson.

Conquest of Granada. 1829. (I)   "A study of history which
. . . conveys not only the pathos but the humor of one of the most
splendid and expressive situations in the experience of the race."—
W. D. Howells.

The Alhambra. 1832. "The book abounds in delightful legends.
. . . The enchantments of this Moorish paradise become part of our
mental possessions without the least shock to our common sense."—
C. D. Warner.

Life of Oliver Goldsmith. 1849. (I)   A congenial subject
for Irving. Many, including Dickens and Landor, have remarked upon
the close literary resemblance between Goldsmith and Irving. They
seem often to have written with quills from the same fowl. C. F.
Richardson called this "one of the best biographies in the whole range
of English literature."

LIFE OF WASHINGTON. 5v. 1855-59. (I) "Although not a biography of the very highest rank, it is in every way worthy of its position as the standard life of a remarkable man and the crowning work of a brilliant literary career."—F. L. Pattee, in 1896.

Isham, Samuel   1855-1914   and **Cortissoz, Royal**   1869-1948

HISTORY OF AMERICAN PAINTING. 1935. (II) Revised edition of the standard work on the subject; illustrated.

Isherwood, Christopher   1904-   English novelist and playwright who has spent most of his recent years in the United States. His work has been highly praised by Edmund Wilson and other American critics.

GOODBYE TO BERLIN. 1939. Six sketches picturing life in Berlin just prior to the rise of Hitler.

PRATER VIOLET. 1945. Novel about a German film director in Vienna who is a refugee from the Nazis.

Jackson, Charles   1903-   American novelist. He became a teetotaler on realizing that alcohol interfered with his writing.

LOST WEEKEND. 1944. (IV) Psychological study of a young man of good intent who finds himself a pitiful drunkard on a five-day binge, and not for the first time.

Jackson, Helen Hunt   1831-85   American author and crusader for justice to the Indian.

RAMONA. 1884. (I) Story of Spanish and Indian life in the California of nearly a century ago. It is the strongest fictional presentation ever made of the wrongs suffered by the Indian at the hands of the white man.

Jackson, Shirley   1920-   American fictionist.

THE LOTTERY. 1942. Twenty-five ironic short stories. "Even if she is using a story that has a New (Yorker) Look, she still belongs to the literary line that goes back to Katherine Mansfield and Chekhov."—*Saturday Review of Literature.*

Jacobs, W. W.   1863-1943   Author of humorous and occasionally macabre stories, mostly of the London dock area and its denizens.

CRUISES AND CARGOES.

THE NIGHTWATCHMAN. Both are omnibus volumes of Jacobs' stories; recommended by *An English Library*.

Jaffe, Bernard   1896-   American author, chiefly of books on scientists, by reading which one may acquire some knowledge of the fields in which his subjects have labored.

CRUCIBLES; THE LIVES AND ACHIEVEMENTS OF THE GREAT CHEMISTS. Revised edition, 1948. (III) Glimpses of chemistry from the days of alchemy to those of the tungsten lamp.

MEN OF SCIENCE IN AMERICA. 1944. (IV) In the lives of nineteen savants this book summarizes the role of science in the pageant of American progress.

James, Henry   1843-1916   Subtlest of American novelists; long resident in England. In the year before his death he became a British subject. There was a remarkable revival of interest in the work of Henry James during the years 1930 to 1950.

THE AMERICAN. 1877. (I) Because of the embarrassment caused by differing social codes, the rich American's engagement to the French widow of noble birth is annulled.

THE EUROPEANS. 1877. Debonair young sophisticates from Europe visit the home of their proper Bostonian cousins.

DAISY MILLER. 1878. (I) The heroine of this tragic novelette is a pretty, innocent, but unconventional, young American girl who, visiting Rome, is sadly misunderstood by Europeans she meets there.

PORTRAIT OF A LADY. 1881. (I) "American girl in a European milieu marries a man of exquisite taste and finds that dilettantism cannot offset defects of character."—*Good Reading*.

THE BOSTONIANS. 1886. Satirizes the social life of New England's metropolis, particularly that of certain suffragettes and desiccated but dedicated females.

WINGS OF THE DOVE. 1902. (I and II) Mournful story of the projected marriage and mortal illness of an American heiress who, in London. falls among designing friends.

THE AMBASSADORS. 1903. (I and II) Describes a struggle between the old-fashioned New England conscience and the advanced—some would say decadent—refinement and cultural maturity of Paris. James considered this book "quite the best 'all round' of my productions."

THE GOLDEN BOWL. 1905. (I and II) American millionaire's daughter marries an indigent Italian prince. All is well until first one and then another "eternal triangle" materializes.

TURN OF THE SCREW. 1898. This is perhaps the most famous and puzzling ghost story in all literature. It relates the struggle in a lonely country house between an English governess and two specters from hell, the latter bent upon corrupting the charming children of whom the governess has been left in charge.

AMERICAN SCENE. 1907. (I and II) "Keen and subtle analyses of America, revisited after five-and-twenty years." Involved and difficult. An example of the "amazing and fantastic climax" of the author's later manner.

SMALL BOY AND OTHERS. 1913. (I and II) Reminiscences of boyhood in old New York. Exquisite artistry but not easy reading.

THE MIDDLE YEARS. 1917. (I and II) Rapturous recollections of his first stay in London, with accounts of his meetings with Tennyson, George Eliot, Lowell, etc.

LETTERS. 2v. 1908. (II) Brander Matthews called this "the best book of Henry James." "Bids fair to become a classic in English literature."—J. G. Huneker.

NOTEBOOKS; edited by F. O. Matthiesen. 1947. "Four hundred and eighteen pages of pure joy for the James addict and sure benefit for the practicing craftsman."—*Christian Science Monitor.*

James, Henry 1879-1947 American publicist; son of William James, psychologist, and nephew of Henry James (1843-1916), novelist.

CHARLES W. ELIOT. 2v. 1930. (III) No modern "psychograph" this, but an honest piece of standard craftsmanship, based on an ample supply of original sources.

James, Marquis 1891- American journalist and biographer.

THE RAVEN. 1929. This excellent life of Sam Houston (1793-1863) of Texas won the Pulitzer prize for biography in 1930.

ANDREW JACKSON, THE BORDER CAPTAIN. 1933. (III) Readable and scholarly life, from his birth (1767) to his first retirement at fifty-one. This also won a Pulitzer prize.

ANDREW JACKSON, PORTRAIT OF A PRESIDENT. 1937. (IV.) Sequel to the above. "His Jackson is alive, an Old Hickory of pulsing sap, a man who broke heads while shielding his own heartbreak."— *Saturday Review of Literature.*

CHEROKEE STRIP: A TALE OF AN OKLAHOMA BOYHOOD. 1945. (IV) Autobiography. "Written with delightful charm and skilful simplicity . . . an epic of the cattle kingdom."—*Commonweal.*

James, Will   1892-1942   American cowboy, author, artist; born in one of the last covered wagons.

LONE COWBOY; MY LIFE STORY. 1930. (III) Here's where the West begins—and ends. A grand story, in cowboy vernacular, of a glamorous life in the open spaces.

James, William   1842-1910   American psychologist and philosopher; sponsor of pragmatism; brother of Henry James (1843-1916).

WILL TO BELIEVE AND OTHER ESSAYS. 1897. (I) Collection of philosophical essays which, said *The Nation,* is "popular in no sense that can make it of less service to the specialist."

VARIETIES OF RELIGIOUS EXPERIENCE. 1902. (I and II) Treatise on man as a religious animal, in which the genuineness of the experience known as conversion is shown by numerous examples to be indisputable. Standard work in its field; widely read half a century after publication.

PRAGMATISM. 1907. (I and II) A philosophy proposed for the average man. It may be roughly epitomized as, "Does the theory work? Then it's true."

MEANING OF TRUTH. 1909. (II) Sequel to *Pragmatism*; an answer to its critics.

LETTERS. 2v. 1920. (II) "What letters! The letters of Lamb, of Edward Fitzgerald, are not more delightful."—*The Freeman.*

Jeans, Sir James H. 1877-1946 English scientist who, says Mencken, has "a really extraordinary gift for making the most difficult of scientific concepts understandable."

UNIVERSE AROUND US. 1929. Revised edition, 1931. (III) The Layman's Brief Guide to the Universe would have been another good title. Its text is wonderfully simple—as only a master could safely make it.

MYSTERIOUS UNIVERSE. 1930. Revised edition, 1932. (III) Summary of the modern scientist's problems of cosmology and physics, with overtones of metaphysics and mysticism in the final chapter. It supplements *The Universe Around Us.*

STARS IN THEIR COURSES. 1931. (III) Conversational exposition of the marvels of up-to-date astronomy; based upon a series of radio talks.

Jefferies, Richard 1848-87 English naturalist. "One of the most fascinating of all the writers who have ever set themselves to describe the sights, sounds, and occupations of the English country-side."—H. D. Traill.

GAMEKEEPER AT HOME. 1878.

AMATEUR POACHER. 1879. (I)

PAGEANT OF SUMMER. 1884. "Let us go out of these indoor, narrow, modern days . . . into the sunlight and pure wind. A something that the ancients called divine can be found and felt there still." —Richard Jefferies.

Jeffers, Robinson 1887- American "poet of tragic terror"; member, American Academy of Arts and Letters.

SELECTED POETRY. 1938. (IV) One hundred and twenty-five poems, chosen by the author and his wife from his published writings. "To Jeffers, modern man and his works are without equivocation abominable, and the thing most worthy of admiration is the unconsciousness of nature. Such views underlie most of his writings."— F. B. Millet.

Jefferson, Thomas 1743-1826 Chief author of the Declaration of Independence; political opponent of Alexander Hamilton; third President (1801-09) of the United States.

PAPERS. . . . Vol. 1 (1760-76). 1950. "An achievement as nearly definitive as a human performance can be." "This is the most monumental editorial task ever undertaken in this country."—*Yale Review.* "From every point of view the work is well and soundly done."—C. M. Wiltse, in *American Political Science Review.*

Jehan de Bourgogne   *See* Mandeville, Sir John.

Jennings, Herbert Spencer   1868-1947   American   biologist; Fellow, American Academy of Arts and Sciences.

BIOLOGICAL BASIS OF HUMAN NATURE. 1930. (III) Popular work of sound scholarship, showing the influence of heredity and environment upon personality and society.

Jensen, Johannes V.   1873-1950   Danish poet, novelist, essayist; awarded (1944) Nobel prize for

THE LONG JOURNEY. 3v. in 1. 1933. A vast novel which is in fact an epic of the Teutonic race from its prehistoric beginnings to the discoveries of Columbus, whom the author conceives to have been descended from some Northern pirate. The three volumes are called, respectively, *Fire and Ice, The Cimbrians,* and *Christopher Columbus.*

Jessup, Philip Caryl   1897-   American legal scholar and diplomat.

ELIHU ROOT. 2v. 1938. (IV) Root (1845-1937) was long revered, first as an active leader and later as an elder statesman, in the American legal and political arena. "This is a sympathetic but not extravagantly sentimental biography, detailed but never dull. . . . It is just about what a good biography should be."—*Boston Transcript.*

Jewett, Sarah Orne   1849-1909   American author of novels and short stories dealing usually with the lives and characters of dwellers in Maine coast villages.

COUNTRY OF THE POINTED FIRS. 1896. (I) This book of tales and sketches is "fresh and clean with sea-air and the scent of herbs." It contains perhaps the author's best work.

TORY LOVER. 1901. (II) Historical novel of the American Revolution. Captain Paul Jones is a leading figure.

LETTERS. 1911. (II) Miss Jewett was a letter-writer of rare quality, who deserves to be thought of in the company of such correspondents as Shelley, Scott and Byron, said Richard Burton.

Joad, C. E. M. 1891- English philosopher; "the Mencken of England."

COMMON SENSE ETHICS. 1921. Brief survey of the leading theories of philosophical ethics, followed by a disquisition which has to do with psychology and politics as the realms wherein man struggles for the realization of his desires.

INTRODUCTION TO MODERN PHILOSOPHY. 1924. "Mr. Joad's little book is as good as a short manual of this sort can be."—*Nation and Athenaeum.*

GUIDE TO PHILOSOPHY. 1936. "Lucid, non-technical compendium of philosophic thought."—*Good Reading.*

Johnson, Gerald W. 1890- American author of books on American public men and affairs.

AMERICAN HEROES AND HERO-WORSHIP. 1941. (IV) He considers Washington, Hamilton, Jefferson, Van Buren, Clay, Jackson, Du Pont, Theodore Roosevelt and Wilson; and paints a convincing background of the conditions which formed them.

OUR ENGLISH HERITAGE. 1949. A study of the British tradition in American life. "Its essays on the language, the laws, the religious faith, the arts and the sciences are accurate as well as penetrating."—Allan Nevins, in *Saturday Review of Literature.*

INCREDIBLE TALES; THE ODYSSEY OF THE AVERAGE AMERICAN IN THE LAST HALF-CENTURY. 1950. "Informal history at its best." "A proud and cheerful book, full of humor, as provocative as a buzz-saw."—*New York Herald Tribune.*

Johnson, James Weldon 1871-1938 American Negro poet, anthologist, professor, racial leader.

SELECTED POEMS. 1936. Rich in the traditional folk qualities of his race.

AUTOBIOGRAPHY OF AN EX-COLORED MAN. 1910. Fiction; first published anonymously. The book on which his reputation is based. Probably his best piece of writing.

BOOK OF AMERICAN NEGRO POETRY. 1922. An anthology.

BOOK OF AMERICAN NEGRO SPIRITUALS. n.d. "The best collection of our country's folk poetry."—*Good Reading.* (Compiled with the assistance of his brother, John Rosamund Johnson.)

Johnson, John Rosamund, joint compiler   *See* Johnson, James Weldon.

Johnson, Josephine Winslow   1910-   American novelist, poet, and painter.

Now in November. 1934. (III) Bitterly beautiful and tragic first novel about men and women toiling and suffering on well-loved but pitiless acres in the Middle West. Won the Pulitzer prize, 1935.

Johnson, Osa Helen (Mrs. Martin Johnson; later Mrs. C. H. Getts) 1894-1953 Traveler and animal photographer.

I Married Adventure. 1940. (IV) Splendidly illustrated. "A fine book on many counts. It is a good travel book, a good adventure book, a good book about animals, a good book on photography, and, best of all, it is a good human story about two extremely likable people."—*New York Herald Tribune.*

Johnson, Samuel   1709-84   "The Great Lexicographer"; literary dictator of his day in England. Though hard to read, he is very easy to read about.

Dictionary. 2v. 1755. "Chiefly important because of the picture its subjective definitions give of the personality of the author."

Rasselas, Prince of Abyssinia. 1759. (I) Didactic novel, which has been called "a lay sermon on 'the vanity of human wishes.'" A museum piece.

Lives of the Poets. 10v. 1779-81. (I) A series of critical biographies which are "dated" today, but which were admired by the faithful Boswell and considered by Macaulay Johnson's best work.

Johnson, Walter   1915-   American author.

William Allen White's America. 1947. "A definitive book, thoroughly documented, well-written, entertaining and enlightening."—R. L. Duffus, in *New York Times.* "It re-creates for us both the times and the man."—H. S. Commager, in *New York Herald Tribune.*

Johnston, Mary 1870-1936 American historical novelist, who had the knack of combining historical accuracy with colorful romance.

To HAVE AND TO HOLD. 1900. Roaring tale of Virginia in 1627. This was by far her most popular book, but the critics preferred some of the later ones, like

THE LONG ROLL. 1911. (II) Fictional study of Stonewall Jackson in the Civil War. "Since Zola wrote *La Débâcle* there has been no more vivid story of war."—*Saturday Review*, about 1911.

Joinville, Jean de 1224-1317 French historian.

HISTORY OF SAINT LOUIS. 1305-09. (I) Joinville was a feudal lord who accompanied his friend and master, Louis IX of France (Saint Louis), on the Sixth Crusade. In his book we have an invaluable picture of life in Europe in the Thirteenth Century.

Jonson, Ben 1573-1637 English dramatist; pensioned as "King's poet." Among the great Elizabethans Jonson ranks highest except for Shakespeare and, possibly, Marlowe. Said Dryden, "If I would compare him with Shakespeare, I must acknowledge him the more correct poet, but Shakespeare the greater wit." "Jonson is known for his satire, his classicism, his rigid observance of theoretic principles in his writing, his opposition to the romantic attitude."—*Reader's Encyclopedia*.

PLAYS. The best known are *Every Man in His Humour* (1598), *Volpone* (1606), *Epicene, or the Silent Woman* (1609), and *The Alchemist* (1610).

Josephson, Matthew 1899- American litterateur who turned to economic and political history.

ROBBER BARONS: THE GREAT AMERICAN CAPITALISTS, 1861-1901. 1934. Unfavorable portrayal, from leftist point of view, of the bold, ruthless spirits whom we used to call empire-builders—how the modern system of capitalism was set up during the half-century that followed the Civil War.

POLITICOS: 1865-96. 1938. (IV) Here are all the questionable heroes of our politics who flourished in the last third of the Nineteenth Century, from Ben Butler to Bryan. "A scholarly work. It stands up, a true picture of the times."—William Allen White, in *Saturday Review of Literature*.

PRESIDENT MAKERS: THE CULTURE OF POLITICS AND LEADERSHIP IN AN AGE OF ENLIGHTENMENT, 1896-1919. 1940. (IV) American politics from McKinley to Wilson. The leaders studied are Mark Hanna, Theodore Roosevelt, Colonel House, and George Harvey. "A clear picture of democracy at work, and on the whole a pretty encouraging picture."—*Survey Graphic.*

STENDHAL; OR, THE PURSUIT OF HAPPINESS. 1946. Good criticism and good biography of Henri Beyle ("Stendhal"), the French novelist who died more than a century ago. Neglected in his own time, he has come into his own in this, as he foretold that he would.

Joyce, James   1882-1941   Irish novelist, psychologist, and experimentalist in the use of language; regarded as one of the greatest and most influential authors of the Twentieth Century. He knew seventeen languages and during his later years was nearly blind. Though he lived almost entirely in Paris, Switzerland, or Austria after he was twenty, he wrote always of Irishmen.

DUBLINERS. 1914. Short stories and sketches of incidents in the lives of mean, petty, or tragic people of the Dublin streets. The style is simple and moving. In this early production eccentricity and obscurity had not yet united to bring forth genius.

PORTRAIT OF THE ARTIST AS A YOUNG MAN. 1916. Autobiographic short novel. The hero, Daedalus—Joyce himself—appears prominently also in the succeeding book, *Ulysses.* The author describes "his hero's psychological activity, and experiments in exploitation of his unconscious as well."

ULYSSES. 1922. The first unabridged and uncensored edition was first published in the United States in 1934. With a bow toward Homer's *Odyssey,* this strange book "reveals in exhaustive detail the mental and emotional wanderings of a Jew of Dublin during a single day."

FINNEGAN'S WAKE. 1939. (IV) The cult of initiates is as one in considering this book a masterpiece of the highest genius. But it is possible that to the average reader, without the pale but aware of the author's prodigious learning and protracted labor, the book may seem a long, exhausting nightmare induced by linguistic and psychological indigestion.

Judith   *See* Anglo-Saxon Poetry.

Juvenal   c. 60-140 A.D.   Satirist of the early Roman Empire.

SATIRES. (I) These present a repellent picture, Hogarthian in detail, of the manners and morals of Rome in the First Century.

Kafka, Franz   1883-1924   Bohemian novelist; a mystic obsessed by religion and philosophy.

THE CASTLE. 1930. "Beautifully styled but intricately symbolic spiritual allegory; a modern *Pilgrim's Progress.*"

THE TRIAL. 1937. Fantastic allegory of a harmless bank clerk who is arrested, tried, and unjustly condemned.

Kalevala   The Finnish epic; first compiled in the Nineteenth Century from oral tradition, by the Swedish philologist, Elias Lönnrolt. In unrhymed, alliterative verse, it is the prototype of Longfellow's *Hiawatha.*

Kalidasa   Flourished Fifth (?) Century   Hindu dramatist.

SAKUNTALA. Fairy-tale play about a water-nymph's daughter who marries a king and almost loses him when the wedding-ring disappears.

Kang, Younghill   1903-   Korean-American writer.

GRASS ROOF. 1931. (III) The author's story of his boyhood and youth in Northern Korea, of his pursuit of an education in Japan, and of his final attainment of America—the land of his dreams.

Kant, Immanuel   1724-1804   German philosopher.

CRITIQUE OF PURE REASON. 1781. (I) "An examination of the mind with a view to detect its *a priori* principles. He calls them pure because they are *a priori,* because they are above and beyond experience."

CRITIQUE OF PRACTICAL REASON. 1788. (I) Practical reason is "the determination of the grounds or universal laws of voluntary action by reason."—*Webster's New International Dictionary.*

CRITIQUE OF JUDGMENT. 1790. (I) Deals with aesthetics and the order of nature—a kind of middle ground between pure and practical reason.

Kantor, MacKinlay 1904- American novelist, who confesses to a "permanent fixation on the Civil War."

LONG REMEMBER. 1934. (III) Realistic historical novel; the battle of Gettysburg vividly described by a non-combatant caught between the armies.

Kaufman, George S. 1889- American playwright.

OF THEE I SING, A MUSICAL PLAY. 1932. (III) Hilarious burlesque of our statesmen at Washington, our government, and our politics. Written with M. Ryskind. Pulitzer prize play of 1932.

SIX PLAYS. 1942. All written with Moss Hart. Includes *Once in a Lifetime, You Can't Take It with You, The Man Who Came to Dinner, George Washington Slept Here*, etc.

Kaufman, George S., joint author *See also* Connelly, Marc.

Kaye-Smith, Sheila (Mrs. Penrose Fry) 1888- English novelist.

JOANNA GODDEN. 1921. (II) Story of a vulgar, bouncing, faulty and unlucky, but withal brave and likable woman.

SUSSEX GORSE. 1916. (II) Life story of a Sussex yeoman (1835-1905), recording the changes in English ways and sentiments which occurred in his lifetime.

Kazin, Alfred 1915- American critic; a New Yorker, born and bred.

ON NATIVE GROUNDS; INTERPRETATION OF MODERN AMERICAN PROSE LITERATURE. 1942. (IV) "History of the relation between American prose writers and our developing society" in the years since 1890 which has been recognized by a Guggenheim Fellowship and a grant-in-aid from the Carnegie Corporation. "This book is the signal of a new force in American criticism."—Irwin Edman, in *New York Herald Tribune*.

Keats, John 1795-1821 English poet. Though he died at twenty-six, he still had time to scale poetic heights where Shakespeare walks almost alone.

POEMS. (I) Leigh Hunt—a friend who knew him well—said that Keats was born a poet of the most poetical kind. "He never beheld an oak tree without seeing the dryad."

LETTERS; edited by H. Buxton-Forman. 1895. "In addition to the poignant story of the poet's life which these letters tell, the reader is given an insight to his critical and creative mind which no other book will give in the same degree."—*English Library*.

Keble, John   1792-1866   English clergyman and poet.

CHRISTIAN YEAR. 1827. (I) Thoughts in verse for the Sundays and Holy Days throughout the Anglican church year. Ninety-five editions were issued in the author's lifetime. "It is not necessary, and scarcely becoming, to praise a book that has already become one of the classics of the language."—Cardinal J. H. Newman.

Keith, Agnes Newton   1901-   American wife of an English official in North Borneo.

LAND BELOW THE WIND. 1939. (IV) Informal, amusing account of home life and jungle travel in Borneo before World War II.

Keller, Albert Galloway   1874-   American sociologist.

MAN'S ROUGH ROAD; BACKGROUNDS AND BEARINGS FROM MAN'S EXPERIENCE. 1932. (III) Exposition, for the layman, of the nature and evolution of human society and institutions—property, religion, etc. Based entirely on the monumental *Science of Society* (1927), by William Graham Sumner and this author.

Keller, Gottfried   1819-90   "Switzerland's foremost storyteller." —*Book Review Digest*, 1929.

PEOPLE OF SELDWYLA, AND SEVEN LEGENDS. English translation, 1929. "Picturesque folk stories, with leisurely ways and real charm of narrative."—*Spectator*.

Keller, Helen   1880-   American author and lecturer; blind and deaf from infancy.

STORY OF MY LIFE. 1903. (II) "One of the rare books that not only delight readers but compel attention from students of educational methods."

Kelly, Amy Ruth   1878-   Formerly Associate Professor of History at Wellesley College.

ELEANOR OF AQUITAINE AND THE FOUR KINGS. 1950. "Excellent popular biography of one of the more fascinating characters of the Twelfth Century."—*Nation.* "It makes even the best historical novel seem like pap."—*New Yorker.*

Kelly, George   1887-   American playwright—"the most serious devotee of American domestic comedy."

CRAIG'S WIFE. 1926. "Faithfully realistic and honest in characterization." Awarded Pulitzer prize for 1926.

Kempis, Thomas à   *See* Thomas à Kempis.

Kennedy, Charles Rann   1871-1950   Anglo-American dramatist.

SERVANT IN THE HOUSE. 1908. (II) A generation ago this play startled audiences by its application of the teachings of Jesus to modern life. Said dramatic critic Clayton Hamilton, "Surely this play is literature as well as being drama."

Kennedy, Margaret   1896-   English novelist.

CONSTANT NYMPH. 1925. Chronicles the strange, surprising adventures of the neglected children of a musical genius, and especially of poor little Teresa, the constant nymph.

Keynes, John Maynard (Lord Keynes)   1883-1946   British economist.

ECONOMIC CONSEQUENCES OF THE PEACE. 1920. (II) This ruthless criticism of the Versailles Treaty, however brilliant, remains a controversial book thirty years after publication.

Keyserling, Hermann Alexander, Count   1880-1946   Estonian social philosopher and mystic of German stock.

TRAVEL DIARY OF A PHILOSOPHER. 2v. 1925.(II) Exposition and review of several spiritual cultures: Buddhism, Hinduism, Confucianism, the philosophy of Japan, and that of Western civilization. *New Republic* called it the most important book to appear in Germany since World War I.

Kierkegaard, Soren A.   1813-55   Danish philosopher. The middle of the Twentieth Century witnessed a remarkable revival of interest in his work, thanks to Sartre, Auden, and others.

EITHER-OR. 1843. Analyses of "the razor-edge decision on human free will which determines man's personal relation to God."

Kilmer, Joyce 1886-1918 American poet; killed in action on the Western Front in World War I.

JOYCE KILMER: POEMS, ESSAYS, LETTERS. 2v. 1918. (II) "Some of his poems will go clothed in ink a long time, for they carry a genuine life, and emotion that touches intimate human concerns."—Christopher Morley.

Kimbrough, Emily, joint author *See* Skinner, Cornelia Otis.

Kinglake, A. W. 1809-91 English historian.

EOTHEN, OR TRACES OF TRAVEL BROUGHT HOME FROM THE EAST. 1844. (I) Frank and unconventional record of impressions of the manners and morals of the Mohammedans. Helen Haines calls it "perennial in charm and vitality."

Kingsley, Charles 1819-75 English novelist. "There is not one of his novels that has not the power of Christianity for its theme."—David Masson.

WESTWARD HO! 1855. (I) This story of English seamen in the days of Elizabeth is Kingsley's masterpiece. "A finer, nobler story for boys does not exist" than this "ideal example of the historical romance."

ALTON LOCKE. 1850. (I) An early labor novel; inspired by the bad economic conditions in the England of its day.

HEREWARD THE WAKE. 1866. (I) The hero, an outlaw called "the last of the English," opposed the rule of William the Conqueror in 1070-71.

HYPATIA. 1853. (I) Dramatic tale of the struggle in Fifth-Century Alexandria between the young but already faulty Christian Church and the Greek world that then was old and dying.

Kingsley, Henry 1830-76 English novelist; brother of Charles Kingsley.

RECOLLECTIONS OF GEOFFREY HAMLIN. 1859. Story of adventure, based upon the author's own experiences in the Australian gold fields.

RAVENSHOE. 1861. (I) A family romance of England's West Country. Incidents "rise to a thrilling height of tragic suspense."

Kingsley, Sidney   1906-   American playwright.

MEN IN WHITE. 1933. Play about modern doctors; the stern demands of the medical profession. Pulitzer prize play of 1934.

THE PATRIOTS. 1945. A play about Hamilton and Jefferson. The New York Drama Critics' Circle pronounced it the best of its year.

DEAD END. 1936. Presenting typical incidents which take place in a dead-end street, this play pictures life in New York's slums.

Kinsey, Alfred Charles   1894-   American biologist (and others).

SEXUAL BEHAVIOR IN THE HUMAN MALE. 1948. Much discussed sociological study that was supported by the National Research Council. "The Kinsey report qualifies as an adult text of sex education, although some of its content will prove to be rather rough for the sensitive. However, the spirit of scientific detachment reigns throughout."—*Science and Society.*

Kipling, Rudyard   1865-1936   English writer. *The Spectator,* in 1906, called him "the interpreter of the English-speaking race"; and the *North American Review,* "this supreme genius of his generation."

KIM. 1901. (I and II) Picaresque romance which is a colorful panorama of British India as it was two generations ago. This book has many devotees, some of whom read it at least once every year.

RUDYARD KIPLING'S VERSE. 1940. (II) T. S. Eliot has declared that Kipling's position in the class of great verse writers "is not only high but unique."

TWO JUNGLE BOOKS. n.d. (I) "The Jungle Books are far more than a . . . childhood classic. They are the life of modern India, told in allegory, and in Kaa and Bagheera and all the rest we have the types of native life, with its stored-up wisdom of old, primeval instincts, its simplicity of outlook upon the present-day world."—F. T. Cooper.

JUST SO STORIES. 1902. (II) Here are delightful explanations and illustrations, written and drawn for the author's own children, of how the camel got his hump, where the elephant got his trunk, etc.

PUCK OF POOK'S HILL   (1906)   (II)   and REWARDS AND FAIRIES
(1910) (II) are fascinating books of historical fairy stories,
written for the young folk of Old England.

CAPTAINS COURAGEOUS. 1897. (I) The spoiled son of an
American millionaire falls overboard from an Atlantic liner and
is picked up by a Gloucester fisherman. "By the time the fishing
season is over he has a different and much healthier attitude
towards life."

SOLDIER STORIES. 1899. (I) These seven tales about the in-
separable British Tommies—Mulvaney, Ortheris, and Learoyd—
are among the best and most famous short stories in any language.

SELECTED STORIES; edited by W. L. Phelps. 1921. Judicious
selection of thirteen tales, four of which are also in *Soldier Stories.*

SOMETHING OF MYSELF. 1937. (IV) A somewhat disappoint-
ing book. The latter half of his life remains uncovered. But as we
may expect no more, Kipling's admirers will wish to read this
fragment.

Kittredge, George Lyman, joint author   *See* Greenough, J. B.

Kleist, Heinrich von   1777-1811   German dramatist and novelist.

MICHAEL KOHLHAAS. 1808. Story of Brandenburg in the
Middle Ages. "Considered one of the outstanding works of
German fiction" and "regarded as the best novelette in the Ger-
man language."

Kluckhohn, Clyde   1905-   American anthropologist.

MIRROR FOR MAN; THE RELATION OF ANTHROPOLOGY TO MODERN
LIFE. 1949. "A diagnostic study of our own national character
. . . one of the best that has been made to date. . . . The
reader will not be altogether flattered by the resulting picture,
but it can serve as a basis for some profitable introspection."—
New York Herald Tribune.

Knight, Eric   1897-1943   English novelist.

THIS ABOVE ALL. 1941. (IV) English soldier, his valor already proved in battle, is home on leave. When he is about to
return to the trenches doubts assail him. "One can't say any
longer that no great novel has come out of the second World
War. Eric Knight has written one."—*Boston Transcript.*

Knoblauch, Edward, joint author *See* Bennett, E. A.

Koestler, Arthur 1905- Hungarian novelist, journalist, soldier. A Communist from 1931 till about 1935. Called by reviewers, "the best of the *émigrés*."

THE GLADIATORS. 1939. Realistic novel about the revolt, in 73 to 71 B.C., of the downtrodden in Rome, under the leadership of Spartacus, the gladiator.

DARKNESS AT NOON. 1941. (IV) Psychological study in fiction of the strange purge-trials in Moscow. The *Manchester Guardian* called this book "an anatomy of totalitarianism." George Orwell's comment is that it is "most valuable as an interpretation of the Moscow 'confessions' by some one with an inner knowledge of totalitarian methods."

SCUM OF THE EARTH. 1941. (IV) The author's recollections of what happened in France to him and others between the outbreak of World War II and the fall of France. The *Manchester Guardian* called this title "the best book to come out of the collapse of France."

ARRIVAL AND DEPARTURE. 1943. (IV) Psychological novel about a refugee Communist who, after arrest and torture, escapes from the Nazis. "I cannot too strongly urge *Arrival and Departure* upon you. . . . If Koestler develops, he may quite conceivably become the great writer of our generation."—Clifton Fadiman.

YOGI AND THE COMMISSARS, AND OTHER ESSAYS. 1945. (IV) About literature, Russia, Communism, and the parlous state of the world. "In this war," the author says, "we are fighting a total lie with a half-truth."

THIEVES IN THE NIGHT. 1946. "Sympathetic fiction depicting the confusion of Jewish life in Palestine shortly before the outbreak of World War II."—*Good Reading.* "A bewildering book . . . a magnificent novel."—*Saturday Review of Literature.*

Koran Seventh Century (I) As the Bible means simply the Book, so the Mohammedan sacred scripture, the Koran, means the Reading. It is believed by Moslems to be God's revelation to his third great prophet, Mohammed—the first and second ones having been Moses and Jesus.

Krutch, Joseph Wood 1893- American writer and critic; member, National Institute of Arts and Letters.

EDGAR ALLAN POE: A STUDY OF GENIUS. 1926. (III) Not a conventional "life," but an attempt to explain Poe and his genius in the light of modern psychology.

THE MODERN TEMPER, A STUDY AND A CONFESSION. 1929. Essays.

FIVE MASTERS; A STUDY IN THE MUTATIONS OF THE NOVEL. 1930. (III) The five are Boccaccio, Cervantes, Richardson, Stendhal, and Proust.

SAMUEL JOHNSON. 1944. (IV) Impressive, six-hundred-page biography by an admirer who writes *con amore*. Boswell has been ably supplemented—but not superseded.

HENRY DAVID THOREAU. 1948. "A nearly perfect fusing of biography and critical study."—*New Yorker*. "A biography that ranks with the best work in the field of Thoreau . . . and accepts him as a prophet."—Brooks Atkinson, in *New York Times*.

TWELVE SEASONS; A PERPETUAL CALENDAR FOR THE COUNTRY. 1949. A contemplative and philosophical nature essay for each month in the year. "It is difficult to convey the charm, to identify the quality of this book. . . . It is filled with a delight in the whole natural scene."—Irwin Edman, in *New Republic*.

La Farge, Christopher 1897- American poet and novelist; brother of Oliver La Farge.

THE SUDDEN GUEST. 1946. A tense tale of a New England spinster and the hurricanes of 1938 and 1944, "the woman being drawn with great skill, the hurricanes being described with extraordinary vigor and vividness."

La Farge, Oliver 1901 American novelist and anthropologist.

LAUGHING BOY. 1929. (III) An idyll of the hapless love of a Navajo Indian boy and girl of the Twentieth Century. Won the Pulitzer prize, 1930.

SPARKS FLY UPWARD, A NOVEL. 1931. (III) Central American politics a century ago. In the hero's veins there is strife 'twixt Spanish and Indian blood.

La Fayette, Marie Madeleine, Comtesse de   1634-93   French novelist; one of the *Précieuses*.

PRINCESS OF CLEVES. 1678. As perhaps the earliest psychological novel, this is a landmark in literary history.

La Fontaine, Jean   1621-95   French poet; member, French Academy.

FABLES. 1668-93. (I) Brief and, in the original, versified stories of talking animals "in the tradition of Æsop and the medieval 'beast epic,' presented with humor, grace, and satire." Children love them for their seeming simplicity, students for their perfect art, and wise men for their subtlety as studies in human character.

Lagerlöf, Selma   1858-1940   Swedish novelist. Member, Swedish Academy; the first woman to whom was awarded (1909) a Nobel prize for idealistic literature.

STORY OF GÖSTA BERLING. 1894. "An unfrocked priest, after a career of love-errantry, marries and dedicates himself to a life of service. . . . The novel excels in humor, characterization and dramatically significant Swedish backgrounds."—*Good Reading*.

WONDERFUL ADVENTURES OF NILS. 1906. (II) A Swedish classic for children—and adults. Natural history and travel are combined with a charming love story.

EMPEROR OF PORTUGALLIA. 1916. (II) Story of a Swedish peasant's love for his daughter. Told with rare charm and simplicity.

LILIECRONA'S HOME. 1914. (II) Perhaps because this idyll of village life is spiced with a mystery, the *Nation* believes that this book has a more general appeal than the author's other titles.

La Guardia, Fiorello H.   1882-1947   American politician; Mayor, New York City, 1934-46.

MAKING OF AN INSURGENT; AN AUTOBIOGRAPHY. 1948. His first 37 years, only. "Students of political parties and pressure politics will find this book especially worth while."—*Quarterly Booklist*. "Sketchy as the book is, it discloses a passion for public service. . . . Some of his famed fractiousness comes through here, and so does his standard of political morality."—*Time*.

Lamb, Charles ("Elia," pseudonym) 1775-1834 English author; greatest master of the essay which is often thoughtful and stimulating but always light, graceful, and pleasingly familiar.

ESSAYS OF ELIA. 2v. 1823-33. (I) "Humanly appealing in their utter frankness and naturalness, whimsical in their humor."

LETTERS; edited by E. V. Lucas. 3v. 1935. (I) Lamb's personal charm and easy intimacy are characteristics of his letters no less than of his essays. (The edition named above contains also his tragic sister Mary's letters.)

Lamb, Harold 1892- American historian and biographer.

GENGHIS KHAN; THE EMPEROR OF ALL MEN. 1927. (III) Author tells an interesting and coherent story—describes a striking, yet credible personality (1167-1227). Other historians find little to question in this vivid portrait.

THE CRUSADES; IRON MEN AND SAINTS. 2v.in 1. 1930. "Popular history of the First Crusade, which centers interest on its preachers and leaders, and ends with the death of Baldwin, its last leader."—*Book Review Digest.*

La Motte-Fouqué, F. H. K., Baron de 1777-1843 German author, descended from a French Huguenot family.

UNDINE. 1811. (I) Fanciful tale about a water-fairy. A classic of romanticism, it has charmed millions of readers, having been translated into many languages.

Landon, Margaret 1903- American author.

ANNA AND THE KING OF SIAM. 1944. (IV) Story of Anna Leonowens, a young Welsh widow, who for two years in the 1860's was governess of the King's many daughters. "Not fiction, but skillfully documented biography." "Its fascination lies in the contrast between a splendid Scheherazade background and the tidy-minded Victorian lady period-piece."—*New York Times.*

Landor, Walter Savage 1775-1864 English writer and classical scholar. "Full of dignity and splendor," his works are a touchstone of refined taste.

IMAGINARY CONVERSATIONS. 1824-53. (I) Prose dialogs between famous men and women of past ages.

PERICLES AND ASPASIA. 1836. Imagined correspondence between the great Athenian and his lady love.

Lang, Andrew, translator *See* Aucassin and Nicolette, and Homer.

Lang, Paul Henry 1866- Hungarian musicologist and critic; naturalized in the United States, 1934.

MUSIC IN WESTERN CIVILIZATION. 1941. Professor Lang regards "musical ideas and forms as the expressions of religious, philosophical, and social ideals, from Greek antiquity to the present day."

Langland, William c. 1330-c. 1400 English cleric; reputed author of

THE VISION OF PIERS PLOWMAN. First printed, 1550. (I) Long, alliterative poem by an author or authors contemporary with

Chaucer. Describes many human types and throws much light upon social and religious institutions of the Fourteenth Century. The vices of the priests are pitilessly scourged, as is the covetousness of the rich and powerful.

Langley, Mrs. Adria (Locke) American publicist and novelist.

LION IS IN THE STREETS. 1945. (IV) Story of "Magnolia State" and of the sharecroppers and fishermen of the bayous. The chief character is "strongly reminiscent of the late Huey Long. . . . It is both an intensely readable tale and a social document, for it reveals how mass ignorance and legalized injustice can become grist for the mill of the clever demagogue."—*New York Herald Tribune.*

Lanier, Sidney 1842-81 American poet, critic, compiler of books for boys, and soldier of the Confederacy.

SELECTED POEMS. 1947. (I) Comprises his best work, including *The Marshes of Glyn.*

Lao-tsze Sixth Century, B.C. Chinese philosopher. Reputed author of

THE BOOK OF REASON AND VIRTUE (*Tao-teh-king*). This is the Bible of Taoism, one of the three great religions of China. (*See also* Bynner, Witter.)

Lardner, Ring   1885-1933   American sports-writer and satirist.

PORTABLE RING LARDNER. 1946. "Bitterly humorous and satirical stories and sketches of Twentieth Century American life, told in the characteristic slang and vernacular of baseball-players, chorus-girls, etc., in order to show the stupidity or viciousness of the people involved."—*Reader's Encyclopedia.*

Larkin, Oliver W.   1896-   American professor of art at Smith College.

ART AND LIFE IN AMERICA. 1949. "Discussion of the development of American painting and sculpture, from its beginnings to the present. Architecture, interior decoration, and allied arts are considered less fully."—*Book Review Digest.* "A synthesis in a single volume of the most up-to-date scholarship, it is intended to serve both as a college text and as an introduction to the subject for the general reader."—*New York Herald Tribune.*

La Rochefoucauld, François, Duc de   1613-80   French courtier and cynic.

MAXIMS. 1665. There are about seven hundred of these often translated aphorisms, varying in length from two lines to half a page. No one else has recorded his reflections with so much point and brevity. Each paragraph is packed with meaning and equipped with a cutting edge. The prevailing idea is that self-love is the mainspring of human action.

Laski, Harold   1893-1950   English political scientist and socialist.

AMERICAN PRESIDENCY. 1940. (IV) "It takes its place with de Tocqueville and Bryce as an acute analysis of American political institutions."—*American Political Science Review.*

Latourette, K. S.   1884-   American Orientalist. Faculty member, Yale-in-China, 1910-17.

CHINESE: THEIR HISTORY AND CULTURE. Revised edition, 1946. (III) For the intelligent reader this is perhaps the best background book on the subject.

HISTORY OF JAPAN. Revised edition, 1947. "For those who wish to learn as much about Japan's past as can be learned from one volume, in order to understand her present and make a sensible guess as to her probable future, this is the book."—*Christian Century.*

Lauterbach, Richard E.   1914-50   Formerly American correspondent in Moscow for *Life* and *Time.* He spoke Russian.

THESE ARE THE RUSSIANS. 1945. (IV) Very readable and unusually sympathetic. He thought we could and should work with the Russians.

Law, William   1868-1761   English author of devotional books.

SERIOUS CALL TO A DEVOUT AND HOLY LIFE. 1728. "Written to prod easy-going and indifferent Christians into living more worthily that which they profess to believe. It still fulfills that purpose."—*Religious Book Club Bulletin.*

Lawes, Lewis E.   1883-1947   American penologist.

TWENTY THOUSAND YEARS IN SING SING. 1932. (III) Autobiography of the veteran warden of the famous prison in New York State. Consists largely of his sober, reasonable reflections on crime and criminals, together with a description of the experience upon which his conclusions are founded.

Lawrence, D. H.   1885-1930   English writer; "the idol of the intellectuals." "Known for his lifelong obsession with problems of sexual relations."

SONS AND LOVERS. 1913. (II) "The hero's deep affection for his mother colors his relations with other women, so that he never finds complete satisfaction in their love."—*A.L.A. Catalog*, 1926.

WOMEN IN LOVE. 1920. (II) "This novel sums up the author's mystical theories of sex. They are still tentative . . . obscure . . . and by no means stated in a way to conciliate criticism. . . ." —E. A. Baker.

PLUMED SERPENT. 1926. "Remarkable attempt to penetrate to the essential spirit of modern Mexico as it reveals itself to a lovely, world-weary Irishwoman resident there. The Plumed Serpent is the name of one of the old Aztec gods."—*Cleveland Public Library.*

Lawrence, Thomas Edward (also known as Aircraftsman T. E. Shaw)   1888-1935   British soldier, archaeologist, scholar.

SEVEN PILLARS OF WISDOM. 1935. (Privately printed in 1926.) (III) This account of the time when the author was "the uncrowned king of three nations" in the Near East is a work of genius; but, despite brilliant flashes here and there, the average intelligent reader may find it hard going.

REVOLT IN THE DESERT. 1927. (III) A briefer telling of the Arabian tale first told in *Seven Pillars of Wisdom*. It is a narrative of intrigue and primitive, hand-to-hand fighting. The facts, though imaginatively presented, are true.

Lawrence, Thomas Edward, translator   *See* Homer.

Lawson, Ted W.   1917-   American bomber pilot.

THIRTY SECONDS OVER TOKYO. 1943. (IV) Describes the Doolittle raid, the preliminary training, and its aftermath. "Certainly the most stirring story of individual heroism that the war has so far produced."—W. L. White, in *New York Times* (1943).

Laxness, Halldór   1902-   Icelandic novelist and poet; a farmer's son.

INDEPENDENT PEOPLE. 1946. Long, grim, epic-novel of Icelandic peasant life in a region where living on the land is reduced to a desperate struggle for bare existence. It justifies the Icelanders' boast: "We are the independent people."

Lea, Henry C.   1825-1909   American historian; member, American Academy of Arts and Letters.

HISTORY OF THE INQUISITION OF SPAIN. 4v. 1906-08. (II) Story of the Roman Catholic Church's struggle against heresy in Spain. "The monumental work of a great scholar."—*A.L.A. Catalog*, 1926.

Lea, Tom   1907-   American novelist and painter. Born in Texas, he saw his first bull-fight at eight years old.

BRAVE BULLS. 1949. A fine story that helps one to understand the Spanish mania for the *corrida*. "One of the most dramatic and impassioned treatments of bullfighting that have so far appeared. . . . In addition to his spirited words about the fascination of the great Latin pastime, the author has provided a series of appropriate pen-and-ink decorations."—*New Yorker*.

Leacock, Stephen 1869-1944 Canadian humorist and professor of economics.

CHARLES DICKENS, HIS LIFE AND WORK, 1934. (III) A sincere, hero-worshipping introduction to Dickens and his work, with a quip now and then to make it irresistible. A large part of Leacock's best humorous writings is to be found in the two following collections:

LAST LEAVES. 1945.

LEACOCK ROUNDABOUT. 1946.

Lear, Edward 1812-88 English humorist and artist.

LEAR OMNIBUS. 1938. Selection of nonsense verses and drawings from Lear's published volumes of such material, beginning with the *Book of Nonsense* (1846). Nonsense must have something, to last into its second century!

Learned, W. S. 1876-1950 American specialist in education.

AMERICAN PUBLIC LIBRARY AND THE DIFFUSION OF KNOWLEDGE. 1924. (II) Though much has happened since this book was written it is still a basic work on a subject of vital interest to every reader.

Lecky, W. E. H. 1838-1903 British historian. Justin McCarthy said that "Lecky is always the historian and never the partisan." But it is as well to remember that he had "an undisguised aversion to democratic government."

HISTORY OF EUROPEAN MORALS FROM AUGUSTUS TO CHARLEMAGNE. 1869. (I) A demonstration of the progressive character of moral institutions.

HISTORY OF ENGLAND IN THE EIGHTEENTH CENTURY. 8v. 1878-90. (I) "Remains the best existing record of the social and political activities" of its period, particularly of the years 1760-93.

Lee, Sir Sidney 1859-1926 English scholar and man of letters; one of the principal editors of the *Dictionary of National Biography*.

LIFE OF WILLIAM SHAKESPEARE. (I) First published in 1898, but revised and enlarged by new editions up to 1931. It has long been the standard life; but biographers like Sir E. K. Chambers, J. Q. Adams, and Marchette Chute, have incorporated in their books more of the fruit of modern research.

Leech, Margaret (Mrs. Ralph Pulitzer) 1893- American author.

REVEILLE IN WASHINGTON, 1860-65. 1941. (IV) Panorama of the nation's capital as it was during the Civil War. Awarded the Pulitzer prize in history, 1942. "A faithful mirror of a great and critical time in our history."—*Saturday Review of Literature.*

Lenin, Nikolai 1870-1924 Russian founder of the Bolshevik party and the Soviet state.

LETTERS. 1937. Selection of 340 letters, personal and political, dated from 1896 to 1922. An interesting and important book, though it is said that, owing to the Soviet government's control of the sources, there has been "a studied evasion of those things which will react unfavorably on the present regime."

Leonard, William Ellery 1876-1944 American poet and professor of English.

Two LIVES. 1925. The story of an intimate personal tragedy is here told in three sonnet sequences. "That a poet should at all succeed in a task of such delicacy would be matter for astonishment; the degree to which Mr. Leonard succeeds amazes one."— *New York Times.*

LOCOMOTIVE GOD. 1927. This autobiography is an extraordinary case history which, as Helen Haines says, "holds its deepest values for the psychologist and lover of literature, rather than for the general reader of biography."

Leonardo da Vinci 1452-1519 Italian painter, sculptor, architect, musician, and scientist; the supreme example of "Renaissance Man."

NOTEBOOKS. 2v. 1938. (IV) "Magnificently produced work of great permanent value." *The New Yorker* calls it "a work of supreme importance."

Lessing, G. E. 1729-81 German dramatist and critic.

LAOKOÖN, AN ESSAY UPON THE LIMITS OF PAINTING AND POETRY. 1766. (I) Goethe declared that after the publication of this unfinished work all previous criticism "could be thrown away like a worn-out coat."

MINNA VON BARNHELM. 1767. (I) This, Germany's first great comedy, was a picture of contemporary life and manners. "It liberated the German drama from slavish imitation of the French."

NATHAN THE WISE. 1779. (I) Rather a dramatic poem than a play, this work has been called "one of the finest written in the Eighteenth Century." It is an eloquent plea for religious tolerance. (All three of the titles described above were published (1930) in a single volume in *Everyman's Library*.)

Lever, Charles 1806-72 Anglo-Irish novelist. Though he is now old-fashioned, every male reader should have some acquaintance with this rollicking author—if only to increase his own delight in the contemporary colored sporting-prints.

HARRY LORREQUER. 1837. (I) Story of garrison life—very jocular and very Irish.

CHARLES O'MALLEY. 1841. (I) Rattling, jolly tale of the Peninsular War, when wars apparently, were very good fun; accounted the author's masterpiece.

Levi, Carlo 1902- Italian doctor and painter. He was a political prisoner for a year among the people described in this book.

CHRIST STOPPED AT EBOLI. 1947. "Well-written account by a sensitive and cultivated anti-fascist."—*Saturday Review of Literature*. "A critical and popular success in both Italy and France. I can think of no success more rightly deserved."—H. Basso, in *New Yorker*.

Lewes, George Henry 1817-78 British author; most often remembered today for his long association with George Eliot which began in 1854 and continued until Lewes's death.

LIFE OF GOETHE. 1855. (I) Still an important title in the Goethe bibliography. Longfellow called it "a clever and judicious book" which showed "the great German as he was." And Trollope considered it almost perfect "as a critical biography of one of the great heroes of literature."

Lewis, Clive Staples 1898- English author; Lecturer on English literature at Oxford. "He has a special gift for dramatizing Christian dogma."

SCREWTAPE LETTERS. 1943. "A witty, satiric presentation of the tricks and fallacies by which doubt makes its appeal."—*Good Reading*.

Lewis, Lloyd   1891-1950   American biographer and dramatic critic.

SHERMAN, FIGHTING PROPHET. 1932. (III) Full, straight-forward biography of the Union general who understood and loved the South, even while he relentlessly ravaged it on his "march to the sea."

CAPTAIN SAM GRANT. 1950. A very fine book about the early years (1822-61) of the commander of the Union forces in the Civil War. The author's death has prevented the completion of the story.

Lewis, Sinclair   1885-1951   American novelist and satirist. He refused the Pulitzer prize in 1926, but accepted the Nobel prize in 1930. Member, American Academy of Arts and Letters.

MAIN STREET. 1920. (II) Story of the vain crusade of a young college-bred uplifter against the ingrained inertia of a small Midwestern town. Like the one which follows, this book was a landmark in American literature.

BABBITT. 1922. (II) The booster "gets there" but, to his sad bewilderment, is not happy after he arrives. Thousands today recognize a "Babbitt" when they see one, even though they have never read the book.

ARROWSMITH. 1925. (II) A robust idealist struggles with the materialists who would dominate his medical career. Many consider this the author's best book.

DODSWORTH. 1929. (III) American couple travel and quarrel through Europe. The reader is made to see the foreign countries exactly as they appear to their American eyes.

CASS TIMBERLANE; A NOVEL OF HUSBANDS AND WIVES. 1945. (IV) "Sinclair Lewis has done it again. With that observant, buzz-saw mind of his, he has sliced through the main trunk of American life to lay bare a cross-section more worm-eaten than we like to suppose."—Edward Weeks, in *Atlantic*.

Lewisohn, Ludwig   1882-   German-Jewish-American critic and novelist.

STORY OF AMERICAN LITERATURE. 1937. (III) (Originally published in 1932 as *Expression in America*.) A brilliant interpretation and history that no one seriously interested in the subject

can afford to miss, though F. B. Millett warns that "it is less
a literary history perhaps than a re-interpretation . . . in terms
of its author's Continental liberalism and his temperamental hos-
tility to Puritanism."

Lie, Jonas   1833-1908   Norwegian novelist.

THE PILOT AND HIS WIFE. 1874. A sailor's love story. This
author is at his best when describing the sea and sea-faring men.

**Lieber, Lillian   1886-   American professor of mathematics;
born in Russia.**

EINSTEIN'S THEORY OF RELATIVITY. 1945. "Combines lucid
text, carefully worded for swift and easy reading, and skillful dia-
grams and cartoon drawings that effectively interpret the subject."
—Helen Haines.

**Liebman, Joshua L.   1907-48   American rabbi, Jewish scholar,
and theologian.**

PEACE OF MIND. 1946. A book about social problems, psychology, and religion. "Meant for those who have turned from
traditional religion because they cannot adjust their confidence in
the findings of science to the requirements of orthodoxy—Christian or Jewish."—Atlantic.

Life (magazine)

PICTURE HISTORY OF WORLD WAR II. 1950. The pictures are
arranged chronologically, with explanatory text and some maps.
"It may not be the best conceivable compilation of its sort, but
it is easily the best that has been produced since the war ended."
—J. T. Winterich, in Saturday Review of Literature.

**Lilienthal, David   1899-   TVA Director (1933-46); Chairman
(1941-46); Chairman, United States Atomic Energy Commission
(1946-50).**

THIS I DO BELIEVE. 1949. A prayerful study of democracy
in America and how to preserve it for the world. "A sound, sober
and thoughtful book, a testament of faith in the democratic process
and in the possibility of attaining good ends by good means—and
by no other kind."—Christian Century. "David Lilienthal is one of
America's most useful public servants. . . . What he has to

say about the problems of democracy, the role of government and of the citizen in such enterprises as regional economy and atomic energy merits the closest attention."—H. S. Commager, in *New York Herald Tribune.*

Lin Yu-tang   1895-   Chinese-American author.

My Country and My People. 1935. "Thought-provoking interpretation of the character and philosophy of the Chinese people."—*Good Reading.*

Importance of Living. 1937. (IV) The Chinese philosophy of life, written with a chuckle for Western readers. He calls it "a personal guide to enjoyment"; and it seems a distillation of the canniness of centuries of Chinese sages.

Between Tears and Laughter. 1943. (IV) Book of essays on the "most urgent issues of our times—an enduring peace and the future relations between Asia and the Western world."

Moment in Peking. 1939. (IV) Novel of family life in Peking from 1900 to 1938. "No other novel about China in English approaches the scope of this one, and probably none surpasses it in authenticity and detail."—*Nation.*

Lin Yu-tang, translator   *See* Confucius.

Lincoln, Abraham   1809-65   American statesman and Civil War President. "His heart was as great as the world, but there was no room in it to hold the memory of a wrong."—R. W. Emerson.

Speeches and Letters. (I) Sincerity, simplicity, sympathy, and elemental power: these are the characteristics of Lincoln's printed words. The modest selection in *Everyman's Library* is convenient and satisfactory.

Papers; the Story of the Collection with Selections to July 4, 1861; edited by D. C. Mearns. 2v. 1948. Mostly letters *to* Lincoln. For Lincoln specialists. "Nothing written about the martyred President can ever replace this deeply moving record of what his contemporaries actually said to him."—*Yale Review.*

Lincoln, Joseph C.   1870-1944   American novelist who wrote many pleasing stories about Cape Cod folk. A good sample is

Cap'n Eri. 1904. (II) "Story of three jolly, retired Cape Cod sea captains, forced into matrimony to escape the hardships of their own housekeeping."—*A.L.A. Catalog,* 1926.

Lindbergh, Anne Morrow (Mrs. Charles A. Lindbergh)   1907- American author and aviatrix.

NORTH TO THE ORIENT. 1935. (III) Account of her flight with her husband to China and Japan in 1931. Almost anybody's description of such a bit of pioneering would be interesting. But Mrs. Lindbergh writes exceedingly well—with charm and gleams of poetic feeling or glints of humor, and always with sincerity.

LISTEN, THE WIND. 1938. (IV) Story of ten days spent in a survey flight with her husband, in 1933, from Africa to South America. "Mrs. Lindbergh's books, quite apart from their value as aeronautical history, are small works of art."—*New Yorker.*

Lindsay, Howard, joint author *See* Crouse, Russel.

Lindsay, N. Vachel   1879-1931 American poet, who "united ragtime and religion"; member, National Institute of Arts and Letters.

COLLECTED POEMS. Revised edition, 1925. "He attempted deliberately to bring back poetry to the people, first, by writing on subjects and in a style that might attract the unlettered, and, second, by tramping in person over highways and byways as a vendor of his poetry and an apostle of beauty and idealism. . . . No poet of his time has come so near as Lindsay to being an authentic folk poet, or vehicle of the imagination of the people."—F. B. Millett.

Link, Arthur Stanley   1920- Teacher of history at Princeton University and student of Woodrow Wilson's career.

WILSON: THE ROAD TO THE WHITE HOUSE. 1947. "An important contribution to our historical literature. As top-notch interpretative biography it should prove rewarding to any intelligent citizen who is concerned with America's past and future."—*Christian Science Monitor.*

Lippman, Walter   1889- American journalist and commentator on public affairs, who is also the author of a dozen or more books and a member of the American Academy of Arts and Letters.

PUBLIC OPINION. 1922. (II) Important study of the means for manipulating a great force—for good or evil. John Dewey called this book "the most effective indictment of democracy as currently conceived ever penned."

PREFACE TO MORALS. 1929. (III) As a substitute for religion the author offers the faithless a philosophy of humanism based upon the ideal of disinterestedness. *Yale Review* called this "a sound and valuable book; honest, unafraid, and austere."

UNITED STATES FOREIGN POLICY: SHIELD OF THE REPUBLIC. 1943. (IV) "A definite service to his country. . . . He has undermined all possible arguments for isolationism or for the imperialism to whose standards the isolationists will repair as soon as they find that they are licked."—Clifton Fadiman, in *New Yorker.*

INQUIRY INTO THE PRINCIPLES OF A GOOD SOCIETY. New edition, 1943. "The 'good' society is the liberal society, free from Fascism, Communism, Toryism, and New Dealism. The subject matter, while inherently difficult, is presented with reasonable simplicity."—*Wisconsin Library Bulletin.*

Livy (Titus Livius) 59-17 B.C. Roman historian. He has always been more greatly admired by lovers of literature than by students of history.

HISTORY OF ROME. In 142 books. Only 35 survive *in toto*, covering the period before 293 B.C., and that between 218 and 167 B.C. "No historian with whom we are acquainted has shown so complete an indifference to truth. He seems to have cared only about the picturesque effect of his book, and the honor of his country. On the other hand, we do not know, in the whole range of literature of a bad thing so well done."—Lord Macaulay.

Llewellyn, Richard 1907(?)- Welsh novelist.

HOW GREEN WAS MY VALLEY. 1940. (IV) This first novel is about a family of coal miners in South Wales. "A story as noble as it is simple. It is a beautiful story, too, told in words that have Welsh music in them."—*Atlantic.*

Lloyd George, David 1863-1945 British statesman; Prime Minister, 1916-22.

WAR MEMOIRS. 6v. 1933-36. (III) Author was in the cabinet continuously throughout World War I—an active participant in the events he describes. It is always his side of the story which he tells, and with his vivid personality he has no trouble in making the story a lively one.

Locke, John   1632-1704   English philosopher, known as "the father of English empiricism" and "the intellectual ruler of the Eighteenth Century."

ESSAY CONCERNING HUMAN UNDERSTANDING. 1690. (I) "Locke had the faculty of making philosophy speak the language of ordinary life."—*Cambridge History of English Literature.*

SOME THOUGHTS CONCERNING EDUCATION. 1693. (I) "Of all Locke's work perhaps the most universally approved; in truth a golden treatise, the very incarnation of good sense and right feeling."—Richard Garnett.

Locke, W. J.   1863-1930   English novelist of subtly sterilized bohemianism and vagabondism.

BELOVED VAGABOND. 1906. (II) Almost the first and probably the best of many similar tunes trilled on the same flute. It was called "the outstanding picaresque romance of our day."

Lockhart, J. G.   1794-1854   Scottish author and brilliant but caustic contributor to *Blackwood's* and editor of *The Quarterly Review*; Scott's son-in-law.

LIFE OF SIR WALTER SCOTT. 1836-38. (I) Sir Sidney Lee called this "the second best biography in the language, Boswell's Johnson being the first."

ANCIENT SPANISH BALLADS. 1823. (I) George Ticknor described this translation as "a work of genius beyond any of the sort known to me in any language."

Lockridge, Ross Franklin, Jr.   1914-48   American novelist and professor of English.

RAINTREE COUNTY. 1948. Epic novel, describing one day (July 4, 1892) in Indiana, and its recollections. "An achievement of art and purpose, a cosmically brooding book full of significance and beauty."—*New York Times.*

Lomax, John   1867-1948   **and Lomax, Alan**   1915-   American folklorists. John A. Lomax was President of the American Folklore Society and honorary curator of folk songs at the Library of Congress.

AMERICAN BALLADS AND FOLK SONGS. 1934. (III) A big "bokay" of about three hundred of the wild flowers of American poetry and music.

Cowboy Songs and Other Frontier Ballads.   Revised and enlarged edition, 1938. Words and often music of 150 songs, chiefly from the cattle ranches of the Southwest. (Old English and Scottish ballads as sung in the Southern Appalachians are excluded from both collections.)

111 Best American Ballads: Folk Song, U.S.A. 1948. Words, music and background for each song are included. "The best anthology of singable American folksongs" since Sandburg's (1927).

London, Jack   1876-1916   Tramp, oyster-pirate, seal-hunter, coal-shoveler, longshoreman, factory-hand, gold-seeker, and writer of "red-blooded" fiction, some of it excellent.

Call of the Wild. 1903. (I and II) Tale of a Klondike dog's relapse into wolfhood. Probably the best dog-story ever written.

The Sea Wolf. 1904. (I and II) Story of a brutal sailor-superman. Perhaps it is London's most powerful book.

White Fang. 1906. (II) *The Call of the Wild* in reverse. This time it is a wolf that is tamed into the likeness of a dog.

Martin Eden. 1909. (II) In the guise of fiction London here relates how he transformed himself from sailor to best-selling author.

John Barleycorn. 1913. (II) "The amazingly frank confession of London's own struggle with alcohol."—Carl Van Doren, in *Cambridge History of American Literature.*

Longfellow, Henry Wadsworth   1807-82   Through a great part of the Nineteenth Century this New England college professor was one of the favorite poets of the English-speaking world.

Poems. (I) "Critics have styled him 'the poet of the Commonplace.' It is no mean title. To lift the commonplace into the bright air of poetry is to confer one of the richest boons on dull humanity."— Katharine Lee Bates.

Lönnrolt, Elas, compiler and translator   *See Kalevala.*

Loti, Pierre (pseudonym of L. M. J. Viaud)   1850-1923   French naval officer and author of exotic novels; member, French Academy.

Marriage of Loti. 1880. (I) Story of a transitory love affair between Loti and an ardent damsel of Tahiti.

ICELAND FISHERMAN. 1886. (I) Charmingly sincere story of a Breton girl and her Breton lover, a sailor of the Iceland seas.

MADAME CHRYSANTHÈME. 1887. (I) Romance of a French naval officer and a geisha, in the picture-book Japan of the Nineteenth Century.

DISENCHANTED. 1906. (II) Women of a Turkish harem are described as tired to death of their monotonous life. *The Outlook* described the book as "a story of rare delicacy and beauty, full of refinement and feeling."

Lounsbury, Thomas R. 1838-1915 American philologist; member, American Academy of Arts and Letters.

HISTORY OF THE ENGLISH LANGUAGE. 1879. (I) Presents the important facts in the growth of the English tongue and explains its history with easy-going common sense.

Lover, Samuel 1797-1868 Irish novelist, playwright, and song-writer.

HANDY ANDY. 1842. (I) It is a pity that this rollicking history of the mistakes and mishaps of a raw and awkward Irish gossoon is now so little read. For it is really funny.

Lovett, R. M., joint author *See* Moody, M. V.

Lowell, A. Lawrence 1856-1943 American educator and political scientist; President and President Emeritus of Harvard University, 1909-43; member, American Academy of Arts and Letters.

GOVERNMENT OF ENGLAND. 2v. 1908. (II) "In this imposing book Professor Lowell has done for England what Mr. Bryce did for the American commonwealth."—*English Historical Review.*

Lowell, Amy 1874-1925 American champion and practitioner of free verse and imagism and polyphonic prose; sister of A. Lawrence Lowell. "In the course of present day poets she is a kind of drum-major. . . . Notably American in her zest for argument and in her love for experiment."—Percy H. Boynton, in 1919.

SELECTED POEMS. 1928. Chosen from Miss Lowell's eleven volumes of verse.

JOHN KEATS. 2v. 1925. (II) Monumental work of biography and literary criticism. "As refreshing in its rightness as it is titanic in its proportions."—Mark Van Doren.

TENDENCIES OF MODERN AMERICAN POETRY. 1917. (II) Critical studies of Robinson, Frost, Masters, Hilda Doolittle, and Fletcher— all of whom were personal friends of the author.

Lowell, James Russell 1819-91 Critic, poet, satirist, and college professor, Lowell was perhaps the most distinguished example of the all-round man of letters that America has produced.

COMPLETE POETICAL WORKS. (I) Brander Matthews coupled praise of Lowell's two most famous poems in the following words: "As the *Biglow Papers* is the firmest and the finest political satire yet written in the United States, so the *Fable for Critics* is the clearest and the most truthful literary satire." The beautifully lyrical excursion into Arthurian legends, *The Vision of Sir Launfal*, is stirring and ennobling. *The Courtin'* is a lovely gem of New England dialect, while the *Harvard Commemoration Ode, Democracy,* and several of his other poems have become integral parts of America's literary heritage.

AMONG MY BOOKS. 1870. (II)

MY STUDY WINDOWS. 1871. (II) These titles contain much of Lowell's best literary criticism.

Lowell, Robert 1917- American poet; born in Boston, a great-great-grand-nephew of James Russell Lowell; convert to Catholicism.

LORD WEARY'S CASTLE. 1946. Won Pulitzer prize for poetry, 1947. "There is a great hope for poetry, and indeed for America in these poems. Without Whitman's loose though buoyant optimism, they are directed just as surely at a people and a land of infinite unfulfilled promise."—*New York Times.*

Lowes, John Livingston 1867-1945 Student and teacher of English literature; member, National Institute of Arts and Letters.

CONVENTION AND REVOLT IN POETRY. 1919. "One of the best analyses of the cycle of change in poetry."—Helen Haines.

ROAD TO XANADU. Revised edition, 1930. (III) A unique study of the poet Coleridge. The author has traced and described the conception and gestation of *Kubla Khan* and *The Rime of the Ancient Mariner*. A marvelous and fascinating work on literary embryology

GEOFFREY CHAUCER AND THE DEVELOPMENT OF HIS GENIUS 1937. (III) Study of Chaucer's background—the conditions, men, events, books of his time. A work which will delight anyone with even a moderately keen interest in English literature.

Lowry, Malcolm   1909-   British author.

UNDER THE VOLCANO. 1947. "Large, ambitious, and immensely sad" novel about a British consul in Mexico. Intellectuals pronounced it the finest novel of the year and the *Saturday Review of Literature* declared it a work of genius.

Lubbock, Percy   1879-   British Etonian and litterateur; for many years a personal friend of Edith Wharton.

CRAFT OF FICTION. 1921. "Careful study of the principles which are the bases of all good fiction."—*A.L.A. Catalog,* 1926.

PORTRAIT OF EDITH WHARTON. 1947. "Within its narrow limits as perfect a piece of writing as has been done in our decades. It is not a true biography; it is not a literary critique; it is a portrait of a notable character and personality such as was written more often in the Eighteenth Century than today."—H. S. Canby, in *Saturday Review of Literature.*

Lucas, E. V.   1868-1938   English essayist, humorist, novelist, traveler, biographer, anthologist.

LIFE OF CHARLES LAMB. 2v. New edition, 1921. (II) "He seems born to be Lamb's biographer. He has written of Elia in the most Elian manner."—Graham.

OVER BEMERTON'S. 1908. (II) Leisurely tale—charming, witty, quaint. It breathes an air of lettered ease and humor. "Bemerton's" is a London bookshop.

OPEN ROAD. 1899. Collection of wise and quietly joyous writings, by many men, on the pleasures of walking.

GENTLEST ART. 1907. Anthology of genial, kindly, witty, and interesting letters by many masters of this gentlest art. A wonderful bedside book.

SELECTED ESSAYS. n.d. The compiler's own best essays. Edmund Gosse considered Lucas the most successful essayist since Stevenson.

Luce, Mrs. Clare Boothe *See* Boothe, Clare.

Lucian c. 120- c. 180 A.D. Greek satirist and skeptic.

DIALOGUES OF THE DEAD AND DIALOGUES OF THE GODS. Lucian is perhaps the most entertaining of the ancient writers. "He tilts against old faiths, philosophies and conventions in the most audacious manner."

Lucretius 96(?)-55 B.C. Roman poet and philosopher.

DE RERUM NATURA (ON THE NATURE OF THINGS). (I) An exposition in hexameter verse of the rationalistic philosophy of Epicurus; largely concerned with the mysteries of life and death. Though unfinished, it ranks as one of the world's masterpieces. (Everyman's Library; Loeb Classical library.)

Ludwig, Emil 1881-1948 German biographer.

NAPOLEON. 1926. (III) Not only a history of Napoleon's life, but a dramatic study of his mind and heart.

BISMARCK; THE STORY OF A FIGHTER. 1927. (III) This portrait of the "Iron Chancellor" of Germany who was discarded by the bumptious Kaiser Wilhelm II, is a good example of the psychological biography in which Ludwig was proficient.

Luther, Martin 1483-1546 German religious reformer. It is surprising that the chief architect of the Reformation and the translator of the German Bible should have left so few truly literary monuments behind him. Besides a score or two of hymns, some history-making addresses, letters, and of course many sermons, we find to our purpose only

TABLE TALK (*Tischreden*). (I) "A valuable source of historical and theological detail," enlivened here and there by shrewd thrusts and sallies of wit. (It may be stated for the record, however, that a ponderous set of *Werken* (Works), in 19 volumes, was published, 1539-58 and another, in 67 volumes, in 1826-57.)

Lyly, John   1554-1606   English author of high-flown romances and plays. He is sometimes reckoned to be the earliest of a now mighty horde—the authors of prose fiction in English.

EUPHUES, in 2 parts. 1579-80. "This work marks the beginning of the English novel of manners." Its absurdly affected style— weighed down with countless pointless similes, metaphors and conceits —was so often imitated or parodied, even in its own day, that it added the word *euphuist* and its derivatives to the language. It is listed here as a museum piece, and milestone on the broad highway of English literature.

Lynd, Robert S.   1892-1940   and **Lynd, Mrs Helen M.**   1897-
American sociologists.

MIDDLETOWN; A STUDY IN CONTEMPORARY AMERICAN CULTURE. 1929. (III)

MIDDLETOWN IN TRANSITION; A STUDY IN CULTURAL CONFLICTS. 1937. (IV) Two brilliant surveys of life and thought, of manners and morals, in a typical American city (Muncie, Indiana) of 30,000 population in the Middle West. The earlier study was made not long before the Great Depression, the later one at about its end. In fine, here are two cross-sections of our American civilization skillfully set up for the examination of interested students.

Lyons, Eugene   1898-   Born in Russia, he came to the United States in 1907 and became a citizen in 1919. He was an American correspondent in Russia, 1928-34.

ASSIGNMENT IN UTOPIA. 1937. (IV) "A book that any supporter of any dictator system will find it hard to answer. . . . It will strengthen the movement to put life and fighting spirit into an idealistic liberalism."— R. L. Duffus, in *New York Times*.

Lytton, Edward Bulwer- (Lord Lytton)   1803-73   English novelist, dramatist, statesman.

LAST DAYS OF POMPEII. 1834. (I) A vivid and tragic picture of Roman manners and morals in the early days of the Empire. His most popular novel.

RIENZI. 1835. (I) Romance of the turbulent Rome of the Fourteenth Century.

LAST OF THE BARONS. 1844. (I) Story of England in the Fifteenth Century: the Wars of the Roses, with Warwick the Kingmaker and Edward IV as protagonists.

Mabinogion; translated by Lady Charlotte Guest. 1838-49. Collection of old Welsh stories of the Fourteenth Century or earlier. *Mabinog* means an apprentice bard, and the collection was a sort of textbook for young aspirants to poetic honor. (*See also* Bulfinch, T.)

Macaulay, Rose 1889(?)- English novelist-satirist.

POTTERISM. 1920. (II) This novel tried to add a new word to the language—*potterism;* that is, a sickening combination of sentimentality and hypocrisy. A bitterly sophisticated picture of the home front in England, during and after World War I.

DANGEROUS AGES. 1921. (II) An acute character study of four women—their ages, twenty to sixty-three; and all dangerous. "Perhaps the best novel in which the prim, humorous talent of Miss Macaulay has disclosed iself. . . . No one does this sort of thing better."—Rebecca West.

Macaulay, Thomas Babington (Lord Macaulay) 1800-59 English critic, essayist, historian, poet.

CRITICAL AND HISTORICAL ESSAYS. 2v. n.d. (Everyman's library). (I) Still regarded as models of English style, though they are a bit cold, formal, and ponderous for many modern readers.

HISTORY OF ENGLAND FROM THE ACCESSION OF JAMES THE SECOND. 5v. 1849-61. (I) This work covers only seventeen years but Charles Kendall Adams described it as "the most brilliant and the most popular history in the English language" and believes it has been "more universally read than any other history in English literature."

LAYS OF ANCIENT ROME. 1842. (I) "Their music is as the neighing of steeds, and the tramp of armed heels, their inspiration was the voice of the trumpet."—R. H. Horne.

McCullers, Carson 1917- American woman novelist.

HEART IS A LONELY HUNTER. 1940. The chief character in this strong first novel is a deaf-mute living in a Southern town who becomes the confidante of a series of strangely assorted individuals.

McFee, William 1881- Anglo-American fictionist; formerly an engineer in the merchant marine.

CASUALS OF THE SEA. 1916. (II) Story, realistic and full of detail, of a London brother and sister, who drift and struggle through life rather aimlessly, both afloat and ashore. Highly praised by Huneker, by Mencken, and by Morley.

CAPTAIN MACEDOINE'S DAUGHTER. 1920. (II) A novel of "plotting and intrigue, involving the life and death of an exotic lady." Mediterranean coastal towns form the background.

McFee, William, editor

WORLD'S GREAT TALES OF THE SEA. 1944. An excellent collection of fascinating material.

Machen, Arthur 1863-1948 Welsh novelist of the soul. "He writes of a strange borderland, lying somewhere between dreams and death."

HILL OF DREAMS. 1907. (II) Practically a classic, though never a popular one. The author said he tried to make it a Robinson Crusoe of the soul. Professor Weygandt says it "moons its tenuous length through long pages that only good writing saves from futility."

Machiavelli, Niccolò 1469-1527 Florentine writer on government.

THE PRINCE. 1513. (I) A realistic manual for Renaissance despots. Its doctrine? Man exists to serve the State, not *vice versa*; and the end always justifies the means. *The Prince* will retain special interest and significance for us as long as its principles reign supreme in the minds and hearts of some of the world's rulers.

MacKaye, Percy 1875- American author of poetic dramas and historical pageants.

THE SCARECROW. 1908. (II) His most important historical play. Scene is a New England town at the time of the Seventeenth Century witchcraft hysteria.

CANTERBURY PILGRIMS. 1908. (II) His best comedy. Chaucer himself is a character, and so are the Wife of Bath, the Prioress, and other old friends.

JEANNE D'ARC. 1906. (II) "Rather a series of rich dramatic pictures than a closely welded drama, is this historical play in blank verse of lyric cadence and beauty."—*A.L.A. Catalog*, 1926.

SAPPHO AND PHAON. 1907. (II) This classical poetic drama of "burning Sappho" and the beautiful Greek youth who rejected her was pronounced by *The Nation* "the most notable addition that has been made for many years to American dramatic literature."

MYSTERY OF HAMLET. 1950. Four plays which form a prolog to Shakespeare's great tragedy. "A book to ponder . . . not light reading; but a major contribution to poetic drama."—*Saturday Review of Literature.*

Mackenzie, Henry　1745-1801　Scottish novelist and journalist.

THE MAN OF FEELING. 1771. (I) Called the most sentimental of English novels, this lachrymose tale was very popular in its different day and shows the influence of both Richardson and Sterne. It affords a good picture of its time and will interest those who care to trace the development of English fiction.

MacLeish, Archibald　1892-　American poet. He has been soldier, teacher, lawyer, Librarian of Congress, Assistant Secretary of State, and Boylston Professor of Rhetoric and Oratory at Harvard.

CONQUISTADOR. 1932. (III) A Spanish comrade of stout Cortez tells in virile verse the story of the conquest of Mexico. No worthier narrative poem has been produced in recent years. It was awarded a Pulitzer prize in 1933.

POEMS, 1924-1933. 1933. "What I have done here has been to select from poems already published and from poems not yet published those pieces I can now re-read without embarrassment."— Foreword. (*Conquistador* is included.)

FALL OF THE CITY; A VERSE PLAY FOR RADIO. 1937. (IV) The first play of the kind written in America. "Contains some of Mr. MacLeish's most persuasive work to date."—*Christian Science Monitor.*

PUBLIC SPEECH; POEMS. 1936. (IV) Consists of ten short pieces on current problems, and ten love poems. This little book moved the *Herald Tribune Books* to declare that "he is now, unquestionably, the most important poet writing in America today."

McMaster, J. B.　1852-1932　American historian.

HISTORY OF THE PEOPLE OF THE UNITED STATES FROM THE REVOLUTION TO THE CIVIL WAR. 8v. 1883-1913. (I and II) Distinctly a *social* history. Politics is subordinated. A readable and reliable work. The years covered are from 1783 to 1861.

MacPherson, James　1736-96　Scottish discoverer and translator, or more probably *forger*, of ancient Gaelic poems attributed to one Ossian, son of a Scottish king, Fingal. "The Poems of Ossian"

(I) influenced, with their charmingly savage wildness, the works of Chateaubriand, Goethe, Schiller, and Byron; but Dr. Johnson was an early and characteristically vocal doubter of their authenticity.

McWilliams, Carey   1905-   American champion of the foreign-born, of racial minorities, of migratory workers.

BROTHERS UNDER THE SKIN. 1943. (IV) Discussion of the status of non-white minorities in the United States.

PREJUDICE, JAPANESE-AMERICANS: SYMBOL OF RACIAL INTOLERANCE. 1944. (IV) About our Japanese problem, with emphasis on the so-called relocation centers during World War II.

MASK FOR PRIVILEGE: ANTI-SEMITISM IN AMERICA. 1948. "A penetrating, cool-headed study . . . and certainly a most valuable addition to the literature on this subject."—*New Yorker.*

Macy, John A.   1877-1932   American critic.

SPIRIT OF AMERICAN LITERATURE. 1913. (II) Critical and biographical essays on sixteen authors, from Irving to Henry James, whose books have won distinction for American literature.

STORY OF THE WORLD'S LITERATURE. 1925. (II) "To me the most vital and inspiring popularization of literature yet brought to the American public."—Helen E. Haines.

Madariaga, Salvador de   1886-   Spanish author and diplomat.

HEART OF JADE. 1944. Long historical romance about the Spanish conquest of Mexico. "A colorful tapestry of Sixteenth-Century Aztec civilization."—*Good Reading.*

GENIUS OF SPAIN, AND OTHER ESSAYS ON SPANISH CONTEMPORARY LITERATURE. 1928. "Literary portraits of seven Spanish writers with . . . essays on the character and genius of Spain."—*A.L.A. Catalog,* 1926.

CHRISTOPHER COLUMBUS. 1940. Author believes Columbus to have been an Italian-born Spanish Jew. "Written in a richly imaginative and romantic vein, it will delight the general reader."—*English Historical Review.*

Maeterlinck, Maurice   1862-1949   Belgian naturalist, mystic, dramatist. Awarded the Nobel prize, 1911.

PELLÉAS AND MÉLISANDE. 1892. (I) This somewhat misty play is based on Dante's simple love story of Paolo and Francesca. From this play sprang the libretto of Debussy's opera of the same name.

LIFE OF THE BEE. 1901. (I and II) "An artist's story of the bees, in which philosophy, fancy and natural history join to make a book of rare fascination."—Pratt Alcove.

MONNA VANNA. 1902. (I and II) "His strongest drama of action, and probably his masterpiece. . . . The story of a woman un-dishonored by the sale of her honor."—Graham.

BLUE BIRD. 1908. (I and II) A fairy play telling how the woodcutter's children sought, finally found, but soon lost again the Blue Bird of Happiness. This is Maeterlinck's best known production—a masterpiece of its kind.

Magoffin, Ralph Van Deman   1874-   American scholar and teacher.

MAGIC SPADES; THE ROMANCE OF ARCHAEOLOGY. 1929. (III) Popular account of archaeological treasure trove in Mediterranean lands, Great Britain, Scandinavia, and America. Well illustrated and documented.

Mahabharata and **Ramayana**   (I)   These ancient epics of India are of uncertain date and probably composite authorship, though the perhaps mythical sage, Vyasa, is the reputed author of the former, while the latter is ascribed to Valmiki, who seems to have been a real person. The *Ramayana* is the older and more homogeneous work; the *Mahabharata* is far longer—eight times as long as the *Iliad* and *Odyssey* together—and in it is embedded the *Bhagavadgita*, beloved and revered by Mahatma Gandhi and paraphrased by Sir Edwin Arnold as the *Song Celestial.*

Mahan, Alfred Thayer   1840-1914   American admiral and author of books on naval history.

INFLUENCE OF SEA POWER UPON HISTORY, 1660-1783. 1890. (I) His thesis is that sea power in the past has frequently been the decisive factor in international relations. The book is a sort of Bible to Big Navy men the world over.

LIFE OF NELSON. 2v. 1897. (I) Britain's naval hero is treated with full competence in his personal, professional, and political aspects.

Mailer, Norman 1923- American novelist who served in World War II.

NAKED AND THE DEAD. 1948. Nakedly realistic novel about the invasion of a Japanese island and its aftermath. There are four-letter words in abundance and the book has been called "virtually a Kinsey report on the sex behavior of the GI." But some critics have suggested that it is "perhaps the best novel about World War II."

Maine, Sir Henry 1822-88 English jurist.

ANCIENT LAW, ITS CONNECTION WITH THE EARLY HISTORY OF SOCIETY, AND ITS RELATION TO MODERN IDEAS. 1861. (I) "An epoch-making book; the starting-point of the study of jurisprudence."

VILLAGE COMMUNITIES IN EAST AND WEST. 1871. (I) "One of the most valuable and quite the most interesting of Sir Henry Maine's works."—C. K. Adams.

Mallea, Eduardo 1903- "The outstanding novelist of Argentina," and some say of South America.

BAY OF SILENCE. 1944. Modern Argentina, pictured in the life, thought and emotions of a group of intellectuals in Buenos Ayres.

Malone, Dumas 1892- Professor of history at Columbia; editor, *Dictionary of American Biography*, 1929-36; served in United States Marine Corps in World War II.

JEFFERSON THE VIRGINIAN. 1948. First of the projected four volumes of *Jefferson and His Time.* "If the next three volumes are of the same quality we shall have at last a biography . . . that is worthy of its exciting subject."—H. J. Laski, in *New Republic.*

Malory, Sir Thomas 1430(?)-1471(?) English compiler, editor, and translator of the old Arthurian romances.

MORTE D'ARTHUR. First printed by Caxton in 1485. (I) Said to be the most important English prose work written before the Age of Elizabeth. An idealized picture of chivalric combat and courtly love, rendered into pure English that Frederic Harrison declared to be "hardly second to the English of the Bible."

Malraux, André 1895- French novelist, soldier, and liberal politician.

MAN'S FATE. 1936. A story of the bloody insurrection at Shanghai in 1927, in which the author participated. This novel won the Goncourt prize.

MAN'S HOPE. 1938. (IV) "It is not only a novel of Loyalist Spain he has written, but a study of contemporary man on the field of battle."—A. Kazin, in *New York Herald Tribune.* "There can be only one summing-up. *Man's Hope* is a great book."— *New Republic.*

Malthus, Thomas R. 1766-1834 British economist.

ESSAY ON THE PRINCIPLES OF POPULATION. 1798. (I) A century and a half ago Malthus gave warning through this book that peoples increase in number faster than the food supply. This warning came to be generally scoffed at but today his theories are again very much alive, despite the killings of two World Wars and the marvelous improvements in agriculture, the last two factors being more than overbalanced by recent life-saving advances of medical science.

Mandeville, Sir John Fourteenth Century British explorer and teller of tall tales.

TRAVELS. 1371(?) Most of the material was lifted from earlier imaginative writers. The real editor or compiler may have been one Jehan de Bourgogne. Donald G. Mitchell described this famous and fascinating book as a "budget of delightfully extravagant travelers' tales bearing the Mandeville name."

Mann, Thomas 1875- German novelist; resident in the United States since 1938, he has become an American citizen. His American publisher has shyly admitted that Mann is the world's greatest living author and he was awarded the Nobel prize in 1929.

BUDDENBROOKS. 2v. 1924. (II) Story of the decline and disintegration of a once prosperous commercial family in northern Germany.

MAGIC MOUNTAIN. 1927; revised edition, 1938. (III) The critics have pronounced this a very great book. But, despite its tremendous implications, it impresses some less intellectual readers as both unpleasant and tiresome. "The mountain is a sanitarium from which no one can escape. A remarkable book picturing modern society as a pathologic universe."—*Good Reading*.

BELOVED RETURNS; LOTTE IN WEIMAR. 1940. (IV) Charlotte, the heroine of Goethe's *Sorrows of Werther*, was really Lotte, one of the superman's early loves. She was so indiscreet as to call upon him forty years later. This long novel by Mann was inspired by that indiscretion. The story of this brief visit gleams like a tiny jewel in the broad tapestry of the old giant's pictured personality.

STORIES OF THREE DECADES. 1936. A collection of twenty-four of Mann's short stories, including those in his famous *Death in Venice*.

THE JOSEPH TETRALOGY. Consists of the following:

JOSEPH AND HIS BROTHERS. 1934. (III)

YOUNG JOSEPH. 1935. (III)

JOSEPH IN EGYPT. 2v. 1938. (IV)

JOSEPH THE PROVIDER. 1944. (IV)
"A literary event of the first magnitude."—*New York Times*. "Among the few masterpieces of our time."—*New Republic*. "A vast and leisurely fable of the nature, state and destiny of man." —*Atlantic*. "There can be no doubt . . . that it is one of the greatest imaginative efforts of our time. . . ." *Nation*.

JOSEPH AND HIS BROTHERS. 1948. This includes in one volume all four titles of the Joseph series. In this edition, however, the first title has been changed to *Tales of Jacob*.

DR. FAUSTUS; THE LIFE OF THE GERMAN COMPOSER, ADRIAN LEVERKÜHN. 1948. This somewhat difficult novel is a modern version of the Faust legend. It is saturated with German thought and discussion of German music.

Manning, Anne   1807-79   English author.

HOUSEHOLD OF SIR THOMAS MORE. 1851. This story, written as the diary of the great humanist's daughter, Margaret, paints a vividly authentic picture of manners and important figures in the tragic but thrilling time of Henry VIII. It has been said that the story's "faithfulness to the tone of the period makes it more historical than history."

Mansfield, Katherine 1888-1923 Born in New Zealand, she was the wife of John Middleton Murry. In her unrivaled short stories plot is subordinated to vivid impression, strong characterization, and exquisitely finished writing.

SHORT STORIES. 1937. An omnibus volume of eighty-eight stories, including all those which first appeared in *Bliss* (1921) (II), *Dove's Nest* (1923) (II), and *Garden Party* (1922) (II).

JOURNAL, 1914-1922. 1927. "Delightful reading . . . stamped with that rare individuality which was so innately her gift."— *New York Times.*

LETTERS. 2v. 1929. "Poignant, living letters filled with the details of her daily existence, written during the last ten years of her life."—*Book Review Digest.*

NOVELS AND NOVELISTS. 1930. A collection of her criticism. "Her comment was always clear and sound."—*New York World.* (The last three titles were all edited by her husband.)

Manzoni, Alessandro 1785-1873 Italian novelist.

THE BETROTHED. 1826. (I) This "greatest of Italian romances" is a wondrous panorama of life in Seventeenth-Century Italy among peasants and outlaws, including a dramatic conflict between true love and religion. Some Italians rank this work second in importance only to *The Divine Comedy.* It has appeared in more than five hundred editions. The best English translation is that by Archibald Colquhoun, published in 1951.

March, Harold 1896- American professor of romance languages.

THE TWO WORLDS OF M. PROUST. 1948. A study of the man and his work. "Written with sound scholarship, it is in general an intelligent, compact, logically organized study addressed to the general reader."—C. J. Rolo, in *Atlantic.*

Marcus Aurelius Antoninus *See* Aurelius Antoninus, Marcus.

Marie, Grand Duchess of Russia 1890- Cousin of Czar Nicholas II.

EDUCATION OF A PRINCESS. 1930. (III) Her childhood and youth at the Russian court are described, as are her work as a nurse during World War I, the terrors of the Russian Revolution, and her escape to the haven of a fashion shop on Fifth Avenue, New York.

Maritain, Jacques　1882-　French Catholic philosopher.

TRUE HUMANISM. 1936. "He outlines the principles of a new social order, a 'personalist democracy,' destined to succeed capitalism and to preserve the ideals of freedom and human dignity."— *New Republic.*

CHRISTIANITY AND DEMOCRACY. 1944. Essays "on the rival ideologies of today in which the philosopher affirms once more the dignity of man and the ideals of human brotherhood."

Marlowe, Christopher　1564-93　English dramatist and poet. Generally regarded as inferior only to Shakespeare and possibly Jonson among the great Elizabethans. He was killed at twenty-nine in a tavern brawl.

PLAYS AND POEMS. (Modern editions are to be found in *Everyman's Library* and *World's Classics.*) His plays include *Tamburlaine the Great* (1587), *Doctor Faustus* (c. 1592) (I), *Jew of Malta* (c. 1590), and *Edward II* (1594) (II). His most successful poem is an unfinished paraphrase of Musaeus' *Hero and Leander.*

Marquand, John P.　1893-　American novelist; member, American Institute of Arts and Letters.

LATE GEORGE APLEY. 1937. (IV) "In the disguise and labored style of a minor man of letters undertaking to write the life of a friend whom he admired to idolatry, Mr. Marquand manages to be most hilariously funny."—*American Review.* Won the Pulitzer fiction prize in 1938.

WICKFORD POINT. 1939. (IV) Story of a family run to seed, somewhere near and north of Boston. "He is a novelist—and a real one—with all that the word implies."—S. V. Benét, in *Saturday Review of Literature.*

H. M. PULHAM, ESQ. 1941. (IV) This novel is a pretended autobiography satirizing "the best people" of Boston—those who have the right grandfathers, go to the right school and college, belong to the right clubs, and are slowly bored to death in the name of propriety and loyalty to caste.

So LITTLE TIME. 1943. (IV) A satiric fictional study of America—not just of Boston, this time—on the threshold of World War II. "Mr. Marquand is that rarest of artists, a sympathetic satirist. He satirizes without damning. And it is fitting that the last words of this novel, so far his biggest and his best, should be: 'Forgive us our debts, as we forgive our debtors.'"
—*Saturday Review of Literature.*

POINT OF NO RETURN. 1949. "This is, it seems to me, the best of John Marquand's books since *The Late George Apley.*"— John Woodburn, in *Saturday Review of Literature.* "The shrewdest picture of American middle class life that has appeared since *Main Street.*"—*Chicago Sun.* "Marvelously clever in design and execution . . . a pleasure to read, if in some respects it is painful to think about."—Maxwell Geismar, in *New York Times.*

Marquis, Don 1878-1937 American journalist and humorist; best known for his column, *The Sun Dial*, in the *New York Sun*, 1912-20. "He was not only a nimble epigrammatist and genial satirist of passing literary fads and fashions, but the admired creator of comic characters whose lives his readers insisted on his preserving."—F. B. Millett.

BEST OF DON MARQUIS. 1946. Generous excerpts (670 pages) from the books by which Marquis is best remembered: *Archy and Mehitabel, Old Soak, Hermione and Her little Group of Serious Thinkers, The Almost Perfect State*, etc.

Marryat, Frederic 1792-1848 English novelist of the sea.

MR. MIDSHIPMAN EASY. 1836. (I) "Rollicking adventures of an apprentice officer aboard a British man-of-war."—*Good Reading.*

PETER SIMPLE. 1834. (I) "Journal of a sailor, from the day he is entered as a midshipman to his marriage and retirement. . . . A lively and humorous picture of British naval life."—E. A. Baker.

MASTERMAN READY. 1841. (I) Desert island story, written with the conscious aim of improving upon *Swiss Family Robinson.* This it certainly does. As a boy's never-to-be-forgotten hero, Ready is a "natural."

Marshall, Archibald 1866-1934 English novelist. He wrote pleasant, unexciting stories about County families in England in the first years of the Twentieth Century. W. L. Phelps called him "a reincarnation of Anthony Trollope."

THE SQUIRE'S DAUGHTER. 1909. (II) This is the first book in the *Clinton Series.* If the reader enjoys it and wishes further escapes into the good old days, he can follow it with *The Eldest Son* (1911) (II), *Honour of the Clintons* (1913), and *The Old Order Changeth* (1915) (II).

Marshall, Bruce 1899- British novelist and satirist, who is given to writing reverently humorous tales with a priestly hero.

FATHER MALACHY'S MIRACLE. 1931. By a strenuous exercise of faith he moves an Edinburgh dance-hall to the top of Bass Rock, in the Firth of Forth. But things don't turn out as they should.

THE WORLD, THE FLESH, AND FATHER SMITH. 1945. (IV) "He writes with an open heart, a salty understanding of frailty, and the most delightful, impertinent wit that I have chuckled over this year."—Edward Weeks, in *Atlantic.* "It is difficult to conceive of anyone—Catholic, Protestant or unbeliever, who will not enjoy every page of this book."—*Commonweal.*

Marshall, George Catlett 1880- American soldier, statesman, Secretary of Defense, 1950-51.

WINNING OF THE WAR IN EUROPE AND THE PACIFIC. 1945. (IV) Covers events of World War II from the invasion of Italy to the collapse of Japan. "Greatest state paper of the War . . . 'required reading' for every American citizen . . . required study material for every school and college."—*Saturday Review of Literature.* "If the art of prose lies in the communication of ideas, General Marshall's report is a work of art."—*Chicago Sun.*

Martial (Marcus Valerius Martialis) c. 43-c. 104 Latin epigrammatist. He was born and reared in Spain, but spent his middle years in or near Rome.

EPIGRAMS. 14 books. An unrivaled source of information on every aspect of life in Rome during the First Century. Though many are indecent, most of these thousands of witty squibs reveal the hand of a brilliant literary genius. A prose translation, embellished by renderings in verse by the English poets where these

are available, will be found in the Bohn Library. Two volumes
of the Loeb Classical Library offer a careful text of the original,
together with modern prose translations.

Martin, Everett Dean   1880-1941   American educator, sociologist, clergyman.

MEANING OF A LIBERAL EDUCATION. 1926. (III) Education,
he says, should teach us "to think and act in ways that distinguish
men from animals and higher men from lower. . . . It is a
spiritual awakening and if this does not come a person is not
educated, however much he knows."

Martin du Gard, Roger   1881-   French novelist.

WORLD OF THE THIBAULTS. 2v. 1941. (IV) Originally published over many years in 10 volumes, this is one of the *romans-
fleuve*, so typical of modern French literature. It was awarded
a Nobel prize in 1937. The world described is that of a middle-
class French family in Paris, before and during World War I.
"We are bound to recognize in *The Thibaults* one of the great
novels of our time, a work to be put beside Jules Romains's *Men
of Good Will* and Rolland's *Jean Christophe*."—*New York Herald
Tribune*. The *Nation's* reviewer pronounced it "a masterpiece";
and the *Atlantic* declared it "by far the greatest piece of fiction
done in our time."

Marx, Karl   1818-83   German political philosopher.

CAPITAL. 3v. 1867-94; English translation, 1901-09. "The
Communist Bible." "Dispassionate scholars have tended to regard
Marx as one of the greatest of economic theoreticians, whose
views cannot be lightly discounted but whose system, like all
systems, is vitiated by its rigid doctrinaire nature."—*Columbia
Encyclopedia*, 1950.

COMMUNIST MANIFESTO. 1848. (Written with F. Engels.)

Masefield, John   1878-   English Poet Laureate, 1930- . "Master alike of lyric and adventurous narrative."—John Macy. "Poetry
has been like a religion to him; and he has served it like a priest."
—Stuart P. Sherman.

POEMS: COMPLETE EDITION. 2v. in 1. 1935. "The stamp of
a powerful and impressive personality is upon them."—*Saturday
Review of Literature*. The great naı rative poems are *The Story of*

a *Round House* (called *Dauber* in England) (II), *Reynard the Fox* (II), *The Everlasting Mercy* (I and II), *The Widow in the Bye Street* (II) and *The Daffodil Fields* (II); the two first named are perhaps his most distinctive achievements.

PROSE PLAYS. 1925. (II) Includes *Tragedy of Nan* and five others.

VERSE PLAYS. 1925. (II) Includes *Good Friday* and four others.

JIM DAVIS. 1911. This yarn about smugglers on the Devonshire coast a century and more ago is a grand one for boys.

SARD HARKER. 1927. (II) Story of the far-flung adventures of a sailor who, left behind, tries to catch up with his ship.

BIRD OF DAWNING. 1933. Thrilling tale of adventure during a race of tea-clippers of the China trade, in the Sixties.

GALLIPOLI. 1916. (II) This account of an ill-fated British enterprise in which the author participated is perhaps as fine a piece of literature as any inspired by World War I.

WILLIAM SHAKESPEARE. 1911. (II) An interesting, scholarly, revealing book. It has been called the best short life of Shakespeare.

Mason, Alpheus T. 1899- Professor of political science at Princeton University and author of many books in his field.

BRANDEIS, A FREE MAN'S LIFE. 1946. This full scale biography of a great modern jurist is also "a chronicle of the processes of American democracy at work. On all accounts it deserves a wide audience."

Massinger, Philip 1583-1640 English dramatist. Professor Saintsbury ranks him fourth, after only Shakespeare, Jonson, and Fletcher, among the great Elizabethans.

NEW WAY TO PAY OLD DEBTS. 1633. (I) This play, generally agreed to be his masterpiece, is still occasionally revived. The chief character is Sir Giles Overreach, a scheming and relentless usurer.

Masson, David 1822-1907 Scottish biographer.

LIFE OF JOHN MILTON, NARRATED IN CONNECTION WITH THE POLITICAL, ECCLESIASTICAL AND LITERARY HISTORY OF HIS TIME.

6v. 1859-80. (I) In fact, a *monumental* history from original and independent studies of England's most interesting and most momentous period.

Masters, Edgar Lee 1869-1950 American author and interpreter of the Middle West. Amy Lowell called him "a Dostoievsky in *vers libre*," and J. C. Powys said he was "the only poet with Americanism in his bones."

Spoon River Anthology. 1915. (II) Not an anthology in the common sense, but a collection of imaginary epitaphs in a village graveyard, all written by Masters himself. H. L. Mencken thought it "the most eloquent, the most profound, and the most thoroughly national volume of poetry published in America since *Leaves of Grass.*"

Vachel Lindsay, a Poet in America. 1935. (III) Masters was Lindsay's intimate friend. Both were poets who loved best and wrote most of the American Middle West. Masters was the man best fitted to write of Lindsay's life, mind, spirit, and work. He has done just this and the resultant book is a good one.

Mather, Cotton 1663-1728 American Puritan theologian; "the epitome of the New England Puritan spirit."

Magnalia Christi Americana. 1702. An ecclesiastical history of New England. "Though strongly marked by partialities and prejudices, its somewhat quaint and grotesque character and its admixture of superstition, learning and ingenuity make it still interesting."

Matthews, J. Brander 1852-1929 Student and teacher of dramatic literature at Columbia University, 1900-24; member, American Academy of Arts and Letters.

Molière, His Life and Works. 1910. (I and II) The best biography and the most scholarly study in English of the master of French comedy.

Study of the Drama. 1910. (II) Discussion of play construction and presentation—why plays succeed or fail.

These Many Years, Recollections of a New Yorker. 1917. (I and II) Anecdotes of and witty observations on the literary and dramatic lions of grandfather's day.

Matthiesen, Francis Otto   1902-50   American professor of history and literature.

AMERICAN RENAISSANCE; ART AND EXPRESSION IN THE AGE OF EMERSON AND WHITMAN. 1941. (IV) Discusses chiefly Emerson, Thoreau, Hawthorne, Melville, and Whitman. "Perhaps the most profound work of literary criticism on historical principles by any modern American, with the possible exception of Lowes's *Road to Xanadu* (1927)."—R. E. Spiller, in *Saturday Review of Literature.*

THE JAMES FAMILY. 1947. Consists chiefly of selections, with comment, from their writings. "A magnificent family portrait." —*New York Herald Tribune.*

Matthiesen, Francis Otto, editor

OXFORD BOOK OF AMERICAN VERSE. 1950. The work of fifty-one poets is represented, chronologically arranged. More than half of the 1132 pages is allotted to poetry of the Twentieth Century.

Mattingly, Garrett   1900-   American historical scholar and teacher.

CATHERINE OF ARAGON. 1941. (IV) "Mr. Mattingly has told the story of Henry the Eighth's first wife superbly. . . . An achievement of distinctive and exhaustive scholarship."—*New York Times.*

Maugham, W. Somerset   1874-   English novelist, playwright, physician, who has spent much of his time, of recent years, in the United States. "Smooth irony is his most marked characteristic."—Manly.

OF HUMAN BONDAGE. 1915. (II) Story of a young man's life to about his thirtieth year. "Its ethics are frankly pagan."— *Independent.* "It immediately takes its place beside the masterpieces of personal chronicle in English fiction."—*Boston Transcript.*

THE MOON AND SIXPENCE. 1919. (II) A genius sacrifices himself—and his family—to his art. The story was suggested by the life of the French artist, Gauguin.

CAKES AND ALE. 1930. Satirical story suggesting Hugh Walpole, and the last of the Victorian novelists—Thomas Hardy, perhaps?— and his marriages.

EAST AND WEST. 1934. Collection of thirty short stories which really have "the power to seize and hold the reader's attention."

RAZOR'S EDGE. 1944. (IV) Story of the bewildered world-wanderings of a tired flyer after the first World War. It inspired the *New Yorker's* comment: "If he keeps on writing with his tongue in his cheek it may well become permanently stuck there."

THE SUMMING UP. 1938. (IV) "It is not often that an author writes an honest book about his own life . . . but in this book Mr. Maugham has done so."—*Christian Science Monitor.* "Where the book is of real value is in its analysis of the art of the dramatist and novelist. . . . No man or woman who hopes to be a professional writer can afford to miss those chapters; they are a veritable course in the art of writing."—*Commonweal.*

HOUR BEFORE DAWN. 1942. The story of an aristocratic English family's private conflict in wartime.

WRITER'S NOTEBOOK. 1949. "It is a big book in which to seek and find, and for me a rich one."—*Edward Weeks, in Atlantic.* "There may not be a lot of the milk of human kindness in Mr. Maugham, but there is a remarkable understanding of the human animal and a positively clinical understanding of the scribbling race."—*Vincent Starrett, in Chicago Tribune.*

Mauldin, William H. 1921- American cartoonist of World War II, who served (1940-45) in Sicily, Italy, France, and Germany.

UP FRONT. 1945. (IV) "His text has the same biting humor that goes into his drawings. . . . It makes the whole a 'must' book of the war."—*Saturday Review of Literature.*

BACK HOME. 1947. Comment and cartoons on our home-front problems. "Frank, tough, realistic." "Mauldin often writes better than he draws!"—*Library Journal.*

Maupassant, Guy de 1850-93 French writer of naturalistic short stories; a disciple of Flaubert. He died insane at forty-three. (*See also* Steegmuller, F.)

THE ODD NUMBER. 1889. (I) Collection of thirteen of the best stories. They are well translated, and none of them is "objectionable."

COMPLETE SHORT STORIES. An all-inclusive collection of about 160 stories. (Blue Ribbon Books.)

UNE VIE. 1883. (I) Tolstoi called this the best French novel since *Les Misérables.*

Mauriac, François 1885- French novelist; member of the French Academy and winner of their Grand Prix du Roman.

THÉRÈSE. 1928. "A complete unfolding of the mind of a neurotic woman. In the opening scene Thérèse leaves the court acquitted of the crime of poisoning her husband."—*Book Review Digest.*

Maurois, André 1885- French author, equally at home in English and French, in France, Great Britain, and the United States; served in World Wars I and II; member of the French Academy.

SILENCE OF COLONEL BRAMBLE. 1920. A war story, read with delight in the trenches of World War I.

ARIEL: THE LIFE OF SHELLEY. 1924. (II) "It thrills and throbs with the magic that attaches to one of the most fascinating spirits that ever appeared in this troubled world."—Gamaliel Bradford.

DISRAELI, A PICTURE OF THE VICTORIAN AGE. 1928. (III) This charming book is a distillation of the mountains of material heaped up by Monypenny and other laborious biographers.

ASPECTS OF BIOGRAPHY. 1929. "A biographer writes about biography with the intelligence, clarity and elegance expected in French criticism."—*A.L.A. Catalog,* 1926-31.

BYRON. 1930. "Artistic, thoroughly documented study of Byron the man. His ancestry, his deformity, the Calvinism in his blood warring with his pride and recklessness, are presented as influences in developing his character."—*A.L.A. Catalog,* 1926-31.

ART OF LIVING. 1940. "The highbrow, midbrow and lowbrow will all find something to interest them in this sensible book."—John Cournos, in *New York Times.*

PROUST: PORTRAIT OF A GENIUS. 1950. "The definitive critical biography."—Fanny Butcher. "The best single volume on the subject."—J. W. Krutch.

Maxtone Graham, Joyce Anstruther *See* Struther, Jan, pseudonym.

Maxwell, William 1908- American novelist.

FOLDED LEAF. 1945. (IV) This novel is the story of a friendship between two modern American boys. "A drama of the immature, with no background more glamorous than middle-class apartments and student fraternity houses. It is more moving and more absorbing than any of the romantic melodramas which have been stimulated by the war."—Edmund Wilson, in *New Yorker*.

TIME WILL DARKEN IT. 1948. Sensitive story about an adolescent "crush" in a small Illinois town in 1912. "His people and their period are wonderfully alive."—*Atlantic*.

Mead, Margaret 1901- American anthropologist.

FROM THE SOUTH SEAS. 1939. Studies of adolescence and sex among primitive peoples. Includes: *Coming of Age in Samoa* (1928), *Growing Up in New Guinea* (1930), and *Sex and Temperament in Three Primitive Societies* (1935).

AND KEEP YOUR POWDER DRY: AN ANTHROPOLOGIST LOOKS AT AMERICA. 1942. A thoughtful discussion of what anthropology as a science can offer to implement America's fight for a brighter future. "Margaret Mead's wartime classic."

Mears, Helen 1900- American traveler and writer on Japan.

YEAR OF THE WILD BOAR; AN AMERICAN WOMAN IN JAPAN. 1942. (IV) Describes the daily life of the lower and middle classes in Japan before World War II. "Miss Mears is not out to make us like or dislike the Japanese. She does succeed in making us understand them at least roughly."—*New Yorker*.

Melville, Herman 1819-91 American novelist. He was neglected for more than half a century but after World War I there came a tremendous revival of interest in him and his work.

TYPEE. 1846. (I) Fascinating story of life among the cannibals of the South Seas, as the author experienced it a century ago. In it actual and imaginary adventures are inextricably intertwined.

OMOO. 1847. (I) Sequel to *Typee*: a cut off the same joint.

WHITE-JACKET. 1850. Semi-autobiographical novel picturing the hardships of life in the American navy a century ago.

MOBY DICK. 1851. (I) At once a thrilling picture of whale-hunting and a moral allegory. Captain Ahab's vengeful pursuit of Moby Dick, the White Whale, is a symbol of man's struggle against the metaphysical incongruities of life and his inevitable defeat. "Considered one of the greatest novels in the history of American literature and the literature of the world."—*Reader's Encyclopedia.* (*See also* Vincent's *Trying-Out of Moby Dick.*)

Menander *See* Terence.

Mencken, Henry L. 1880- American iconoclast, satirist, philologist, autobiographer.

AMERICAN LANGUAGE. Revised edition, 1936. (II) SUPPLEMENT I. 1946. (IV) SUPPLEMENT II. 1948. Inquires into the development of the English language in the United States. "Serious studies with enough of the Mencken sparkle to interest even the reader without philological learning."—*The Booklist.*

DAYS OF MR. MENCKEN. 1947. This is a one-volume edition of the three following autobiographical books: *Happy Days, 1880-1892* (1940); *Newspaper Days, 1899-1906* (1941); and *Heathen Days, 1890-1936* (1943). (All of these are in IV.)

MENCKEN CHRESTOMATHY; Edited and Annotated by the Author. 1949. A generous selection (627 pages) from his many books. "This monument to the Wrath of Henry is not improbably the greatest corpus of invective in the English language."—*Quarterly Booklist.*

Menninger, Karl A. 1893- American psychiatrist.

HUMAN MIND. Third edition, 1945. (III) Book about mental abnormality, mental hygiene, and psychotherapy, illustrated by hundreds of actual cases. Written for the intelligent layman and for the physician who is not a psychiatrist.

Meredith, George 1828-1909 English novelist; the last except Hardy of the great Victorians, and the least popular and most intellectual member of the group.

ORDEAL OF RICHARD FEVEREL. 1859. (I) A story of the crumbling away of man's defenses—no matter how carefully prepared—before the onslaught of woman.

EVAN HARRINGTON. 1861. "Masterly novel, in which the author gives a fiction study of the family whence he sprang, and exhibits certain aspects of English snobbery that make it a true mirror of its time."—J. A. Hammerton.

ADVENTURES OF HARRY RICHMOND. 1871. (I) The most vigorous and romantic of his novels.

BEAUCHAMP'S CAREER. 1876. Gives a broad view of English politics a century ago, in the light of Carlyle's teaching. This is the background for the emotional life of Beauchamp, who is successively enamored of three women.

THE EGOIST. 1879. (I) A great character study of man's inherent selfishness. R. L. Stevenson said that to provide the author of *The Egoist* God had first to create a gentleman and then to give him genius.

DIANA OF THE CROSSWAYS. 1885. (I) The Irish heroine is perhaps the best of Meredith's splendid women, fine in brain and strong in body.

POETICAL WORKS. 1912. "Meredith's verse is dramatic and realistic, but occasionally ventures upon a classical or romantic study."—E. C. Stedman.

Meredith, Roy   1908-

MR. LINCOLN'S CAMERA MAN. 1946. This first full biography of Mathew Brady is factual and competent, but uninspired. The four hundred pictures by Brady, however, are wonderful; and many are now here published for the first time.

Merejkowski, Dmitri S.   1865-1941   Russian novelist, poet, and critic; a violent opponent of the Russian Revolution of 1917.

CHRIST AND ANTICHRIST. 3v. 1901-05. (II) Trilogy of novels on the eternal conflict between Christian and pagan elements in human nature. The Roman emperor Julian the Apostate is the central figure of Volume 1, which is called *The Death of the Gods*; Volume II is *The Romance of Leonardo da Vinci*; while the story of Peter the Great is told in Volume III, *Peter and Alexis*.

Mérimée, Prosper   1803-70   French novelist. "One of the greatest masters of Nineteenth-Century imaginative prose."

CARMEN. 1847. In this short novel, the source of Bizet's opera of the same name, "a Spanish soldier is destroyed body and soul by the gypsy girl who ensnared him."

COLUMBA. 1840. Short romance of the vendetta in Corsica.

LETTERS TO AN UNKNOWN. 1873. These letters, actually written to a female friend over thirty years, constitute Mérimée's most admired work. They record almost daily the writer's subjective impressions of contemporary persons and events, and paint a vivid picture of their time in France.

Merriam, John Campbell   1869-1945   American geologist and paleontologist.

LIVING PAST. 1900. (III) Popular, well-illustrated essays on prehistoric animal and plant life in America, as revealed in its fossil remains.

Merrick, Leonard   1864-1939   English fictionist; called "the novelists' novelist," perhaps because Howells, Barrie, Wells, Hewlett, Locke, Chesterton, Pinero, Granville Barker, and others each wrote a warmly appreciative introduction to his favorite volume in the collected edition of Merrick's works.

CONRAD IN QUEST OF HIS YOUTH. 1903. (II) Considered by many his best book. Barrie said of it, "I know scarcely a novel by any living Englishman, except a score or so of Mr. Hardy's, that I would rather have written."

WHILE PARIS LAUGHED. 1918. (II) Short stories—French contes in their brevity and crispness."—A.L.A. Catalog, Supp. 2.

CHAIR ON THE BOULEVARD. 1919. (II) Gaily satirical little stories of French life.

Merton, Thomas (in religion, Brother M. Louis)   1915-   American poet, who was converted to Catholicism and became a Trappist monk.

SEVEN STOREY MOUNTAIN. 1948. This autobiography is "an extraordinary record of religious experience." "Essentially the odyssey of a soul. A more human document than the comparable Apologia Pro Vita Sua of John Henry Newman."—Saturday Review of Literature.

WATERS OF SILOE. 1949. "A history, a description and an interpretation of the meaning and purposes of Cistercian monasticism."— Quarterly Booklist. "Only Thomas Merton could have written single-handed this history of Trappist monks, for it is a work of diverse gifts and skills, an ardent collaboration of scholar and story-teller, past and present."—Fulton Oursler, in New York Times.

Meyer, Conrad F.   1825-98   Swiss novelist and poet.

THE SAINT. 1879. Story of the life and tragic death of Saint Thomas à Becket, in the days of Henry II (1154-89). "The style is vivid, swift and powerful and the diction of wonderful force and color." (Cf.Eliot's *Murder in the Cathedral.*)

Meyer, Cord   1920-   American soldier (1942-45), writer, and publicist; president, United World Federalists, 1947-49.

PEACE OR ANARCHY. 1947. Author considers present United Nations ineffective, and advocates world federalism. Raymond Swing urged "that twenty million Americans may somehow be brought to read this book. It could save civilization."

Meynell, Alice   1847-1922   English poet and essayist, whose work was greatly admired by literary friends such as Patmore, Thompson, Rossetti, Ruskin, Browning, and Meredith.

POEMS. Complete edition, 1940. (II)   She followed only Kipling as the popular choice for Poet Laureate.

ESSAYS. 1923. (II)   Bessie Graham, author of *The Bookman's Manual*, considered Mrs. Meynell a better essayist than poet. "Every essay," said *The Spectator*, "is worth reading several times over."

Michener, James Albert   1907-   American teacher, editor, and author. Served in the South Pacific in World War II.

TALES OF THE SOUTH PACIFIC. 1947. Stories of the island-hopping war in the South Pacific. Won Pulitzer prize, 1947. "Magnificently entertaining."—*Yale Review.* "The finest fiction to come out of the South Pacific war."—*New York Herald Tribune.*

Mill, John Stuart   1806-73   English philosopher and economist. "A wiser and more virtuous man I have never known and never hope to know."—John Morley.

SYSTEM OF LOGIC. 1863. (I)   This book "must take its rank among the great treatises on logic of all times. Mill is frequently called the founder of the inductive logic."—Richard T. Ely.

ON LIBERTY. 1859. (I)   Teaches "that self-protection is the sole end for which society is warranted in interfering with individual liberty of action."—Frederic Harrison.

REPRESENTATIVE GOVERNMENT. 1861. (I) Mill is "individualistic democracy's greatest protagonist."—*Good Reading.*

UTILITARIANISM. 1863. (I) The criterion of right and wrong is "the tendency of an action to produce the happiness of mankind."

SUBJECTION OF WOMEN. 1869. "Earnest plea for the equality of the sexes."—*Good Reading.*

AUTOBIOGRAPHY. 1873. (I) "A fascinating book it is from beginning to end."—Edward Everett Hale. "It can scarcely be called an exaggeration to call his autobiography . . . a wonderful book."—Richard T. Ely.

Millar, George Reid 1910-   Scottish soldier and war correspondent in World War II.

HORNED PIGEON. 1946. Personal experiences in the North African campaign and in Axis prisons. "A book that would be hard to beat in the field of either fiction or non-fiction for excitement, suspense, character and just plain ordinary good writing."—*Commonweal.*

Millay, Edna St. Vincent 1892-1950   American poet; member, American Academy of Arts and Letters. "Verse as clear as crystal and as sad as life."—Agnes Repplier. "Rarely since Sappho has a woman written as outspokenly as this."—Carl Van Doren.

COLLECTED LYRICS. 1943. Includes most of the lyrics published in earlier volumes.

COLLECTED SONNETS. 1941. (IV) Includes 161 sonnets; all but two published previously. "She remains today the greatest living master of the sonnet in the English language."—W. R. Benét, in 1950.

KING'S HENCHMAN. 1927. (III) Lyrical drama of Saxon England, written as a libretto for Deems Taylor's opera, produced at the Metropolitan, New York City.

Miller, Alice Duer 1874-1942   American author.

WHITE CLIFFS. 1940. (IV) Short novel in verse. Story of an American woman who married an Englishman and lived in England, adventurously but loyally, during two World Wars. It was the most popular book of poetry in many years.

Miller, Arthur 1915- American playwright; born in New York City.

DEATH OF A SALESMAN. 1949. Received New York Drama Critics' Award, Pulitzer prize, etc. "A deeply affecting tragedy."—*New Yorker*. "The most distinguished event in the theatre of this decade." —*Kirkus*. "The drama of disillusion without the catharsis of faith." —*Catholic World*. "Mr. Miller's is a terrific wallop, as furious in its onslaught on the heart as on the head."—John Mason Brown.

Miller, Caroline 1903- American novelist.

LAMB IN HIS BOSOM. 1933. (III) Story of pioneer life in the back country of Georgia preceding and during the Civil War. Won Pulitzer prize, 1934.

Miller, Douglas 1892- American Rhodes Scholar, economist, and diplomat. In the years before World War II he was a commercial attaché in the American embassy in Berlin.

YOU CAN'T DO BUSINESS WITH HITLER. 1941. (I) The author tried but found it impossible. In this book he tells why. While totalitarian dictatorships exist the book's lesson should not be forgotten.

Miller, John Chester 1907- American historian.

ORIGINS OF THE AMERICAN REVOLUTION. 1943. (IV) Reviews the background of our history from George III's accession to the Declaration of Independence. "A thoroughly scholarly piece of work, precisely documented, and still lively and spirited enough for a best-seller list."—*Saturday Review of Literature*.

Millikan, Robert A. 1868- American physicist; won Nobel prize, 1923.

AUTOBIOGRAPHY. 1950. "An important book for all scientists, historians, philosophers and educators."—*New York Herald Tribune*.

Millis, Walter 1899- American journalist; Second Lieutenant, Field Artillery, 1918.

MARTIAL SPIRIT, A STUDY OF OUR WAR WITH SPAIN. 1931. (III) How and why the American people were incited and cajoled into making war unnecessarily.

Road to War, America, 1914-1917. 1935 and 1939. (III) A study of the influences which brought America into World War I. The power of propaganda is skillfully demonstrated.

Why Europe Fights. 1940. (IV) Résumé of Europe's economic and political history during "the long armistice" between World Wars I and II. In this book the author's viewpoint is not at all that of either a pacifist or an isolationist. "I know no better primer of the background of World War II."—Lewis Gannett, in *Boston Transcript*.

This Is Pearl. 1947. The story of Pearl Harbor and the year before it. "Has the interest and suspense of a novel." "Chapter by chapter, the suspense mounts, the tragedy deepens and the irony grows more pregnant."—Owen Lattimore, in *New York Herald Tribune*.

Milman, H. H.   1791-1868   English historian and churchman.

History of Latin Christianity. 1855. (I) Impartial account of the establishment and growth of monastic institutions and orders. "To the student of the Middle ages," says C. K. Adams, "this work is secondary in importance only to that of Gibbon. One told the story of the Empire's gradual fall, the other the contemporary development of a new institution, first the victim, then the rival, and ultimately the successor of the first."

Milne, A. A.   1882-   English dramatist, novelist, children's poet.

Three Plays. 1922. Includes *Dover Road, Truth about Blayds, Great Broxopp.*

Red House Mystery. 1922. Excellent murder mystery. Scene, an old English manor house.

When We Were Very Young. 1924. (II) A delightful piece of childishness. "Mr. Guiterman said this was a book to get for 'a kind child who will let you read it aloud.' That is exactly true."— E. L. Pearson.

Milton, John   1608-74   English poet. Emerson called him "the stair or tableland to let down the English genius from the summits of Shakespeare."

Complete Poetical Works. (I) Cambridge edition. n.d. Includes *Paradise Lost* (1667), "the greatest epic in any modern language"; its sequel, *Paradise Regained* (1671), superior to its predecessor in technique, though inferior in inspiration; *Comus* (1634), a masque; *Lycidas* (1637), an elegy; *L'Allegro* and *Il Penseroso* (1632), pastoral poems; *Samson Agonistes* (1671), a sacred drama; and many others of very high quality.

AREOPAGITICA. 1644. (Everyman's Library of World's Classics.) This, the best known of Milton's prose works, is his masterly argument for freedom of the press.

Mitchell, Margaret 1900(?)-49 American novelist.

GONE WITH THE WIND. 1936. (IV) The century's most phenomenally successful book is this novel of Georgia before, during, and after the Civil War. It had been translated into sixteen foreign languages at last accounts. It won the Pulitzer prize in 1937. Two million copies had been sold by 1939. The reader's interest never falters through 1,037 pages. J. D. Adams, in the *New York Times*, declared it "the best Civil War novel that has yet been written." And Helen E. Haines's comment is that it is "one of those rare novels that in sheer story-telling quality commands absorbed interest and spontaneous emotional response."

Mitchell, S. Weir 1829-1914 American novelist and neurologist; member American Academy of Arts and Letters.

ADVENTURES OF FRANÇOIS, FOUNDLING, THIEF, JUGGLER, AND FENCING MASTER DURING THE FRENCH REVOLUTION. 1898. (I) A vivid picture of low life in Paris during the Terror.

HUGH WYNNE, FREE QUAKER. 1897. (I) Excellent historical novel of Philadelphia in the days of the American Revolution.

THE RED CITY, A NOVEL OF THE SECOND ADMINISTRATION OF PRESIDENT WASHINGTON. A sequel to *Hugh Wynne.* 1908. (II)

Mitford, Mary Russell 1787-1855 English writer.

OUR VILLAGE. 1824-32. (I) These collected magazine sketches present a quiet picture of the English countryside which is delightfully and nostalgically old-fashioned. M. F. Egan called it "fresh and sweet as the English daisies." Saintsbury ranked it with Gilbert White's *Selborne.*

Mohammed *See* Koran.

Molière (pseudonym of Jean Baptiste Poquelin) 1622-73 French writer of social comedies which have made his name perhaps the most illustrious one in French literature.

COMEDIES. (I) "Realistic or humorously exaggerated pictures of the follies of mankind."—*A.L.A. Catalog*, 1926. Among his best plays are *Tartuffe* (his masterpiece, in which he scored hypocrisy), *The Doctor in Spite of Himself* (*Le Médecin Malgré Lui*), *The Miser* (*L'Avare*), *The Bourgeois Gentleman*, *The Hypochondriac* (*Le Malade Imaginaire*), *The Ridiculous Misses* (*Le Précieuses Ridicules*), *The School for Wives* (*L'École des Femmes*), *Don Juan*, *The Misanthrope*, and *The Learned Ladies* (*Les Femmes Savantes*).

Molnár, Ferenc 1878-1952 Hungarian dramatist; a refugee from Nazism, he came to the United States in 1940.

LILIOM. 1921. (II) A play, fantastic and bizarre, with some unforgettable scenes. The principal character is a roughneck barker for a merry-go-round.

Montague, Lady Mary Wortley 1689-1762 English diplomat's wife and writer of remarkable letters. Famed also for her bitter quarrel with Pope, and for having introduced smallpox inoculation into England.

LETTERS. 1777. (I) "A lively picture of manners in a picturesque age of English life, including a unique series of impressions from foreign courts." Saintsbury said, "Her rank as the best letter-writer of her sex in England is undisputed."

Montague, C. E. 1867-1928 Man of letters; for many years chief editorial writer for the English *Manchester Guardian*.

DISENCHANTMENT. 1922. (II) One of the best written and most fearlessly honest commentaries on World War I, in which the author fought as a private.

RIGHT OFF THE MAP. 1927. (III) Satirical novel about a war between two imaginary countries, showing how it was brought about and conducted by the silly, noble, selfish creatures we call men.

Montaigne, Michel Eyquem de 1533-92 Inventor and, many think, world-master of the familiar essay.

ESSAYS. 1582-88. (I) Casual, intimate, and candid commentaries by an urbane skeptic on men, books, religion, ethics, manners, and politics. They have fascinated many first-class minds. Florio's contemporary (1603) English translation is the one most widely known. It was used by Bacon and by Shakespeare. The one by Izaak Walton's friend, John Cotton (1685), is a more correct if less picturesque translation, especially in the editions revised by W. Hazlitt (1842-65) and W. C. Hazlitt (1889-1903).

Montesquieu, C. L. de Secondat, Baron de La Brède et de 1689-1755 French philosopher and man of letters.

SPIRIT OF LAWS. 1748. (I) Investigation of the origin of laws and the principles which mold them. Designed to awaken desire for freedom, condemnation of despotism, and hope of political progress. One of the slow matches which ignited the train of thought and feeling leading to the explosion of the French Revolution.

PERSIAN LETTERS. 1721. (I) Satire on contemporary manners purporting to consist of a series of outspoken letters exchanged between two travelers from Persia.

Moody, William Vaughn 1869-1910 American dramatist and poet; member, American Academy of Arts and Letters.

THE GREAT DIVIDE. 1909. (I and II) A "Western" that was nominated for consideration as "the Great American Play." The divide is the gulf that seemed likely to separate the cultured Eastern heroine from the wild and woolly Western hero.

HISTORY OF ENGLISH LITERATURE. 1907. Revised edition, 1930. A good short history, used as a textbook in many schools and colleges. (Written with R. M. Lovett.)

Moore, George 1852-1933 Irish author. A hypochondriacal celibate, whose keen appreciation for beauty in every form went far to atone for his exaggerated ego and perverse, cold-blooded character. "His prose flows like conversation, but no conversation was ever so well shaped and worded."—J. C. Squire.

ESTHER WATERS. 1894. (I) "The misfortunes and brief happiness of a servant girl, portrayed with sympathetic realism by an English follower of Zola's naturalism."—*Good Reading*.

EVELYN INNES. 1898. (I) Story of a prima donna's struggle between worldly and spiritual yearnings. In the sequel,

SISTER TERESA. 1901. (II) The author describes Evelyn's spiritual history after she has become a nun.

MEMORIES OF MY DEAD LIFE. 1906. (II) Sentimental reminiscences in which—to quote Chesterton—he loves to contemplate "the ruins of George Moore by moonlight."

THE BROOK KERITH. 1916. (II) Story founded on a legend of Christ's resuscitation after the crucifixion. The tale is told, supposedly by Joseph of Arimathea, with simplicity, tenderness, dignity, and beauty.

HÉLOISE AND ABELARD. 1921. (II) The old, unhappy story of the medieval scholar and his love, retold "with realism and great imaginative force."

HAIL AND FAREWELL. 3v. in 2. Revised edition, 1925. (II) Autobiographical maunderings—but such maunderings—about the Irish Renaissance, literature, music, Protestantism, Catholicism, Yeats, "A.E.," Lady Gregory, etc. While he lived the thought that he might produce more of the same brought gray hairs to the heads of his terrified acquaintances.

Moore, Marianne   1887-   American poet of the objectivist school; editor, *The Dial*, 1925-29.

SELECTED POEMS. 1935. "Miss Moore's poems form part of the small body of durable poetry written in our time."—T. S. Eliot. "Don't expect it to be like anything else you ever read, because it isn't."—W. R. Benét, in *Saturday Review of Literature*.

More, Paul Elmer   1864-1937   American critic, Sanskrit and classical scholar, editor, leader of the movement in philosophy and criticism known as humanism or the new humanism; member, American Academy of Arts and Letters.

SHELBURNE ESSAYS. 11v. 1904-21. (II) Critical essays on literary and philosophical subjects. "The much abused Paul Elmer More remains our only professional critic whose learning is really great and whose efforts are ambitious."—Edmund Wilson.

More, Sir Thomas   1478-1535   British statesman and author; beheaded by his former friend, Henry VIII; canonized, 1935.

UTOPIA. 1516. (I) Written in Latin; first English version, 1551. (I) Everyman's Library, 1948. If we except Plato's *Republic*, this is the first of many books which describe an imaginary commonwealth wherein society is ideally organized. This one's central idea is the triumph of altruism over egoism.

**Morgan, Charles 1894- English novelist; George Moore's literary executor.

THE FOUNTAIN. 1932. (III) Story of an English officer's illicit love. Like his hero, the author had been taken prisoner by the Germans and interned in Holland "for the duration." This novel won the Hawthornden prize, 1933.

**Morgenthau, Henry, Jr. 1891- American agriculturist, financier, and former public official; Secretary of the Treasury, 1934-45. His New Deal diary (unpublished) runs to hundreds of manuscript volumes.

GERMANY IS OUR PROBLEM. 1945. (IV) This book was the basis of the "Morgenthau Plan" for turning Germany into a harmless agricultural nation. "The Morgenthau Plan will never be adopted *in toto.* It can be, however, a yardstick to measure our flagging will to render Germany impotent for war."—Leon Henderson, in *Nation.*

**Morier, James 1780-1849 English author and diplomat.

ADVENTURES OF HAJJI BABA OF ISPAHAN. 1824. Picaresque romance which paints a vivid picture of Persian manners. "The book is witty, entertaining, and shows a marvelous adaptation to Oriental ways of thought and a thorough acquaintance with Oriental institutions."—Keller.

**Morison, Samuel Eliot 1887- American historian, named by the United States Navy to write the official history of its part in World War II.

ADMIRAL OF THE OCEAN SEA; A LIFE OF CHRISTOPHER COLUMBUS. 1942. (IV) Himself a sailor, Morison, before writing this book, followed faithfully all the routes of the Admiral's ships on his voyages to and from America, in sailing craft of about the same size as the old caravels. "There is no danger at all in saying that this is the best book about Columbus so far printed."—G. Mattingly, in *New Republic.* Won a Pulitzer Prize, 1943.

BATTLE OF THE ATLANTIC, 1939-43. 1947. (Vol. 1 of *United States Naval Operations in World War II.*) "Our best account of anti-submarine warfare, waged for the protection of shipping, supply and troop transport."—*Library Journal.* Includes excellent illustrations and maps, and the *New Yorker* declares it "very well written."

Rising Sun in the Pacific, 1931-April 1942. 1948. (Vol. 3 of *United States Naval Operations in World War II.*) "By far the best account to date of the period when adversity beset the United States Navy in the Pacific."—*Christian Science Monitor.*

Struggle for Guadalcanal, August 1942-February 1943. 1949. (Vol. 5 of *United States Naval Operations in World War II.*) This book describes the beginning of the offensive. The *Saturday Review of Literature* called it "the most exciting war book of the year." "One of the great studies and great stories of the second world War."—Walter Millis, in *New York Herald Tribune.*

Morley, Christopher 1890- American man of letters, "who in his early years," says Helen Haines, "brought the modern 'familiar essay' to near perfection in American literature."

Parnassus on Wheels. 1917. (II) Good-humored and amusing tale of a vagabonding bookshop.

Thunder on the Left. 1925. (II) A whimsical allegory. "It is difficult to know what the story means but it is impossible not to be moved by it," says the *Book Review Digest.*

Where the Blue Begins. 1922. (II) In more than one way, with its gentle satire and humor, this story recalls Kenneth Grahame's *Wind in the Willows.* The characters are mostly dogs, or men in the guise of dogs.

Human Being, a Story. 1932. (III) Morley knows a lot about men, women, books, the publishing business, and show business. He likes them and in a comradely way has been amused by them. Much of his knowledge, liking, and amusement has been worked into this tale, which the *Nation* called "the ripest and most full-flavored of all his books."

John Mistletoe. 1931. A book written, the author says, "to celebrate (or deplore) his own fortieth birthday. . . . An early example of what is now a universal passion, the autobiographies of young men." R. L. Duffus likens it to "the cheerful whistling of an excellent companion."

Kitty Foyle. 1939. (IV) A novel, autobiographical in form, about a young Philadelphia working-girl. It carries her into her late twenties. "As a woman, we take the liberty of congratulating Mr. Morley on his expert knowledge of our thoughts and emotions."—Rose Feld, in *Boston Transcript.*

ESSAYS, 1918-27. 1928. (II) Mostly selected from his books *Shandygaff, Mince Pie, Pipefuls, Travels in Philadelphia, Plum Pudding, Powder of Sympathy,* and *Romany Stain.*

Morley, John (Viscount Morley of Blackburn) 1838-1923 English editor, biographer, critic, philosopher, and statesman.

LIFE OF WILLIAM EWART GLADSTONE. 3v. 1903. (II) In the army of Twentieth-Century books this title marches with the heavy artillery. But it is a masterpiece of historical writing in which interest is absorbing, authority indisputable, and skill consummate.

Morris, Lloyd R. 1893- American biographer, playwright, historian.

POSTSCRIPT TO YESTERDAY: AMERICA, THE LAST FIFTY YEARS. 1947. "A shining book on a melancholy subject. . . . A less doleful book on American history has never been written."

Morris, William 1834-96 English author, artist, craftsman, socialist.

EARTHLY PARADISE. 1868-70. (I) Collection of old Norse and Greek tales which he has put into verse.

STORY OF SIGURD THE VOLSUNG. 1876. (I) "Stands among the foremost poems not only of this century but of our literature."— H. Buxton Forman.

Motley, John Lothrop 1814-77 American historian who specialized in studies of Holland's Sixteenth-Century struggle for liberty.

RISE OF THE DUTCH REPUBLIC. 1856. (I) "A history as complete as industry and genius can make it. . . . The book is one which will take its place among the finest histories in this or any other language."—J. A. Froude.

Mottram, Ralph H. 1883- British novelist.

SPANISH FARM TRILOGY. 1927. (III) Consists of *The Spanish Farm* (1924), which won the Hawthornden prize, *Sixty-four, Ninety-four* (1925) and *Crime at Vanderlynden's* (1926). Fine, objective stories of life as it was lived just behind the British lines in French Flanders, during World War I. Dramatized in the moving picture, *Roses in Picardy.*

Muir, John   1838-1914   Scottish-American mountain-man, explorer, naturalist and man of letters; member, American Academy of Arts and Letters.

MOUNTAINS OF CALIFORNIA. 1894. Enlarged edition, 1911. (I) A revelation of mountain beauty, together with a masterly description of the region's geology, flora, and fauna.

STORY OF MY BOYHOOD AND YOUTH. 1913. (I and II) "One of the great pieces of writing of its kind."—Percy F. Bicknell. Most boys delight in it.

MY FIRST SUMMER IN THE SIERRAS. 1911. It was a case of love at first sight, and this book is its worthy offspring.

A THOUSAND MILE WALK TO THE GULF. 1916. (II) Account of a tramp from Indiana to Florida in the year 1867.

Mulock, Dinah Maria (Mrs. Craik)   1826-87   English novelist.

JOHN HALIFAX, GENTLEMAN. 1856. (I) A good, old-fashioned, quiet story, characterized by optimism, high ideals and simplicity of diction. It was immensely popular with our simple-hearted grandparents.

Mumford, Lewis   1895-   American social, literary, and art critic.

STICKS AND STONES. 1924. Architecture in the light of its dependence on a good economic system; "the reflection of the American spirit through architecture."

GOLDEN DAY; A STUDY OF AMERICAN EXPERIENCE AND CULTURE. 1926. (III) Panorama of our culture, and especially of that high time when Emerson, Thoreau, Whitman, Hawthorne, and Melville were the stars in our literary firmament.

HERMAN MELVILLE. 1929. (III) Biography and criticism of the creator of *Moby Dick*. Mr. Mumford believes that Melville "shares with Whitman the distinction of being the greatest writer that America has produced."

BROWN DECADES, 1865-1895. 1931. (III) The re-appraisal of a misunderstood period in our cultural history. The roots of today, he says, are drawing sustenance from a long contemned yesterday.

TECHNICS AND CIVILIZATION. 1934. Discussion of "the social changes brought about by the development of the machine, its power for good and ill, and how its benefits may be assimilated and brought more completely in harmony with human needs and desires."—*Book Review Digest.*

CULTURE OF CITIES. 1938. (IV) This historical study of cities from the Middle Ages to the present, with proposals for their betterment, has been described as "a plea for the spiritual regeneration of America." Nobody can read this book without finding his public interest heightened in potential. And what more can ever be said for a book?"—Alvin Johnson, in *Yale Review*.

GREEN MEMORIES. 1947. A beautiful book about his son, Geddes, killed at nineteen in World War II. "The tone is affectionate and restrained. It is a sunlit book. . . . It should have something of consolation for others who have lost their sons."—*New York Times*.

Münchhausen, K. F. H., Baron von. 1720-97 German officer in the Russian army; reputed author of

TRAVELS AND ADVENTURES. 1785. Perhaps the most amusing collection of tall tales ever published. The original yarns were collected, enlarged and embellished by R. E. Raspe and other monumental liars.

Munro, Hector Hugh (Saki, pseudonym) 1870-1916 Scottish author of humorous fiction, and especially short stories; killed in World War I.

SHORT STORIES OF "SAKI" COMPLETE. 1930. Light, facetious, and amusing tales.

Munthe, Axel 1857-1949 Swedish physician, who retired to the island of Capri after a wandering life of medical practice and adventure.

STORY OF SAN MICHELE. 1929. (III) Extraordinarily interesting autobiography. Fantastic, bizarre, with a vein of mysticism and some very tall stories which will offend only the literal-minded.

Murasaki Shikibu, Baroness Eleventh Century Japanese novelist and poet.

TALE OF GENJI; a novel in 6 parts, translated by A. Waley. n.d. 1135 pages. "The gallantries and love adventures of Prince Genji, son of the emperor. . . . A Japanese classic written by a lady-in-waiting."

Murray, R. H. editor *See* Creasy, Sir Edward S.

Myrdal, Gunnar Karl 1898- **and others.** Swedish sociologist.

AMERICAN DILEMMA; THE NEGRO PROBLEM AND MODERN DEMOC-
RACY. 2v. 1944. (IV) "A book which nobody who tries to face
the Negro problem with any honesty can afford to miss."—*New York
Times.*

Nansen, Odd 1901- Norwegian architect; son of Fridtjof Nansen, Arctic explorer.

FROM DAY TO DAY. 1949. Diary (1942-45) of a prisoner in a
German concentration camp. "There is little . . . that cannot be found
in a hundred other books. The one difference is that it is a masterpiece."—*Times* (London). "You will never know what hate makes
possible until you have read this book."—*Chicago Sun.*

Nash, Ogden 1902- American writer of humorous verse, often
based upon sophisticated New York or New Yorkers.

SELECTED VERSE. 1946. His own choice of 165 of his most representative poems. In them, "nonsense, wit and satire appear in varying degrees, and most of them are notable for startling eccentricities
of meter, line-length, and rhyme."

Nashe, Thomas 1567-1601 English satirist and romancer.

UNFORTUNATE TRAVELLER, OR THE LIFE OF JACK WILTON. 1594.
A piece of antique fiction which preceded Daniel Defoe, "Father of
the English novel," by more than a hundred years.

Nathan, George Jean 1882- American dramatic critic; friend
and associate of H. L. Mencken on *The Smart Set* and *American
Mercury.*

THEATRE BOOK OF THE YEAR . . . A RECORD AND AN INTERPRETA-
TION. 1943- . "Statistical record and critical appreciation of the
plays produced annually in the American theatre."

ENCYCLOPEDIA OF THE THEATRE. 1940. "The American stage
of today, with some consideration of its past, its overseas ramifications,
and its probable future."—*Standard Catalog,* 1940.

Nathan, Robert 1894- American teller of fantastic tales, often
sentimental, sometimes satirical.

ROAD OF AGES. 1935. "Mr. Nathan has imagined a final exile
of all Jews from all countries, and this is the story of their slow march
eastward across Europe towards Asia and the Gobi desert, offered
by the Mongols as a haven."—*Booklist.*

PORTRAIT OF JENNIE. 1940. Story of a discouraged artist and a strange and lovely girl whom he meets one wet winter's evening in Central Park.

ONE MORE SPRING. 1940. "In this charming, gentle and ironic story Mr. Nathan offers subtle and wise reflections on the depression of 1929."—*Booklist*.

Needler, H. A., translator *See* Nibelungenlied.

Neff, Emery Edward 1892- Professor of English at Columbia University.

EDWARD ARLINGTON ROBINSON. 1948. A biographical and critical study. "An appreciative work, written with sympathy and understanding."—*Library Journal*.

Nehru, Jawaharlal 1889- Indian statesman; Prime Minister, 1947-

TOWARDS FREEDOM; AUTOBIOGRAPHY. 1941. (IV) "One of the most absorbing personal histories of modern times."—*Nation*. "This book presents more effectively than any other the Indian point of view in the long strained relations with the government in London."—*Christian Science Monitor*.

Neihardt, John G. 1881- American poet of the Missouri country.

CYCLE OF THE WEST. 5v. in 1. 1949. Includes *Song of Hugh Glass* (1915) (II), *Song of Three Friends* (1919) (II), *Song of the Indian Wars* (1925), *Song of the Messiah* (1935), and *Song of Jed Smith* (1941). "Classic telling of a great story that will never be outdated. . . . Mr. Neihardt's epic is a splendid monument in literature."—*Springfield Republican*.

Neruda, Pablo (pseudonym of Neftalí Ricardo Reyes) 1904-
Chilean writer of the Left Wing. "He has exerted wide influence in Hispanic America."—*Columbia Encyclopedia, 1950*.

RESIDENCE ON EARTH, AND OTHER POEMS. 1946. "An excellent translation." "The first large-scale introduction to the American public of a truly important contemporary poet. The general excellence of the poems selected is high; the range, if not fully representative, is wide."—*New York Herald Tribune*.

Nevins, Allan   1890-   American historian and biographer; twice a Pulitzer prize-winner; member, National Institute of Arts and Letters.

GROVER CLEVELAND; A STUDY IN COURAGE. 1932. Revised edition, 1933. (III) A conscientious, adequate, scholarly, and readable presentment of "The Man Four-Square."

HAMILTON FISH; THE INNER HISTORY OF THE GRANT ADMINISTRATION. 1936. (IV) Fish was Grant's Secretary of State. "One of the best of the author's works, and that in itself is the highest praise."—*Saturday Review of Literature.*

GATEWAY TO HISTORY. 1938. "A helpful discussion of historiography and methods of research."—*Social Studies.* "The enthusiasm of a lover of history is combined with the knowledge and experience of a distinguished historian."—Helen Haines.

JOHN D. ROCKEFELLER; THE HEROIC AGE OF AMERICAN ENTERPRISE. 2v. 1940. (IV) The most important biography of its year. It is neither partisan nor apologetic. Has stronger claims to consideration as a work of art than either his Cleveland or his Hamilton Fish, although they both won Pulitzer prizes.

ORDEAL OF THE UNION. 2v. 1947. History of the United States, 1847-57: the causes of the Civil War. "The most authentic and unbiased history of the time."—Burton J. Hendrick, in the *New York Herald Tribune.* (Won Scribner's Ten Thousand Dollar prize in American History.)

EMERGENCE OF LINCOLN. 2v. 1950. "A tremendous amount of detailed research has been presented with the skill that makes the name Allan Nevins synonymous with history at its best."— *New York Times.*

Nevins, Allan, joint author and editor   *See* Commager, H. S.

Nevinson, Henry Wood   1857-1941   British journalist.

FIRE OF LIFE. 1935. His three-volume autobiography condensed to one by H. Ellis Roberts. "No better autobiography has been written in English in the last hundred years. . . . He can reflect that he has been a friend to every worthy cause that has stirred men's hearts in his time."—John Masefield.

Newman, John Henry (Cardinal Newman) 1801-90 Anglican theologian who became a cardinal of the Catholic Church.

Apologia Pro Sua Vita, Being a History of His Religious Opinions. 1864. "Deals partly with controversies now forgotten, but the writer's style has made the book a classic of English literature. As a spiritual autobiography, moreover, it has few equals in English."—*English Library.*

Newton, Alfred Edward 1863-1940 Prince of American amateur bookmen.

Amenities of Book-Collecting. 1918. (II) Nectar and ambrosia for booklovers; followed by gossip about Boswell, Lamb, Trollope, and other good old fellows with inky fingers.

Magnificent Farce and Other Diversions of a Booklover. 1921. (II) More jaunts and joustings amid the leafy coverts of Bookland.

Newton, Sir Isaac 1642-1727 English scientist, mathematician, philosopher.

Principia. 1685. (I) An important landmark in the history of science, in which the author expounds his newly formulated theory of gravitation.

Nexö, Martin Anderson 1869- Danish proletarian novelist.

Pelle the Conqueror. 4v. in 1. 1930. (II) Life story of a Danish peasant who became a labor leader. "Surely," said Randolph Bourne, in *New Republic,* "*Pelle* is one of the great novels of the world."

Ditte. 3v. in 1. n.d. (II) Heartrending story of the hard life in a Danish fishing village of a brave, fine, loving girl and woman.

Nibelungenlied. (I) Epic of Siegfried, the Germanic hero. It was written in Middle High German near the end of the Twelfth Century and is now regarded as largely the work of a single unknown author. There have been several English translations, notably that into rhymed verse in the original metrical form by H. A. Needler (1904), and the exact prose translation by D. B. Shumway (1910).

Niebuhr, Reinhold   1892-   "Our best-known English-speaking theologian"; professor of Applied Christianity at Union Theological Seminary, New York, since 1930.

NATURE AND DESTINY OF MAN: A CHRISTIAN INTERPRETATION. 2v. 1941-3. "Perhaps the most notable Christian apologia of our times in the English language."—Ordway Tead, in *Ethics*.

FAITH AND HISTORY; A COMPARISON OF CHRISTIAN AND MODERN VIEWS OF HISTORY. 1949. "A brilliant piece of Christian apologetics."—*Quarterly Booklist*. "An excellent introduction to the work of one of the outstanding thinkers of our time."—*Christian Century*.

Nietzsche, F. W.   1844-1900   German philosopher.   He died insane after twenty years of illness.

PHILOSOPHY. 5v. in 1. 1937. (I) Nietzsche might be termed the dictators' philosopher. He believed that "good and evil are only relative. . . . There is one morality for the vigorous, efficient man . . . another for the weak, average, subordinate man"; and that Christianity is a slave's religion. *Thus Spake Zarathustra*, his most famous work, is included with six other titles in the Modern Library edition noted above.

Nijinsky, Romola (De Pulszky)   Hungarian actress and dancer.

NIJINSKY, BY HIS WIFE. 1934. (IV) An important book on many counts: as a study of the genius which is so often near to madness, as an exposition of a great art-form but recently come into its own, as a poignantly interesting love story, and as the reflection of a great tragedy.

Nock, Albert Jay   1880-1945   American journalist and iconoclast.

JEFFERSON. 1926. (III) Not a biography, says the author, just a study of conduct and character. Yet there emerges a convincing portrait of his subject, as philosopher and man of culture and vision.

MEMOIRS OF A SUPERFLUOUS MAN. 1943. (IV) These "Memoirs" are really essays propounding the author's "philosophy of informed common sense." Said Clifton Fadiman in the *New Yorker*, "I have not since the days of the early Mencken read a

more eloquently written blast against democracy or enjoyed more
fully a display of crusted prejudices. Mr. Nock is a highly civilized
man who does not like our civilization and will have no part in it."

Nordhoff, Charles Bernard 1887-1947 and **Hall, James Norman** 1887-1951 American comrades in the Lafayette Escadrille
in World War I and afterwards as writers in the islands of the
South Pacific.

THE BOUNTY TRILOGY. 1940. (III) Vivid reconstruction of a
true tale of the sea by two modern adventurers by sea and air.
The trilogy consists of *Mutiny on the Bounty* (1932), *Men
Against the Sea* (1934), and *Pitcairn's Island* (1934).

Norris, Frank 1870-1902 American novelist. Though he
died at thirty-two, he produced four books that have a permanent
place in American literature.

McTEAGUE. 1899. (I) Realistic story of slum life in San
Francisco, with the usual accompaniments of brutality and degeneracy.

THE OCTOPUS. 1901. (I and II) Fictional presentment of the
railroads' stranglehold on the California farmers of two generations
ago. (This is the first volume of his unfinished trilogy, *The Epic
of the Wheat.*)

THE PIT. 1901. (I and II) Fictional indictment of the specu-
lators in the Chicago grain market. (Second volume of *The Epic
of the Wheat.*)

VANDOVER AND THE BRUTE. 1914. (I and II) His first novel,
put aside for revision and published twelve years after his death. An
immensely powerful story of the gradual moral deterioration and
disintegration of a well-meaning young man.

Norris, George W. 1861-1944 A strictly honest and stalwart—
though limited—American public servant; for thirty years a United
States Senator from Nebraska. He opposed American entry into
World War I, and he led the fight for the establishment of the Tennessee Valley Authority.

FIGHTING LIBERAL; THE AUTOBIOGRAPHY OF GEORGE W. NORRIS.
1945. (IV) "Bare alike of literary graces and the nursed rancors
of so many memoirs, this life story holds you by its unconscious revelation of a magnificent human being; strong, incredibly honest, growing and learning until he died at eighty-three."—*Springfield Republican.*

Northrop, F. S. C. 1893- American editor; student and teacher of philosophy; author of books on world affairs.

MEETING OF EAST AND WEST; AN INQUIRY CONCERNING WORLD UNDERSTANDING. 1946. "This is a Great Book."—*New York Times.* "Those who go in for education by reading the 'great books' may well make this one of them."—*Christian Century.*

Noyes, Alfred 1880-1945 English author chiefly of narrative verse, and ballads dealing with English history; professor of English literature at Princeton University, 1914-23.

COLLECTED POEMS. 703 pages. 1947. (II) Americans know him as a poet whose verse is easy to read and also decidedly worth reading.

O'Casey, Sean 1884- Irish proletarian playwright.

JUNO AND THE PAYCOCK. 1924. Exemplifying Dublin life; one of his best plays, it won the Hawthornden prize in 1926.

WITHIN THE GATES. 1933. "Combining poetic fantasy, pageant, epic, and melodrama into what might be called a futurist morality play."—Helen E. Haines.

INISHFALLEN, FARE THEE WELL. 1949. "In this part of his autobiography the slum-born, slum-reared, self-educated dramatist says farewell to Inishfallen and sails away to make his home in England."—*Christian Century.* "There is humor in the book, most of it bitter, and there are humanity and awareness, too, but above all there is the ever-new magic of the author's language."—*New Yorker.*

Odets, Clifford 1906- American proletarian dramatist; "an avowed revolutionary" in the early 1930's, he is now more conventional in his views.

SIX PLAYS. 1939. Includes the well-known *Waiting for Lefty* (1935), a play of trades-unionism which won the Yale drama prize of 1935.

O'Faolain, Sean 1900- Irish author.

NEST OF SIMPLE FOLK. 1934. (III) A beautifully and sensitively written first novel, mirroring three generations of Irish life, from 1854 to 1916—not always a quiet and happy time.

O'Flaherty, Liam 1897- Irish novelist.

THE INFORMER. 1925. "Story of Dublin during the Insurrection . . . a melodrama of the soul as well as of action."—*Good Reading.*

FAMINE. 1937. Story of Irish peasant life in the days of the potato blight which started the mass migration of the 1840's to America.

Omar Khayyám Died 1123 Persian poet-philosopher.

THE RUBÁIYÁT. A series of quatrains about life, love, wine, and death. Edward FitzGerald's translation (1859)—at least as much FitzGerald as Omar—became extraordinarily popular, after being long neglected.

O'Neill, Eugene 1888- America's most outstanding playwright. Thrice winner of a Pulitzer prize; the second American—there have been but four—to be awarded the Nobel prize; member, American Academy of Arts and Letters.

BEYOND THE HORIZON. 1920. (II) One of two brothers gives up his chance of a larger life "beyond the horizon," marries, and finds himself trapped on the farm in a narrow round of chores and family cares. (Won a Pulitzer prize.)

ANNA CHRISTIE. 1922. (II) A chronicle of regeneration. O'Neill knows well the sea—and sea folk. Anna is a bosun's daughter. (Won a Pulitzer prize.)

EMPEROR JONES. 1921. (II) Study of the psychology of fear in a braggart and bully.

THE HAIRY APE. 1922. (II) Drama of class-consciousness: life as lived in the stokehold.

DESIRE UNDER THE ELMS. 1925. Evil and hatred on a farm in Puritan New England in the year 1850.

STRANGE INTERLUDE. 1928. (IV) This long, original, Freudian play has been hailed by some critics as America's greatest contribution to dramatic literature.

MARCO MILLIONS. 1928. About Marco Polo, the Venetian traveler of the Thirteenth Century.

GREAT GOD BROWN. 1926. In this play masks are used to show the characters as they are and as they appear to others.

LAZARUS LAUGHED. 1927. The imagined life and death of Lazarus after his resurrection by Jesus.

ALL GOD'S CHILLUN GOT WINGS. 1924. The theme of inter-racial marriage is herein explored.

MOURNING BECOMES ELECTRA. 1931. (IV) Classic Greek drama of Orestes and Electra, re-created against a background of decadent New England.

PLAYS. 3v. 1951. Published by Random House; includes 30 plays.

Ortega y Gasset, José 1883-   Spanish philosopher and critic.

REVOLT OF THE MASSES. 1932. "Analysis of society in the terms of what he considers loss of cultural values through the rise of a mass mind."—Whit Burnett.

Orwell, George (pseudonym of Eric Blair) 1903-50   English author and critic.

ANIMAL FARM. 1946. Political satire in the guise of allegory. "It is absolutely first-rate. It even seems very creditable if we compare it with Swift or Voltaire."—Edmund Wilson.

1984. 1949. "A profound, terrifying and wholly fascinating book."—*New Yorker.* "A dramatization of Lord Acton's apothegm, 'Power tends to corrupt and absolute power corrupts absolutely.' "—*New York Times.* "Novel about a future time when people living in a collectivist society are persuaded by Thought Police into thinking that ignorance is strength and war is peace."—*Saturday Review of Literature.*

BURMESE DAYS. 1950. Pictures the life of the white man in Burma before World War II. "The finest thing in its field since *A Passage to India.*"—C. J. Rolo, in *Atlantic.*

Osborn, Fairfield 1887-   American naturalist and conservation-ist; president, New York Zoological Society.

OUR PLUNDERED PLANET. 1948. The author sums up his mes-sage in a single sentence: "The tide of the earth's population is rising, the reservoir of the earth's living resources is falling." "Prime stuff for statesman and citizen alike. Its importance can hardly be exag-gerated."—*New York Herald Tribune.*

Osborn, Henry Fairfield 1857-1935 American paleontologist.

MEN OF THE OLD STONE AGE. Third edition, 1918. (II) Interesting summary for the general reader of what is known of the history, customs and art of our ancestors of 25,000 years ago.

Osborne, Dorothy (Lady Temple) 1627-95 English letter-writer.

LOVE LETTERS. n.d. (Everyman's Library.) These letters, addressed to her future husband, Sir William Temple, have retained their freshness and charm for over three centuries.

Ossendowski, Ferdinand 1876- Polish professor and scientist.

BEASTS, MEN AND GODS. 1922. (II) Describes the author's flight in 1920-21 from the army of the Soviets through Siberia, Mongolia, Tibet, and Manchuria. Melodramatic pictures of wild and perilous nomadic life in far places.

Ossian See Macpherson, James.

O'Sullivan, Maurice 1903(?)- Irish author.

TWENTY YEARS A-GROWING. 1933. (III) Record of the author's youth on Great Blasket, a storm-swept island off the Irish western coast, where even today medieval culture lingers. The narrative is full of naïve beauty, freshness, and spontaneity.

Ottley, Roi 1906- American Negro author; Harlem-born student of race relations.

NEW WORLD A-COMING: INSIDE BLACK AMERICA. 1943. (IV) The book tells what the Harlem Negro is thinking, feeling, saying— and expecting. "In depicting the color and rhythm of Harlem, Roi Ottley is at his best."—New Republic.

Otway, Thomas 1652-85 English dramatist.

VENICE PRESERVED. 1682. "Next to Shakespeare, the greatest genius England ever produced in tragedy."—Oliver Goldsmith. "The best tragedy of the Restoration . . . a sort of prose Shakespeare."— Edmund Gosse.

Oursler, Fulton   1893-1952   American author, lecturer, broadcaster.

GREATEST STORY EVER TOLD; A TALE OF THE GREATEST LIFE EVER LIVED. 1949. Life story of Jesus, compiled from the author's radio programs. "An account in modern form of those dramatic, long-past, seemingly obscure events that have somehow changed the world."—*New York Times.*

Overstreet, Harry Allen   1875-   American psychologist.

INFLUENCING HUMAN BEHAVIOR. 1925. "His directions are explicit and to the point."—G. M. Dorsey, in *Saturday Review of Literature.*

Ovid (Publius Ovidius Naso)   43 B.C.-17 A.D.   Latin poet of the Augustan Age.

METAMORPHOSES. (I) Poems describing all the classical myths involving transformations, from the world's beginnings to Caesar's metamorphosis into a star. These beautiful verses strongly influenced English poetry and offered subjects to many Renaissance painters. Arthur Golding's famous translation appeared in 1567 and was reprinted in London in 1904.

Page, Elizabeth   1889-   American author.

TREE OF LIBERTY. 1939. (IV) Historical novel in which three generations of an American family play their parts in the nation's story from 1754 to 1806.

Page, Thomas Nelson   1853-1922   American fictionist; member, American Academy of Arts and Letters. His work has preserved for future generations true, kindly and lively pictures of the Old South.

IN OLD VIRGINIA. 1887. (I) Short stories, including the famous and delightful *Meh Lady* and *Marse Chan.*

RED ROCK; A CHRONICLE OF RECONSTRUCTION. 1898. (I) Novel of Southern life in the days of the Carpet-baggers and Ku Kluxers.

Page, Walter H.   *See* Hendrick, Burton J.

Paine, Albert Bigelow 1861-1921 Mark Twain's biographer, personal friend, literary executor; editor of Twain's Letters and Speeches.

MARK TWAIN, A BIOGRAPHY. 3v. (II) Long, gossipy, uncritical—yes, but very interesting. The authorized life.

Paine, Thomas 1737-1809 Anglo-American radical pamphleteer of the American and French Revolutions.

COMMON SENSE. 1776. "A pamphlet that had prodigious success."—Benjamin Franklin, in 1787. "Paine did more to cause the Declaration of Independence than any other man."—Robert G. Ingersoll, in 1874.

RIGHTS OF MAN. 1791. "Mr. Paine's answer to Burke . . . would bring England itself to reason and revolution if it was permitted to be read there."—Thomas Jefferson, in 1791.

Palmer, George Herbert 1842-1933 Harvard professor; philosopher; translator of the *Odyssey*; husband of an ex-president of Wellesley College.

LIFE OF ALICE FREEMAN PALMER. 1908. (II) Among shining tributes offered by husbands to wives this book perhaps ranks second only to Shah Jehan's Taj Mahal.

Papashvily, George 1895(?)- and **Papashvily, Helen** 1906- He was born in Georgia, on the Black Sea; she, in California, of English extraction.

ANYTHING CAN HAPPEN. 1945. (IV) A tasty dish from the melting-pot. Mr. Papashvily reads and speaks but does not write English. He "told" this book to his wife. "With its charming violence to English and its ridiculous adventures it can be read for sheer entertainment. . . . But it is also a deeply satisfying American document which can teach while it delights us."—*Springfield Republican.*

Papini, Giovanni 1881- Italian philosopher, who became a zealous convert to Catholicism.

LIFE OF CHRIST; translated by Dorothy Canfield Fisher. 1923. (II) "The humble expression of a new-found Christianity."—*The Outlook.*

Parker, Dorothy   1893-   American satirist; one of the most brilliant wits of the New York literary world.

THE PORTABLE DOROTHY PARKER. 1944. "Sparkling collection of prose and verse." The tone of her verse has been said to be "that of an embittered and journalistic Millay."

Parker, Sir Gilbert   1862-1932   Canadian novelist.

SEATS OF THE MIGHTY. 1896. (I) Historical romance of the French and Indian War, culminating in the struggle of Montcalm and Wolfe upon the Plains of Abraham.

RIGHT OF WAY. 1901. (I and II) A story of Canada. Through strangely changed conditions and a great love, a brilliant, conscience-less barrister, "Beauty" Steele, develops heroic qualities in a humble role.

Parkman, Francis   1823-93   American historian who wrote of the struggle of France and England for North America. Said James Ford Rhodes, "I suspect his is the only work in American history that cannot and will not be written over again."

OREGON TRAIL. 1849. (I) This, his first book, describes his wandering and buffalo-hunting, in 1846, with a band of Sioux Indians.

CONSPIRACY OF PONTIAC. 1851. (I) "Will remain the favorite. Here and constantly in dealing with the Indian, with the primeval American landscape and its primeval inhabitants, his touch is masterly and irreproachable."—James Schouler.

PIONEERS OF FRANCE. 1865. (I) Histories of the Huguenots in Florida and Champlain in the North.

LA SALLE AND THE DISCOVERY OF THE GREAT WEST. 1869. Exploration of the Mississippi Valley by La Salle, Joliet, Hennepin, and Marquette.

MONTCALM AND WOLFE. 1884. (I) The end of the struggle: Wolfe defeats Montcalm at Quebec.

JOURNALS; edited by Mason Wade. 2v. 1947. The historian's diaries and work-books, discovered by the editor in a Boston garret. They are of great historical and biographical interest, of course, but here is also "an excellent travel book, full of vivid pictures of men, scenes and manners."

Parrington, Vernon L. 1871-1929 American literary scholar.

MAIN CURRENTS IN AMERICAN THOUGHT; AN INTERPRETATION OF AMERICAN LITERATURE TO 1920. 3v. in 1. 1930. The first two volumes won the Pulitzer prize in 1928. "For twenty years Parrington's great work has held its place as a foundation stone of modern American literary criticism."—Helen Haines. (The author's untimely death prevented the completion of the work. It extends only to 1900.)

Parrish, Anne 1888- American novelist.

PERENNIAL BACHELOR. 1925. (II) The old story of woman's sacrifice for the unworthy man of the house. "A panoramic comedy of American manners . . . the fads and the fashions which characterized the success've periods since 1860."

Parsons, Geoffrey 1879- Chief editorial writer, *New York Herald Tribune*; won Pulitzer prize for editorials, 1942.

STREAM OF HISTORY. Revised edition, 1933. (III) A well-proportioned outline history of the world. The narrative is interesting, often even dramatic.

Partridge, Bellamy 1878- American lawyer, critic, foreign correspondent.

COUNTRY LAWYER; THE STORY OF MY FATHER. 1939. (IV) Humorous narrative of a life lived (1870-1920) in up-state New York. It was the most popular non-fiction book of its year. "Grand reading and grand documentation. Here is Main Street and the cross streets and the furtive alleys and the little lanes that slide out into the country. Here are both sides of the tracks."—John T. Winterich.

Pascal, Blaise 1623-62 French mathematician, physicist, theologian. Nietzsche called him "the one logical Christian."

PENSÉES (THOUGHTS). 1670. (I) Unique in their combination of deep religious feeling and insight, with mathematical precision, philosophic grasp, and epigrammatic skill.

Paston Letters. Collection of letters, etc., written by or to members of the Paston family of Norfolk, England, between 1422 and 1509. These frank and homely documents cover the period of the Wars of the Roses and paint an interesting picture of English

manners and customs in the Fifteenth Century. The standard
edition, 6v., is edited by Dr. J. Gairdner. There is another, 2v., in
Everyman's Library.

Pater, Walter   1839-94   English humanist and stylist.

STUDIES IN THE RENAISSANCE. 1873. (I) "Seems to me sometimes to be the most beautiful book of prose in our literature."—
Arthur Symons.

MARIUS THE EPICUREAN. 1885. (I) *Philosophical* romance of
a young Roman patrician in the days of Marcus Aurelius, when
Christianity was beginning to win converts among the upper classes
in Rome.

GREEK STUDIES. 1895. (I) Aesthetic criticism of a high order,
dealing with mythology, poetry, sculpture, and architecture.

Paton, Alan   South African writer.

CRY THE BELOVED COUNTRY. 1948. Greatly praised novel of life
in South Africa. The main character is a Zulu minister. "Mr.
Paton's novel is the finest I have ever read about the tragic plight of
black-skinned people in a white man's world. It lacks entirely the
bitterness, dogmatism and exaggerated melodrama which disfigure
most fictional treatments of race relations."—Orville Prescott, in *Yale
Review*.

Patton, George S.   1885-1945   American soldier, from Second
Lieutenant (1909) to General (1945), when killed in a motor ac-
cident in Germany.

WAR AS I KNEW IT. 1947. "A fascinating self-portrait of an
American professional soldier of top ability."—W. Millis, in *New
York Herald Tribune*.

Paul, Elliott Harold   1891-   American writer; permanently in
love with *la vie de Bohème*, both at home and abroad.

LIFE AND DEATH OF A SPANISH TOWN. 1937. (IV) The first
half of the book describes the idyllic life of a little Spanish town in
the Balearic Islands, where the author spent five happy years. Then
came war (July 1936) and the spirit of the book changes.

LAST TIME I SAW PARIS. 1942. (IV) An American expatriate's nostalgic portrait of the Paris that was. "For all that knew
Paris and loved her—and those who did not love her did not know
her—this is an intolerably heart-breaking book."—*Saturday Review
of Literature*.

Paxson, Frederic Logan 1877-1948 American historian.

HISTORY OF THE AMERICAN FRONTIER. 1924. (II) The saga of the conquest of the American wilderness, from 1763 to 1893. Won the Pulitzer prize for history in 1925.

Payne, Robert 1911- English author of novels and other books dealing with China, India, and Russia.

MAO TSE-TUNG; RULER OF RED CHINA. 1950. "Major contribution to our understanding of the Chinese Revolution."—*San Francisco Chronicle.* "Sympathetic but critical biography of the most powerful revolutionist since Lenin."—*Saturday Review of Literature.*

Peacock, Thomas Love 1785-1866 English novelist and poet.

HEADLONG HALL. 1816. Satiric novel, negligible in plot, but with much witty dialog.

NIGHTMARE ABBEY. 1818. Satirizes its day's recently popular "Gothic romances." Among the characters are caricatures of Coleridge, Shelley, and especially Byron.

Pearson, Hesketh 1887- English actor, soldier, biographer.

G. B. S., A FULL LENGTH PORTRAIT. 1942. (IV) "Robustly critical" and "immensely amusing" life of Bernard Shaw. "A book of uncommon importance and uncommon delight."—*Saturday Review of Literature.*

OSCAR WILDE, HIS LIFE AND WIT. 1946. "The first book anyone should read on the subject."—*New Republic.* "Mr. Pearson is sympathetic . . . but never blinded by his sympathy. His book is fair, careful, wise and temperate. . . . A must for admirers or students of Wilde and his times."—*Atlantic.*

DICKENS; HIS CHARACTER, COMEDY AND CAREER. 1949. "A well-balanced, as well as very readable, book which will be of interest to anyone with even a partial knowledge of the novels."—George Orwell, in *New York Times.* "In comparison, the standard, three-volume biography of Dickens's Boswellian friend, Forster, seems pedestrian indeed."—*Christian Science Monitor.*

Peary, Robert E. 1856-1920 American Arctic explorer.

THE NORTH POLE, ITS DISCOVERY IN 1909. 1910. (II) One of the classics of exploration, with interesting accounts of Eskimo customs.

Peattie, Donald Culross 1898- American naturalist and nature-writer.

ALMANAC FOR MODERNS. 1935. Essays—one for every day in the year—on nature and naturalists. Their style is such that they will be read for pleasure quite as much as for information.

GREEN LAURELS: THE LIVES AND ACHIEVEMENTS OF THE GREAT NATURALISTS. 1936. (IV) "He has read and digested what is known about his subjects and has then in the most excellent and smooth language given them vivid consideration."—William Beebe, in *Saturday Review of Literature*.

ROAD OF A NATURALIST. 1941. (IV) Autobiographical essays written by one who has both the trained eye of a scientist and the vision of a poet. He discusses natural beauty chiefly, and the quiet pleasures it brings to the botanist and zoologist.

Peattie, Donald Culross, editor *See* Audubon, John James.

Pennell, Mrs. Elizabeth Robins 1855-1936 **and Pennell, Joseph** 1857-1926 Americans both, long resident in England; she was the writer, he a celebrated etcher.

LIFE OF JAMES MCNEILL WHISTLER. 6th edition, 1920. (II) The personality of the expatriate American artist was a most interesting if not entirely a pleasant one. The Pennells, long his intimate friends, manage to transmit every atom of its pungent flavor.

Pennell, Joseph Stanley 1908- American novelist.

HISTORY OF ROME HANKS AND KINDRED MATTERS. 1944. (IV) "A work of unusual talent and, among other things, the best novel about the Civil War I have read with the natural exception of *The Red Badge of Courage*."—Hamilton Basso, in *New Yorker*.

Pepys, Samuel 1633-1703 English official in the days of the Stuart Restoration.

DIARY. (I) Covers the years 1660-69, during which London was grievously smitten by both plague and fire. Richard Garnett said that no other work of this kind in the world's literature is half as fascinating, while Andrew Lang called Pepys "the most amusing of gossips and . . . the only one who tells the truth." The diary was written in cipher and remained unprinted for more than 150 years. (It is readily accessible in Everyman's Library and Modern Library editions.)

Percy, Thomas, editor 1729-1811 English bishop and antiquarian scholar.

RELIQUES OF ANCIENT ENGLISH POETRY. 1765. (I) This priceless collection of the old ballads and songs of England "marks an important stage in literary history, the starting-point of the modern study of ancient poetry." (A modern edition, in two volumes, was added to Everyman's Library in 1906.)

Percy, William Alexander 1885-1942 American lawyer, poet, soldier.

LANTERNS ON THE LEVEE; RECOLLECTIONS OF A PLANTER'S SON. 1941. (IV) A Southern aristocrat's quiet assertion of his stoic faith. "You may not agree with all Mr. Percy says, but you have rarely heard his side stated with so much wisdom, gentleness and wit. . . . A very creditable swan-song."—*New Republic.*

Perelman, Sidney Joseph 1904- American humorist.

BEST OF PERELMAN. 1947. Fifty essays, plentifully seasoned with the condiments that add zest to Perelman's zany confections.

Pérez Galdós, Benito 1845-1920 Spanish novelist and dramatist; probably the foremost novelist of his day in Spain.

DOÑA PERFECTA. 1876. "This exquisite romance is a vivid description of life in a Spanish provincial town just before the Carlist War."—Keller.

Perkins, Frances (Mrs. Paul Wilson) 1882- United States Secretary of Labor, 1933-45; the first woman cabinet officer.

THE ROOSEVELT I KNEW. 1946. "The best thing that has been written about Roosevelt and I doubt that it will be improved on for a long time. . . . Miss Perkins knows that he wasn't a sun god. Consequently she is able to see him without getting spots before her eyes."—H. Basso, in *New Yorker.*

Perkins, Maxwell E. 1884-1947 Famous American editor; patiently encouraged Wolfe, Fitzgerald, Hemingway, and other writers.

EDITOR TO AUTHOR; selected and edited by J. H. Wheelock. 1950. "This collection of letters . . . takes us out of the library or book store straight into the publisher's inner office and the author's study." —John Mason Brown, in *Saturday Review of Literature.* "Here is a self-portrait of a man who through years of grinding effort gave the utmost to inspiring and perfecting the work of others."—Geoffrey Parsons, in *New York Herald Tribune*.

Perry, Ralph Barton   1876-   American professor of philosophy at Harvard.

PURITANISM AND DEMOCRACY. 1944. "This is the best thing of its kind since Santayana's *Character and Opinion in the United States.*"—H. Basso, in *New Yorker*. "As a weighty contribution to the intelligent appreciation and understanding of Americanism and the traditional bases thereof, this book deserves a high priority rating." —*American Historical Review*.

Pershing, John J.   1860-1948   Commander-in-Chief, American Expeditionary Force, in World War I.

MY EXPERIENCES IN THE WORLD WAR. 2v. 1931. (III) This must always be an interesting and important book in the field of American history. It is more straightforward than most war memoirs. Won the Pulitzer prize for history.

Pertinax (pseudonym of André Géraud)   1882-   French journalist.

GRAVEDIGGERS OF FRANCE. 1944. (IV) "The most authoritative and informative account of the French military and political collapse and of the establishment of the feeble Vichy dictatorship."— W. H. Chamberlin, in *Atlantic*.

Peterkin, Julia Mood   1880-   American novelist who specializes in sympathetic stories of the plantation Negroes she knows so well.

BLACK APRIL. 1927. (III) Scene: a plantation in the South Carolina lowlands; chief character: a gigantic Negro foreman; other characters: all Negroes. "Certainly the finest work produced thus far dealing with the American Negro."—*Nation*, 1927.

BRIGHT SKIN. 1932. (III) Striking story of modern Negro life on a Carolina sea-island plantation.

SCARLET SISTER MARY. 1928. (III) The reader fully shares the author's interest in and respect for the lively Negress of unconventional morals, who is her heroine. Won a Pulitzer prize in 1929.

Peters, Arthur A. (Fritz Peters) 1913- American author.

WORLD NEXT DOOR. 1949. "Story of a young man's fight back to sanity as a patient in a veterans' hospital."—*Book Review Digest.* "A magnificent novel. . . . A first book, it is probably largely autobiographical; but no qualifications are necessary because of either of these facts. To my mind it is the best piece of fiction yet produced by a veteran of the recent war."—Hollis Alpert, in *Saturday Review of Literature.*

Peterson, Florence 1894-

AMERICAN LABOR UNIONS; WHAT THEY ARE AND HOW THEY WORK. 1945. "This comprehensive handbook is written in as popular a style as serious discussion of the subject would allow; it is highly informative."—*Commonweal.*

Petrie, Sir William Flinders 1853-1942 English archaeologist.

SOCIAL LIFE IN ANCIENT EGYPT. 1923. "Clear and concise account of the way men lived in the Nile Valley in ancient times."— *A.L.A. Catalog,* 1926.

MAKING OF EGYPT. 1939. "Terse, forceful exposition, characteristic of the doyen of Egyptology."—*Manchester Guardian.*

Petronius Arbiter, Gaius Died 66 A.D. Director of entertainments at Nero's court.

SATYRICON. A romance which paints a realistic picture of the social manners and vices of the Imperial Age in Rome, with specimens of the *plebeius sermo,* or language of the common people. It is interesting also as a very early specimen of fiction. English translations are available in Modern Library and Black and Gold Library editions.

Petry, Ann Lane 1911-

THE STREET. 1946. A novel about the Negro in Harlem. "A fine piece of realistic writing conveying what it means to be a Negro in this white world. Comparable to 'An American Tragedy' in stature and execution."—*Library Journal.*

Phelps, William Lyon 1865-1943 Notably benevolent and enthusiastic American literary critic.

ADVANCE OF THE ENGLISH NOVEL. 1916. (II) Readable survey of more than a hundred English and American novelists from Daniel Defoe to William De Morgan.

ESSAYS ON RUSSIAN NOVELISTS. 1911. (II) Discussions of Gogol, Turgenev, Dostoievski, Tolstoi, Gorki, Chekhov, Artsybashev, Andreev, and Kuprin.

SOME MAKERS OF AMERICAN LITERATURE. 1923. Sympathetic, readable lectures on Franklin, Jonathan Edwards, Cooper, Hawthorne, Webster, Lincoln, Emerson, and Mark Twain.

AUTOBIOGRAPHY WITH LETTERS. 1939. (IV) "As the pages roll on, the wonder grows that any one human being should have been able to do so many different things and get such fun out of all of them. . . . Few men since Samuel Pepys have had such unflagging zest for life."—S. V. Benét, in *New York Herald Tribune.*

Phillips, Stephen 1868-1915 English poet, dramatist, actor, whose work, overpraised in his youth, came later to be undervalued. His best play is probably

PAOLO AND FRANCESCA. 1897. (II) A four-act tragedy in blank verse on a theme from Dante; beautiful and stately.

Phillpotts, Eden 1862- Prolific English novelist—a lesser Hardy—who took Devonshire and Dartmoor for his province, even as Hardy took Wessex (Dorset).

CHILDREN OF THE MIST. 1899. (I) A good example of his best work. "Many of the dialogs and witticisms are very comic and racy in their broad Devon."—E. A. Baker.

THE GREY ROOM. 1920. (II) Mystery story. A series of deaths occur in the grey room. (Highly commended by "S. S. Van Dine," a very competent judge.)

Pieshkov, A. M. *See* Gorki, Maxim, pseudonym.

Pinckney, Josephine 1895- American novelist; born in Charleston, S.C.

THREE O'CLOCK DINNER. 1945. (IV) Story about two families in Charleston; one had money, the other breeding. These differences were but trifles to Dan Cupid. "A thoroughly satisfying novel.

. . . Miss Pinckney's success with an old formula shows how good old formulas can be when they are processed by a knowing hand."—*New York Times.*

Pindar 520(?)-443(?)**B.C.** Chief lyric poet of the ancient Greeks. His stately measures were imitated by Dryden in *Alexander's Feast.*

ODES. Their beauty is to some extent lost in translation, but Sir J. E. Sandys has achieved notable success in his version which appears with parallel Greek text in the Loeb Classical Library.

Pinero, Sir Arthur Wing 1855-1924 English author of social comedies, and of early "problem plays."

SECOND MRS. TANQUERAY. 1893. (I) This play about a woman with an unsavory past is Pinero's most famous production.

Pirandello, Luigi 1867-1936 Italian dramatist and novelist.

THREE PLAYS. 1922. (II) They are *Three Characters in Search of an Author, Henry IV,* and *Right You Are!* (*If You Think So!*)

THE LATE MATTIA PASCAL. 1905. In this novel the hero (a librarian) incautiously sheds his identity and is dismayed to find himself unable to resume it. In both plays and novels the author's theme is generally the riddle of personality and the power and prevalence of illusion as the dominant factor in all lives.

Plato 427-347 **B.C.** Greatest of Greek philosophers; disciple of Socrates, teacher of Aristotle. His works are mostly cast in the form of

DIALOGUES (I) in many of which his old master, Socrates, is cast as the questioner. The most famous of these are *The Republic* (a long treatise on the ideal state, often regarded as a separate work): *The Symposium,* or *Banquet,* which considers ideal love; *The Phaedo,* on immortality; *The Timaeus,* on the nature of the physical world; *The Apology*—the defense of Socrates; *The Laws; Crito;* and *Meno.* Standard translations of Plato are the one by Dr. Benjamin Jowett, and that by Fowler in the Loeb Classical Library.

Plautus 254(?)-184 **B.C.** Roman author of numerous

COMEDIES—of which about twenty survive. The best known are *The Captives, Trinummus, Menaechmi* (Shakespeare's *Comedy of Errors* is adapted from it), and *Aulularia* (the original of Molière's *L'Avare*).

Plievier, Theodor　　1892-　　German novelist.

STALINGRAD. 1948. Fictional account of the siege of Stalingrad, from the German point of view. "The most clinically realistic, the most horrifying novel about modern war. . . . A book which bears comparison with *All Quiet on the Western Front.*"—C. J. Rolo, in *Atlantic.*

Pliny the Younger　　62-114 A.D.　　Roman author and administrator.

LETTERS. (I) Though somewhat lacking in spontaneity—they were written with an eye on the general reader of the day—they are "the best extant contemporary authority for an important period of Roman history." See especially his account of the death of his uncle, Pliny the Elder, which was caused by the eruption of Vesuvius that destroyed and buried Pompeii; also his letter to the Emperor Trajan, with its information on the manners and customs of the primitive Christians and their treatment by the Roman administration.

Plotinus　　205(?)-270　　Neo-Platonism's chief exponent in Rome; born in Egypt.

THE ESSENCE OF PLOTINUS, compiled by Grace Turnbull. 1934. Includes extracts from the six *"Enneads."*

Plutarch　　46(?)-120(?) A.D.　　Greek biographer.

LIVES. Sometimes his work is called the *Parallel Lives*, because he arranged his biographies in pairs, a Roman's career set opposite a Greek's; *e.g.,* Alexander and Caesar, or Demosthenes and Cicero. Plutarch is always readable. Shakespeare drew upon him freely for classical plots and for striking descriptive passages. (*Cf.* the picture of Cleopatra's barge in *Antony and Cleopatra* with its description in the life of Marc Antony in Plutarch.)

Poe, Edgar Allan　　1809-49　　American short story writer, poet, and critic, whose life was as unhappy as it was short. One of the primary American authors. His work brought distinction to American letters during the second quarter of the Nineteenth Century, both at home and abroad.

TALES. (I) Their action takes place "in that dim region which stretches from the utmost limits of the probable to the weird confines of superstition and unreality." They are decked with beauty a-plenty of an unearthly sort. But humor is lacking unless one can find fun in the grinning mask of a death's-head.

POEMS. (I) "No other American poet," says John Macy, "has been so unanimously accepted by all the poets of the world." His verse, though often morbid, is always melodious.

CRITICAL ESSAYS. These are interesting, though often bitter or at least insufficiently objective. His *Philosophy of Composition* and *The Poetic Principle* are outstanding.

Pollard, John Albert   1901-

JOHN GREENLEAF WHITTIER, FRIEND OF MAN. 1949. Whittier as abolitionist, poet, philosopher, and political leader; with critical chapters on his writing. "This study views Whittier primarily as a social thinker, who used poetry incidentally as a weapon in his fight for social justice."—*Quarterly Booklist.*

Pollock, Sir Frederick   *See* Holmes, Oliver Wendell (1841-1935).

Polo, Marco   1254(?)-1324(?)   Venetian traveler.

BOOK OF MARCO POLO. 1496 (First Italian edition). (I) Account of his life and travels in Asia during the years 1271-95. He was for some years an official of Kublai Khan's empire. The passing of the centuries has raised rather than lowered this author's reputation for veracity.

Polybius   204-125(?) B.C.   Greek historian.

HISTORY OF ROME FROM 266 TO 146 B.C. This history was in forty books of which only the first five, plus some fragments, survive.

Poole, Ernest   1880-1950   American novelist.

THE HARBOR. 1915. (II) In this story of the Brooklyn waterfront the harbor is really the chief character. Its aspects, activities, and strife mold the hero's life from boyhood to manhood.

HIS FAMILY. 1917. (II) "An extraordinarily fine summary of the broad and perplexing theme of sex."—Percy Boynton. Carl Van Doren praised both this book and the more popular *The Harbor,* but thought this the better novel of the two. It won the Pulitzer prize for fiction in 1918.

Pope, Alexander   1688-1744   English poet and literary dictator of his age. Artificial, spiteful and often little, this indefatigable polisher of couplets has been called "the greatest of the world's machine poets." Yet there was greatness in him too, else it could not have been said probably with truth that only Shakespeare is more frequently quoted, often unconsciously, by the English-speaking peoples.

COMPLETE POETICAL WORKS. Cambridge edition, 1903. (I) Includes the *Essay on Man*—source of numberless popular quotations; *The Rape of the Lock*—"filagree work . . . the apotheosis of foppery and folly"; *The Dunciad*—in which he revenged himself upon and so immortalized sundry envious Grub Street hacks; *Epistle to Dr. Arbuthnot*—a satirical dialog in which he judges his own writings and abuses those of his rivals; *Essay on Criticism*—which won him fame, though written, he said, at the age of twelve; and many others. His translations of *The Iliad* and *The Odyssey* were immensely successful commercially, though stark old Homer could never recognize himself set forth in such mincing guise.

Poquelin, Jean Baptiste   *See* Molière, pseudonym.

Porcupine, Peter, pseudonym   *See* Cobbett, William.

Porter, Jane   1776-1850   English novelist.

SCOTTISH CHIEFS. 1810. (I) Romantic tale of love and war in the Scotland of the Thirteenth and Fourteenth Centuries. It should always be remembered to this author's credit that this book appeared before and not after the once phenomenally popular Waverley Novels of Sir Walter Scott.

Porter, Katherine Anne   1894-   American writer of short stories and short novels. "Miss Porter's style is, so to speak, perfection."—Glenway Wescott, in *New York Times*. "Although she errs in the direction of supersubtlety, her writing has a very rare poetic power, and her suggestiveness in this form is incomparable." —F. B. Millett. "The nearest American equivalent to Katherine Mansfield."—*Twentieth Century Authors*. "Katherine Anne Porter moves in the illustrious company headed by Hawthorne, Flaubert, and Henry James."—*Saturday Review of Literature*. "It is perhaps natural for an Englishman to compare her stories with those of Katherine Mansfield—and not entirely to Miss Porter's disadvantage."—Christopher Isherwood.

PALE HORSE, PALE RIDER; THREE SHORT NOVELS. 1939.

FLOWERING JUDAS, AND OTHER STORIES. 1935. "Brilliant technique in a variety of themes and settings."—*Good Reading*.

Leaning Tower, and Other Stories. 1944. (IV) "Miss Porter is absolutely a first rate artist."—Edmund Wilson, in *New Yorker*.

Porter, William Sydney   *See* Henry, O., pseudonym.

Pound, Ezra   1885-   American poet, born in Idaho; resided in Europe from 1907 till the end of World War II, when he was tried for treason as an active Fascist, acquitted on grounds of insanity, and committed to a mental hospital. Possessed of a brilliant mind, of great originality and extraordinary erudition, Pound has done more, said Carl Sandburg, "to incite new impulses in poetry than any other writer in the English language."

Personae: Collected Poems. 1926. "Pound has sought to communicate his poetry to us and failed. It is a tragedy since he is our best poet."—W. C. Williams.

Cantos. 1948. (Includes all of them, even the much discussed *Pisan Cantos*, written in prison.) "The monumental epic poem on which Pound has been at work for twenty years."

Letters. 1950. "This stimulating and illuminating collection of [384] letters, covering 1908-41, is essential to any study of Pound."— *Kirkus*. "Extremely helpful reading for any one who wants to write poems that are more than echoes or heart throbs. . . . Nobody who writes poems can afford to miss reading this book."—Malcolm Cowley, in *New York Herald Tribune*.

Pratt, Fletcher   1897-   American author, chiefly of war books.

The Marines' War: an Account of the Struggle for the Pacific, from Both American and Japanese Sources. 1948. "A fine service history written with clarity and intelligence; one that the Marines will welcome as an authoritative corrective to their own unit histories."—*Time*.

Prescott, William H.   1796-1859   American historian. As Motley took Holland's history for his province, and Parkman the struggle of England and France for North America, so Prescott's name will always recall his histories of the Spanish discoveries and conquests in the Americas, and their backgrounds.

Reign of Ferdinand and Isabella. 1838. (I) Considered his best work by some judges, this book has scarcely the appeal for Americans as have his *Mexico* and *Peru*.

CONQUEST OF MEXICO. 1843. (I) Dickens was enthusiastic about this book. Said he, "From beginning to end the whole history is enchanting and full of genius."

CONQUEST OF PERU. 1847. (I) "Boys read his *Mexico* and *Peru* as they read the *Arabian Nights*; critics can point to few flaws in the accuracy of his judgment."—John Nichol.

Prévost, Antoine François (Abbé Prévost) 1697-1763 French novelist and Benedictine *abbé*.

MANON LESCAUT. 1731. Story of a young man ruined by an extravagant passion for a beautiful but unworthy woman. It has been the subject of operas by both Puccini and Massenet.

Priestley, John Boynton 1894- English novelist and playwright.

GOOD COMPANIONS. 1929. (III) Long, humorous and sentimental novel in the Dickens tradition and with picaresque qualities.

ANGEL PAVEMENT. 1930. (III) Ample, leisurely novel about the shabby denizens of a London office. Many critics consider it a better book than *The Good Companions*, though not so well tailored to the popular taste.

Pringle, Henry Fowler 1897- American journalist and biographer.

THEODORE ROOSEVELT. 1931. (III) A biography, not a panegyric. It tells the whole story, and is probably the best of many books on the subject. It won a Pulitzer prize.

LIFE AND TIMES OF WILLIAM H. TAFT. 2v. 1939. (IV) This biography was highly praised by William Allen White in *Saturday Review of Literature*, by Ellery Sedgwick in *Atlantic*, by M. A. DeWolfe Howe in *Harvard Law Review*, by H. S. Commager in *New York Herald Tribune*, and many others.

Proust, Marcel 1871-1922 French novelist. "With James Joyce and Thomas Mann he is ranked among the greatest novelists of the Twentieth Century."—*Reader's Encyclopedia*, 1948.

REMEMBRANCE OF THINGS PAST. 7 parts. 1923-32. (II and III) A vast digressive novel, largely autobiographical, of Parisian life. "Exhibits and analyzes the many-fibered texture of French society, particularly in its upper strata. The protagonist is the hypersensitive author; the method, largely revery; the result, a tapestry for scene lovers, psychologists, and philosophers."—*Good Reading.* The seven parts of the work were separately published in English as follows: *Swann's Way* (1923), *Within a Budding Grove* (1924), *The Guermantes Way* (1925), *Cities of the Plain* (1928), *The Captive* (1929), *The Sweet Cheat Gone* (1930), and *The Past Recaptured* (1932).

Pupin, Michael   1858-1935   Serbian immigrant and American physicist.

FROM IMMIGRANT TO INVENTOR. 1923. (II) Intensely interesting autobiography, whose author had a gift for making science intelligible to the layman. Won a Pulitzer prize in 1924.

Pushkin, Alexander Sergeyevitch   1799-1837   Russian poet, dramatist, fictionist. "Undeniably and essentially the great national poet of Russia," and indeed the first great author Russia produced.

BORIS GODUNOV. 1826. Historical tragedy of a czar of Russia in the early Seventeenth Century. An opera by Moussorgsky founded on this tragedy was first presented in America in 1913.

EUGENE ONEGIN. 1931. Somewhat Byronic narrative poem, later dramatized in Tchaikovsky's opera of the same name. An English translation of the poem appeared in 1881.

CAPTAIN'S DAUGHTER, AND OTHER TALES. The translation, by Natalie Duddington contains five representative stories. It is included in Everyman's Library.

Pyle, Ernie (Ernest Taylor Pyle)   1900-1945   The most widely read and widely beloved correspondent of World War II; killed in action on Ie, a Pacific islet.

HERE IS YOUR WAR. 1943. (IV) Describes the campaign in North Africa, emphasizing as always the human qualities of the American infantryman.

BRAVE MEN. 1944. (IV) Describes the fighting of our men in Europe from the landing on Sicily, June 1943, to the liberation of Paris, September 1944.

Quick, Herbert   1861-1925   American lawyer, journalist, novelist.

VANDEMARK'S FOLLY. 1922. (II) Fine novel describing pioneer journeys to Iowa in the 1840's and 1860's, partly by way of the Erie Canal, with interesting adventures by the way, caused by claim-jumpers, frontier law, the underground railway, etc. The first volume in an excellent trilogy, it is followed by *The Hawkeye* (1923) and *The Invisible Woman* (1924).

Quiller-Couch, Sir Arthur T.   1863-1944   English critic, essayist, novelist, anthologist, professor of English literature.

SPLENDID SPUR. 1889. Adventures of King Charles's messenger on a hazardous journey from Oxford to Cornwall in 1642. An excellent historical novel.

STUDIES IN LITERATURE. 3v. 1918-30. (II) Intimate, unacademic essays on English literature.

ON THE ART OF WRITING. 1916. Friendly talks to undergraduates which, said *The Times*, "constitute the beginnings of a liberal education in literary style."

Quiller-Couch, Sir Arthur T., editor

OXFORD BOOK OF ENGLISH VERSE. New edition, 1939. (I) A standard anthology, and an excellent one; but only a few American poets are included.

Quinn, Arthur Hobson   1875-   Scholar, teacher, and writer on American literature.

HISTORY OF THE AMERICAN DRAMA FROM THE CIVIL WAR TO THE PRESENT DAY. Revised edition, 1945. An excellent survey which follows his *History of the American Drama from the Beginning to the Civil War*, Second edition, 1943.

Rabelais, François   1495(?)-1553   French satirist and Renaissance scholar.

GARGANTUA AND PANTAGRUEL. 1532-62. (I) An immense, rambling, burlesque fairy tale of two giants, father and son, in which "the author's amazing humor runs riot amidst the wildest extravagances and the grossest indecencies." Rabelais was one of the most learned men and advanced thinkers of his time. He used his jester's privilege to express opinions which, without the diverting jingle of his cap and bells, would have brought serious trouble upon him. The book as we have it today was some thirty years in the writing, and was published bit by bit. There have been several English translations, but that by Urquhart and Motteux, published 1653-94, remains a favorite.

Racine, Jean 1639-99 French neoclassic, tragic dramatist.

PLAYS. 1663-91 (I) The most important, perhaps, are *Andromache* (1667), his first great success; *Iphigénie* (1674), "considered by Voltaire the greatest work that the French stage has produced"; *Athalie* (1691), "often spoken of by French critics as the most perfect of his works"; and the particularly painful *Phèdre* (1677).

Radcliffe, Mrs. Ann 1764-1823 British novelist; "the Queen of Horror."

MYSTERIES OF UDOLPHO. 1794. (I) One of the best of the Gothic romances. Warranted to make the flesh creep if the reader is very young and not overburdened with a sense of humor. Some say that Lord Byron spent a lifetime trying to act like one of Mrs. Radcliffe's villains.

Raleigh, Sir Walter 1552-1618 English soldier, sailor, courtier, colonist, and author.

HISTORY OF THE WORLD. 1614. "This huge composition is one of the principal glories of Seventeenth-Century literature, and takes a very prominent place in the history of English prose."—Edmund Gosse. It was written, with the help of Ben Jonson and others, during the dozen years of Raleigh's imprisonment in the Tower of London. He was released shortly after *The History* was first published, but beheaded four years later. Many readers have been surprised and a few disappointed to find that the work extends only to about 200 B.C.

Ramayana *See* Mahabharata.

Randall, James Garfield 1881- American student, teacher, and author of books on American history.

LINCOLN THE LIBERAL STATESMAN. 1947. An interesting and successful book. "Professor Randall well sustains his commanding position as a Lincoln scholar."

Raspe, R. E., editor *See* Münchhausen, K. F. H., Baron von.

Rawlings, Marjorie Kinnan 1896- American novelist; member, National Institute of Arts and Letters.

THE YEARLING. 1938. (IV) Story of one year in the life of a Florida boy and his beloved fawn—a year that ended in tragedy. As Jody said, "Life knocks you down but you stand up again." The *Atlantic* pronounced this "a distinguished book," and it won the Pulitzer prize for fiction in 1939.

CROSS CREEK. 1942. (IV) Describes the life and people of the tiny and remote Florida hamlet where for a long time the author has lived, raised oranges, and written stories.

Reade, Charles 1814-84 English novelist. Many of his stories were attacks on social abuses prevalent in his Victorian day. These books were always benevolent, sometimes beneficent as well. But they have disappeared from the public consciousness. Only his masterpiece is read today. This is the

CLOISTER AND THE HEARTH. 1861. (I) Presents a lively and unforgettable panorama of Fifteenth-Century Europe in the course of the hero's journeys through Holland, France, Germany, and Italy. Stirring adventures follow one another in brisk succession, and through the whole runs the thread of a noble and moving love story. This book remains, after nearly a hundred years, one of the very best of historical novels.

Reinach, Salomon 1858-1932 French archaeologist and art historian.

APOLLO: AN ILLUSTRATED MANUAL OF THE HISTORY OF ART THROUGHOUT THE AGES. New revised edition, 1935. (I and II) This book has no rival in its combination of completeness and compactness. Includes hundreds of marginal illustrations.

Remarque, Erich Maria 1897- German novelist. Fought in German army in World War I. Deprived of citizenship by the Nazis in 1938, he came to America the following year and became an American citizen in 1947.

ALL QUIET ON THE WESTERN FRONT. 1929. (III) Tale of a German private and his stoical endurance of the horrors of World War I. The book has been translated into dozens of languages and millions of copies have been sold.

THE ROAD BACK. 1931. (III) Story of German soldiers after World War I and the hardships of their readjustment to civilian life.

FLOTSAM. 1941. Story of World War I's political exiles—men without a country.

ARCH OF TRIUMPH. 1945. Paris, just before the German occupation in World War II, is the scene of this novel describing what the Germans' smashing temporary success did to Europe.

Renan, Ernest   1823-92   French scholar, historian and critic. He studied for the priesthood but lost his faith in Catholic orthodoxy.

LIFE OF JESUS. 1863. (I) He believed Jesus to have been, morally, the most perfect *man* the world has ever known, but considered the miraculous and supernatural elements of the Gospels "unconscious distortions of natural incidents." The landscape, costume, and manners of the Holy Land are described by word-painting of great warmth and richness of color.

Repplier, Agnes   1855-1950   No American has excelled her in mastery of the familiar essay.

PHILADELPHIA: THE PLACE AND THE PEOPLE. New edition, 1925. With charm and clarity she describes her native city and tells its story.

FIRESIDE SPHINX. 1901. (II) Sprightly discussion of the cat's role in legend, literature, and history.

HAPPY HALF-CENTURY. 1908. (II) "Reflections, spiced with smiling malice, on the pious, ornate, and sentimental products of the years 1775-1825."—*Best Books*, 1908.

PÈRE MARQUETTE. 1929. (III) Engaging book about the Jesuit missionary who explored the headwaters of the Mississippi. His story is both moving and ennobling and it is here told with quietly restrained enthusiasm.

IN PURSUIT OF LAUGHTER. 1936. Traces the history of humor in English life and literature from the Middle Ages to the present day. "A book of delight, to be read and digested with smiles."— *Atlantic*.

EIGHT DECADES. 1937. The sixteen essays here presented from her earlier volumes are preceded by a sketch in which the author recalls some of the events of her life, decade by decade, up to her eightieth birthday.

Reymont, Wladyslaw   1868-1925   Polish novelist.

THE PEASANTS. 4v. 1924-25. (II) A long novel whose pages give us a close-up of great and small events in the daily life of a group of Polish villagers. Each volume presents the developments of one of the four seasons, from autumn round to summer. Won the Nobel prize for literature in 1924.

Reynolds, Sir Joshua   1723-92   English portrait painter; first president, Royal Academy.

DISCOURSES ON ART. 1778. (I) The author was one of the world's great painters and his advice is said still to be of value and "expressed in language which could scarcely be improved." As Edmund Gosse remarked, "It was doubtless through his lifelong companionship with Johnson, Burke and Goldsmith that Reynolds learned to write the English language only a little less brilliantly than they."

Rhodes, James Ford   1848-1927   American historian; member, American Academy of Arts and Letters.

HISTORY OF THE UNITED STATES FROM THE COMPROMISE OF 1850 TO THE END OF THE [THEODORE] ROOSEVELT ADMINISTRATION. 9v. 1893-1922. (I and II) "Full, exact, and impartial."—*English Historical Review*.

HISTORY OF THE CIVIL WAR. 1917. (I and II) "Excellent one-volume history, not an abridgment of the author's previous work, but a fresh study based in part on later material. An achievement . . . in condensation and readableness."—*Best Books*, 1917.

Riasanovsky, Antonina   *See* Federova, Nina, pseudonym.

Ricardo, David   1772-1823   British economist.

PRINCIPLES OF POLITICAL ECONOMY AND TAXATION. 1817. (I) The masterpiece of "the classical school" of political economy. Its most important section is the detailed and profound exposition of the theory of rent.

Rice, Mrs Alice Hegan   1870-1942   Popular American novelist.

MRS. WIGGS OF THE CABBAGE PATCH. 1901. (II) An unpretentious little classic of optimism which has been translated into several foreign languages. Its cheery picture of human courage and kindness in the face of trouble tugs at the heart-strings of wise and simple alike.

Rice, Elmer L. 1892- American playwright.

ADDING MACHINE. 1923. "Expressionistic 'play,' with its under-scored implications of the deadening effects of industrialism on the petty bourgeoisie."

STREET SCENE. 1929. A sordid, realistic drama, it runs the whole gamut of human life in a tenement house in the slums of New York. Awarded a Pulitzer prize in 1929.

Richard de Bury 1278-1345 Book-lover *in excelsis*; Bishop of Durham; Chancellor of Edward III. He endowed a lending library at Oxford.

PHILOBIBLON. 1345. A treatise on books and the loving care of them. The cornerstone of every orthodox bookman's library. Writ-ten in Latin, it was first translated into English some five centuries later.

Richardson, Dorothy M. 1882- English novelist.

PILGRIMAGE. 4v. in 12 parts. 1916-35. (II) Each part, with its own title, is an instalment in the soul-story of the heroine, as presented in a study of her "stream of consciousness." "This novelist aims at a sincere criticism of life, and to obtain perfect sin-cerity and a complete expression of herself she sacrifices many ac-cepted canons."—*Athenaeum.*

Richardson, Henry Handel (pseudonym of Mrs. Henrietta Richard-son Robertson) 1880(?)-1946 Australian novelist.

FORTUNES OF RICHARD MAHONY. 1930. (III) A trilogy con-sisting of *Australia Felix* (1917), *The Way Home* (1917), and *Ultima Thule* (1929). This very long story describes the rise and gradual decline of an Irish physician who emigrated to Australia at the time of the Gold Rush. It has been compared to Rolland's *Jean Christophe* and Mann's *Buddenbrooks.*

Richardson, Samuel 1689-1761 "The Father of the English Novel." "If you were to read Richardson for the story, your im-patience would be so much fretted that you would hang yourself. But you must read him for the sentiment, and consider the story as only giving occasion to the sentiment."—Samuel Johnson. But just how does one escape *drowning* in that sentimental ocean?

PAMELA, OR VIRTUE REWARDED. 1740. (I) Struggling fran-tically, the handsome servant-girl keeps her ardent master at arm's length for hundreds of perilous pages. To get her, he has to marry her. Thus was canny "virtue" rewarded. *Pamela* provoked Fielding to write his first novel, *Joseph Andrews*, a well-deserved parody of Richardson's sensational success.

CLARISSA. 1749. (I) Considered Richardson's masterpiece. This book also is in the form of myriads of very long letters written by the heroine to her confidante. And here too the virtue of a persecuted paragon of her sex is a thousand times endangered. She dies in the end, though, worn out by her troubles. Lady Mary Wortley Montagu confessed that she "was such an old fool" as to weep when she heard the news. As for Lord Macaulay, he confessed that a hundred years later he nearly cried his eyes out when he read the last volume.

SIR CHARLES GRANDISON. 1753. (I) The hero of this book is the author's *beau idéal* of an Eighteenth-Century gentleman. But most readers from Richardson's day to ours have strongly resented his priggishness. Hazlitt called him "the prince of coxcombs."

Richter, Conrad 1890- American novelist.

THE TREES. 1940. (IV) Historical novel about the long, slow trek of the pioneers over the Alleghanies through Pennsylvania to Ohio. "We close the book convinced that this is how the woodsmen in the great forests of the Northwest Territory really lived."—*Saturday Review of Literature*.

THE FIELDS. 1946. This story of farm life in old Ohio—a sequel to *The Trees*—is called by the *Yale Review* "a truly distinguished book"; and by the *United States Quarterly Booklist*, "a sensitive recreation of a passage in our history."

THE TOWN. 1950. The *United States Quarterly Booklist* called this concluding volume of the Richter trilogy "even richer and subtler than its predecessors." It was awarded the Pulitzer prize for fiction in 1951.

Riis, Jacob 1849-1914 American reformer-journalist; born in Denmark; friend and admirer of Theodore Roosevelt.

MAKING OF AN AMERICAN. 1901. (I and II) Autobiography of a good and useful man who was also a skillful writer. It is full of interest and inspiration.

Riley, James Whitcomb 1853-1916 American "Hoosier Poet."

COMPLETE POETICAL WORKS; preface by Donald Culross Peattie. n.d. (II) "He wrote humorously of the everyday life of rustic America. . . . He had genuine sympathy for ordinary folk and especially children, for animals, for nature. . . . He appeals urgently to the normal thoughts and feelings of the divine average."—*Cambridge History of American Literature.*

Roberts, Elizabeth Madox 1885-1941 American novelist who wrote usually about the people of Kentucky, her native state.

TIME OF MAN. 1926 and 1946. (III) Story of the hard life of a poverty-stricken Kentucky farm girl whose inborn nobility and love of beauty are in pathetic contrast with a sordid environment. The author's first novel and perhaps her best. It was translated into German, Swedish, and Norwegian.

GREAT MEADOW. 1930. (III) Fine, poetic, pioneer novel of the Dark and Bloody Ground—Kentucky, from 1774 to 1781.

BLACK IS MY TRUELOVE'S HAIR. 1938. (IV) "Chiefly rewarding for its excellent language wrought from the quaintness and rhythm of Kentucky speech."—*Christian Science Monitor.* It will repay a second reading. There are depths of significance that do not yield all their treasure at first glance.

Roberts, Kenneth 1885- American historical novelist; member, National Institute of Arts and Letters.

ARUNDEL. 1930. Benedict Arnold's secret expedition against Quebec is described in this dramatic story.

RABBLE IN ARMS; A CHRONICLE OF ARUNDEL AND OF THE BURGOYNE INVASION. 1933. (III) Sequel to *Arundel.* A stirring and realistic novel of the American Revolution. Benedict Arnold looms heroic. The Congress at Philadelphia is the villain of the piece.

NORTHWEST PASSAGE. 1937. (IV) Historical novel about Robert Rogers and his Rangers and the battles they fought with the Indians two centuries ago.

OLIVER WISWELL. 1940. (IV) Tale of the Revolutionary War with—strange!—a Tory hero. Carl Van Doren said this absorbing novel would revise the opinions held by most of its readers about the Revolution.

Roberts of Kandahar, Earl (Frederick Sleigh Roberts)   1832-1914   British soldier.

FORTY-ONE YEARS IN INDIA; FROM SUBALTERN TO COMMANDER-IN-CHIEF. 1897; new edition, 1915. (I) This book, covering the years 1852 to 1893, is the factual background for Kipling's stories and poems. Here is not the shadowy realm of mysticism and romance, but the matter-of-fact India of the soldier and the administrator. Yet in the everyday life of the sahib there was indeed romance and color enough to suit anybody.

Robertson, Mrs. Henrietta Richardson   See Richardson, Henry Handel, pseudonym.

Robinson, Edwin Arlington   1869-1935   American poet; thrice a winner of the Pulitzer prize for poetry; member, American Academy of Arts and Letters.

COLLECTED POEMS. 1946. (II and III) Perhaps because Robinson's verse is four parts intellect to one part emotion he has been called the Henry James of American poetry. Amy Lowell described his work in three words—*difficult and beautiful.* But in comparison with some of our later poets his "difficultness" is hardly formidable at all.

UNTRIANGULATED STARS: LETTERS TO DE FOREST SMITH, 1890-1906. 1948. "The book is a record of the building of Robinson's character and habits, and it is also the record of the making of a major poetic mind. Both are fascinating to watch."—*Springfield Republican.*

Robinson, James Harvey   1863-1936   American historian.

MIND IN THE MAKING: THE RELATION OF INTELLIGENCE TO SOCIAL REFORM. 1921 and 1936. (II) Plea for an open mind and honest thinking: why men fail to solve the problems of the day. H. G. Wells called it "a cardinal book."

HUMANIZING OF KNOWLEDGE. 1926. (II) A call for the popularization of scientific knowledge. E. E. Slosson, who knew about such things, said that in a hundred pages this book contains more about the things that matter than many a thousand-page book.

Roeder, Ralph   1890-   American historical scholar and writer.

JUAREZ AND HIS MEXICO; A BIOGRAPHICAL HISTORY. 2v. 1947. Covers the whole story of the Mexican struggle for independence.

It is a book for the scholar rather than the general reader. "Probably the most definitive work on Mexico ever written in English."—*American Historical Review*.

Rogers, Agnes (Mrs. Frederick Lewis Allen)   1893-   and Allen, Frederick Lewis   1890-   American author and editor.

I REMEMBER DISTINCTLY; A FAMILY ALBUM OF THE AMERICAN PEOPLE. 1947. Five hundred pictures and 37,000 words of text that present the United States as it was between the World Wars, 1918-41.

Rolland, Romain   1866-1944   French author and musicologist.

JEAN CHRISTOPHE. 3v. in 1. Modern Library. n.d. (I) The hero is a musical genius. This is the story of him and of his mind, from birth to death. Originally published (1905-12) in ten volumes, it is the first of the many modern *romans-fleuve* which have since appeared, and was hailed by the critics as the most important title published in the Twentieth-Century's first decade. It won the Nobel prize in 1915.

Rölvaag, Ole Edvart   1876-1931   Norwegian-born immigrant who became an American college professor and novelist.

GIANTS IN THE EARTH; A SAGA OF THE PRAIRIE. 1927. (III) Story of the struggles of a group of Norwegian settlers in South Dakota. One of those strange books which are American in setting and in point of view, while wholly European in their art. (Like all its author's works, this book was originally written in Norwegian.)

Romains, Jules (pseudonym of Louis Farigoule)   1885-   French novelist; member, French Academy.

MEN OF GOOD WILL. 14v. 1933-46. (III and IV) This monster *roman-fleuve* is an attempt to present another *Comédie Humaine*— this time a survey of all sections of Parisian life in the Twentieth Century. The fourteenth and last volume, called *Seventh of October*, is "notable for its recreation of the atmosphere of anxiety in France in 1933," while the first volume describes some of the happenings of 1908. *Verdun*, the strongest novel of the series, shows us French society as it was during the grim second winter of World War I.

Roosevelt, Eleanor   1884-   Wife of Franklin Roosevelt; niece of Theodore Roosevelt. Always interested in social welfare and after her husband's death prominent in the worlds of journalism, radio, television, and the United Nations.

This I Remember. 1949. The second part of her autobiography; the first having been *This Is My Story* (1937). "Its fascination comes almost less from its sidelights on F.D.R. than from its candid and beguiling revelation of a woman who is in her own right one of the most remarkable figures of our time."—Arthur Schlesinger, Jr., in *Saturday Review of Literature.*

Roosevelt, Franklin Delano   1882-1945   American statesman; Thirty-second president of the United States, 1933-45.

Public Papers and Addresses; compiled and edited by Samuel I. Rosenman. 5v. 1938. (IV) "A source book indispensable to any student of the recent past or of the near future."—*Saturday Review of Literature.*

F.D.R.: His Personal Letters; edited by Elliott Roosevelt. Vols. 1-2. 1947-48. This first volume covers his first years, to his engagement at twenty-two; the second covers the years 1905-28. The *New Yorker* calls them "engaging books; the young Roosevelt had the knack of putting his personality into his letters."

Roosevelt, Theodore   1858-1919   Twenty-sixth president of the United States; member, American Academy of Arts and Letters.

Winning of the West. 4v. 1889-96. (I) History of the advance of the pioneers beyond the Alleghanies.

Strenuous Life. 1900. (I) Stimulating essays, with title characteristic of the author.

Theodore Roosevelt, an Autobiography. 1913. (II) "A book of extraordinary personal fascination."—*Boston Transcript.*

Letters to His Children. 1919. (II) These delightful letters, written by the most interesting personality of his generation, reveal him in many new aspects. They will please both old and young readers.

Ross, Leonard Q., pseudonym   *See* Rosten, Leo C.

Rossetti, Christina 1830-94 English poet of Italian parentage. The sister of Dante Gabriel Rossetti, she was a member of the Pre-Raphaelite group.

POETICAL WORKS. "Her most characteristic strain is where . . . pathos blends with, or passes into, the utterance of religious awe, unstained and unweakened by any craven fear."—George Saintsbury.

Rossetti, Dante Gabriel 1828-82 English poet and painter, of Italian parentage; the most distinguished of the Pre-Raphaelite Brotherhood. (See Winwar's *Poor Splendid Wings.*)

POEMS AND TRANSLATIONS. 1850-70. (I) "Rossetti's luscious lines seldom fail to cast a spell."—Augustine Birrell. William Morris considered his sonnets "unexampled in the English language since Shakespeare's, for depth of thought and felicity of expression."

Rostand, Edmond 1868-1918 French dramatist and poet; member, French Academy.

CYRANO DE BERGERAC. 1897. (I) This play in verse (whose big-nosed hero is a historic character—a poet and duellist of the Seventeenth Century) was one of the greatest stage successes of the late Nineteenth and early Twentieth Centuries, both in France and America.

L'AIGLON. 1900. (I) A play about the Eaglet—Napoleon's pathetic, ill-starred son. It was only less successful than *Cyrano*, both in France and the United States.

CHANTECLER. 1910. (I and II) A strange but delightful fantastic allegory about a rooster. It was not a popular stage success because it needed not only artistry in scenery and costume, but also a deal of explaining.

Rosten, Leo C. (Leonard Q. Ross, pseudonym) 1908- Polish-born American sociologist and humorist.

EDUCATION OF HYMAN KAPLAN, by Leonard Q. Ross. 1937. (IV) The education was achieved in the "American Night Preparatory School for Adults," and this book about it was said to be "the funniest and kindest book of the year."

HOLLYWOOD, THE MOVIE COLONY; THE MOVIE MAKERS. 1941. "He has no axes to grind or vitriol to throw, and the industry as a whole is bound to find a great deal of useful information in the pages of this penetrating analysis."—*Nation.*

Rostovtzeff, Michael Ivanovich　　1870-　　Russian-born American historian.

SOCIAL AND ECONOMIC HISTORY OF THE ROMAN EMPIRE. 1926. "Professor Rostovtzeff's book will probably rank among the most notable contributions to the subject since Gibbon's."—A. J. Toynbee, in *Nation and Athenaeum*.

Roth, Cecil　　1899-　　English scholar and historian.

JEWISH CONTRIBUTION TO CIVILIZATION. 1940. "For all who have an open mind the book should be a valuable corrective of the racial nonsense that is poisoning European thought."—*Manchester Guardian*.

Rourke, Constance M.　　1885-1941　　American author, generally of biographies.

AMERICAN HUMOR; A STUDY OF THE NATIONAL CHARACTER. 1931. (III) History, description and interpretation of the comic spirit in America, from Sam Slick to Will Rogers. A rare fruit of scholarship; ripe, juicy, and flavorsome.

AUDUBON. 1936. (IV) Superbly illustrated. "In this life Miss Rourke has done for Audubon what he did for the birds of his new country. She has painted him in his habitat, and alive."—S. V. Benét, in *New York Herald Tribune*.

Rousseau, Jean Jacques　　1712-88　　French author and philosopher; perhaps the Eighteenth Century's most influential personality.

JULIE, OR THE NEW HÉLOISE. 1761. Chiefly interesting as the prototype of the novel which stresses both the sentimental and the picturesque.

ÉMILE. 1762. (I) Pedagogical romance, advocating *natural* religion and *natural* methods of instruction. It influenced Pestalozzi, Froebel, and other educational theorists, and may be said to be the germ—or Pandora's box—whence sprang progressive education.

THE SOCIAL CONTRACT. 1762. (I) Theoretical treatise on the origins and organization of government and the rights of citizens. It became one of the bases for the democratic revolutions which followed during the next hundred years.

CONFESSIONS. 1781-88. (I) Till Boswell's diary was published this book could be called the most shameless revelation of the human soul ever recorded. But the reader should be warned that it ranks higher in frankness than in veracity. In style and in human interest, however, *The Confessions* leave nothing to be desired. This was the favorite book of both Emerson and George Eliot.

Royce, Josiah 1856-1916 American philosopher, whose clear, distinguished style helps to make his books readable.

PROBLEM OF CHRISTIANITY. 2v. 1913. (I) "A philosopher's able statement and defense of his faith."

PHILOSOPHY OF LOYALTY. 1908. (I) "Consideration of loyalty as the central spirit of the moral and reasonable life of man."— *A.L.A. Catalog.*

Rukeyser, Muriel 1913- American poet and biographer.

WILLARD GIBBS: AMERICAN GENIUS. 1942. (IV) Definitive biography of the little known physicist whom the author ranks with Lincoln, Melville, and Whitman as among the greatest men of his time. Clifton Fadiman hails him as "the greatest intellect in our country's history." The book won an award from the American Academy of Arts and Letters.

Rusk, Ralph Leslie 1888- American author, editor, and professor of English at Columbia University.

LIFE OF RALPH WALDO EMERSON. 1949. Based largely on Emerson's manuscripts, journal, and letters. The *Quarterly Booklist* declares it to be "the fullest and most painstakingly accurate biography of Emerson yet attempted." And Odell Shepard, in the *Yale Review*, describes it as "the amplest and most fully documented biography of the Concord sage . . . a highly readable book, seldom brilliant or exciting or profound, but sufficiently enlivened by quiet humor and warmed by an enthusiasm that stops well short of idolatry."

Ruskin, John 1819-1900 English critic and theorist upon the fine arts, literature, ethics, and political economy. "The cardinal principle that runs through all his teaching can be stated in a line. It is that men—men and not the works of men, men and not materials, or machines, or gold, or even pictures or statues or public buildings—should be the prime objects of our care and reverence and love."—Edward Dowden.

SEVEN LAMPS OF ARCHITECTURE. 1849. (I) "The first treatise in English to teach the real significance of architecture as the most trustworthy record of the life and faith of nations."—Charles Eliot Norton.

KING OF THE GOLDEN RIVER. 1851. A charming fairy tale, written in 1841, for the little girl whom he married seven years later.

STONES OF VENICE. 3v. 1851-53. (I) "His greatest work." "The germ of all his teaching as a social reformer is found in that chapter on The Nature of Gothic."—Washington Gladden.

MODERN PAINTERS. 5v. 1843-60. (I) "The author's most important and safest writing on art. Nowhere else are the moralist's and the nature-lover's view of fine art so well expressed as in the third and fourth volumes."—Sturgis and Krehbiel.

SESAME AND LILIES. 1865. (I) Lectures on books and their uses, on the education and influence of women, and on the mystery of life and its arts.

PRAETERITA. 1885-88. Autobiographical. Leslie Stephen called it "one of the most charming examples of the most charming kind of literature." It contains the story of his religious development.

Russell, Bertrand (Earl Russell) 1872- English philosopher and radical thinker; imprisoned as a pacifist during World War I. Often in conflict with the authorities, but perhaps the greatest of England's living thinkers.

WHY MEN FIGHT: A METHOD OF ABOLISHING THE INTERNATIONAL DUEL. 1917. (II) "Seeks the influences which must be developed to avoid future conflicts."—*A.L.A. Catalog*, 1926. (Banned in England as pacifistic.)

WHAT I BELIEVE. 1925. (II) "An ethical creed from the scientific standpoint . . . maintains that moral rules ought not to be such as to render instinctive happiness impossible."—*Booklist*, 1925.

OUTLINE OF PHILOSOPHY. 1927. (III) "Philosophy as it has been affected by the most recent discoveries of science, both physical and psychological. Includes a summary of Mr. Russell's own philosophical system which he calls 'a neutral monism.'"

CONQUEST OF HAPPINESS. 1930. (III) A guide to the fuller enjoyment of life. "The author knows just what he wants to say, and says it brilliantly. . . . The worth of a guide is in its omissions as much as in its contents."—*Spectator*.

FREEDOM VERSUS ORGANIZATION, 1814-1914. 1934. "Brilliant epitome of the teachings of Nineteenth-Century exponents of economic doctrine."—Helen Haines.

POWER; A NEW SOCIAL ANALYSIS. 1938. (IV) "A brilliant book, one of the most stimulating, as well as one of the most horrifying that I have read for some time. The horror is in the subject matter; the stimulus, in its treatment."—C. E. M. Joad, in *New Statesman.*

HISTORY OF WESTERN PHILOSOPHY. 1945. "A critical review of philosophy's social background."—*Good Reading.* "The masterwork of the ablest philosopher of our day."—Helen Haines.

HUMAN KNOWLEDGE; ITS SCOPE AND LIMITS. 1948. A book about man and the universe. Many will find it difficult reading; but, as the *New Yorker* says, "It's something just to have been up that high."

Russell, George William ("A. E.") 1867-1935 Irish mystic, poet, painter, critic, and political reformer.

SELECTED POEMS. 1935. (II) "It has the stamp of permanence."—*Saturday Review.* "The soul of poetry, the rapture, the spiritual exaltation, the glad consciousness of kinship between the mind of man and the moods of the earth."—Harold Williams.

Russell, W. Clark 1844-1911 British sailor and novelist.

WRECK OF THE *Grosvenor.* 1875. (I) At once a stirring tale of romantic adventure and a realistic picture of the life of the old-time sailor.

Rylee, Robert 1908- American novelist; born in Memphis.

DEEP, DARK RIVER. 1935. (III) This fine story of Negro life in Mississippi—a first novel—is sometimes called a modern *Uncle Tom's Cabin.* But it is a much finer book than Mrs. Stowe's history-making piece of propaganda.

Ryskind, Morris, joint author *See* Kaufman, George S.

Sabatier, Paul 1858-1928 French Protestant scholar and cleric.

LIFE OF ST. FRANCIS OF ASSISI. 1893. (I) Sympathetic study of the age (1182-1226) and of the man who exemplified its noblest tendencies. Based on original documents never previously used in research.

Sabatini, Rafael   1875-1950   Italian-born English author of spirited gadzooks romances that make wonderfully successful movies. "In his hand historical fiction becomes a thing of life."—*Boston Transcript.*

SCARAMOUCHE. 1921. (II)   Colorful, dramatic, Dumas-like tale of love and adventure in the French Revolution.

CAPTAIN BLOOD. 1922. (II)   A pirate story of the Spanish Main, with a good plot.

SEA HAWK. 1915. (II)   English gentleman of Elizabeth's day is kidnapped and sold as a slave to the Barbary pirates.

Sackville-West, Victoria Mary   1892-   English novelist; writes of aristocrats with authority, but is equally at home with the Bloomsbury intelligentsia.

ALL PASSION SPENT. 1931. (III)   A delicate fantasy. "Age on a summer evening muses in a walled garden while the peaches ripen." The heroine is charming at four score and eight.

THE EDWARDIANS. 1930. (III)   Story of the privileged class in England in the decadent glory of their sunset years.

Sadi   1194(?)-1291(?)   Persian poet.

GULISTAN (THE ROSE-GARDEN). 1258(?)   A miscellany of prose and verse, containing essays on old age, contentment, taciturnity, etc., together with stories, maxims, philosophizings, and puns. There are English translations of this, Sadi's best known work, by Ross (1923) and Eastwick (1880).

Saint-Exupéry, Antoine de   1900-1944   French essayist, novelist, and aviator. Missing since November, 1944.

WIND, SAND AND STARS. 1939. (IV)   About flights over Spain in wartime and over deserts and waste places in Africa and South America; about what happened to the flyer and, more important, what he was thinking as he flew, and now and then beheld Death coming up to meet him.

FLIGHT TO ARRAS. 1942. (IV)   Story of his last reconnaissance flight during the final days of the French *débacle.* "A truly noble attempt to think out his war experiences as a philosopher would, not as a soldier would, or a mere writer. *Flight to Arras* is a credo, the credo of a fighting man to whom the ordinary reasons for fighting have proved unsatisfactory."—Clifton Fadiman, in *New Yorker.*

Saint-Pierre, Bernardin de 1737-1814 French author and friend of Rousseau.

PAUL AND VIRGINIA. 1789. (I) Idyllic tale of the pure but passionate and unfortunate love of two young people brought up together from childhood, in a state of nature, on the tropical island of Mauritius. Shows the strong influence of Rousseau's *Émile*.

Saint-Simon, Duc de (Louis de Rouvroy) 1675-1755 French statesman, whose fame rests on his

MEMOIRS ON THE REIGN OF LOUIS XIV AND THE REGENCY. 1839. (Abridged translation in English, by B. St. John; new edition, 1901). (I) "Priceless record of the most brilliant and powerful court of Europe." Saintsbury said, "No writer of memoirs has ever approached him in vividness, originality and irregular power."

Sainte-Beuve, Charles Augustin 1804-69 Perhaps the greatest of all literary critics; regarded as the originator of *biographical* criticism, in which the author, his mind and intention, are considered as carefully as his writing.

CAUSERIES DU LUNDI (MONDAY TALKS), translated by E. J. Trechmann. 8v. 1909-11 (I) A veritable treasury of superlative criticism. The majority of the essays deal with French writers, a sizable minority with other European authors.

PORTRAITS OF THE SEVENTEENTH CENTURY; translated by K. P. Wormeley. 1925. (I)

PORTRAITS OF THE EIGHTEENTH CENTURY; translated by K. P. Wormeley and G. G. Ives. 1925. (I) The last two titles contain brilliant portraits of French literary and historical personalities from 1585 to 1755.

Saintsbury, George E. 1845-1933 English critic of English and French literature. "Probably the best-read man of his time; few could excel him in the art of briefly summing up the characteristics of an age or an author."—*English Library*.

HISTORY OF NINETEENTH CENTURY LITERATURE (1780-1895). 1896. (I) "Clear general statements, orderly arrangement, little prejudice, much knowledge, and a general sound acceptance of average sensible opinion."—*A.L.A. Catalog*, 1926.

HISTORY OF CRITICISM AND LITERARY TASTE IN EUROPE. 3v. 1900-04. (I) "Scholarly treatise from early Greek criticism to the end of the Nineteenth Century."—*A.L.A. Catalog*, 1926.

ENGLISH NOVEL. 1913. (I and II) "Rarely has a more illuminating and pleasant textbook of literature been offered to the public."—*Athenaeum*.

HISTORY OF THE FRENCH NOVEL (TO THE CLOSE OF THE NINETEENTH CENTURY). 2v. 1917-19. (I and II) "Traces with a certain joyousness the history of the pleasures which fiction has given to its readers."—*A.L.A. Catalog*, 1926.

Saki, pseudonym   *See* Munro, H. H.

Salten, Felix   1869-1944   Austrian man of letters.

BAMBI, A LIFE IN THE WOODS; translated by Whittaker Chambers. 1928. (III) Simple, quiet, yet graceful and poetic life-story of a buck in the greenwood. Some adults and some children will find it charming.

Sand, George (pseudonym of Mme. Dudevant)   1804-1876 French novelist. Her life was tempestuous, her style sometimes diffuse; "but her books will always be remembered as both the reflection and the inspiration of the Utopian visions of her time." (See Winwar's *Life of the Heart*.)

CONSUELO. 1842-44. (I) Her masterpiece. The career of the heroine, a prima donna, is fantastically sensational.

FRANÇOIS THE WAIF. 1846. (I)

DEVIL'S POOL. 1847. (I)

FANCHON THE CRICKET. [or, FADETTE.] 1848. Three pastoral idylls of great simplicity and grace. (The first two of this trio are published in a single volume of Everyman's Library.)

Sandburg, Carl   1878-   "Folk-singer of America." Poet and biographer; born in Illinois, the son of Swedish immigrants, he left school at thirteen and became a casual laborer; but worked his way through college after serving in the Spanish-American War.

COMPLETE POEMS. 1950. (II) "He insists that anything in the great pageant of modern life is worth attention, whether it be ugly or beautiful, expressed in music or in jazz; it is all part of today."—*A.L.A. Catalog, Supplement 2*.

ROOTABAGA STORIES. 1922. (II) These "fairy stories in a new vein" merit a place on the shelf of "authentic literature for children." "It is a rare treat to be a child and read it for the first time. . . . It makes America thrilling."—*New York Herald Tribune.*

ABRAHAM LINCOLN: THE PRAIRIE YEARS. 2v. 1926. (III)

ABRAHAM LINCOLN: THE WAR YEARS. 4v. 1939. (IV) These two titles constitute a great biography. In the first, "Lincoln is pictured against his natural background—the prairie"; in the second, "the tragedy of the greatest American has been reported by a poetic historian." (The second was awarded the Pulitzer prize for biography and history.)

AMERICAN SONGBAG. 1927. (III) A compilation of the words and music of 280 ballads and folksongs collected from all parts of the country: the songs of pioneers, immigrants, sailors, lumberjacks, Negroes, hoboes, and college boys.

REMEMBRANCE ROCK. 1948. This prose epic is a trilogy of The Pilgrim Fathers, The Revolution, and The Pioneers to the Civil War. "It is the book of a poet, an historian, a biographer, a storyteller," and above all, it may be added, a *folklorist.* "Here, for the first time, is an American novel comparable with the greatest—one which should certainly take its place beside Tolstoi's *War and Peace.*"—*Christian Science Monitor.*

Sandoz, Mari 1901- American writer, born in the sandhills of Nebraska.

OLD JULES. 1935. (III) A Swiss emigrant pioneered to western Nebraska in 1884, and settled there. He was brutal, vindictive, conceited, yet strong and somehow wise. One of his daughters wrote this book. In it is not only a speaking likeness of the terrible old man but a dramatic account of how incoming farmers and outgoing cattlemen lived and fought each other in that time and place.

Santayana, George 1863-1952 Philosopher, poet, and novelist. Of Spanish birth and parentage and American education, he lived mostly in Europe after 1912, following twenty-two years of teaching philosophy at Harvard.

LIFE OF REASON. 5v. 1905-06 and 1922. (I and II) "Nobly conceived and adequately executed."—John Dewey. "A profound, shrewd, stirring, and beautiful synthesis of human existence."—Carl Van Doren.

WINDS OF DOCTRINE. 1913. (I and II) Essays on other philosophers, etc., by a lover of wisdom "who has the poet's vision and power of expression."

CHARACTER AND OPINION IN THE UNITED STATES. 1920 and 1934. (I and II) "Keen analysis of American character and summing up of philosophical tendencies." The *Spectator* called it "one of the most fascinating books imaginable."

SOLILOQUIES IN ENGLAND. 1922. (II) Essays on many subjects; "packed," as John Farrar says, "with knowledge, wisdom, and beauty."

SCEPTICISM AND ANIMAL FAITH; INTRODUCTION TO A SYSTEM OF PHILOSOPHY. 1923. "A book of rare distinction, both in style and thought."—*A.L.A. Catalog*, 1926. (An introductory volume to *Realms of Being.*)

REALMS OF BEING. 4v. in 1. 1942. Includes *Realm of Essence* (1927), *Realm of Matter* (1930), *Realm of Truth* (1938), and *Realm of Spirit* (1940). Here, in one pair of covers, is the statement of the author's entire philosophy.

THE LAST PURITAN. 1936. (IV) A first novel, published when the author was 73. "The Bostonian hero convinced himself, on puritan grounds, that it was wrong to be a puritan. . . . He thought it to be his clear duty to give up puritanism, but couldn't." —*New Republic.*

PERSONS AND PLACES. 2v. 1944-45. (IV) Autobiography. The first volume closes with his graduation from Harvard; the second covers graduate study, travels, and over twenty years of teaching at Harvard. "An autobiography with a metaphysical plot; it stands somewhere between Proust's great novel and *The Education of Henry Adams.*"—Edmund Wilson, in *New Yorker.*

Saroyan, William   1908-   American author of stories and plays. Born in California, of Armenian parentage; member, National Institute of Arts and Letters.

DARING YOUNG MAN ON THE FLYING TRAPEZE, AND OTHER STORIES. 1934. Rambling, original, amusing, youthful yarns. "Mr. Saroyan flies through the air with the greatest of ease."— *Saturday Review of Literature.*

MY NAME IS ARAM. 1940. (IV) Tales about the boyhood of Aram in the Armenian colony at Fresno, California. "I should vote for this story of an American boyhood as the most typically American book of the year."—H. S. Canby, in *Saturday Review of Literature*.

HUMAN COMEDY. 1943. (IV) Tender tale of a California family. "Glowing, original, heart-warming."—Bennett Cerf.

THREE PLAYS. 1940. Includes *Time of Your Life*; *My Heart's in the Highlands*; and *Love's Old Sweet Song*. The first named was awarded the Pulitzer prize for drama in 1940, but the author declined it.

Sartre, Jean-Paul   1905-   French philosopher, playwright, novelist. High priest of existentialism, whose motto is "Throw aside all restraint and enjoy your pessimism."

EXISTENTIALISM. 92 pages. 1947. A statement in relatively clear and direct language of the outlines of his philosophy.

AGE OF REASON. 1947. "Sordid but entertaining" are the adjectives chosen by a critic to characterize this novel picturing Paris in 1938. It is the first in the tetralogy *Roads to Freedom*, and is followed by

REPRIEVE. 1947. This novel is a brilliant kaleidoscope of the eight days which led to the Munich Pact and the rape of Czecho-slovakia. The story is continued in

TROUBLED SLEEP. 1950. This fictional narrative describes the reactions of a group of people to the news of the fall of France in June, 1940. "The virtues of Sartre are superbly exemplified in *Troubled Sleep*."—*New Republic*.

Sassoon, Siegfried   1886-   English poet, soldier, pacifist, biographer, novelist.

MEMOIRS OF GEORGE SHERSTON. 3v. in 1. 1937. A long auto-biographical novel which includes *Memoirs of a Fox-hunting Man* (1929) (III); *Memoirs of an Infantry Officer* (1930); and *Sherston's Progress* (1936).

MEREDITH. 1948. "Admirable critical biography of the last of the Victorian novelists and poets, which treats its subject with clarity, humor, and insight."—*Library Journal*. "The reader lays the book down with the feeling that a great author has become one of his close neighbors."—*New York Herald Tribune*.

COLLECTED POEMS. 1949. A liberal selection from the poems written between 1908 and 1940. "Sassoon's poems are more rewarding now than they were ten years ago."—H. Breit, in *New York Times.*

Schachner, Nathan   1895-   American biographer.

ALEXANDER HAMILTON. 1946. Based largely upon documents hitherto unused by writers on Hamilton. "This book is likely to remain the definitive biography . . . for a long time to come. Mr Schachner spent more than ten years in its preparation."—*American Political Science Review.*

Scheffel, Joseph Victor von   1826-86   German poet and novelist.

EKKEHARD. 1872. (I) This charming love story—a fictitious biography of a poet-monk of the Tenth Century—presents a vivid picture of German medieval life in court and cloister.

Schiller, J. C. F. von   1759-1805   Probably the greatest of German dramatists, he was also eminent as historian, poet, and philosopher. "His name, linked habitually with Goethe's, stands for all that is best in the best epoch of German letters."

WALLENSTEIN (1799) (I) and WILLIAM TELL (1804) (I) are probably his greatest plays. The Bohn Library collection of his Dramas (1901) contains *Don Carlos, Mary Stuart, The Maid of Orleans,* and *The Bride of Messina.*

Schlesinger, Arthur M.   1888-   American historian; professor of history at Harvard.

PATHS TO THE PRESENT. 1949. Essays on American history and political Americans. "Combines scholarship and popular appeal."—*American Historical Review.* "Stamps him anew as the leading interpreter of America's past."—*Saturday Review of Literature.*

Schlesinger, Arthur M., Jr.   1918-   American historian and publicist.

AGE OF JACKSON. 1945. (IV) A thoughtful and scholarly book which the *New Republic* praised as "a major contribution to American historiography." It won the Pulitzer prize for history.

THE VITAL CENTER; THE POLITICS OF FREEDOM. 1949. "A liberal's analysis of our democratic evolution." "Mr. Schlesinger is expertly clear and navigates smoothly a treacherously complicated course."—*Atlantic.*

Schmitt, Gladys (Mrs. Simon Goldfield) 1909- American novelist.

DAVID THE KING. 1946. A novel in modern style, based upon the Old Testament accounts in *Samuel, Kings,* and *Chronicles.* "A worthy successor to such biblical adaptations as Asch's *The Nazarene* and Mann's *Joseph* series."—L. Untermeyer, in *Saturday Review of Literature.*

Schnitzler, Arthur 1862-1931 Viennese author of sophisticated plays, stories, and sketches. Essentially a dramatic impressionist, the one-act play is his special *métier.*

STORIES AND PLAYS. 1930. Full of bright, witty, and quite amoral dialog. See especially *Anatol* and *Professor Bernhardi.*

Schopenhauer, Arthur 1788-1860 German philosopher; "chief expounder of philosophical pessimism."

WORLD AS WILL AND IDEA. 1819. (I) His doctrine, roughly, is that, life being full of suffering, the will to live is the root of evil; yet life has its palliatives: the contemplation of art and the practice of morality, based on sympathy.

Schreiner, Olive (Ralph Iron, pseudonym) 1855-1920 English author and feminist; born in South Africa, with pro-Boer sympathies.

STORY OF AN AFRICAN FARM. 1883. (I) Semi-autobiographical study of a sensitive temperament against the harsh background of South African farm-life and a lonely landscape.

Schulberg, Budd 1914- American author who is intimately acquainted with both Hollywood and Broadway.

THE DISENCHANTED. 1950. "Halliday," the chief figure in this novel, "is of course the very essence of 'the lost generation.'" This is not surprising as it is no secret that Halliday is a portrait of F. Scott Fitzgerald. "One feels torn between shame that the country should not have read with more enthusiasm so great a man, and shame that so great a man should let his career be twisted by the superficial power of too soft a standard of living." —*Chicago Tribune*.

Schuster, M. Lincoln　1897-　American compiler and publisher.

TREASURY OF THE WORLD'S GREAT LETTERS. 1940. (IV) A selection from the best correspondence of all ages. "A delectable bundle. . . . He has made an absorbingly interesting collection." —Royal Cortissoz, in *New York Herald Tribune*.

Schweitzer, Albert　1875-　Alsatian philosopher, physician, organist, musicologist, author; missionary in Equatorial Africa. He has been hailed by some as the best and greatest man of the Twentieth Century. His guiding star is Reverence for Life. "Good consists in maintaining, assisting, and enhancing life . . . to destroy, to harm or to hinder life is evil." (*Cf.* Schopenhauer's doctrine.)

ON THE EDGE OF THE PRIMEVAL FOREST (1931) and MORE FROM THE PRIMEVAL FOREST (1938). Records of his experience and observation as a medical missionary in Equatorial Africa.

INDIAN THOUGHT AND ITS DEVELOPMENT. 1936. Discusses Indian mysticism as it may be studied in Buddhism and Hinduism, in contrast to the ideas of Western philosophies.

OUT OF MY LIFE AND THOUGHT; AN AUTOBIOGRAPHY. 1949 (First published in 1933). A simple and amazingly vivid book by and about the versatile genius who has been called the modern Leonardo. "This book, in which Dr. Schweitzer discusses each of his many lives, is a stirring lesson in the humanities."—*New Yorker*.

Scott, Evelyn (Mrs. John Metcalfe)　1893-　American novelist, born in Tennessee.

THE WAVE. 1929. (III) Prose fiction about the Civil War. "With great imaginative force, she shows the effect of the war, not on the aristocracy alone but on the rank and file of persons touched by the conflict. It is a fictional history of the people in wartime, and as such it is unrivaled by its earlier or later competitors."—F. B. Millett.

Scott, Michael　1789-1835　Scottish novelist of the sea.

TOM CRINGLE'S LOG. 1834. (I)

CRUISE OF THE *Midge*. 1836. (I) Classic tales of the sea that are said to rank with or surpass those of the contemporary yarn-spinners, Cooper and Marryat. Saintsbury said that they "contain some of the best of fighting, fun, tropical scenery and description generally, to be found outside of the greatest masters."

Scott, Robert Falcon 1868-1912 English antarctic explorer who reached the South Pole, January 18, 1912, five weeks after its discoverer, Amundsen, and died of hunger and exposure on the return trip to his base.

SCOTT'S LAST EXPEDITION: JOURNALS AND REPORTS; arranged by L. Huxley. 2v. 1913.

Scott, Robert Lee, Jr. 1908- American flyer who distinguished himself in World War II.

GOD IS MY CO-PILOT. 1943. (IV) The striking title somewhat misrepresents this true tale of hazardous duty with the Flying Tigers in China. It has been called "the best writing to come from any flyer with the exception of Saint-Exupéry."—*Chicago Sun.*

Scott, Sir Walter 1771-1832 Scottish historical novelist and poet. Though the name of the Great Romantic invariably appears in all the older lists of best books, it had fallen sadly out of favor and fashion by the middle of the Twentieth Century. Yet Helen Haines said stanchly in 1950, "His genius is the greatest force that has appeared in English fiction."

COMPLETE POETICAL WORKS. (I) The most famous are *Marmion* (1808), *The Lay of the Last Minstrel* (1805) and *The Lady of the Lake* (1810) —all long poems. "He has always been the poet of youthful, and high-hearted, readers."—W. M. Rossetti.

WAVERLEY. 1814. (I) First of Scott's historical novels, this is a tale of Bonnie Prince Charlie and the romantic struggle which ended with his defeat at Preston Pans in 1745.

GUY MANNERING. 1815. (I) A novel of England at the time of the American Revolution, with plenty of gipsies, smugglers, and other disreputable but picturesque characters.

OLD MORTALITY. 1816. Historical novel of Scotland during the rise of the Covenanters in 1679. It was the favorite, among Scott's novels, with both Tennyson and Andrew Lang.

HEART OF MIDLOTHIAN. 1818. (I) Effie and Jeanie Deans, daughters of the humble "cow-feeder," Douce Davie, are the main characters in this novel of Scotland and England in the Eighteenth Century.

IVANHOE. 1820. (I) A stirring tale of chivalry—of Richard the Lionheart and Robin Hood—of Saxon and Norman in Twelfth-Century England.

KENILWORTH. 1821. (I) Story of Queen Elizabeth and her favorite, the Earl of Leicester, whose unhappy wife, Amy Robsart, may be said to be the heroine. Raleigh, Burleigh, Shakespeare, and other great personalities of the period are introduced.

QUENTIN DURWARD. 1823. (I) Story of Fifteenth-Century France and of sly and penurious King Louis XI. The hero is a dashing member of his Scottish Guard.

Seabrook, William B.   1886-1945   American teller of tall tales of his travels in exotic lands.

MAGIC ISLANDS. 1929. (III) Vivid description, well illustrated, of the black republic of Haiti, with emphasis upon Voodooism, in which cult the author participated, as perhaps no other white man has done.

Seagrave, Gordon Stifler   1897-   American surgeon and medical missionary, born in Burma. During and after World War II he served as surgeon with the British and American armed forces till he came into conflict with the authorities.

BURMA SURGEON. 1943. (IV) "Epitomizes a life of service, a life in which religion becomes a practical demonstration of science and devotion."—Science Book Club. "He can make you see, smell and feel the jungle. . . . He gives the word courage a new and deeper meaning."—*Chicago Sun.*

Sedgwick, Anne Douglas (Mrs Basil de Sélincourt)   1873-1935 American-born novelist who lived her adult life in England and France. Her stories reflect her own international background and economic status. Member, National Institute of Arts and Letters.

TANTE. 1911. (II)

LITTLE FRENCH GIRL. 1924. (II) These two novels, says F. B. Millett, "revealed an enviable power to infuse emotion into essentially well-bred fiction, and to exploit with insight and conviction the vagaries of artistic or alien temperaments."

THE OLD COUNTESS. 1927. (III) Tragic story of three women—one an old one—and an attractive man, set against the background of a sinister little French town. An ugly element in the situation is handled with skill and delicacy.

Sedgwick, Ellery 1872- American man of letters; editor, *Atlantic Monthly*, 1908-38.

THE HAPPY PROFESSION. 1946. "A good book, full of human interest, about writers."—Walter Prichard Eaton.

Seghers, Anna 1900- German novelist; Anti-Nazi, with proletarian sympathies. As a Jewish refugee she fled to Paris in 1933. Her husband was sent to a concentration camp.

SEVENTH CROSS. 1942. (IV) "It is more than a compelling story of a man's escape from a concentration camp; it is a testament to the grandeur and beauty of the human soul."—*New York Herald Tribune*. "This is not only the most compelling contribution to world literature made, so far, by any exiled German author, but also one of the most remarkable books to come out of these times of chaos and mortal danger."—*Saturday Review of Literature*.

Sender, Ramón José 1902- Spanish novelist and political nonconformist; appears as "Manuel" in Malraux's novel, *Man's Hope*.

PRO PATRIA. 1935. Novel about desert warfare and the dismayed disillusionment of a patriotic Spanish soldier. "War as it is: heroic, unjust; idealistic, treacherous; and unavailing."—*Good Reading*.

SEVEN RED SUNDAYS. 1936. Story of an unsuccessful rising in 1934 in Revolutionary Spain.

MAN'S PLACE; translated by Oliver La Farge. 1940. What happened in a small Spanish town when an obscure young man mysteriously disappeared, but re-appeared fifteen years later.

Seneca, Lucius Annaeus 4 B.C.-65 A.D. Roman Stoic philosopher and dramatist. In Nero's youth Seneca had been his tutor, but he fell from favor and finally killed himself at the Emperor's command.

MORALS. (I) These essays on such subjects as Consolation, Providence, The Happy Life, Peace of Mind, Anger, Clemency, etc., constitute his masterwork. In them the Stoic virtues of calmness, fortitude, forbearance, and justice are nobly set forth.

Serge, Victor 1890-1947 Former Russian communist. He lived his last decade as a refugee in France and Mexico.

CASE OF COMRADE TULAYEV. 1950. A novel of the Purge, written in 1940-42; highly praised by the reviewers. "This book is in the great tradition of the European novel. It is the Human Comedy of a police state . . . where the innocent confess their guilt and punishment falls on the guiltless."—*Christian Science Monitor*.

Service, Robert W. 1876- Canadian poet; celebrated as the Canadian Kipling.

COMPLETE POEMS. 1942. (II) Virile, forthright ballads of the out-of-doors. The soldiers of World War I loved them.

Sevareid, Eric 1912- American journalist and radio correspondent.

NOT SO WILD A DREAM. 1946. A story of personal experiences in World War II. "First rate reporting, both of action and of those rear areas which are apt to be the ugliest aspects of war."—Elmer Davis, in *Saturday Review of Literature*.

Sevigné, Marquise de (Marie de Rabutin-Chantal) 1626-96 French writer of incomparable letters to her daughter and friends.

LETTERS. 2v. 1937. (I) A mirror of Seventeenth-Century France and a classic of French literature.

Shakespeare, William 1564-1616 English dramatist and poet. "The Monarch of Mankind."—Georg Brandes. "Shakespeare has already exhausted the whole of human nature in all its tendencies, in all its heights and depths . . . in fact there remains for . . . the aftercomer, nothing more to do."—Goethe. "Homer, Job, Æschylus, Isaiah, Ezekiel, Lucretius, Juvenal, St. John, St. Paul, Tacitus, Dante, Rabelais, Cervantes, Shakespeare. This is the avenue of the immovable giants of the human mind."—Hugo.

Of the many editions of Shakespeare's complete works in one volume, the following are among the more satisfactory:

OXFORD SHAKESPEARE; the complete works; edited, with a glossary, by W. J. Craig. 1350 pages. Oxford Press. (I)

COMPLETE PLAYS AND POEMS; a new text edition, with introduction and notes by W. A. Neilson and C. J. Hill. 1420 pages. New Cambridge Edition. 1942. (I)

Of the accepted canon of 37 plays the following 21 are those which the critics have praised most consistently. Most of the remaining 16 are collaborations or adaptations in which the magic of the master's hand is but intermittently manifest.

Successful Experiments

ROMEO AND JULIET (1592?)
RICHARD III (1594?)

Genius Transfigures the Craftsman

RICHARD II (1594?)
MIDSUMMER NIGHT'S DREAM (1594?)
MERCHANT OF VENICE (1596?)
TAMING OF THE SHREW (1596?)
HENRY IV, PART I (1597?)
HENRY IV, PART II (1598?)
MUCH ADO ABOUT NOTHING (1598?)
JULIUS CAESAR (1599?)
AS YOU LIKE IT (1599?)
TWELFTH NIGHT (1601?)

The Great Tragedies

HAMLET (1602?)
OTHELLO (1604?)
KING LEAR (1605?)
MACBETH (1606?)
ANTONY AND CLEOPATRA (1607?)
CORIOLANUS (1608?)

The Great Romance-Plays

CYMBELINE (1609?)
WINTER'S TALE (1610?)
THE TEMPEST (1611?)

The Poems

These include chiefly the mysterious SONNETS (1609?), VENUS AND ADONIS (1593?), and THE RAPE OF LUCRECE (1594?): listed here in the order of their importance.

Shapiro, Karl Jay   1913-   American poet and critic.

V-LETTER, AND OTHER POEMS. 1944. "His poems are the best which (so far, at least) this war has produced."—Louis Untermeyer, in *Yale Review*, 1945. Won the Pulitzer prize, 1945.

ESSAY ON RIME. 1945. (IV) "Brilliant, provocative, critical summary in verse of contemporary English and American poetry in form, content and language."—Helen Haines.

Shapley, Harlow   1885-   American astronomer.

FLIGHTS FROM CHAOS; A SURVEY OF MATERIAL SYSTEMS FROM ATOMS TO GALAXIES. 1930. (III) A scientist's attempt to classify the universe for laymen. Modern concepts of matter are set forth; not simply, but probably as simply as possible.

Sharp, Margery   1905-   English author of light, amusing, and sophisticated novels.

CLUNY BROWN. 1944. (IV) The droll young witch, Cluny, is not only the heroine but also a plumber's niece. She is competent in both roles.

Shaw, George Bernard   1856-1950   Anglo-Irish dramatist, socialist, critic, and wit. He was educated, he said, because he escaped from school at fourteen. "With his last gasp he will make a phrase to flabbergast a dolt."—H. L. Mencken. "My way of joking is to tell the truth: it is the funniest joke in the world." —G. B. Shaw. "A combination of faun and philosopher, of Peter Pan and St. Francis, of Puck and Euripides."—Archibald Henderson.

The nine plays listed below are among his most important. They are listed alphabetically.

ANDROCLES AND THE LION. 1913. (II) "The Shavian view of primitive Christianity."

ARMS AND THE MAN. 1898. (1) Satire on the romantic attitude toward war.

BACK TO METHUSELAH. 1921. (I and II) Starting in the Garden of Eden this satiric, time-gobbling fantasy goes on through the ages to the Twentieth Century and far into the future.

CAESAR AND CLEOPATRA. 1898. (I) Shaw's challenge to Shakespeare. Some consider it his greatest play.

CANDIDA. 1897. (I)   An outspoken comedy. The wife, desired by two men, chooses her husband; not because he is her husband, but because his need for her is greater than his rival's.

MAN AND SUPERMAN. 1903. (I and II)   The theme is the pursuit of man by woman. This play too is often called Shaw's masterpiece.

MRS. WARREN'S PROFESSION. 1898.   It was harlotry. "The daughter, when the discovery is made, freezes up into an iceberg of contempt . . . the mother [Mrs. Warren] explodes into pulverizing cynicism and practicality."—G. K. Chesterton.

PYGMALION. 1912. (II)   Sets forth the transformation of a cockney flower-girl into a duchess through the magic of a few weeks' expert training in phonetics.

SAINT JOAN. 1923. (II)   "Mr. Shaw's heart has been touched; and he has surrendered. Joan of Arc bowled him over." —*Times* (London). (So Mark Twain and Shaw had at least one thing in common.)

INTELLIGENT WOMAN'S GUIDE TO SOCIALISM AND CAPITALISM. 1928. (III)   Although "dated," this book expounds with wit and brilliance the Fabian variety of socialism and pleads for equality of income as the panacea for the world's critical and economic ills.

EVERYBODY'S POLITICAL WHAT'S WHAT. 1944. (IV)   Here, says Jacques Barzun, is "the entire Shavian system, the word and thought of half a century, not only of criticism but of what amounts to constitution-making."

PREFACES. 1934.   Thirty-seven introductions to as many of Shaw's plays. They embody at some length his views on politics and social problems.

Shaw, George Bernard, joint author   *See* Terry, Dame Ellen.

Shaw, Irwin   1913-   American playwright and fictionist.

YOUNG LIONS. 1948.   This first novel is a picture of three young men gripped in the toils of World War II. "With the publication of his first novel, Irwin Shaw, dramatist, short-story writer and ex-scenarist becomes one of the most important of American novelists."—*New York Herald Tribune*. "A fine, full, intelligent book, packed with wonderful talk and crackling writing. We have waited a long time for this novel of Irwin Shaw's."—*Saturday Review of Literature*.

Sheean, Vincent 1899- American foreign correspondent, autobiographer, novelist. His wife is Diana Forbes-Robertson.

PERSONAL HISTORY. 1935. (III) The autobiography of a man of 34. His book is an account of interesting things he saw and heard and thought during several crucial years. Very earnest, it is as innocent of conceit as of humor.

SANFELICE. 1936. Historical novel of the revolutionary uprising in Naples in 1799, when Lord Nelson and Lady Hamilton were the city's notorious lovers.

NOT PEACE BUT A SWORD. 1939. (IV) Describes the tragic background of World War II when, from March 1938 to March 1939, Sheean watched the growth of fascism in visits to Spain, Vienna, and Prague.

Sheen, Fulton J. 1895- Catholic prelate and proselyter; today's most persuasive speaker for Catholicism in America.

PEACE OF SOUL. 1949. "How one faith resolves some of its holders' mental conflicts and frustrations."—*Saturday Review of Literature.* "He points the troubled away from Freud and toward God."—*Quarterly Booklist.*

Shelley, Mary Wollstonecraft 1791-1851 English writer; daughter of William Godwin, the philosopher, and wife of Shelley the poet.

FRANKENSTEIN. 1818. (I) Striking story of mystery and horror. The hero creates a mechanical man-monster, human in form but of course lacking a soul. This frightful creature relentlessly dogs his creator about the world. Curiously enough, in literary allusions, the name *Frankenstein* is often mistakenly applied to the monster instead of to his maker.

Shelley, Percy Bysshe 1792-1822 He lived and thought erratically and was drowned at 30; yet his place is secure in the foremost rank of English poets. "A beautiful *and ineffectual* angel, beating in the void his luminous wings in vain."—Matthew Arnold. "He is often too much in the clouds for me."—Tennyson.

COMPLETE POETICAL WORKS. (I) Cambridge edition. 651 pages. "Had Shelley possessed humor, his might have been the third name in English poetry."—E. P. Whipple.

Shepard, Odell   1884-   American scholar and teacher of literature.

PEDLAR'S PROGRESS; THE LIFE OF BRONSON ALCOTT.   1937.   (IV)
Alcott was a rustic Yankee pedlar. He became the philosopher
and teacher whom Emerson called "the most refined and the most
advanced soul we have had in New England." Fortunately for him
he was also the father of the less exalted but more practical author
of *Little Women*. "Mr. Shepard's book reflects faithfully the Arcadian innocence of this transcendental pedlar who had the heart
of a child and the mind of a seer."—H. S. Commager, in *New York
Times*. Won the Pulitzer prize for biography in 1938.

Sheridan, Richard Brinsley   1751-1816   Irish-born English
dramatist and statesman.

PLAYS.   (I)   These comedies, "full of deft characterization,
wit, and satire," are mirrors of the hollow, glittering, heart-
breaking society for which they were written. *The Rivals* (1775)
and *The School for Scandal* (1777), his masterpieces, are still often
seen on the modern stage.

Sherman, Stuart P.   1881-1926   American scholar and critic.
Editor of *Books* (the *New York Herald Tribune's* book review section) ; co-editor, Cambridge History of American Literature.

CRITICAL WOODCUTS.   1926.   (III)   Brisk yet responsible estimates of 26 literary personages, from Laurence Sterne to Willa
Cather.

THE MAIN STREAM.   1927.   (III)   Essays—22 of them—on
books in the main stream of modern—for the most part, American
—literature.

Sherwood, Robert E.   1896-   American dramatist and publicist.
Overseas Director, Office of War Information, in World War II;
friend and assistant to President Roosevelt in the war years.

REUNION IN VIENNA.   1932.   "A perfect infusion of Viennese
sentiment and pathos, cynicism, worldliness, and sophistication."—
F. B. Millett.

IDIOT'S DELIGHT.   1936.   "A portent of the grim war shadow
then rising over Europe."—Helen Haines.   Won the Pulitzer prize.

ABE LINCOLN IN ILLINOIS. 1939. (IV) "Mr. Sherwood is one of the few who have grasped and held firm the elusive personality which is Lincoln's. . . . His soul speaks in these lines."—*Saturday Review of Literature.* (Pulitzer prize, 1939.)

THERE SHALL BE NO NIGHT. 1940. (IV) Play about the Russian invasion of Finland in 1939. "Rich in wisdom and pity," it won the Pulitzer prize in 1941.

ROOSEVELT AND HOPKINS, AN INTIMATE HISTORY. 1948. "This is an amazing book. . . . Immediately it takes its place—a high honor —on the same slim shelf with Winston Churchill's *Gathering Storm.*"—*Saturday Review of Literature.* "A triumph in the difficult field of contemporary history. In years to come it will be a basic work for all who seek to understand the age of Roosevelt."—A. M. Schlesinger, Jr.

Shirer, William L.   1904-   American war correspondent.

BERLIN DIARY; THE JOURNAL OF A FOREIGN CORRESPONDENT, 1934-41. 1941. (IV) The best of all the books which describe the coming and first years of World War II. W. L. White said in the *Saturday Review of Literature*, "I have yet to find anyone who picked this book up who was able to put it down unfinished."

Sholokhov, Mikhail   1905-   Russian novelist; said to be the most widely read novelist in the U.S.S.R.

THE SILENT DON. 1934-41. (IV) This long, powerful, naturalistic novel is a panorama of the Russian civil war (1917-21) and the years which followed before World War II. The first part is called *And Quiet Flows the Don* and the second, *The Don Flows Home to the Sea.* In both, the chief characters are Don Cossacks— "a primitive, virile and unbelievably brutal people."

Shumway, D. B., translator   *See* Nibelungenlied.

Sidney, Sir Philip   1554-86   English poet. Gallant and chivalrous gentleman; courtier of Queen Elizabeth. "The idol of his time. . . . Perhaps no figure reflects the age more fully and beautifully."—J. R. Green.

ARCADIA, AND OTHER WORKS. 4v. (I) Cambridge Press. n.d. Include

ARCADIA. 1590. (I)   This extremely artificial pastoral romance, in verse and tortured prose, is almost unreadable today; yet it merits attention from lovers of fiction, for it is an ancestor of the English novel.

ASTROPHEL AND STELLA. 1591. (I)   Palgrave said that "after or beside Shakespeare's Sonnets" these poems "offer the most intense and powerful picture of the passion of love in the whole range of our poetry."

APOLOGIE FOR POETRY. 1595.   "No other work, Italian, French or English, can be said to give so complete and noble a conception of the temper and the principles of Renaissance criticism."—J. E. Spingarn.

Siegfried, André   1875-   French author and scholar; member of the Institut de France.

AMERICA COMES OF AGE; A FRENCH ANALYSIS. 1927. (III) Survey of American conditions and problems in the decade after World War I.   Still helpful as background for the study of the more complicated problems of the mid-century.

FRANCE, A STUDY IN NATIONALITY. 1930. (III)   Portrait of France in 1930.   An aid to the understanding of the more bewildering and less inspiring mid-century France.

Sienkiewicz,   Henryk   1846-1916   Leading   Polish   novelist; awarded Nobel prize in 1905.

QUO VADIS. 1897. (I)   Melodramatic novel of ancient Rome in which gladiatorial combats, Christian martyrdoms, and the burning of Nero's city are described.   An immensely popular story, it has been translated into many languages besides English.

WITH FIRE AND SWORD. 1884. (I)

THE DELUGE. 1886. (I)

PAN MICHAEL. 1887. (I)   These three historical novels form a trilogy which tells the story of Poland and its invasions (1647-74) by Cossacks, Russians, Swedes, Turks, and Tartars.

Silone, Ignazio   1900-   Italian novelist; always anti-Fascist, he was for a time (till 1930) a Communist.

FONTAMARA. 1934.   "Bitter, realistic novel of the working of Fascism in a village of northern Italy. . . . Coarse humor, ribaldry and tragedy mingle."—*Booklist.*

BREAD AND WINE. 1937. (IV) "A quiet, shrewd, humorous and bitter book about the Italian peasantry under Fascism."—P. M. Jack, in *New York Times*. "Reveals Silone's full stature; he must now be recognized as one of the most truly contemporaneous and significant writers of our time."—*Nation*.

Simmons, Ernest Joseph   1903- Chairman of the Department of Slavic Languages at Columbia University, and writer on Russian literature.

LEO TOLSTOI. 1946. A monumental book, on which the author worked for many years. "It can be said to replace and displace virtually all the biographical studies of Tolstoi available in English."—*New York Times*.

Simonds, Frank H.   1878-1936 American journalist, and extraordinarily able interpreter of military science.

HISTORY OF THE WORLD WAR. 5v. 1917-20. (II) Interesting, competent, well illustrated. With the inevitable limitations of contemporary history, this will always be a useful work of reference on World War I.

Simonov, Konstantin   1915- Russian novelist.

DAYS AND NIGHTS. 1945. (IV) Novel about the siege of Stalingrad in World War II; unspoiled by propaganda. John Hersey called it "the truest book we have yet had on the Russian war." "The superb merit of the book is its series of portraits of men in battle." —*New York Times*.

Simonson, Lee   1888- American designer of stage settings; director of the Theatre Guild.

STAGE IS SET. 1932. (III) Discusses principles and practice of designing scenery, with an account of the historical background and development of the art theatric from the Greeks to the present day.

Sinclair, May   1870(?)-1946 English novelist. W. L. Phelps, in 1916, with characteristic enthusiasm, called her the greatest living English writer; even H. L. Mencken thought her surpassed by only two or three living Englishmen.

DIVINE FIRE. 1904. (I and II) Novel about a cockney poet. This is the favorite among her books, alike with critics and with general readers.

MR. WADDINGTON OF WYCK. 1921. (II) H. S. Canby considered this "Miss Sinclair's most brilliant novel" and Heywood Broun called it "the finest study of a windbag in literature."

Sinclair, Upton 1878- American novelist and reformer. His unflattering descriptions of American political, economic and social conditions have been greedily devoured in European translations, especially in the U.S.S.R. "Without attempting to pass judgment on the validity of his theories or his findings, one can admire his indefatigable idealism, his indomitable vitality and his selfless devotion to what he believes to be in the realm of politics and economics, the good and the true."—F. B. Millett.

THE JUNGLE. 1906. (II) This outspoken novel which exposed disgraceful conditions in the Chicago meat-packing industry is supposed to have been largely instrumental in improving them.

BOSTON. 2v. 1928. (III) Based on the Sacco-Vanzetti case, this book is propaganda first and novel afterwards. But the decent reader must respect this reformer who, for our own good, shouts into our ears so many unpleasant things.

OIL. 1927. (III) A good story about the oil industry a quarter-century ago, and a picture of the manners and customs of Americans in southern California.

WORLD'S END SERIES; popularly known as the LANNY BUDD series. 10v. In this ocean of story the author writes more as an historical novelist than as a propagandist. The change has been welcomed by the critics, though critics and readers may groan together when they contemplate the thousands upon thousands of pages with which they are here confronted.

1. WORLD'S END. 1940. (IV) About Europe and Americans in Europe in the years 1913-19.

2. BETWEEN TWO WORLDS. 1941. (IV) Begins with the Versailles Treaty; ends with the financial crash of 1929.

3. DRAGON'S TEETH. 1942. America and Europe, 1929-34: the rise of Hitler. Pulitzer prize novel, 1943.

4. WIDE IS THE GATE. 1943. The years between the Nazi Blood Purge and the Spanish Civil War.

5. PRESIDENTIAL AGENT. 1945. The gathering Nazi war-clouds of 1937-38.

6. DRAGON HARVEST. 1945. Lanny Budd acts as F.D.R.'s agent in seething Germany.

7. WORLD TO WIN. 1946. The hero confers with Laval at Vichy and with Stalin in Russia, during 1940-42.

8. PRESIDENTIAL MISSION. 1947. Budd in North Africa before the invasion, and later in Germany.

9. ONE CLEAR CALL. 1948. Budd as a pretended Nazi sympathizer in Italy, France, Spain, and Germany.

10. O SHEPHERD, SPEAK! 1949. Closing months of the war, Nuremberg trials, visit to Stalin as F.D.R.'s agent.

Sitwell, Edith　1887-　English poet, biographer, and critic.

VICTORIA OF ENGLAND. 1936. "With delicate irony and vivid pictorial details, Miss Sitwell sketches the queen's relations with her family, her ministers and her subjects."—*A.L.A. Catalog*, 1937-41.

SONG OF THE COLD. 1948. "A magnificent selection from a poet who has now attained the full development of her powers."—*Library Journal.* "This latest volume . . . makes her claim as the outstanding woman poet of England incontrovertible."—*Kirkus.*

CANTICLE OF THE ROSE. 1949. Selection from her poems, 1917-49.

Sitwell, Sir Osbert　1892-　English author of satirical poems, plays, novels, and autobiography.

SCARLET TREE. 1946. The second volume of his autobiography, covering his seventh to seventeenth year. "A child's-eye picture of Edwardian England, a portrait of a great family, and an astringent commentary on the adage that school days are 'the happiest of our lives.' "

LAUGHTER IN THE NEXT ROOM. 1948. The fourth volume of the autobiography; covers 1918-44. "Hardly a page . . . is without portraits of extraordinary people . . . speaking portraits. That of Virginia Woolf took my breath away. She was alive again, her biography implicit."—E. Evans, in *New York Herald Tribune.*

Other volumes of the autobiography are *Left Hand, Right Hand,* 1944, (Vol. 1); *Great Morning!,* 1947, (Vol. 3); and *Noble Essences,* 1950, (Vol. 5).

Sitwell, Sacheverell　1900-　English lyric poet and art critic.

HUNTERS AND THE HUNTED. 1947. "An outpouring of imagery, fantasy and strange and scattered learning. It has no subject; it is a very elaborated expression of the author's enjoyment of the splendid and the fantastic."—*Spectator.*

Skinner, Constance Lindsay   1882-1939   Canadian writer.

BEAVER, KINGS AND CABINS. 1933. (III) A colorful chapter in American history: the story of the fur trade and traders, from their early beginnings to the present time.

Skinner, Cornelia Otis   1901-   and **Kimbrough, Emily**   1899-
Miss Skinner is actress and humorist; Miss Kimbrough, editor and lecturer. Both are married.

OUR HEARTS WERE YOUNG AND GAY. 1942. (IV) Reminiscences of a hilarious trip to Europe just after World War I. "We defy anyone to read it without laughter or recall it without a smile." —*Saturday Review of Literature.*

Slocum, Joshua   1844-1908(?)   Sailor from Nova Scotia. He disappeared at sea in 1908.

SAILING ALONE AROUND THE WORLD. 1900. "Actual experiences during cruise around the world in the sloop *Spray*, with a crew of one."—*A.L.A. Catalog,* 1926.

Smiles, Samuel   1812-1904   British author and social reformer.

SELF-HELP. 1859. (I) Courage is required to admit so old-fashioned a book to these pages. It is a mine of pithy extracts, anecdotes, shining examples, and practical suggestions to assist aspiring youth in making the most out of life—a classic in inspirational books.

Smith, Adam   1723-90   Scottish economist.

INQUIRY INTO THE NATURE AND CAUSES OF THE WEALTH OF NATIONS. 1776. (I) On this rock was founded the science of classical economics. The author believed in freedom of action—within limits—for the individual trader and in free trade between nations.

Smith, Alexander   1830-67   Scottish essayist and poet.

DREAMTHORPE. 1863. (I) Twelve graceful essays describing life in an English village a century ago. For those who yearn for peace and quiet in a hectic age.

Smith, Betty   1904-   American actress, playwright, novelist.

TREE GROWS IN BROOKLYN. 1943. (IV) Story of a German-Irish-American family of the tenements in the Williamsburg section of Brooklyn, during the first years of the Twentieth Century. Two million copies were sold. The *Yale Review* described it as "a first novel of uncommon skill, and an almost uncontrollable vitality and zest for life, the work of a fresh, original and highly gifted talent."

Smith, F. Hopkinson   1838-1915   American author, engineer, artist; member, American Academy of Arts and Letters.

COLONEL CARTER OF CARTERSVILLE. 1891. "Describes with humorous and loving touch, an unreconstructed Virginia gentleman and the friends he endeared himself to."—*Nation.*

Smith, Goldwin   1823-1910   British historian; advocated union of the United States and Canada.

THE UNITED STATES: AN OUTLINE OF POLITICAL HISTORY, 1492-1871. 1893. (I) "Brilliantly written sketch, well proportioned and marvelously condensed. While critical, distinctly sympathetic."—J. N. Larned.

Smith, Horatio   1779-1849   and   **Smith, James**   1775-1839   English wits.

REJECTED ADDRESSES. 1812. This curiosity of English literature is a collection of parodies of then contemporary poets: Wordsworth, Southey, Coleridge, Scott, Byron, Crabbe. All the "addresses" were supposedly offered at the re-opening of the Drury Lane Theatre, in London, after its destruction by fire.

Smith, John   1580-1631   English soldier and colonist. "Perhaps the last professional knight-errant that the world saw."—Moses Coit Tyler. "The most picturesque figure in the early history of America. His writings are like him—bold, free, highly colored."—Brander Matthews.

TRUE RELATION OF . . . OCCURRENCES . . . IN VIRGINIA. . . . (Also called NEWES FROM VIRGINIA.) 1608. The story of Pocahontas was unaccountably omitted from this book, but it appears in *General Historie of Virginia, New England and the Summer Isles.* 1624.

DESCRIPTION OF NEW ENGLAND. 1616. Listed among his most important works; contains the best early map of the region.

Smith, Lillian   1897-   American novelist; a Southerner, born and bred.

STRANGE FRUIT. 1944. (IV) Realistic story of white and black, and miscegenation in the Deep South. It ends with a lynching. "Written honestly and with a fine bitterness against the inhumanity of Southern whites to blacks. . . . Edifying and saddening reading."— *New Yorker.*

Smith, Logan Pearsall   1865-1946   American expatriate author, long resident in England.

ALL TRIVIA. New, revised edition. 1945. (II and IV) Contains *Trivia, More Trivia, Afterthoughts* and *Last Words.* "I know nothing since Lord Bacon quite like these ineffably dainty little paragraphs of gilded whim, these rainbow nuggets of wistful inquiry, these butterfly wings of fancy, these painted sparrows of wit."—E. F. Edgett.

ON READING SHAKESPEARE. 1933. (III) Informal, humorous introduction to Shakespeare by a scholarly but enthusiastic amateur. Should go far to destroy antagonisms set up in the young by the dry-as-dust pomposities of uninspired schoolbooks.

Smith, Preserved   1880-1941   American historian and biographer. "A thin dark mild shy edge of a man."—Max Eastman.

HISTORY OF MODERN CULTURE. 2v. 1930-34. From the death of Luther to the birth of American independence (1543-1776). "A work which no scholar or student or intelligent layman can afford to miss from his shelves."—Geoffrey Bruun, in *Social Studies.*

Smith, Walter Bedell   1895-   American soldier who served through the grades from private (1910) to major-general (1945). Ambassador to the U.S.S.R., 1946-49.

MY THREE YEARS IN MOSCOW. 1950. "Happily combines personal stories with interpretations of trends and institutions."—*Commonweal.* "Another of those first-hand glimpses, becoming ever more rare, of the economy of Soviet Russia and the life of its people."— *Journal of Political Economy.*

Smollett, Tobias George   1721-71   English surgeon and novelist; translator of Le Sage, Voltaire, and Cervantes. Dickens claimed to know Smollett's rowdy books by heart.

RODERICK RANDOM. 1748. (I) Somewhat autobiographical novel of adventure by land and sea; an *exposé* of brutal conditions in the Royal Navy, in which he served as surgeon's mate at the siege of Cartagena.

PEREGRINE PICKLE. 1751. (I) Novel of travel and amorous exploits on the Continent and in London. Humorous, coarse, unedifying.

HUMPHREY CLINKER. 1771. (I) Novel about the adventures of a family traveling with an invalid through England and Scotland. Usually considered Smollett's best book. Thackeray pronounced it "the most laughable story that has ever been written."

Smyth, Henry DeWolf   1898-   American physicist.

ATOMIC ENERGY FOR MILITARY PURPOSES; THE OFFICIAL REPORT ON THE DEVELOPMENT OF THE ATOMIC BOMB UNDER THE AUSPICES OF THE UNITED STATES GOVERNMENT, 1940-45. 1945. (IV) "Virtually a textbook on nuclear physics."—*New York Times.* "Can be understood by any person who has had a high school or college education in physics."—Waldemar Kaempffert.

Snow, Edgar   1905-   American foreign correspondent; expert on China. "The first foreigner to have penetrated to the Chinese Soviet regions, to have lived with the Red armies, and to have made a study of every phase of life in Soviet China."—*New Statesman.*

RED STAR OVER CHINA. 1937. (IV) Revised edition with epilog, 1944. Valuable as a book of travel in unknown territory, exciting as a book of dangerous adventure, important as a study of politics and history, including the kidnapping of Chiang Kai-shek. But it should be emphasized that even the revised edition appeared as early as 1944.

Sologub, Feodor (pseudonym of F. K. Teternikov)   1863-1927 Russian fictionist. His sphere is the life of small provincial Russian towns. A fine stylist, his work has been compared to that of Chekhov, Poe, and Dunsany; and it seems guiltless of ideological coloring.

LITTLE DEMON. 1907. (II) In Russia, an extremely popular novel about a perverted schoolteacher.

SWEET-SCENTED NAME. 1915. (II) Fairy tales, fables and stories.

Somervell, D. C. S., editor *See* Toynbee, Arnold Joseph.

Sophocles   496-406 B.C.   Greek dramatist. The successor of Æschylus and the predecessor of Euripides in Greek tragedy's triumvirate. In the dazzling Periclean Age he was the most highly esteemed of the three.

TRAGEDIES, translated by R. C. Jebb. 1940. (I) Of more than one hundred plays that Sophocles fathered only seven have come down to us. Of these the favorites are the Œdipus trilogy: *Œdipus Tyrannus, Antigone,* and *Œdipus at Colonus;* the other extant plays are *Electra, Trachinias, Ajax,* and *Philoctetes.* (See also the notable translations by Edward FitzGerald and by William Butler Yeats.)

Southey, Robert   1774-1843   British Poet Laureate, 1813-43. Byron said of him, "His prose is perfect; of his poetry there are various opinions." Time has in general sustained Byron's judgment. The only work of Southey's that is still highly praised is the

LIFE OF NELSON. 1813. (I) "A peerless model among short biographies."—Richard Garnett.

Spencer, Herbert   1820-1903   English philosopher and social scientist. "In universality of knowledge he rivals Aristotle and Bacon at a time when the sphere of learning is immensely larger than in their epochs."—Clement Shorter. John Burroughs described Spencer as "mainly a systematizer and organizer of ideas— a sort of intellectual clearing-house on a scale befitting the Nineteenth Century." *Synthetic Philosophy* is the author's name for the ten volumes that comprise his *magnum opus.* Of these the most important is

FIRST PRINCIPLES. 1862. (I) The foundation on which the structure of the *Synthetic Philosophy* is erected.

EDUCATION: INTELLECTUAL, MORAL AND PHYSICAL. 1861. (I) This is usually considered his most important work, though it is not a part of the *Synthetic Philosophy.* The monoliths which complete that ponderous structure are

PRINCIPLES OF BIOLOGY. 1864. (I)

PRINCIPLES OF PSYCHOLOGY. 1872. (I)

PRINCIPLES OF SOCIOLOGY. 1876-96. (I)

PRINCIPLES OF ETHICS. 1869-92. (I)

The doctrine of evolution underlies Spencer's whole philosophy and explains, he believed, all phenomena, from those of astronomy to those of sociology.

Spengler, Oswald   1880-1936   German philosophical historian.

DECLINE OF THE WEST. 2v. 1920-22. New revised edition, 1945. (II and III) "A philosophy of world history conceived as an unending cycle of race-groups . . . each passing through the same successive phases—emergence, which is pre-culture; fulfillment, which is culture; and death, which is civilization, bringing extinction, and leaving no vital, enduring influence on any other race-group."—Helen Haines. (*Today and Destiny* (1940) is an intelligent condensation in one volume.)

Spenser, Edmund   1552-99   English poet. A true child of the Renaissance, who "combines the ardor of the old knightly romance with the awakening national pride of the Elizabethan age."

FAERIE QUEENE. 1590-1611. (I) Allegorical romance of chivalry. Its place is secure in the canon of English literature, though today it is more praised than read. Modern readers find allegory tiresome and the text abounds, not only with forbidding archaisms, but with references to men and events of the time which, after the passing of three or four centuries, mean little to the average reader of today.

Spiller, R. E.   1896-   **and others, editors**

LITERARY HISTORY OF THE UNITED STATES. 3v. 1948. "A landmark of criticism." "Likely to be consulted a quarter-century hence. . . . A must item for all historians of the United States." "No reader interested in American life and letters can afford to be without these three volumes."—*Quarterly Booklist.*

Spinoza, Benedict de   1632-77   Dutch philosopher of Portuguese-Jewish parentage. In his philosophy, says *Good Reading,* "Mysticism and mathematics blend to make a transcendental world."

PHILOSOPHY, SELECTED FROM HIS CHIEF WORKS. Modern Library. 1927.

ETHICS. His greatest work. There is an adequate condensation of it (84 pages) in *Masterworks of Philosophy*, edited by S. E. Frost, and published by Doubleday, 1927.

Staël, Mme. de (Anne Louise Germaine Necker) 1766-1817 Franco-Swiss bluestocking of the Napoleonic era. Her salon was famous and Napoleon feared her influence. Of her many books the following are perhaps the most noteworthy:

CORINNE. 1807. At once a romance, a book of Italian travel, and a bit of autobiography.

GERMANY. 1813. Introduction to German thought and literature, written after visits to Goethe, Schiller, and Schlegel. Though Napoleon destroyed the first edition the book was widely read both in France and England.

Stafford, Jean (Mrs. R. T. S. Lowell, Jr.) 1915- American novelist. "An extraordinarily talented novelist."—Alfred Kazin. "Miss Stafford is a commanding talent, who writes in the great tradition of the English novel."—*Saturday Review of Literature*.

BOSTON ADVENTURE. 1944. (IV) Sonia is the poverty-stricken child of immigrants—a German father and a flighty Russian mother. But when the story closes she is established in Boston as the protegé of a wealthy bluestocking spinster.

MOUNTAIN LION. 1947. "A story of two children, brother and sister, and their years of bitterness between childhood and adolescence."—*Book Review Digest*. "Hard to match . . . for subtlety and understanding. . . A sharply focused study . . . of adolescence, written wittily, lucidly, and with great respect for the resources of language."—*New Yorker*.

Stallings, Laurence 1894- American playwright; as a marine, he lost a leg in World War I.

FIRST WORLD WAR, A PHOTOGRAPHIC HISTORY. 1933. (III) Five hundred war pictures, arranged chronologically, with captions and an introduction. The book is effective because of its evident sincerity and restraint.

Stallings, Laurence, joint author *See* Anderson, Maxwell.

Starkey, Marion Lena American author.

THE DEVIL IN MASSACHUSETTS; A MODERN INQUIRY INTO THE SALEM WITCH TRIALS. 1949. "How this terrible hysteria swelled and in less than a year was dead Miss Starkey tells with a passion and veracity that will hold any reader spellbound."—Esther Forbes, in *New York Times*.

Starling, Edmund Wilson 1875-1944 American Secret Service officer.

STARLING OF THE WHITE HOUSE. 1946. "Remarkably readable memoirs."—*Time*. How he guarded five presidents: Wilson, Harding, Coolidge, Hoover, Franklin Roosevelt. His book throws new light on the personalities of all of them.

Steegmuller, Francis 1906- American author of many books; a frequent contributor to the *New Yorker*.

MAUPASSANT: A LION IN THE PATH. 1949. A biography, a critical study, and four of his subject's stories, in their first English versions. "He has sent me back to Maupassant. This is the surest test of good criticism."—Albert Guérard, in *Nation*.

Steele, Max 1924(?)- American author.

DEBBY. 1950. The heroine of this first novel is an appealing, affectionate woman with a child's mind. It won the Harper prize in 1950. "One of the most rewarding first novels I have ever read. . . . He has managed to get warmth, compassion, sympathy, irony, humor, and deep insight into his pages."—H. Basso, in *New Yorker*.

Steele, Wilbur Daniel 1886- American fictionist and dramatist who has won distinction for the quality of his short stories.

LAND'S END. 1918. (II) Stories of Portuguese fishermen on Cape Cod. "Somber . . . fascinating . . . strange."

URKEY ISLAND. 1926. "These stories are anything but delightful, pastoral effusions. Life in Urkey appears to be almost as tragic as life in 'Spoon River'. . . . But the book as a whole has the mesmeric qualities which cause the reader to return to it again and again."—*International Book Review*.

Steffens, Lincoln   1866-1936   American publicist. He was the leader of the useful group Theodore Roosevelt called Muckrakers.

AUTOBIOGRAPHY. 2v. 1931. (III) A genial prophet of disillusion, Steffens watched public affairs closely for almost half a century—and pondered them. His conclusions, as here stated, are both interesting and important.

LETTERS. 2v. 1938. (IV) Written to his family and friends, 1889-1936. "I can hear his voice in these letters as clearly as if he were in the room. . . . Steffens wrote as he spoke. There was no effort to be the 'man of letters'! He was just his own self."—O. G. Villard, in *The Nation*.

Stegner, Wallace   1909-   American novelist of the Middle West and Northwest.

BIG ROCK CANDY MOUNTAIN. 1943. (IV) Gripping story of a foot-loose family in the Far West (1906-42), and their life of cruel hardships, violence, and poverty, alternating with scenes of simple family happiness.

ONE NATION. 1945. In this book hundreds of fine photographs and a brief text present vividly the lives of minority groups in America today. "The book is unsentimental, hard-hitting and practical."— Walter White, in *Saturday Review of Literature*.

Stein, Gertrude   1874-1946   Expatriate American; reckless experimenter in writing peculiar English and in trying the patience of the public; a curiosity of American literature who perhaps influenced it considerably.

THREE LIVES. 1909. Early experiment in fiction, somewhat tentative and restrained, in "the substitution of the rhythm and diction of speech for the rhythm and structure of literary prose, and the repetitiousness and unselectivity of oral discourse for the rational selectivity of formal prose."

AUTOBIOGRAPHY OF ALICE B. TOKLAS. 1933. (III) Gertrude Stein's autobiography, pretending to be that of her companion. Deceptively naïve, it sketches informatively and inimitably the birth and growth of new art and literature in Paris, 1905-35.

Steinbeck, John   1902-   American novelist, "of German and Irish extraction"; member, National Institute of Arts and Letters.

TORTILLA FLAT. 1935. Story of a group of carefree *paisanos*, of many races, who lived happily in a tumbledown section of Monterey, California.

OF MICE AND MEN. 1937. (IV) Story of two drifting ranch-hands, one a Hercules who is also one of "God's fools." "A thriller, a gripping tale running to novelette length. . . . It is more than that; but it is that."—*New York Times.* "Its style is right for its subject-matter, and that subject-matter is deeply felt, richly conceived and perfectly ordered. That is praise enough for a book."—H. S. Canby, in *Saturday Review of Literature.*

LONG VALLEY. 1938. (IV) Consists of 15 short stories, including *Red Pony*—"a heart-breakingly true picture of boyhood." "I think it's a masterpiece," says Clifton Fadiman.

GRAPES OF WRATH. 1939. (IV) Story of the "Okies," driven to California by the dust-storms of 1934 and the pressure of the big, mechanized corporate farms. "The summation of 18 years of realism. . . . The book is profane and sometimes shocking in detail. So is that segment of America which Steinbeck describes. . . . This is no book for the timid."—Edward Weeks, in *Atlantic.* "It belongs high in the category of the great angry books like *Uncle Tom's Cabin* that have roused a people to fight against intolerable wrongs."—*New Republic.*

THE MOON IS DOWN. 1942. (IV) Story about the German occupation of Norway in World War II—the resistance of the inhabitants of an occupied village. "The lesson this book carries should be known to every American. It is one of the best short novels I have ever read."—John Gunther, in *New York Herald Tribune.*

Stendhal (pseudonym of Marie Henri Beyle)   1783-1842 French novelist. At mid-century his stock was enjoying a boom in the marts of letters.

RED AND THE BLACK. 1830. This very early psychological novel —Stendhal's masterpiece—is the study of a personality at war with itself over revolutionary and reactionary impulses. It pictures the period in French history which followed the downfall of Napoleon.

CHARTERHOUSE OF PARMA. 1839. Realistic novel of political and amorous intrigue in a reactionary Italian court, after the fall of Napoleon. "The book opens with a famous narrative of the Battle of Waterloo."

Stephen, Sir Leslie   1832-1904 English biographer and critic; first editor of the *Dictionary of National Biography*; father of Virginia Woolf. George Meredith said that his was "the profoundest and most sober criticism that we have had in our time. Its only sting was an inoffensive and humorous irony."

HOURS IN A LIBRARY. 3v. New edition, 1892. (I) Collection of essays on writers and books of the Eighteenth and Nineteenth Centuries.

Stephens, James   1882-1950   Irish story-teller and poet. "Best known for his whimsical tales and adaptations from ancient Irish legend."

CROCK OF GOLD. 1912. (II) Tale of men, gods, and fairies—for adults. His best known book.

MARY, MARY. 1912. (II) Charming and humorous story of Dublin life. (Called *The Charwoman's Daughter* in England.)

HERE ARE LADIES. 1913. (II) Here is nonsense—but amusing, heart-touching, wise.

ETCHED IN MOONLIGHT. 1928. (III) His elfin spirit of graceful whimsy is not, as of old, to be found in these stories, but rather a tragic beauty and intensity which are more impressive.

COLLECTED POEMS. 1931. "A poet of fancy and imagination, a blender of incongruous elements, who interests, charms, and warms us."—*Good Reading.*

DEIRDRE. 1923. (II) New and effective rendering of this tragic story of Irish folklore.

Stern, Gladys Bronwyn   1890-   English novelist.

MATRIARCH CHRONICLES. 4v. 1936. (II) This tetralogy tells the story, for 130 years, of a gay, cosmopolitan family of (originally) Viennese Jews. It has many good qualities, including "liveliness, breadth, unity and distinction."

Sterne, Laurence   1713-68   English novelist and clergyman. His style is original and almost indescribable. There is a deal of sentiment, or rather sentimentality, in his work, and also humor which is sly almost always and now and then nasty. In characterization he is superb.

TRISTRAM SHANDY. 1759-67. (I) This, his masterpiece, is described as "a heterogeneous sort of whimsical, humorous memoirs." It is teasingly outrageous and above all original.

SENTIMENTAL JOURNEY. 1768. (I) "A vehicle for sentimental or ludicrous moralizing on the absurdities, elusive humor and pathos of human life and character. The traveler is a reflection of Sterne himself."—E. A. Baker.

Stettinius, Edward R. 1900-1949 American industrialist and statesman; a leader in the organization of the United Nations.

ROOSEVELT AND THE RUSSIANS; THE YALTA CONFERENCE. 1949. "A contribution to the history of the second war of absolutely first importance."—Walter Millis, in *New York Herald Tribune.*

Stevens, Wallace 1879- American "objectivist" poet, and insurance executive.

TRANSPORT TO SUMMER. 1947. "He has been called the poets' poet here in America. His new volume will be welcomed by all poets and poetry lovers."—*Kirkus.* "Reinforces the accuracy of the appraisal—which is now at last current—that Stevens is a most deservedly respected poet."—*Saturday Review of Literature.*

Stevenson, Robert Louis 1850-94 Scottish fictionist, essayist, and poet.

TREASURE ISLAND. 1883. (I) Perennially fascinating tale of adventure, with buried gold, pirates, mutiny, and a dauntless cabin boy.

DR. JEKYLL AND MR. HYDE. 1886. (I) Dramatic tale of the war between good and evil that is waged within every human personality.

KIDNAPPED. 1886. (I) A gallant young Scot's romantic adventures on sea and land, in the year 1751.

DAVID BALFOUR. 1893. (I) A worthy sequel to *Kidnapped.* (Called *Catriona* in England.)

MASTER OF BALLANTRAE. 1889. (I) Cloak and sword romance of two Scottish brothers, whose bitter hatred for each other resulted in the death of both, far from home amid Adirondack snows.

WEIR OF HERMISTON. 1896. The author died while this work was in progress. "This fragment of a novel is looked upon as Stevenson's masterpiece . . . the foundation on which a very great novel might have been built."—*A.L.A. Catalog,* 1926.

TRAVELS WITH A DONKEY IN THE CEVENNES. 1879. (I) Many consider this account of a lonely walking trip Stevenson's most charming book of travel.

FAMILIAR STUDIES OF MEN AND BOOKS; and VIRGINIBUS PUERISQUE (I), both published in 1881, contain most of his best essays.

CHILD'S GARDEN OF VERSES. 1885. (I) "These poems show such unsophisticated memory and intimate understanding of childhood as to make its author the poet laureate of the nursery."—Clayton Hamilton.

LETTERS, 1868-94; edited by Sir Sidney Colvin. 4v. New edition, 1911. Will delight the admirers of "Tusitala" (Teller of Tales) as he was called by his Samoan friends. "You see the very heart of the man."

Stewart, George Rippey 1895- American author, teacher, soldier.

NAMES ON THE LAND; A HISTORICAL ACCOUNT OF PLACE-NAMING IN THE UNITED STATES. 1945. (IV) "A sort of informal history of America, written around his central theme. . . . Highly readable."— *Nation.* "Mr. Stewart has performed a very useful job in a very competent manner."—H. L. Mencken, in *New York Herald Tribune.*

STORM. 1941. (IV) Something new in fiction—a biographical novel about a storm named Maria. "The freshness and vividness of Mr. Stewart's background give it novelty and the storm gives the characters something to fight. . . . Maria herself is a very decided character."— S. V. Benét, in *New York Herald Tribune.*

FIRE. 1948. This novel by the author of *Storm* relates the life history of a forest fire. "The writing is superb—hard, lean, expressive prose. It's an exciting story . . . and so real it's hard to believe the Spitcat never existed."—*Christian Science Monitor.*

Stewart, Randall 1896- American professor of English at Brown University.

NATHANIEL HAWTHORNE. 1948. A biography with all the facts, but not much criticism; though what there is moves the reader to wish there were more. "The nearest to a standard *life* of Hawthorne yet produced."—*Quarterly Booklist.*

Stilwell, Joseph Warren 1883-1946 American soldier.

STILWELL PAPERS; arranged and edited by T. H. White. 1948. A very frank account of the general's part in World War II, as waged in India, China, and Burma (December 1941-October 1944). "These papers (never meant to be published) give us Stilwell in the raw. They add up to a self-portrait of a remarkable man who faced an impossible task and grappled with it pugnaciously until it beat him down."—*New York Herald Tribune.*

Stimson, Henry Lewis 1867-1950 American cabinet officer under Presidents Taft, Hoover, Roosevelt, and Truman.

ON ACTIVE SERVICE IN PEACE AND WAR. 1948. Half the book deals with the years of World War II. "One of the most important biographical works of our generation."—*Foreign Affairs.* "A truly notable personal history. It is the record of a man of high honor and integrity, told with meticulous fairness and honesty."—*Saturday Review of Literature.*

Stockton, Frank R. 1834-1902 American writer of humorous fiction. Original, whimsical, incongruous, absurd—these adjectives occur at once to one seeking to describe the quality of Stockton's stories.

CASTING AWAY OF MRS. LECKS AND MRS. ALESHINE. 1886. (I) The amusing and folksy, but most improbable maritime adventures of two respectable New England widows of middle age.

RUDDER GRANGE. 1879. (I) Account of a summer spent by a young suburban couple, keeping house in a stranded canal-boat.

THE LADY OR THE TIGER? 1882. (I) His best known story. There's a trick in it.

Stoker, Bram 1847-1912 British writer and critic.

DRACULA. 1897. Some experts say that this frightful tale of modern vampires and werewolves is the best horror story ever written.

Stone, Irving 1903- American biographer.

SAILOR ON HORSEBACK. 1938. (IV) The life of Jack London. "A vivid and exciting history of a vivid and exciting personality."— *Times* (London).

Stowe, Harriet Beecher   1812-96   American novelist; sister of
Henry Ward Beecher.

Uncle Tom's Cabin. 1852. (I) Mediocre but momentous story
of life on a Southern plantation before the Civil War. Howells pronounced it "one of the great novels of the world, and of all time."

Oldtown Folks. 1869. (I)

Minister's Wooing. 1859. (I) Two good stories of New England life and character at the beginning of the Nineteenth Century.

Strachey, Lytton   1880-1932   English biographer; the leader, in
England, of a recent school of biography, practicing a becoming
brevity which excludes everything redundant but nothing significant.

Eminent Victorians. 1918. (I and II) "Pungent criticism of
the Victorian Age," set forth in lively sketches of Cardinal Manning,
Dr. Thomas Arnold, Florence Nightingale, and General Gordon.

Queen Victoria. 1921. (I and II) "There is no such short
biography in English."—J. C. Squire. "The book is a masterpiece
which will influence the art of biography."—*New Statesman*.

Elizabeth and Essex. 1928. (III) Not irony but intrigue and
romance are the keynotes of this masterly portrayal of glamorous figures in England's Golden Age.

Streit, Clarence   1876-   American publicist.

Union Now, a Proposal for the Federal Union of the Democracies of the North Atlantic. 1939. (IV) A forceful and
convincing book. Never for a moment of its life has its author
stopped fighting chivalrously for its high principles. "Its great value
lies in the fact that it will prepare public opinion for what must ultimately be the solution of the problem of peace."—*Nation*.

Stribling, T. S.   1881-   American novelist; "known for his realistic studies of crime, injustice, ignorance, poverty, and economic
domination in the South, especially in Alabama."—*Reader's Encyclopedia*, 1948.

The Forge. 1931. Story of an Alabama family in Civil War
and Reconstruction days, "the background of social history being
rather more important than the characters themselves."

THE STORE. 1932. This sequel to *The Forge* was the Pulitzer prize novel in 1933. It carries the story through a second generation of the Vaiden family.

UNFINISHED CATHEDRAL. 1934. Concludes this saga of three generations of an Alabama family.

Strindberg, August   1849-1912   Swedish dramatist and novelist. He has been called the arch misogynist and, because of his unrelenting pessimism, the Swedish Schopenhauer. H. L. Mencken described him as "a lunatic with a gift for turning the preposterous into the shocking."

PLAYS. 4v. 1912-16. (I and II)

Strode, Hudson   1893-   American teacher, lecturer, author of books about foreign countries.

TIMELESS MEXICO. 1944. (IV) A history of Mexico from Montezuma to 1944. "Scholarly without being pedantic, factual without being dull, and readable without being superficial. In short an excellent one-volume survey of Mexico."—*New Yorker.*

Struther, Jan (pseudonym of Joyce Anstruther Maxtone Graham) 1901-   English novelist and poet.

MRS. MINIVER. 1940. (IV) Story-sketches of small domestic matters in upper middle-class England. "This is mandarin writing, beautifully selected with hardly a superfluous phrase."—Edward Weeks in *Atlantic.* "Mrs. Miniver, like Charles Lamb, will place a gentle hand on your elbow and bid you stop to observe something quite insignificant, and lo! it is not insignificant at all."—Clifton Fadiman, in *New Yorker.*

Stuart, John, joint author   *See* Hicks, Granville.

Sturluson, Snorri   *See* Heimskringla.

Suckow, Ruth   1892-   Author of novels and short stories dealing realistically with life in Iowa.

THE FOLKS. 1934. (IV) In this long novel the author depicts with photographic realism the life of a middle-class, American, small-town family. The book's objectivity "is considerably modified by an infusion of kindly sentiment."

Sudermann, Hermann   1837-1928   German novelist and dramatist.

DAME CARE. (FRAU SORGE). 1892. (I) Pathetic and beautiful story of misfortune manfully borne. His most famous novel.

SONG OF SONGS. 1908. (I) Story of the downfall of a well-meaning but weak and unfortunate woman. Merciless analysis, step by step, of the degeneration of character.

MAGDA. 1893. (I) The heroine of this, Sudermann's most famous play, is a woman with a past—also a prima donna. It has been often revived. Every emotional actress has yearned to try her hand at the leading role.

Suetonius   70-140   Roman writer; secretary to the Emperor Hadrian.

LIVES OF THE TWELVE CAESARS. 120 A.D. (I) Little real history is to be gleaned from these gossiping accounts of the Roman emperors from Caesar to Domitian. But they make racy reading as a nearly contemporary collection of personalities and anecdotes.

Sullivan, Sir Arthur *See* Gilbert, Sir William S.

Sullivan, Mark   1874-1952   American journalist.

OUR TIMES; THE UNITED STATES, 1900-1925. 6v. 1926-35. (III) A sprightly chronicle, with lots of pictures, of our recent history and behavior. None of these pages is profound and some are superficial; but all are precious to nostalgic old-timers.

Sumner, William Graham   1840-1910   American sociologist.

FOLKWAYS; A STUDY OF THE SOCIOLOGICAL IMPORTANCE OF USAGES, MANNERS, CUSTOMS, MORES, AND MORALS. 1906 and 1940. He believed that the power of the forces named in his title rendered useless attempts at social reform.

Sumner, William Graham, joint author *See* Keller, A. G.

Swift, Jonathan   1667-1745   The greatest of English satirists.

GULLIVER'S TRAVELS. 1726. (I) This remarkable book is at once a satire—brilliant, bitter, profound and terrible; a fascinating fairy tale, for children, of marvelous travels; and a model of English style.

TALE OF A TUB. 1704. (I) A satire on Peter (Roman Catholicism), Jack (Protestant Extremism), and Martin (Lutheranism and Anglicanism). Some critics consider it Swift's masterpiece.

BATTLE OF THE BOOKS. 1704. (I) Discussion of the eternal question as to the comparative value of ancient and modern authors. Swift champions the former.

JOURNAL TO STELLA, 1710-31. "A wonderful medley, in which grave reflections and important facts are at random intermingled with trivial occurrences and the puerile jargon of the most intimate tenderness."—Sir Walter Scott.

Swinburne, Algernon Charles 1837-1909 English poet. "The most fertile lyric poet of the Victorian era, whose unequaled versatility in the use of the lyric form was amazing in its brilliance."—*Cambridge History of English Literature.*

COMPLETE POETICAL WORKS. 2v. 1924. (I) "The music of his verse was as new to Victorian ears as its subject-matter. He wrote as Tannhäuser might have sung, with the madness of the Venusberg upon him, of strange sins, and exotic passions and mad eroticism. His measures were not new but they sounded on his lyre as though they had never been heard before. Swinburne represents genius without talent, passion without reason." —*Doubleday's Encyclopedia.*

Swinnerton, Frank 1884- English novelist, critic, biographer.

NOCTURNE. 1917. (II) His best known novel. H. G. Wells called it "a book that will not die." With an art that never falters he compresses the significance of years into events that occur within a few hours.

SEPTEMBER. 1919. (II) Love story of a married woman, aged thirty-eight. "The book is one that almost any English novelist might have been proud to write."—*Saturday Review.*

Swinnerton, Frank, editor *See* Bennett, Arnold.

Swisher, Carl Brent 1897- American university professor, student, scholar, and writer on American constitutional history.

GROWTH OF CONSTITUTIONAL POWER IN THE UNITED STATES. 1946. "Good reading for the people in whose hands rests the future of federalism."—*Commonweal.* "In addition to its many other good qualities Professor Swisher's book has the merit of being exceedingly readable."—*American Historical Review.*

Symonds, John Addington 1840-93 English scholar, critic, biographer. "Culture has done its perfect work and endowed him with its greatest gift—the sense of proportion."—Richard Le Gallienne.

RENAISSANCE IN ITALY. 5v. 1875-86 and 7v. 1897-98. (Summary in 1 v. by A. Pearson.) (I) Sympathetic and scholarly record of one of the most fascinating periods of European history. The scholar may read it with profit, the general reader with enjoyment.

STUDIES OF THE GREEK POETS. 1873-76. (I) "He has the art of making the Greek poets live to our eyes as if we saw in pictures the scenes they sing."—Frederic Harrison.

LIFE OF MICHELANGELO. 2v. 3d edition, 1925. (I) A biography of the great sculptor which is as massively brilliant as the work of its subject.

Synge, John M. 1871-1909 Irish dramatist. First influenced by Baudelaire and other French decadents, he later became associated with the Irish Renaissance and with the Abbey Theatre, Dublin.

COMPLETE WORKS. 1935. (I and II) Especially *Playboy of the Western World* (1907), and *Riders of the Sea* (1911). His work is characterized by strength and rugged beauty, combining realism with imagination. Another successful play is *Deirdre of the Sorrows* (1910), "a beautiful and poetic dramatization of the tragic Celtic legend."

ARAN ISLANDS. 1907. (II) Striking and sympathetic yet faithful record of the life, customs, tales, songs, and superstitions of the primitive dwellers on those wave-beat isles.

Tacitus 55(?)-117(?) A.D. Roman author and statesman.

WORKS. (I) These consist chiefly of, first, the *Histories* and *Annals*, both incomplete histories of Rome under the emperors; second, *Germania*, a treatise dealing principally with the manners and customs of the German tribes, whom the author considered rather virtuous and manly barbarians; and, third, *Agricola*, an admiring life of his father-in-law, the governor of Britain. This last affords us an interesting glimpse of the early days of Roman Britain, as it appeared to a cultivated citizen of the Empire.

Tagore, Rabindranath   1861-1941   Hindu mystic, poet, teacher; received Nobel prize in 1913; knighted in 1915, he resigned his knighthood three years later as a protest against British repressive measures.

COLLECTED POEMS AND PLAYS. 1936. (II) "As one reads these poems and plays, there is a soft, diffused feeling of beauty and truth. . . . One is conscious of the absence of all effort . . . of the presence only of simple loveliness."—*Crozer Quarterly.*

MY REMINISCENCES. 1917. "Record of the author's mental, spiritual and religious development in an India unknown to most Europeans. Marked by its literary quality and by a spirit of kindliness and humor."—*A.L.A. Catalog,* 1926.

Taine, H. A.   1828-93   French historian and critic; member, French Academy.

HISTORY OF ENGLISH LITERATURE; translated by H. Van Laun. 4v. 1872-74. (I) Brilliant and suggestive study, emphasizing the influence of national character, inherited culture, and environment upon literature.

ANCIENT RÉGIME. 1875. (I) Study of France as it was in 1789—"of great value for the history of France and for judgment of the future of the French Republic."

FRENCH REVOLUTION. 1878. (I) The argument as usual is based upon Taine's formula of "race, time and circumstance." But "the pages hold the reader with an irresistible fascination."

Tallmadge, Thomas Eddy   1876-   American architect; fellow, American Institute of Architects.

STORY OF ARCHITECTURE IN AMERICA. New enlarged and revised edition, 1936. (III) Popular, readable history from Captain John Smith's time to the Williamsburg restoration and the Century of Progress exposition. Outstanding personalities from Thomas Jefferson to Louis Sullivan are emphasized.

Tarbell, Ida M.   1857-1944   American editor, biographer, publicist.

LIFE OF ABRAHAM LINCOLN. 2v. 1900. New edition, 1924. "Comprehensive, authoritative biography . . . of undoubted value." —*A.L.A. Catalog,* 1926. Readability is its most outstanding quality.

Tarkington, Booth 1869-1946 American fictionist; second president, American Academy of Arts and Letters.

GENTLEMAN FROM INDIANA. 1899. (I) The book which first brought the author fame and success. It describes the struggles of its hero, a young lawyer, with political corruption; and will probably impress the modern reader by its *naïveté*.

MONSIEUR BEAUCAIRE. 1900. (I) This costume piece is a charming romance of Eighteenth-Century France.

PENROD, HIS COMPLETE STORY. n.d. (I and II) Includes *Penrod* (1914), *Penrod and Sam* (1916), and *Penrod Jashber* (1929). Irresistibly funny stories of the young American male at his most barbarous age.

SEVENTEEN. 1916. (I and II) Amusing picture of what happens when, adolescence coming to the young American male, he begins to take a lively interest in the moon.

MAGNIFICENT AMBERSONS. 1918. (I and II) Story of the sudden rise and gradual decline of a Middle West family. The spoiled son of the house is disciplined by misfortune. (Pulitzer prize, 1919.)

ALICE ADAMS. 1921. (II) This is the critics' favorite among Tarkington's books. It tells, without compromise, the story of the unsuccessful social-climbing of a small-town American girl. (Pulitzer prize, 1922.)

Tasso, Torquato 1544-95 Italian epic poet.

JERUSALEM DELIVERED. 1581. (I) Epic poem on the First Crusade. Godfrey of Bouillon is the hero. The best English translation is that by Edward Fairfax, 1600. Though it has been described as "one of the chief treasures of modern literature," it is finding few readers in the Twentieth Century.

Tate, Allen 1899- American poet, novelist, critic, biographer. His antecedents, sympathies, and interests are mostly Southern. "One of the best writers of the century."—*Quarterly Booklist.*

POEMS, 1922-47. 1948. "A literary event of the first importance."—*New York Times.* "He is a cerebral writer, incisive, pugnacious, erudite and witty."

Taylor, Francis H. 1903- American art critic; director, Metropolitan Museum of Art, New York City.

THE TASTE OF ANGELS; A HISTORY OF ART COLLECTING FROM RAMESES TO NAPOLEON. 1948. "The general reader will find the text and its lavish illustrations highly interesting."—*Quarterly Booklist*. "Mr. Taylor's documentation is thorough and ordered; yet his book is popular history in its best sense."—*Atlantic*.

Taylor, Henry Osborn 1856-1941 American student of the past.

MEDIEVAL MIND. 2v. 4th edition, 1925. "Profound and sympathetic study of the development of thought and emotion in the Middle Ages."—*A.L.A. Catalog, 1926*.

Taylor, Jeremy 1613-67 English prelate; chaplain to Charles I. Emerson called him "the Shakespeare of divines."

HOLY DYING. 1651. (I) "Colloquial treatise of Christian exposition and exhortation."—Edmund Gosse.

HOLY LIVING. 1650. (I) "His *Holy Living and Dying* is a divine pastoral. He writes to the faithful followers of Christ, as the shepherd pipes to his flock."—William Hazlitt.

Teasdale, Sara 1884-1933 American lyric poet. "Her favorite form was the brief lyric of personal emotional experience."—F. B. Millett.

COLLECTED POEMS. 1937. (II, III, and IV) Contains most of the poems from eight of her books.

Temple, Dorothy Osborne, Lady *See* Osborne, Dorothy.

Tennyson, Alfred, Lord 1809-92 Poet Laureate of England, 1850-92. "I regard him as the noblest poet who ever lived. . . . No poet is so little of the earth, earthy."—Edgar Allan Poe. "Lovers of poetry will always read him as they will read Wordsworth, Keats, Milton, Coleridge and Chaucer. . . . He is with Milton for learning, with Keats for magic and vision, with Virgil for graceful re-casting of ancient golden lines."—Andrew Lang.

COMPLETE POETICAL WORKS. Cambridge edition. n.d. (I) Tennyson was the great and very characteristic poet of the Victorian era. Of all the Poets Laureate he best merited the distinction. But—"he accepted obvious or accepted truth with rare felicity, but discovered no new truth."

His chief long poems are *Locksley Hall* (1842), *The Princess* (1847), *In Memoriam* (1850), and *Idylls of the King* (1859-72). Many of his immensely popular short poems have been recited with gusto by generations of schoolboys and some of them are enshrined in our hymnals.

Terence (Publius Terentius Afer)   195(?)-159 B.C.   Roman author of comedies which he translated and adapted from originals by the Greek author, Menander.

COMEDIES. Terence has been called the founder of polite comedy, and "his influence has been felt throughout the whole history of literature; but only six of his plays have survived. (There is a good translation of these in the Loeb Classical Library.) They are *Andria, Eunuchus, Heautontimorumenos, Phormio, Hecyra,* and *Adelphi.*

Terhune, Alfred McKinley   1899-   Professor at Syracuse University.

LIFE OF EDWARD FITZGERALD. 1947. FitzGerald was not only a quaint character and the translator of *The Rubáiyát*, he was the lifelong friend of Thackeray, Tennyson, and other eminent Victorians. "On the basis of his research, the author has been able to give a more detailed and accurate history of FitzGerald's life than has hitherto been possible, and one which is filled with glimpses of the society in which FitzGerald moved."—*U.S. Quarterly Booklist.*

Terry, Dame Ellen   1848-1928   English actress and **Shaw, George Bernard   1856-1950**   Irish dramatist.

ELLEN TERRY AND BERNARD SHAW; A CORRESPONDENCE. 1931. (III) This extraordinary sentimental correspondence went on for thirty years. It is one of the more delightful curiosities of literature. Though both lived in or near London the writers very seldom or perhaps never met, except across the footlights.

Thackeray, William Makepeace   1811-63   English novelist and satirist.

VANITY FAIR. 1847-48. (I) This picture of English society at the beginning of the Nineteenth Century has been called, by a good many competent critics, the greatest novel ever written in English. The chief character, green-eyed, fascinating Becky Sharp, is perhaps the best known and least loved heroine in all fiction.

PENDENNIS. 1848-50. (I) This novel, wrote Brander Matthews, "is at once the delight and the despair of all young men who seek to lead the literary life." It may be added that it is a book for all who are *interested* in genteel young men and wish to understand them. For one reason or another many readers belong in that category.

HENRY ESMOND. 1852. (I) The greatest and most charming of all historical novels. England in the Seventeenth Century is the scene. Walter Pater called it "a perfect fiction," and Saintsbury considered it "the greatest book of its own special kind ever written."

THE NEWCOMES. 1853-55. (I) Of this genial description of English society as it was a century ago Dean Hole declared that "none of his books shows so clearly, but not in the least priggishly, his love of goodness and his contempt for evil." Some consider it his masterpiece.

THE VIRGINIANS. 1857-59. Sequel to *Henry Esmond.* While it is not quite equal to the four great novels which preceded it, Americans will enjoy its descriptions of life in colonial Virginia, where one of Colonel Esmond's twin grandsons fought for and the other against General Washington.

ENGLISH HUMORISTS OF THE EIGHTEENTH CENTURY. 1851. (I) Few men have known Eighteenth-Century England as thoroughly as Thackeray. His lectures on *The Four Georges* are proof of this and so are these sprightly discourses on Swift, Congreve, Addison, Prior, Gay, Pope, Hogarth, Smollett, Fielding, Sterne, and Goldsmith.

THE FOUR GEORGES. 1855-56. "Truculent enough in their general satire . . . but full of generous passages about individuals."—George Ticknor. "An airy, humorous and brilliant picture of English life and manners."—*Athenaeum.*

Tharp, Mrs. Louise (Hall)   1898-   American author.

PEABODY SISTERS OF SALEM. 1950. One sister founded the American kindergarten, another married Horace Mann, and the third became Mrs. Nathaniel Hawthorne. "These people mattered largely in their day, and we enjoy that day and feel their vitality in this leisurely and attractive book."—Edward Weeks, in *Atlantic.*

Thayer, William Roscoe   1859-1923   Student and able practitioner of the art of biography; member, American Academy of Arts and Letters.

LIFE AND LETTERS OF JOHN HAY. 2v. 1915. (I and II) Readable and reliable book about an interesting man. In his youth Hay was Lincoln's secretary and friend; in middle age a popular dialect poet (*Little Breeches*) and novelist; and in his maturity a successful diplomat and statesman, and Lincoln's biographer.

ART OF BIOGRAPHY. 1920. (I) Interesting study of "the development of biographical writing, with instances and illustrations drawn from the entire field of biographical literature."

Theocritus   Flourished about 270 B.C.   Greek poet: the originator of rustic verse; imitated by Virgil in his *Eclogues*.

IDYLLS. (I) Charming idealizations of the life of the Sicilian peasants of the author's day. Andrew Lang's is a good prose translation.

Thomas, Augustus   1859-1934   American playwright; member, American Academy of Arts and Letters.

WITCHING HOUR. 1907 and 1916. (II) In this very successful stage play effective use is made of telepathy and hypnotism.

AS A MAN THINKS. 1911. (II) Herein the author develops strikingly "the power of mind over matter."

Thomas à Kempis   1380-1471   German ecclesiastic and mystic.

IMITATION OF CHRIST. 1418-24. (I) "For more than four centuries the chief manual of devotion for Christian lands." Matthew Arnold called it "the most exquisite document after those of the New Testament, of all that the Christian faith has inspired." More than five hundred editions were published in the Nineteenth Century. It has been "more widely translated than any book except the Bible."

Thomas Aquinas, Saint   *See* Aquinas, St. Thomas.

Thomason, John William   1893-1944   American soldier, author, illustrator.

FIX BAYONETS! 1926. (III) Probably the best of the personal narratives of World War I soldiers, its vividness being heightened by the author's own vigorous sketches.

**Thompson, Francis   1859-1907   English poet and mystic who "learned in suffering what he taught in song." "Truly an ascetic, he stood alone among contemporary poets, both for beauty of thought and beauty of expression."

POEMS. Revised edition, 1941. (I and II) *The Hound of Heaven* is his best known poem. In the pursuit of the hare by the hound it symbolizes "the eternal pursuit of reluctant mankind by the grace and redemption of God."

Thomson, James   1700-48   British poet.

THE SEASONS. 1726-30. (I) Poems that led the movement back to nature, away from the artificiality of the Age of Pope.

CASTLE OF INDOLENCE. 1748. (I) Excellent allegorical poem in Spenser's style.

Thoreau, Henry David   1817-62   American author and naturalist. "It is what Thoreau whispered that Whitman so uproariously bawled."—R. L. Stevenson. "Compared with his, all other books of similar vein, even White's *Selborne*, seem dry as a country clergyman's meteorological journal in an old almanac."—J. R. Lowell.

WEEK ON THE CONCORD AND MERRIMACK RIVERS. 1849. (I) "This, his first book, is less a narrative than a collection of essays and discussions."

WALDEN. 1854. (I) "A book for those who love nature, for those who love courageous thinking, courageous acting, and all sturdy, manly virtues."—Bradford Torrey.

MAINE WOODS. 1864. Though *Walden* is Thoreau's best known book, this is the favorite of many readers. It is "full of strange doings of the Indians who talk with the musquashes (muskrats) as with friends, of the varied panorama of nature and the picturesque lives of the busy lumbermen and the hardy pioneers."

WORKS; selected and edited by H. S. Canby. 1937.

PORTABLE THOREAU. 1947. Each of these contains in a single volume a wise and generous selection from all of Thoreau's work, including the massive and fascinating *Journal*.

Thousand and One Nights   *See* Arabian Nights' Entertainment.

Thucydides   470(?)-400 B.C.   Greek historian.

PELOPONNESIAN WAR. (I) Extraordinary things have been said about this account of the war between Athens and Sparta. Consider Macaulay's enthusiasm, for example: "What are all the Roman historians to the great Athenian? There is no prose composition in the world that I place so high as the seventh book of Thucydides. It is the *ne plus ultra* of human art."

Thurber, James   1894-   American humorist, playwright, cartoonist; since 1926 a contributor to the *New Yorker*.

THURBER CARNIVAL; written and illustrated by James Thurber. 1945. Omnibus of the writings of a modern satirist who, as D. S. Norton said in the *New York Times*, "tosses a bomb while he appears to be tipping his hat."

Tibullus, Albius   54(?)-19(?) B.C.   Roman poet.

ELEGIES. "Among the most perfect of their kind which have come down to us from classical antiquity." Four "books" were attributed to him, but the third and fourth are now regarded by scholars as wholly or in part spurious.

Ticknor, George   1791-1871   American scholar and man of letters.

HISTORY OF SPANISH LITERATURE. 3v. 1849. 4th edition (the last revised by the author), 1872. (I) "Remains authoritative . . . perhaps the first American book to establish throughout the learned world the position of any American scholar."—Barrett Wendell, in 1900.

Tilton, Eleanor M.   1914-   Professor of English at Temple University.

AMIABLE AUTOCRAT; A BIOGRAPHY OF DR. OLIVER WENDELL HOLMES. 1947. Scholarly life of the poet, doctor, lecturer, teacher, and wit. "Miss Tilton handles this outrageous and perplexing career with a commendable sobriety and a rather neat, dry style, not without humor."—Maxwell Geismar, in *Saturday Review of Literature*.

Tocqueville, Alexis de   1805-59   French author and politician.

DEMOCRACY IN AMERICA. 2v. 1945. (Originally published, 1835-39.) (I) "The first impartial and systematic study of American institutions." Few books have been so much discussed and quoted. James Bryce pronounced it "one of the few treatises on the philosophy of politics which has risen to the rank of a classic."

Tolstoi, Count Leo 1828-1910 Russian fictionist, dramatist, and moral, social, and religious reformer.

WAR AND PEACE. 3v. 1865-72. (I) Panorama of Russian life, public and private, during the Napoleonic Wars. Many critics consider it the greatest novel ever written.

ANNA KARENINA. 2v. 1875-76. (I) A profoundly tragic work of fiction in the course of which Russian manners and customs under the old régime are presented in great detail. Thomas Mann says it is the greatest novel of society in the world's literature.

NINE STORIES, 1855-63. 1934. (World's Classics.) A good selection of the best short stories.

COMPLETE PLAYS. n.d. (World's Classics.) "Powerful dramatic expressions of Tolstoi's social beliefs."—*Good Reading.*

RESURRECTION. 1899. This novel is also "a moral and social tract enunciating the author's gospel of brotherhood. It tells the story of an aristocrat brought face to face with the girl he has ruined, his repentance and struggle for her redemption."—*A.L.A. Catalog,* 1926.

ESSAYS AND LETTERS. n.d. (World's Classics.) A careful selection from these phases of Tolstoi's writing.

Tomlinson, H. M. 1873- British stylist; known for his brilliant sketches and stories of life at sea.

SEA AND THE JUNGLE. 1913. (II) Sketches of life in the Brazilian jungle and aboard a British tramp steamship. "Established the author's reputation as a writer of real literature."— *Reader's Encyclopedia,* 1948.

GALLION'S REACH. 1927. (III) Not an especially good novel, but a fine book about the sea and the jungle and what they did to the soul of a London clerk.

ALL OUR YESTERDAYS. 1930. (III) A leisurely, reflective war novel which follows the course of British empire from 1900 to 1918. For adult minds, capable of appreciating and assimilating good writing.

GREAT SEA STORIES OF ALL NATIONS FROM ANCIENT GREECE TO MODERN JAPAN. 1930. A magnificent collection (1108 pages) by many authors, assembled by one with an expert's knowledge and love, both of the sea and good writing.

Toynbee, Arnold Joseph 1889- English historical scholar and writer.

STUDY OF HISTORY; abridgment of Vols. 1 to 6, by D. C. S. Somervell. 1947. The original work—an analysis of the rise and fall of civilizations—is so monumental as to overwhelm all but the most determined of general readers. "It is difficult to see how the abridgment could have been done more loyally or more adroitly."—*Annals of the American Academy of Political and Social Science.*

CIVILIZATION ON TRIAL. 1948. Thirteen essays and lectures contributing to the clarification of *A Study of History.*

Trelawney, Edward John 1792-1881 British adventurer.

RECOLLECTIONS OF THE LAST DAYS OF SHELLEY AND BYRON. 1858. Readable memoirs of two great literary figures, set down by a close friend and companion.

Trench, R. C. 1807-86 English philologist, prelate, and poet.

ON THE STUDY OF WORDS. 1851. (I) "The most popular of scholarly and the most scholarly of popular books on the subject."— G. E. Saintsbury.

Trevelyan, George Macauley 1876- British historian; son of Sir George Otto Trevelyan, also a historian.

ENGLAND IN THE AGE OF WYCLIFFE. 1899. (I) Presents the political, social and religious life of the Fourteenth Century in a manner acceptable alike to the student and general reader.

ENGLAND UNDER THE STUARTS. 1904. (I) "The best single-volume history of the Seventeenth Century."—*American Historical Review.*

HISTORY OF ENGLAND. 1926. An outline history to World War I that has been widely praised for both scholarship and style.

**Trevelyan, Sir George Otto   1838-1928   British historian, biographer, statesman; nephew of Lord Macaulay, historian, essayist and poet.

LIFE AND LETTERS OF LORD MACAULAY. 1876. (I) Ranked by many with Boswell's *Johnson* and Lockhart's *Scott*. Praise can scarce go higher.

EARLY HISTORY OF CHARLES JAMES FOX. 1880. (I) "The best picture ever drawn of the transition from the old to the new methods of statesmanship." Has the fascination of a romance.

THE AMERICAN REVOLUTION. 6v. 1899-1914. (I and II) Both good history and good literature, doing full justice to the American side.

**Trevena, John (pseudonym of Ernest J. Henham)   1870-   British novelist whose work is serious to grimness. "He spares his reader nothing."

FURZE THE CRUEL. 1907. (II) The first and best title in his Dartmoor trilogy, the others being *Heather* (1908) and *Granite* (1909). The *Academy* declared *Furze* "undoubtedly a great book— almost a masterpiece."

**Trevor-Roper, Hugh R.   1914-   Oxonian; intelligence officer in the British army, 1945.

LAST DAYS OF HITLER. 1947. "Many strange books have emerged from the recent European war. None are stranger or more horribly fascinating than this footnote to history."—*Atlantic*. "It may be a poor compliment to say of a historical work that it is more readable than a novel, but in this case it is true."—*Manchester Guardian*.

**Trollope, Anthony   1815-82   English novelist. As each generation reaches middle life, sober Trollope is "rediscovered" and his reputation "revived." He excelled in portrayal of the clerics in the Established Church of his time and the humdrum life of the cathedral close and the rural parish. Many of his best books are included in the Barchester Series (I) which comprises *The Warden* (1855), *Barchester Towers* (1857), *Dr. Thorne* (1858), *Framley Parsonage* (1861), *Small House at Allington* (1864), and *Last Chronicles of Barset* (1867). Of the six Parliamentary Novels, the best is probably *Phineas Finn* (1869); and of the Manor House Novels the favorite is *Orley Farm* (1861-62).

AUTOBIOGRAPHY. 1885. Trollope, the bluff, matter-of-fact postal official and foxhunting squire, makes no effort to glamorize his personality or literary labors. He wrote so many words a day to get

the money to pay his bills. That was all there was about it. And yet
this book is one of the most fascinating, as well as astonishing, of
autobiographies.

Trollope, Mrs Frances M.   1780-1863   English author of many
novels, now forgotten; mother of Anthony Trollope.

DOMESTIC MANNERS OF THE AMERICANS. 1832. (New edition
by Knopf, 1952). Her first book. It gave great offense to many
Americans although the justice of some of her strictures is now
recognized. Perhaps it is significant that Dickens wrote his unflattering *American Notes* and *Martin Chuzzlewit* only a few years later.
He was not sorry, it seemed, when he found what Mrs. Trollope had
told English travelers to expect.

Trotsky, Leon   1879-1940   Russian revolutionist. Banished
from Russia in 1929, he lived in Mexico from 1937 till he was murdered there.

HISTORY OF THE RUSSIAN REVOLUTION. 3v. 1932. Important
though biased account by a leading participant. The volumes are sub-
titled *Overthrow of Tzarism, Attempted Counter-Revolution*, and *Triumph of the Soviets.*

Trumbull, Robert   American journalist.

THE RAFT. 1942. (IV) True story of three United States
Navy flyers who made a forced landing in the Pacific and spent thirty-
four days on an eight-by-four raft which finally drifted ashore on an
atoll. "A far greater epic than Bligh's voyage, as the three Americans
who performed this feat are better men than Bligh. Told in plain
prose by a journalist—not one of the raftsmen—who gets everything
out of the tale and puts nothing in."—*New Yorker.*

Tully, Grace George   Miss Tully spent seventeen years in Albany, Washington, and Hyde Park as secretary to Franklin Roosevelt.

F.D.R., MY BOSS. 1949. "The most personal account of Roosevelt as a human being that is likely to be written."—*Chicago Sun.*
"Surprisingly interesting and informative."—*Saturday Review of Literature.*

Turner, Frederick J.   1861-1932   American historian; president,
American Historical Association, 1910-11.

FRONTIER IN AMERICAN HISTORY. 1920. Discusses the characteristics and influence of the shifting frontier. Will interest both student and general reader.

Twain, Mark, pseudonym   *See* Clemens, Samuel L.

Tweedsmuir, Lord   *See* Buchan, John.

Ullman, James Ramsey   1907-   American journalist, novelist, playwright, mountaineer.

WHITE TOWER. 1945. (IV)   Novel about the near conquest of a virgin mountain in Switzerland by five men and one woman, while World War II, in which they had all been involved, was rumbling on not far away. The six characters are, respectively, American, English, German, Austrian, French, and Swiss.

Unamuno, Miguel   1864-1936   Spanish philosopher, essayist, novelist, poet; called by Madariaga "the greatest literary figure in Spain"; exiled in 1923.

TRAGIC SENSE OF LIFE. 1921. (II)   A modern expression of Spanish mysticism. Mark Van Doren said it is "very absurd, but it is a tremendous work and fun for the mind." "To miss reading this book would be as great a loss as not to have read *Sartor Resartus*".— *North American Review.*

Undset, Sigrid   1882-1949   Norwegian novelist. For many years the most distinguished of Scandinavian fiction writers; awarded Nobel prize in 1928; converted to Catholicism in 1924; a refugee in Brooklyn during World War II.

KRISTIN LAVRANSDATTER. 3v. in 1. 1929 and 1935. (III) Trilogy consisting of *Bridal Wreath* (1923), *Mistress of Husaby* (1925), and *The Cross* (1927). Its background is a pageant of Fourteenth-Century life in Norway and a glorification of the Catholic Church in the Middle Ages. Against this background moves the epic of a woman's complete experience as daughter, mistress, wife, and mother.

Untermeyer, Louis   1885-   American anthologist, poet, biographer, parodist and translator.

HEINRICH HEINE: PARADOX AND POET: THE LIFE. 1937. (IV) "A definitive piece of work."—Percy Hutchison, in *New York Times.*

HEINRICH HEINE: PARADOX AND POET: THE POEMS. 1937. More than five hundred poems, many of which the compiler has here translated into English for the first time.

TREASURY OF GREAT POEMS, ENGLISH AND AMERICAN. 1942. In this book of 1,288 pages the compiler characterizes each poet, appraises his work, and gives some biographical facts concerning him.

Valmiki *See* Mahabharata.

Valtin, Jan (originally **R. J. H. Krebs**) **1904-1951** Born in Germany, he was for many years a spy by turns for the German Gestapo and the Russian Ogpu.

OUT OF THE NIGHT. 1941. (IV) "Its sincerity is manifested by the utter cynicism with which the author acknowledges his crimes, and by the tone in which he tells, without shame and without pride, of the various frauds, falsifications, and even assassinations which were everyday routine in his trade."—*Current History.*

Vance, Ethel (Mrs. Grace Zaring Stone) **1896-** Born in New York City; a great-granddaughter of Robert Owen.

ESCAPE. 1939. (IV) The escape was from imprisonment by the Nazis. "An exciting, fast-moving story that most readers won't believe and won't think any the less of for that."—*New Republic.* "The thrills of the story are managed with triumphant skill. . . . Deeply revealing of the emotional tension of life in Nazi Germany."—*Times* (London).

Van Doren, Carl **1885-1950** American teacher, author, critic, editor.

AMERICAN NOVEL, 1789-1940. Revised edition, 1940. An enlargement of the author's contribution to the *Cambridge History of American Literature.* "The book does not seem very likely soon to be superseded."—*New Republic.*

SWIFT. 1930. (III) Life of Swift, and interpretation of his character and personality. Probably the best book on Swift.

THREE WORLDS. 1936. (IV) Autobiography of Middle West schoolboy, teacher, and man of letters, in the periods before and after World War I, and during the Depression. "Should be read by every student of our times."—*Catholic World.* "It is a pleasure, in these days of autobiographical tear-squeezing, to discover an author who had a grand time, as a boy, and plenty to eat, and no Freudian hallucinations."—H. L. Mencken.

BENJAMIN FRANKLIN. 1938. (IV) Won Pulitzer prize in 1939. "The most comprehensive and the most intelligently sympathetic biography of Franklin that we have."—H. S. Commager. "A biography in the best classic traditions of that art."—Burton J. Hendrick, in *Atlantic*.

SECRET HISTORY OF THE AMERICAN REVOLUTION; AN ACCOUNT OF THE CONSPIRACIES OF BENEDICT ARNOLD AND NUMEROUS OTHERS, DRAWN FROM THE SECRET SERVICE PAPERS OF THE BRITISH HEADQUARTERS IN NORTH AMERICA, NOW FOR THE FIRST TIME EXAMINED AND MADE PUBLIC. 1941. (IV) "A most valuable contribution to the history of the Revolution, and a most interesting narrative, scholarly, thorough, and admirably written."—Allan Nevins, in *New York Herald Tribune*.

GREAT REHEARSAL; THE STORY OF THE MAKING AND RATIFYING OF THE CONSTITUTION OF THE UNITED STATES. 1948. "An exact account of the most creative political achievement in the recorded chronicles of government. It will challenge . . . men of good will in every land. And the story it tells cannot help inspiring those architects who at some future time assemble to work out the instruments of government which will substitute law for war in the international field."— W. O. Douglas, in *New York Herald Tribune*.

Van Doren, Mark   1894-   American poet, critic, educationalist; brother of Carl Van Doren; member, National Institute of Arts and Letters.

COLLECTED POEMS, 1922-30. 1939. (IV) Won a Pulitzer prize in 1940. "The subject-matter is almost always the American scene . . . landscape and climate, animals and people, incidents and legends and faiths."—*New York Herald Tribune*.

LIBERAL EDUCATION. 1943. (IV) Written at the request of the Association of American Colleges. "So suitable is his style to his theme that he has done more than explain what liberal education is. He has also exemplified it."—Alexander Meiklejohn, in *New Republic*.

NATHANIEL HAWTHORNE. 1949. A critical biography: Hawthorne as a person, and Hawthorne as an artist. "The most powerful theme to be found in his stories is that of confession. The high point of the book, then, is quite properly its brilliant description of *The Scarlet Letter*."—*Quarterly Booklist*. "The atmosphere of a hundred years ago is reflected in Van Doren's unhurried style."— *Current History*.

Van Doren, Mark, editor   *See* Whitman, Walt.

Van Dyke, Henry   1852-1933   American diplomat, divine, and man of letters; member, American Academy of Arts and Letters. He wrote gracefully of pleasant, wholesome things, in a world remote from the harsh dissonances of the Atomic Age.

LITTLE RIVERS. 1896. (I) Angling sketches—a chronicle of sober pleasures and friendly observation of men and things.

Van Loon, Hendrik Willem   1882-1944   American historian and illustrator of man, his world, and his arts. Born in Holland; member, National Institute of Arts and Letters.

STORY OF MANKIND. 1921 and 1947. (I and II) Survey from the cave man to 1920, illustrated by the author. Won the first award of the Newbery Medal, as the year's most distinguished contribution to American literature for children; but it is one of those rare "juveniles" which are enjoyed as much or more by adults. "A great book, one that will endure."—C. A. Beard, in *New Republic.*

VAN LOON'S GEOGRAPHY. 1932 and 1946. (III) "A study of man in search of food and shelter and leisure for himself and his family," enlivened by the author's numerous and effective (though scraggy) drawings.

THE ARTS. 1937. (IV) His subject includes all the arts from cave-dwelling times to the Renaissance. "Any reader of this book will have absorbed the fundamentals concerning the intention of art throughout the ages, and the place of the artist in human history."— W. R. Benét, in *Saturday Review of Literature.*

VAN LOON'S LIVES. 1942. (IV) Witty essays about forty historical personages from Confucius to Jefferson and from Queen Elizabeth to Emily Dickinson, who are entertained in small groups at Van Loon's Saturday night dinners. "This volume leaped at once into the best-seller group. The author's rollicking humor enlivens most of his pages, and in this volume his humor is at its best."—*Churchman.*

Van Paassen, Pierre   1895-   Holland-born journalist and foreign correspondent.

DAYS OF OUR YEARS. 1939. (IV) An autobiography. Spiritual and intellectual adventures in France, Germany, Russia, Italy, Spain, Morocco, Syria, Palestine, and Ethiopia, between World Wars I and II.

Van Vechten, Carl   1880-   American musical, dramatic, and literary critic; fictionist. "Recalls Huneker, and Cabell, and Arthur Machen."—E. L. Pearson.

Peter Whiffle. 1922. (II) Sparkling, witty fantasy of a charming idler among modern sophisticates. Some real persons are introduced under their own names.

Nigger Heaven. 1925. Harsh story of passionate modern Negro life in the greatest Negro city in the world—Harlem.

Vasari, Giorgio   1511-74   Italian architect, painter, and biographer of the Italian Renaissance artists.

Lives of the Artists; Biographies of the Most Eminent Architects, Painters and Sculptors of Italy. 1946. (Originally published in 1550.) "Full of anecdote and picturesque narrative and brilliant pictures of life in Italy during this epoch."—Sturgis and Krehbiel.

Veblen, Thorstein Bunde   1857-1929   American sociologist, and critic of established social and economic theories and institutions.

Theory of the Leisure Class. 1899. Does the leisure class make a substantial economic contribution to modern society? After a cool, objective study of this question Veblen's answer is an unexcited *no*. This is his best known and most influential book.

Engineers and the Price System. 1921. "Arguments in behalf of production for use rather than for profit."—*Good Reading.*

Absentee Ownership and Business Enterprise in Recent Times; the Case of America. 1923. "Theoretical, analytical, iconoclastic and stimulating."

Vega Carpio, Lope Félix de   1562-1635   Spanish playwright, soldier, priest. Incredibly prolific, he wrote nearly two thousand plays, not to mention epics and prose romances. Chief founder of the national drama of Spain, he was a master of spirited dialog, displayed infinite invention, and a wonderful gift for drawing lifelike pictures of public manners.

Four Plays in English Versions. 1936. Includes: *A Certainty for a Doubt; The King the Greatest Alcalde; The Gardener's Dog; Fuente Avejuna (The Sheep Well).* "Admirably translated. Certain to awake the gratitude of . . . people who love the world's classics, but have hitherto found Lope's dramas as a sealed book, and his genius a thing to be taken on faith."—*Catholic World.*

Verga, Giovanni   1840-1922   Italian fictionist.

House by the Medlar Tree (*I Malavoglia*). 1890. "Realistic and touching story of lower class life in an Italian fishing-village."— Keller.

Cavalleria Rusticana and Other Stories; translated by D. H. Lawrence. 1928. Tales of the Sicilian peasantry. From the title story Mascagni borrowed the plot of his famous opera.

Vergil   *See* Virgil.

Verne, Jules   1828-1905   French author of pseudo-scientific romances, some of which have proved prophetic of actual developments in modern science and technology. He was the precursor of the space-ship authors of the mid-twentieth century.

Around the World in Eighty Days. 1882. (I) Exciting narrative of what was then considered an incredibly rapid journey, undertaken on a wager, by the English hero, Phileas Fogg, and his French valet, Passepartout.

Twenty Thousand Leagues under the Sea. 1870. (I) Adventures of intrepid Captain Nemo in his wonderful electric submarine.

Mysterious Island. 1870. (I) Sequel to the above. Besides perils of the sea, there are pirates and wild beasts in this tale.

From the Earth to the Moon. 1873. "An adventurous party in America have a monster gun cast, and are shot to the moon."— E. A. Baker.

Viaud, L. M. J.   *See* Loti, Pierre, pseudonym.

Villard, Oswald Garrison   1872-1949   American liberal journalist; editor, *Nation* and *Evening Post*.

Fighting Years; Memoirs of a Liberal Editor. 1939. (IV) The years covered include the first four decades of the Twentieth Century. "A human document through which one may accurately interpret the liberal attitude of . . . forty years."—C. G. Bowers, in *New York Times*.

Vincent, Howard Paton   1904-   American student of the career and work of Herman Melville.

Trying-out of Moby Dick. 1949. Study of the evolution of a masterpiece. "The reader who has re-read *Moby Dick* in order to be ready to read Professor Vincent's book will be moved to return and re-read *Moby Dick* again."—R. L. Duffus, in *New York Times*. "As a piece of literary detective work it merits comparison with *The Road to Xanadu* by John Livingston Lowes, under whom Vincent once studied."—*Springfield Republican.*

Vitruvius Pollio, Marcus   Flourished about 40 B.C.   Roman architect.

CONCERNING ARCHITECTURE. About 16-13 B.C. Practically the only surviving original authority on classical architecture, it exercised enormous influence when classical architecture was revived during the Renaissance.

Villiers, Alan J.   1903-   British sailor and writer about the sea.

BY WAY OF CAPE HORN. 1930. (III) True story of a "windjammer's" voyage that was hazardous and full of old-fashioned hardships. It seems likely to take its place as one of the classics of the sea.

Villon, François   1431-   ?   French criminal and literary artist, whose reckless life and beautiful poems have been favorite subjects for exposition and translation at the hands of modern men of letters.

POEMS. The translations by H. De V. Stacpoole (1914) and by John Payne (Modern Library, 1918) are recommended by the *A.L.A. Catalog, 1926.*

Virgil (Publius Virgilius Maro)   70-19 B.C.   Greatest of Roman poets.

ÆNEID. About 35 B.C. (I) The national epic of Rome, in twelve "books." It narrates, chiefly, the adventures of Æneas on his journey home to Italy after the fall of Troy. Its purpose was the glorification of the Julian family (then represented by the Emperor, Augustus), the reputed founder of which was Ascanius, son of Æneas.

THE ECLOGUES. 42-37 B.C. (I) Pastoral poems, directly inspired by the Greek *Idylls* of Theocritus.

THE GEORGICS. 37-30 B.C. (I) Suggested by Hesiod's Greek *Works and Days,* these poems sing the homely arts of cultivating the soil, pruning trees and vines, animal husbandry, and bee-keeping.

There is a good translation of all Virgil's Works, by H. R. Fairclough in the Loeb Classical Library. Standard translations of *The*

Aeneid are those by C. J. Billson, and by John Conington; and there is a good recent one by Rolfe Humphries (1951).

Vogt, William 1902- American ecologist, conservationist, Malthusian.

ROAD TO SURVIVAL. 1948. "The most eloquent, provocative, and informative book that has been written thus far in the United States on conservation or the lack of it."—*Saturday Review of Literature.* "A challenge to every American. . . . In fact, if I could afford it I'd buy a copy for every member of Congress and then spend the next few months arguing each member of Congress into reading it."—J. H. Jackson, in *San Francisco Chronicle.*

Voltaire (pseudonym of François Marie Arouet) 1694-1778 French skeptic and man of letters.

HISTORY OF CHARLES XII. 1731. (I) Story of the Swedish king's wars, chiefly with Poland and Russia. Considered Voltaire's best historical work.

CANDIDE. 1759. (I) Short novel written to satirize the belief that "All is for the best in this best of all possible worlds." Probably more read today than any other of Voltaire's writings. Almost equally popular is the similar

ZADIG. 1748. (I) A satirical tale about the troubles of a wealthy young Babylonian who devotes himself to altruistic causes.

LETTERS ON THE ENGLISH. 1753. (I) Simple in style and diction, these letters discuss such subjects as English Protestant sects, the government, contemporary science and philosophy, and English literature. Of Shakespeare he says, "He was natural and sublime, but had not so much as a single spark of good taste."

VOLTAIRE IN HIS LETTERS. 1919. Translations of letters, particularly to Frederick the Great, most of which have autobiographical interest.

Vyasa *See* Mahabharata.

Wade, Mason, editor *See* Parkman, Francis.

Wald, Lillian 1867-1940 American social worker; vice-president, American Association for Labor Legislation.

HOUSE ON HENRY STREET. 1915. Story of twenty years' work in the Henry Street Settlement on New York's lower East Side.

WINDOWS ON HENRY STREET. 1934. (III) "She has written informally and humanly of the endless phases of her social work."— *New York Evening Post.*

Waley, Arthur D.   1889-   English orientalist.

Translations from the Chinese. 1941. Most of these 218 poems have never before been translated. "They represent a China of delightfully romantic philosophy."—*A.L.A. Catalog.* (*See also* Murasaki, S. *and* Bynner, Witter.)

Wallace, Alfred Russell   1823-1913   British naturalist and traveler.

MALAY ARCHIPELAGO; A NARRATIVE OF TRAVEL, WITH STUDIES OF MAN AND NATURE. 1869. (I) "The style is felicitous, making a scientific treatise as fascinating to read as a story."

CONTRIBUTIONS TO THE THEORY OF NATURAL SELECTION. 1870. Ten essays originally published separately from 1855 to 1869. The first two of these, give an outline of the origin of species as conceived by Wallace before he knew anything of Darwin's ideas on the subject. The latter's *Origin of Species* was published in 1859. But there is no reason to think that Darwin had then heard of Wallace's studies.

MAN'S PLACE IN THE UNIVERSE, A STUDY OF THE RESULTS OF SCIENTIFIC RESEARCH IN RELATION TO THE UNITY OR PLURALITY OF WORLDS. 1903. (I) Aims to prove that "earthly man is the only living and thinking being in the whole universe."

Wallace, Henry A.   1888-   American political leader and agronomist; former cabinet officer and vice president of the United States.

NEW FRONTIERS. 1934. (III) "An exposition and defense of the New Deal."—*Book Review Digest.*

Wallace, Lew   1827-1905   American soldier, official, novelist.

BEN HUR; A TALE OF THE CHRIST. 1880. (I) Best-selling historical novel of its day; a stirring tale of Rome in the First Century. Countless millions have been breathless while reading of the hero's chariot race, or watching it on stage or screen.

Waln, Nora 1895- American author; member of the Society of Friends. She married an Englishman (Edward Osland-Hill) in 1922, and has lived many years abroad, first in China and later in England and Germany.

House of Exile. 1933. (III) Story of the author's residence (1920-22) as an adopted daughter in the feudal home of an ancient Chinese family of landed proprietors with whom her own family of Quaker merchants had traded for a century.

Reaching for the Stars. 1939. (IV) Picture of life in Germany under the Nazis, 1934-38, by an eye-witness who strenuously attempts tolerance and objectivity. All three copies of this book's manuscript, though mailed from Germany separately, were "lost"; so the book had to be rewritten.

Walpole, Horace 1717-97 English dilettante and letter-writer; son of Sir Robert Walpole.

Selected Letters. (I) (Everyman's Library.) "Gossipy revelation of English life under the Georges." Byron called the letters "incomparable," and Scott pronounced Walpole "the best letter-writer in the English language." (There are ponderous, monumental, many-volumed editions by both the Oxford and the Yale University presses.)

Castle of Otranto. 1765. (I) A literary curiosity. The first of the "Gothic romances" or "novels of terror." Though grand, gloomy, and peculiar, Walpole's tale no longer frightens readers very much.

Walpole, Sir Hugh 1884-1941 English novelist. "His wit and perspicacity are mitigated by a genial human kindliness," and his books are ethically sound, as well as entertaining and well-written. But some of the more sophisticated critics have treated his work and personality with something less than enthusiasm.

Fortitude. 1913. (II) A wholesome novel, as well as artistically a fine one. It sets forth, as the shining goal of life, the building of character and high-heartedness. Probably the author's best known work.

The Cathedral. 1922. (II) Describes the struggle at the end of the Victorian era, between the old ways and the new. The battleground is a little English city, with the massive old cathedral as the dominant character. "*The Cathedral* is his best . . . a splendid Anglo-Saxon novel."—Joseph Hergesheimer.

THE DUCHESSE OF WREXE. 1914. (II)   Another story picturing the passing of the Victorian tradition. This time the protagonists are a duchess and her rebellious granddaughter. The first in a series of four novels, the others being *The Green Mirror, The Young Enchanted,* and *Wintersmoon.*

DARK FOREST. 1916. "A symbolic novel . . . pictures Red Cross work on the Russian battlefront . . . unusual, vivid and convincing." —*A.L.A. Catalog,* 1926.

JEREMY. 1919. (II)   "Delightful chronicle of the joys and sorrows of a small boy in an English cathedral town."—*A.L.A. Catalog.*

THE CAPTIVES. 1920. (II)   "Makes Mr. Walpole's previous books look like agreeable fragments. . . . Scarcely ranks below *Clayhanger* and not very greatly below *Of Human Bondage.*"—*The Nation.*

ROGUE HERRIES. 1930. (III)   A big, lusty, novel of life in Eighteenth-Century England. This is the first title in the Herries Chronicle, the others being, *Judith Paris, The Fortress,* and *Vanessa.*

Walton, Izaak   1593-1683   English fisherman, linen-draper, and biographer.

COMPLEAT ANGLER; OR CONTEMPLATIVE MAN'S RECREATION: BEING A DISCOURSE ON RIVERS, FISH-PONDS, FISH AND FISHING. 1653. (I)   This flavorsome volume makes devotees even of indoor book-lovers. It was one of the first English nature books and is still one of the most popular—fit, as J. R. Lowell said, to stand beside the *Natural History of Selborne.*

Ward, Barbara   1914-   English economist.

THE WEST AT BAY. 1948. A well-informed Englishwoman's plea for a Union of the West. Its gist: "Unity can be established and America must help."

Ward, Mrs. Humphry (Mary Augusta Arnold)   1851-1920   English novelist who was both popular and much respected during the two decades before and after the turn of the century. She was a niece of Matthew Arnold and a granddaughter of Thomas Arnold of Rugby.

ROBERT ELSMERE. 1888. (I)   This story of a clergyman's struggle between faith and agnosticism caused great excitement when published.

LADY ROSE'S DAUGHTER. 1903. (I and II) "Novel of manners depicting English society in the Eighteenth Century. Said to be based on the letters of Mlle. de Lespinasse."—*Fiction Catalog*.

MARRIAGE OF WILLIAM ASHE. 1905. (II) Story of a British statesman and his unruly wife. Suggested, probably, by events in the lives of Lord Melbourne, Lady Caroline Lamb, and Lord Byron. *The Spectator* called it "the most brilliant and attractive of all her novels."

Ward, Mary Jane (Mrs Edward Quayle)   1905-   American author.

SNAKE PIT. 1946. Novel about a patient's experience in a mental hospital. "The whole story is absorbing and told with consummate skill in understatement."—*New Republic*. "Obviously an incomplete picture but an extremely moving one."—*New Yorker*.

Warner, Sylvia Townsend   1893-   English novelist and poet.

LOLLY WILLOWES. 1926. (III) Slyly humorous fantasy. The adventures of an old maid who runs away from dependence and dull drudgery, to find delights agreeably tinctured with diabolism.

Warren, Robert Penn   1905-   American novelist, poet and critic, most of whose writings deal with some aspects of Southern life or history.

ALL THE KING'S MEN. 1946. Story of the career of a Southern demagog who in some ways suggests Huey Long. Won Pulitzer prize, 1947. "All together it is the finest American novel in more years than I would like to have to remember."—George Mayberry, in *New Republic*.

Washington, Booker T.   1856?-1915   American Negro educator. Born a slave, he was appointed in 1881 head of Tuskegee Institute. Later, he stood before kings and sat at meat with presidents.

UP FROM SLAVERY. 1901. (I and II) One of the greatest, most interesting, and most inspiring of biographies.

Wassermann, Jakob   1873-1934   Austrian Jewish novelist.

WORLD'S ILLUSION. 2v. 1930-36. (II) Written during World War I, this sombre novel is a terrible picture of rich and poor in the Central European society of that day.

Watts, Mrs. Mary Stanbery   1868-   American novelist.

NATHAN BURKE. 1910. (II) This leisurely novel tells the life story of an Ohio backwoodsman who serves in the Mexican War. Hero is modest and likable, his love affair sane and wholesome.

Waugh, Evelyn   1903-   English man of letters. He became a Catholic convert about 1930 and, later, volunteered for service in one of the first Commando units of World War II. *Sophisticated* is the adjective most often used to describe both his personality and his writing. His novels have been called "hectic pieces of savage satire."

EDMUND CAMPION. 1935. "A book about the Elizabethan martyr and recusant, which won the Hawthornden prize."

BRIDESHEAD REVISITED. 1946. "Satirical sidelights on an age and a society, in the story of a wealthy Catholic family between the two World Wars."—*Good Reading.*

Webb, Mrs. Mary Gladys (Meredith)   1881-1927   English novelist, of Welsh and Scottish parentage. Her fame is almost wholly posthumous. She was the author of five novels, the most praised being the two listed below. "Her native Shropshire is the scene of all her novels, which are somber and passionate and infused with an intense feeling for the countryside."—*Columbia Encyclopedia,* 1950. Said G. K. Chesterton, "Much of the noble work of Mary Webb might be called the prose poems of a Shropshire lass."

PRECIOUS BANE. 1924. "Powerful, tragic tale of sorrow, passion and evil-doing, combined with one of the most beautiful and moving of love stories. . . . Comparable only to the work of Hardy in its grim beauty and love of the soil, it is gentler and more emotional."— Cleveland Public Library. (Won the Femina—Vie Heureuse prize for 1924-25.)

GONE TO EARTH. 1917. The half-gipsy heroine is a passionate child of nature and a lover of all weak and hunted things. She has two suitors. One appeals to her spiritual, the other to her physical nature. "One becomes her husband, the other her lover, and her life ends in tragedy."

Webster, John 1580(?)-1625(?)   English tragic dramatist. Swinburne placed him next in rank to Shakespeare among the great Elizabethans.

WHITE DEVIL. 1612. (I) "Methinks, a very poor play."— Samuel Pepys, in 1661. "One of the most glorious works of the period. . . . Its real charm is the wholly miraculous poetry . . . which it contains."—George Saintsbury.

DUCHESS OF MALFI. 1623. (I) Webster's masterpiece . . . the finest tragedy in the English language outside the works of Shakespeare."—Edmund Gosse.

Wecter, Dixon 1906-50 American literary and historical scholar; an associate editor, *Literary History of the United States,* 1948.

WHEN JOHNNY COMES MARCHING HOME. 1944. (IV) "Study of the return of American soldiers from three wars; the Revolution, the Civil War, and the first World War."—*Book Review Digest.* "The most interesting pages are the lengthy quotations from Civil War letters and diaries."—*New Republic.*

AGE OF THE GREAT DEPRESSION. 1948. A judicious and absorbing treatise on life in the United States from 1929 to 1941. "A masterpiece of condensation. . . . The general reader may read this volume with pleasure and profit; social scientists with admiration and perhaps a little envy."—*American Political Science Review.* "Mr. Wecter is a very able social historian and his evaluation of the New Deal's peaceful revolutionary processes that transformed the country in the 1930's is one of the fairest and most mature we have had yet."—*New Yorker.*

Weizmann, Chaim 1874-1952 Born in Russia; became British subject, 1910; a biochemist; chosen provisional president of the new state of Israel, 1948.

TRIAL AND ERROR. 1949. An autobiography which is also the story of the world Zionist movement. "Wonderfully rewarding reading."—*Christian Science Monitor.* "It fulfills Carlyle's dictum that 'biography is the true history.' The reader will also find that it is well-written."—*Survey.*

Welles, Sumner 1892- American student of foreign affairs; former State Department official.

TIME FOR DECISION. 1944. (IV) Discussion of American foreign policy and the author's plan for the peace. It involves world organization based on regional systems. The *New Statesman* called it "the most important work on American foreign policy in the last twenty-five years." It still merits that description.

INTELLIGENT AMERICAN'S GUIDE TO THE PEACE. 1945. (IV) "Brief picture of every independent nation and of every major dependent people in the world."—Introduction. Seven years after publication this is still a useful work of reference.

WHERE ARE WE HEADING? 1946. "Certainly one of the most forceful, hard-hitting documents ever written by an American public servant."—*Atlantic.* "In discussing the formulation of a proper foreign policy, he is constructive, though sometimes didactic."—*New Yorker.*

Wells, Herbert George   1886-1946   British man of letters, publicist, scientist. "In his day he was easily the most brilliant, if not always the most profound, of contemporary English novelists."— H. L. Mencken, in 1919.

OUTLINE OF HISTORY. 1920. Revised edition, 1930. (I and II) Received more votes than any other title in the referendum conducted in 1924 by the *International Book Review* to determine the best ten books of the Twentieth Century. And the *Boston Transcript* said, "Mr. Wells has never written a more important book than this."

MR. BRITLING SEES IT THROUGH. 1916. (I and II) (World War I was "It.") The *New York Times* said, "Beyond question the greatest novel of the year"; and the *Nation*, "Mr. Britling is a transparent portrait of Mr. Wells—an amazingly frank portrait."

TONO-BUNGAY. 1909. (I and II) The invention and promotion of a patent medicine brings a fortune to a small-town druggist. "In many ways the best of Wells' novels . . . probably the most popular."— Carl Van Doren.

KIPPS: THE STORY OF A SIMPLE SOUL. 1905. (I and II) Tale of a suddenly enriched counter-jumper: "one of his best four books." Henry James called it "the first intelligently and consistently ironic or satiric novel."

SEVEN FAMOUS NOVELS. 860 pages. n.d. Includes: *Time Machine* (1895); *Island of Dr. Moreau* (1896); *Invisible Man* (1898); *War of the Worlds* (1898); *First Men in the Moon* (1901); *Food of the Gods* (1904); *In the Days of the Comet* (1906). "The stories are printed in chronological order, and, curiously enough, in the order of merit."—*New York Times.*

HISTORY OF MR. POLLY. 1910. (II) Humorous and sympathetic narrative of the misadventures of a small tradesman; considered by some critics his best book.

MODERN UTOPIA. 1905. (II) Describes an improved and progressive world-state, with a common language, on a planet the physical counterpart of this. The *Athenaeum* went so far in praise as to declare that "there has been no work of this importance published for the last thirty years."

EXPERIMENT IN AUTOBIOGRAPHY. 1934. (III) A clever man writes informally and honestly about himself, the events and setting of his life and the development of his ideas, with emphasis upon internationalism and the planned world.

SCIENCE OF LIFE. 2v. 1931. (III) Summary review for the layman of the biological sciences. Generally approved for its skillful selection, and felicitous, even dramatic, presentation of material. Written with Julian Huxley and George Philip Wells.

Welty, Eudora 1909- American fictionist, whose writings usually are based upon the life and manners of Mississippi.

DELTA WEDDING. 1946. Study of a Mississippi family in its decline. "There isn't any plot. There isn't any action. There isn't any suspense or crisis or noticeable sex appeal. There is atmosphere only and in delicious gulps."—*Christian Science Monitor.*

GOLDEN APPLES. 1949. "In a series of short stories the author chronicles the passing of some forty years in a little Mississippi town. The same people appear in many of the chapters, the whole adding up to a novel told in brief episodes."—*Book Review Digest.*

Werfel, Franz 1890-1945 Austro-Czech-Jewish novelist and man of letters.

FORTY DAYS OF MUSA DAGH. 1934. (III) Armenian villagers defend their mountain fastness against the Turkish army. An engrossing story, whose plot and characters live in one's consciousness and memory as though personally experienced.

SONG OF BERNADETTE. 1942. (IV) During the author's visit to Lourdes as a refugee from World War II, he vowed to write this novel as his declaration of "the divine mystery and holiness of man." "Enchants us with the magic of children's voices raised in a medieval hymn."—*Saturday Review of Literature.* "It seems to me impossible for anyone to read this book without being completely convinced of the reality of the series of apparitions of Our Lady seen by the fourteen-year-old girl in 1858."—Theodore Maynard, in *Commonweal.*

PASCARELLA FAMILY. 1932. "His most mature and most beautiful achievement. . . . Werfel has been able to compress into the molds of everyday relations a tremendous drama, comparable in amplitude to a Greek tragedy."—Angel Flores, in *New York Herald Tribune*.

Werner, Morris Robert 1897- American author of lively studies of striking American characters.

BARNUM. 1923. "A magical book recounting many amazing and amusing incidents in Barnum's career as showman, editor, legislator, manufacturer, author, real estate operator and philanthropist."— *A.L.A. Catalog*, 1926.

BRIGHAM YOUNG. 1925. "A genial but just and not unsympathetic biography of the Mormon Moses."—Cleveland Public Library.

Wertenbaker, Thomas Jefferson 1879- Virginia-born professor of history at Princeton; author of many books on colonial America.

PURITAN OLIGARCHY; THE FOUNDING OF AMERICAN CIVILIZATION. 1947. "The best study of the New England Puritans."—*New York Herald Tribune*. "A fine, painstaking study of the early Massachusetts colony."—*New Yorker*.

Wescott, Glenway 1901- American novelist. Born in Wisconsin, he has lived much in Germany, Italy, and France.

GRANDMOTHERS. 1927. (III) Fictional study of Wisconsin pioneers whose portraits appear in the family album. (Harper prize novel.)

PILGRIM HAWK. 1940. (IV) Love in a Paris suburb in the late 1920's. "Extremely interesting. A tightly bound little tale that has depths and flights far beyond the surface of the human entanglement it covers."—*New York Herald Tribune*.

APARTMENT IN ATHENS. 1945. (IV) Novel dealing with the Nazi occupation of Greece in 1943. It was called the best novel of its year. "It holds you spellbound, as you see into the hearts of the Greeks in their effort to fathom the character of the German."—*Library Journal*.

Wesley, John 1703-91 British preacher and reformer; founder of Methodism.

HEART OF JOHN WESLEY'S JOURNAL. 1903. (I) A condensation in one volume. The full journal also is available in four volumes of Everyman's Library. "Happily for us his journals remain, and from them we can learn better than anywhere else what manner of man he was and the character of the times during which he lived."—Augustine Birrell.

West, Rebecca (pseudonym of Cicily Isabel Fairfield)   1892- English novelist and critic; also, "the world's greatest woman reporter."

THE JUDGE. 1922. (II) Tragic story: the scene, Edinburgh and Sussex. The hero's love for his sweetheart is overshadowed by his almost abnormal love for his mother.

BLACK LAMB AND GREY FALCON; A JOURNEY THROUGH JUGO-SLAVIA. 2v. 1941. (IV) The author—no sluggard—spent five years writing this book of 1,200 pages—a work of philosophic history and travel in Jugoslavia. It has been called its year's "finest book of non-fiction," "one of the great books of a troubled century," etc. But the reader had best gird his loins before tackling it. This is no hammock book to while away an idle hour.

MEANING OF TREASON. 1947. "The most admirable and important book Miss West has written. . . . She belongs to the small communion of those who constantly grow. Experience is invariably transmuted into further wisdom. She speaks now with the purest, finest, and most modern English voice there is."—Struthers Burt, in *Saturday Review of Literature*.

**Westcott, Edward Noyes   1847-98   Banker of Syracuse, New York. He wrote one book, and only one, published after his death, which was so popular that it became one of the earliest American fiction "best-sellers," being preceded and surpassed in sales only by Ben Hur and Tom Sawyer.

DAVID HARUM. 1898. (I) "Not a novel of plot but a character sketch. David Harum is a shrewd country banker in Central New York, sharp at a bargain, kindhearted, with an unfailing flow of dry humor."—*New York State Library*.

**Weston, Christine   1904-   Born, reared, and married in India, she came to the United States in 1923, and became a citizen in 1928.

INDIGO. 1943. (IV) A novel, chiefly concerned with the relations between educated Hindus and Europeans, in the India of 1889 to 1918. Louis Bromfield considers it "one of the best novels ever written about India."

Weyman, Stanley J.　1855-1928　Able English practitioner of the art of cloak-and-sword romance, in a French setting.

GENTLEMAN OF FRANCE. 1893. (I) Rousing story of the gallant days of Henry of Navarre.

UNDER THE RED ROBE. 1894. (I) A romance of Cardinal Richelieu's day.

Wharton, Edith　1862-1937　American novelist. Born in New York City, half of her seventy-five years were spent in Europe, chiefly in France. Member, American Academy of Arts and Letters.

"The Sargent of American fiction."—H. S. Canby.

"She has more intelligence than Henry James, her principal master in fiction."—Carl Van Doren.

Her work is characterized by rare feeling for intricacies of motive, character, and emotion. Her point of view is that of the cultured class with wide social experience on both sides of the Atlantic.

VALLEY OF DECISION. 1902. (I and II) "Fictional study of Italian society on the verge of the French Revolution." Neither very readable nor characteristic of the author, but worked up conscientiously with immense labor. A *tour de force*.

HOUSE OF MIRTH. 1905. (I and II) Story of the gradual downfall of a New York society girl who is handicapped chiefly by her own lack of high principles. A fine book, and the author's greatest popular success.

ETHAN FROME. 1911. (I and II) "In *Ethan Frome* she reaches her highest pitch of tragic passion. . . . Not since Hawthorne has a novelist built on the New England soil a tragedy of such elevation of mood."—Carl Van Doren.

XINGU, AND OTHER STORIES. 1916. (II) Eight short stories of splendid artistry.

AGE OF INNOCENCE. 1920. (I and II) Acid delineation of New York society in the 1870's—a society that had not yet acquired self-consciousness. Won a Pulitzer prize.

OLD NEW YORK. 1924. (II) Four novelettes of New York society life: *False Dawn, The Old Maid, The Spark*, and *New Year's Day*. They are dated respectively in the '40's, the '50's, the '60's, and the '70's. Each "presents a tragedy which has its origin in the social bondage and in the deadly pressure of convention." *The Old Maid* is the best, being pronounced by the *Bookman* to be "as good as— if not, for its kind, a little better than—*Ethan Frome*." (See also its dramatization by Zoë Akins.)

BACKWARD GLANCE. 1934. (III) A book of well-mannered, gracious reminiscences. The New York of the '70's and '80's is charmingly described, as are Henry James and others of the Anglo-American scene.

Whistler, James McNeill 1834-1903 American painter and etcher, long resident in England.

GENTLE ART OF MAKING ENEMIES. 1890. "The wasp still stings, the arrows of wit still find their targets, although it is more than fifty years since this piece of masterly invective against bourgeois standards and fake art first caused its victims to writhe in helpless anger."—*English Library*.

White, Edward Lucas 1866-1934 American historical novelist and teacher of the classical languages.

EL SUPREMO. 1916. (I and II) Long historical romance about politics and the dictatorship of Dr. Francia, in Paraguay, in the years 1813-40. The praise of the critics was practically unanimous.

UNWILLING VESTAL. 1918. (I) A tale of Rome in A.D. 161-191, the time of Marcus Aurelius and his son, Commodus, both of whom appear prominently.

ANDIVIUS HEDULIO. 1921. (I and II) Adventures of a Roman nobleman in the time of Commodus. He is driven from Rome under suspicion of treason.

White, Elwyn Brooks 1899- American humorist, poet, journalist; editor and principal author of the *New Yorker* "Talk of the Town."

ONE MAN'S MEAT. Enlarged edition, 1944. (IV) Fifty-five quiet, intelligent, amusing essays written from the country. "Extraordinarily fresh and permanent pieces."—Irwin Edman, in *New York Herald Tribune*.

WILD FLAG. 1946. Plea for a world government as distinct from the international league which is now functioning under the name, United Nations. "Both statesman and skeptic should read him. Particularly when they are one and the same person."—*New York Times*.

White, Elwyn Brooks, editor

SUB-TREASURY OF AMERICAN HUMOR. 1941. (IV) (Edited and compiled with his wife, Katharine Sergeant Angell, who was formerly literary editor of the *New Yorker*.) Funny pieces from Benjamin Franklin to "F.P.A."—814 pages of them. "The best assortment of laughable Americana I have ever seen."—Edward Weeks, in *Atlantic*.

White, Gilbert   1720-93   English naturalist and clergyman.

NATURAL HISTORY OF SELBORNE. 1789. (I) An old-fashioned naturalist's account of the topography, physiography, meteorology, fauna, and flora of a single parish—his own—in Hampshire, England. It shares with Walton's *Compleat Angler* the honor of being the best loved nature book written by an Englishman. "One of the most delightful books in my father's library was White's *Natural History of Selborne*. . . . It takes you out of doors."— J. R. Lowell.

White, Margaret Bourke *See* Caldwell, Erskine.

White, Newman Ivey   1892-1948   American scholar and biographer.

SHELLEY. 2v. 1940. (IV) After twenty years of study the author produced this life, which has been generally recognized as the definitive one. (A readable condensation in one volume was published in 1945.) "A genuine contribution to literature, a book I intend to keep and to re-read and to introduce to other readers." —Richard Aldington, in *Saturday Review of Literature*.

White, Stewart Edward   1873-1946   Outdoor man and writer of many outdoor books of fiction, travel, etc.

BLAZED TRAIL. 1902. (II) The first of a trilogy of stories about lumbering in Michigan and California in the 1870's. They describe life in the lumber camps and the hero's struggles with unscrupulous "big business" and with government officials. After this story came

THE RIVERMAN. 1908. (II) and

RULES OF THE GAME. 1909. (II)

GOLD. 1913. (II) This is the first of a trilogy of historical novels about California. It deals with the Gold Rush, covered wagons, and Indians, and is followed by *The Gray Dawn*, showing the early and somewhat wobbly establishment of law and order in San Francisco. This in turn is followed by *The Rose Dawn*, with its pictures of the passing of the Spanish old settlers, the coming of irrigation and the land booms of the 1880's.

THE GRAY DAWN. 1915. (II)

THE ROSE DAWN. 1920. (II)

SILENT PLACES. 1904. (II) Story about the lonely lives of the Hudson's Bay Company's traders. Similar books of description of the wild and lonesome places, in which his thread of story is more tenuous, are *The Forest* (1903), *The Mountains* (1904), and *The Pass* (1906). (All in II.)

White, Terence Hanbury   1906-   English author of fantasies inspired by the legends of King Arthur.

SWORD IN THE STONE. 1939. (IV) Brand-new story about the young King Arthur, "replete with humor, scholarship, nature lore, and comments on modern civilization."

White, Walter Francis   1893-   Secretary, National Association for the Advancement of Colored People. His whole life has been spent battling for the rights of Negroes.

A MAN CALLED WHITE. 1948. Autobiography. "Should be read by every white man who cares about human dignity. . . . It is time we learned the facts."—H. A. Overstreet, in *Saturday Review of Literature*.

White, William Allen   1868-1944   American novelist and biographer; the most famous of small-town editors. His books, instinct with idealism, evidence his sympathetic understanding of American men and women, his realization of their weaknesses, and his confidence in their fundamental soundness.

CERTAIN RICH MAN. 1909. (II) Story of the growth of ethical callosities upon a likable and originally sensitive character, with a growing Kansas town for a background.

IN THE HEART OF A FOOL. 1918. (II) Pictures the development of a Kansas town between the Civil War and World War I. The story is a vehicle for the exposition of the author's idealistic religious and sociological opinions.

WOODROW WILSON, THE MAN, HIS TIMES AND HIS TASK. 1924.
(II) "The final estimate is fair and probably true."—*New York
World*. He shows us "the real Woodrow Wilson, whom he knew
and loved and found imperfect."—*A.L.A. Catalog*, 1926.

PURITAN IN BABYLON; THE STORY OF CALVIN COOLIDGE. 1938.
(IV) "The gist of the story is that Mr. Coolidge was a 'museum
piece' who survived into an age with which in the end he was
not competent to deal."—*New York Times*. "I enjoyed this book
better than any biography that I've read during the past quarter-
century."—J. F. Dineen, in *Saturday Review of Literature*.

AUTOBIOGRAPHY. 1946. "This is a book which this reviewer
believes may be a permanent part of our social history."—*Saturday
Review of Literature*. "The whole nation will know and love
William Allen White better and it will know itself better when
it has read the Autobiography. . . . I am sure this is his greatest
book."—*Christian Science Monitor*.

SELECTED LETTERS, 1889-1943. 1947. "Never was there a more
readable book nor a more exhilarating one."—Dorothy Canfield
Fisher, in *Yale Review*. "As a source-book for an analysis of the
first forty years of the Twentieth Century this volume will long
be invaluable to the historian."—*Annals of the American Academy
of Political and Social Science*.

White, William Lindsay   1900-   American journalist; war correspondent in World War II. Son of William Allen White.

THEY WERE EXPENDABLE. 1942. (IV) True story of an
American squadron of motor torpedo boats in the Philippine
campaign of World War II. It was told the author by four of
the squadron's young officers. "A short, grim, glorious book."—
New Yorker. "It ranks with the great tales of war."—S. V. Benét.

Whitehead, Alfred North   1861-1947   "English mathematician
and philosopher tending toward mysticism."

SCIENCE AND THE MODERN WORLD. 1925. "With a brilliance
of scientific competence joined to broad insight into the values
of poetry and art, Mr. Whitehead carries on the development
of science to our own day."—*Nation*.

RELIGION IN THE MAKING. 1926. Four essays: *Religion in History, Religion and Dogma, Body and Spirit, Truth and Criticism*.
"He provides exclusively strong meat for grown men. He must
be taken slowly and digested at leisure."—*Times* (London).

Whitman, Walt 1819-92 American poet. "That glorious man Whitman will one day be known as one of the greatest sons of earth, a few steps below Shakespeare on the throne of immortality." —W. M. Rossetti, 1869, in a letter to Mrs. Gilchrist.

LEAVES OF GRASS. 1855. (I) "I find it the most extraordinary piece of wit and wisdom that America has yet contributed. I am very happy in reading it as great power makes us happy."— R. W. Emerson. The official edition, with the text sponsored by Whitman's literary executors, was published by Doubleday in 1924. *Walt Whitman; Selected and Edited by Mark Van Doren* was issued by Viking in 1945. Besides *Leaves of Grass* it contains selections from the prose works.

Whittier, John Greenleaf 1807-92 "Quaker Poet" and Abolitionist. "The poet of New England: his genius drew its nourishment from her soil; his pages are the mirror of her outward nature, and the strong utterance of her inward life."—Francis Parkman.

COMPLETE POETICAL WORKS. Cambridge Edition. n.d. (I) Of his poems, all of *Snow-Bound* should be read first. As G. E. Woodberry said, "It is perfect in its conception and complete in its execution; it is the New England home, entire, with its characteristic scene, its incidents of household life, its Christian virtues."

Widsith *See* Anglo-Saxon Poetry.

Wiener, Norbert 1894- American professor of mathematics at the Massachusetts Institute of Technology.

HUMAN USE OF HUMAN BEINGS; CYBERNETICS AND SOCIETY. 1950. A book about the effect of technology on men and women.

Wiggin, Kate Douglas (Mrs. Riggs) 1856-1923 American author of *good*, if now somewhat old-fashioned, light fiction.

BIRDS' CHRISTMAS CAROL. 1888. (I) "Little tale breathing the tenderest spirit of love and human kindness."—E. A. Baker.

CATHEDRAL COURTSHIP; AND PENELOPE'S ENGLISH EXPERIENCES. 1893. (I) Three charming Americans have humorous and sentimental adventures while sight-seeing in England.

REBECCA OF SUNNYBROOK FARM. 1903. (I and II) The experiences of this original, attractive child in prim New England are amusing to both young and old readers.

My Garden of Memory. 1923. (II) Humorous, spontaneous autobiography. The author met and straightway became friends with a great many interesting people.

Wilde, Oscar 1856-1900 Irish-born English poet, playwright, novelist, aesthete.

Picture of Dorian Grey. 1891. (I) This novel is a moral allegory. Dorian is miraculously permitted to keep the unsullied splendor of his youth, but only until the gradual deterioration of his *portrait* reveals his accumulating secret depravity.

Plays. (I) The Modern Library edition includes five plays. Among them are his wittiest comedies: *The Importance of Being Earnest, Lady Windermere's Fan,* and *A Woman of No Importance.* Shaw, it is said, learned the trick of writing sparkling dialog from a study of Wilde's comedies.

Poems. (I) There are satisfactory collections in both Everyman's Library and the Modern Library. Note especially the fantastically lovely *Nightingale and the Rose,* the poignant *Ballad of Reading Gaol,* and *De Profundis.* (Part of the manuscript of the last is still unpublished—locked up in the British Museum till January 1, 1960.)

Wilder, Thornton 1897- American novelist and playwright; thrice the winner of a Pulitzer prize; member, National Institute of Arts and Letters.

Bridge of San Luis Rey. 1927. (III) Tells the story of "entangled lives converging to a tragic destiny in Peru four hundred years ago." Won a Pulitzer prize and—to the honor of American readers—led the group of "best sellers" for a whole year.

Woman of Andros. 1930. (III) Idyll of ancient Greece with a tragic ending. Pensive and beautiful in its own right, it would seem to have been suggested by rather than based upon the *Andria* of Terence.

Heaven's My Destination. 1934. This story about a traveling salesman who is a religious convert was a new departure for Mr. Wilder. "It is what the comic strip might be if a man of some genius lifted it into art. Its subject is that almost forgotten theme . . . morality."—H. S. Canby, in *Saturday Review of Literature.* "Mr. Wilder's best novel. . . . The tone is always comic or matter of fact—with the result that his vision of an imperfect humanity comes through a great deal more tellingly than in his earlier books."—Edmund Wilson, in *New Republic.*

OUR TOWN. 1938. (IV) Uplifting drama of life and death in a small New Hampshire village in the early 1900's. (Pulitzer Prize play, 1938.)

SKIN OF OUR TEETH. 1942. "About one ordinary human man and his ordinary human wife whose ordinary humanness carries on through the most fantastic vagaries of history." (Pulitzer Prize play, 1943.)

IDES OF MARCH. 1948. Historical novel about the last few months in Julius Caesar's life. The incidents are reported entirely through invented documents, letters, and journals. "An amazing feat of the imagination."

Wilkins, Mary E. *See* Freeman, Mrs Mary E. Wilkins.

Williams, Ben Ames 1889- American novelist.

HOUSE DIVIDED. 1947. This Civil War novel of 1,500 pages is a massive family chronicle from the Southern viewpoint, but with little of the sentimentality that colors most of such accounts.

Williams, Charles 1886-1945 English author of metaphysical Christian novels.

DESCENT INTO HELL. 1949. Story about a group of people engaged in the production of a summer pageant in a London suburb. "The most profound, difficult and serious of his novels. It is also one of the most frightening books ever written."—*Time.*

Williams, Kenneth P. 1887- American university professor of mathematics.

LINCOLN FINDS A GENERAL; A MILITARY STUDY OF THE CIVIL WAR. 4v. vols. I-II. 1949. Concerns the selection of Grant. "The present volumes are enough to establish that this work is the most authoritative military history of the Civil War yet written. That is a strong statement but it is not likely to be challenged."—Bernard De Voto, in *New York Herald Tribune.*

Williams, Tennessee 1914- American playwright; representative of the drama that applies ruthless shock treatment to a society seen as festering in greed, or despair, or self-created tragedy.

GLASS MENAGERIE. 1945. A strange play which "combines tragedy with flashes of humor and poignant characterization."

STREETCAR NAMED DESIRE. 1947. Unwholesome but very successful play about a group of more or less sex-crazed degenerates in a New Orleans slum. Won a Pulitzer prize in 1948, and John Mason Brown declares, "It is an achievement of unusual and exciting distinction."

Williams, William Carlos 1883- American poet, critic, fictionist and practicing physician. Won the National Book Award for poetry in 1950.

PATERSON, books I and II. 1946-48. "Epic in free verse and prose of a medium-sized industrial town in New Jersey." *"Paterson* is Whitman's America; grown pathetic and tragic, brutalized by inequality, disorganized by industrial chaos, and faced by annihilation. No poet has written of it with such a combination of brilliance, sympathy and experience, with such alertness and energy."—Robert Lowell, in *Nation.*

SELECTED POEMS. 1949. Selection from all his previously published books of verse except *Paterson.* Williams feels, says F. B. Millett, "that the proper use of the American, rather than the English, language is essential for modern American poetry, and he believes that all art depends for its assurance and firmness upon local and immediate tradition."

Willison, George Findlay 1896- American soldier, scholar, teacher; editor-in-chief, American Guide Series, Federal Writers' Project.

SAINTS AND STRANGERS. 1945. (IV) History of the Pilgrims, beginning with the youth of William Brewster in Scrooby, Nottinghamshire, England, in the late 1500's, and ending a hundred years later with the absorption of the Plymouth Colony into Massachusetts. "No one since Bradford has done the job so well." —*New Republic.*

Willkie, Wendell 1892-1944 American lawyer and statesman; Republican candidate for President in 1940.

ONE WORLD. 1943. (IV) More than three million copies of this book were sold. It was based upon the radio talks that followed the author's forty-nine-day world tour in 1942. "Its basic emphasis is upon the nearness and interdependence of the peoples of all countries, the importance of strengthening the ties between the United Nations now, and the need of following through in a definite, continuing United Nations organization for peace, justice and progress."—Harold E. Stassen, in *New York Times.*

Wilson, Edmund 1895- American literary and social critic.

AXEL'S CASTLE: A STUDY IN THE IMAGINATIVE LITERATURE OF 1870 to 1930. 1931. (III) Masterly and illuminating study of symbolism in literature, and especially in the work of its modern exponents: Yeats, Valéry, T. S. Eliot, Proust, Joyce, and Gertrude Stein.

TO THE FINLAND STATION; A STUDY IN THE WRITING AND ACT-ING OF HISTORY. 1940. (IV) Discussion of radicals and radical thought from the French Revolution to Bolshevism. Includes excellent character studies, especially of Marx, Engels, Lenin, and Trotsky. "There emerges from the story of communism a stern verdict upon those who, beginning with slogans of liberation, have ended by constructing new instruments of enslavement."— *Christian Century.*

WOUND AND THE BOW; SEVEN STUDIES OF LITERATURE. 1941. (IV) Critical essays and psychological studies of Sophocles, Dickens, Kipling, Casanova, Wharton, Hemingway, and Joyce. "Mr. Wilson is about the best literary critic now at work in our country, and this is one of his most penetrating books."—*New Yorker.*

Wilson, Forrest 1883-1942 American man of letters.

CRUSADER IN CRINOLINE: THE LIFE OF HARRIET BEECHER STOWE. 1941. (IV) This book won the Pulitzer prize for biography in 1942. The author died six days after receiving it. He believed that Mrs. Stowe was, as Lincoln (perhaps) said, "the little woman who made a great war."

Wilson, Harry Leon 1867-1939 Author of stories, often bois-terous and unrestrained, but funny and very American.

RUGGLES, BUNKER AND MERTON. n.d. Includes *Ruggles of Red Gap*, 1915 (fun with an English valet); *Bunker Bean*, 1913 (who discovered he had been Napoleon in a previous incarnation); and *Merton of the Movies*, 1922 (a masterpiece of humor and hidden pathos).

Wilson, Margaret   1882-   American novelist.

THE ABLE MCLAUGHLINS. 1923. Story of a family of hardy Scotch settlers in Iowa. A first novel, it was awarded the Harper prize for fiction in 1923 and the Pulitzer prize for the best novel in 1924.

Wilson, Mrs. Paul *See* Perkins, Frances.

Wilson, Woodrow   1856-1924 President of the United States during World War I; member, American Academy of Arts and Letters.

HISTORY OF THE AMERICAN PEOPLE. 5v. 1902. (I and II) A not quite successful attempt to do for American history the superlative job that Green did for the history of the English people. "Valuable for its broad outlines, general accuracy, and interpretation of events."—*A.L.A. Catalog*, 1904.

Winant, John Gilbert   1889-1947 Governor of New Hampshire; American ambassador to Great Britain, 1941-45.

LETTER FROM GROSVENOR SQUARE; AN ACCOUNT OF A STEWARDSHIP. 1947. A picture of England with her back to the wall, from February 1941 to Pearl Harbor. "It is easy to see why Winant was the most popular ambassador the United States ever sent to Britain. He genuinely and unsentimentally appreciated the British."—*New Republic*.

Winters, Yvor   1900-   American critic and poet, "known for the classical orientation of both his verse and his critical studies."

PRIMITIVISM AND DECADENCE. 1937. Defense of classicism "against the eccentricities of the metaphysicals and the idiosyncracies of the excessively personalized experimenters."

IN DEFENSE OF REASON. 1947. Essays on American literature. "Mr. Winters's criticism is powerful, informed, consistent, and for the most part just."—*Nation*.

Winthrop, Theodore   1828-61 American author and pioneering traveler; killed at the head of an assaulting column in the first engagement of the Civil War.

CANOE AND THE SADDLE. 1863. (I) Narrative of personal experiences in the early days of the Pacific Northwest, and in Panama.

Winwar, Frances (originally **Francesca Vinciguerra**) 1900-
Italian-born American biographer and literary historian.

POOR SPLENDID WINGS. 1933. (III) Readable and prize-winning book about the Pre-Raphaelite Brotherhood in Nineteenth-Century England, with emphasis on Dante Gabriel Rossetti.

OSCAR WILDE AND THE YELLOW 'NINETIES. 1940. "Miss Winwar has performed a valuable service. Her Wilde emerges as a social being rather than an esoteric excrescence. The incredible Oscar becomes credible."—M. Geismar, in *Nation*.

LIFE OF THE HEART; GEORGE SAND AND HER TIMES. 1945. "As easy to read as a detective story and as clear as a Somerset Maugham novel. . . . Frances Winwar has done it again. . . . A most satisfactory reading adventure."—*Saturday Review of Literature*.

Wister, Owen 1860-1938 American novelist; friend of Theodore Roosevelt; member, American Academy of Arts and Letters.

THE VIRGINIAN. 1902. (I and II) One of the earliest and best of "Westerns," about a bold but gentle young cowboy and an attractive schoolmarm from the East.

Wolfe, Thomas 1900-38 American novelist. Critics find treasure buried in the mountainous masses of his always autobiographical pages; but readers, unless they be unusually patient and docile, may feel overwhelmed by them. Wolfe's novels, like *Leaves of Grass, Moby Dick*, and the Grand Canyon, are very American. All these phenomena are impressive, wild, and very large; and all lack utterly the pleasing civilized qualities of Greek art; namely, moderation, balance, proportion.

LOOK HOMEWARD, ANGEL. 1929 and 1947. Long, digressive and rhapsodic first novel about the youth of Eugene Gant (Wolfe), in a commonplace Southern hill-town (Asheville, North Carolina).

OF TIME AND THE RIVER. 1935. (III) Sequel to *Look Homeward, Angel*. In 912 pages it carries the hero through the years 1920-25: at Harvard, teaching in New York City, and traveling in England and France.

THE WEB AND THE ROCK. 1939. (IV) More of the same, for 695 pages though "Gant" is now called "Webber." "At once the best and the worst of Wolfe's novels."—A. Kazin, in *New York Herald Tribune*. "Like the curate's egg . . . *parts* of the book are excellent."—*Commonweal*.

You Can't Go Home Again. 1940. (IV) This sequel (743 pages) to *The Web and the Rock* is a story about the collapse of false values in the late '20's and the half-dozen subsequent years.

Woodward, William E. 1874-1950 American biographer and historian.

George Washington, the Image and the Man. 1926. (III) This is no book for idolators. It is the portrait of a human being, much like others—a man, to be sure, of undoubted strength, integrity, fortitude, shrewdness, but one with less admirable qualities too.

The Way Our People Lived: an Intimate American History. 1944. (IV) Contains eleven story-essays. Each presents a time, a place, and a group of appropriate Americans—from Boston in 1640, to New York in 1908. "The basic idea is excellent—a portrait of the average American down the ages."—*Nation.*

Woolf, Mrs Virginia 1882-1941 English novelist and essayist; daughter of Sir Leslie Stephen, distinguished scholar. Some critics consider her the foremost woman writer of her time.

Mrs. Dalloway. 1925. Describes the events—including scenes floating past on her stream of consciousness—during a single day in the life of an English society woman.

Flush, a Biography. 1933. (III) Flush is a cocker spaniel. The book gives us a dog's-eye view of the courtship of his mistress (Miss Elizabeth Barrett) by Robert Browning.

Orlando. 1928. (III) Deeply beautiful and poetic novel. Incidentally it is a fantastic one. The hero begins as a gentleman of Queen Elizabeth's time and ends as an up-to-date young *woman* in modern London.

Common Reader. 1925. and

Second Common Reader. 1932. (III) Excellent literary criticism, together with successful experiments in the resuscitation of defunct English literary notables and re-creation of the scenes amid which they lived. "Little masterpieces—firm, rapid, brilliant and sympathetic."—*Saturday Review.*

To the Lighthouse. 1927. (III) Intense transcript of life and the passage of time. Story and plot are negligible. Not so, characterization.

THE WAVES. 1931. Regarded by some critics as the author's masterpiece. Deals with the personal relationships and psychological development of six English folk from childhood to middle age, with much symbolism of sun and sea.

BETWEEN THE ACTS. 1941. (IV) Her last novel. Describes England on a summer's day, with a county family, their guests, and the villagers who present a pageant.

DEATH OF THE MOTH, AND OTHER ESSAYS. 1942. (IV) "The riches of the book are both overwhelming and companionable."— *Christian Science Monitor.*

HAUNTED HOUSE, AND OTHER STORIES. 1944. (IV) Eighteen short stories. "Mrs. Woolf proved through the years that she could do almost anything with words, and in these brief stories you will find her skill."—*Saturday Review of Literature.*

THE YEARS. 1937. (IV) This "novel" is a pattern of a half-century of upper-middle-class English life, 1880-1930. "The writing throughout has a serene distinction . . . and for anyone whose tale of days coincides with that of the Pargiters, the early chapters, more especially, must evoke an almost unbearable nostalgia."— Wilfrid Gibson, in *Manchester Guardian.*

Woollcott, Alexander 1887-1945 American critic and wit; known to the radio audience of his time as the Town Crier.

WHILE ROME BURNS. 1934. (IV) Collection of the ebullient, yeasty emanations of the Town Crier: essays, sketches, anecdotes, critiques.

Woolman, John 1720-72 Tailor and Quaker missionary of Pennsylvania.

JOURNAL OF THE LIFE, GOSPEL, LABOURS, AND CHRISTIAN EXPERIENCES OF JOHN WOOLMAN. 1774. (I) One of the most attractive of Christian biographies. Charles Lamb said, "Get the writings of John Woolman by heart and love the early Quakers."

Wordsworth, Dorothy 1771-1855 Sister and lifelong companion of her famous brother, the English poet.

JOURNAL; edited by E. de Selincourt. 2v. 1942. "All these journals have the warmth of the lovely heart from which they came."—Edith Sitwell, in *Spectator.*

Wordsworth, William   1770-1850   Leader of "the Lake School" and chief author of the *Lyrical Ballads* (1798). At once one of the greatest and dullest of English poets, Wordsworth needs more than any other poet equally great the cruel kindness of the judicious anthologist.

WORDSWORTH ANTHOLOGY; selected with an introduction by Laurence Housman. 1946. (I) Based on a critical estimate which appeared in the *Atlantic.*

Wright, Frank Lloyd   1869-   American architect; leader of the movement sometimes called in America "the new school of the Middle West" and known in Europe as "the American expression in architecture."

AUTOBIOGRAPHY. 1932. (Second edition, 1943.) (III) The frank and absorbing apologia both of Wright the man and Wright the architect.

FRANK LLOYD WRIGHT ON ARCHITECTURE; SELECTED WRITINGS, 1894-1940. 1941 and 1943. Includes six essays and a bibliography.

WHEN DEMOCRACY BUILDS. 1945. "Suggestions for an ideal city in a new world."—*Good Reading.*

GENIUS AND THE MOBOCRACY. 1949. Includes both a biographical sketch of his "master," Louis Sullivan, and a pungent exposition of Wright's views of the conflict between society and men of genius.

Wright, Richard   1908-   American Negro fictionist; mostly self-educated; worked on Federal Writers' Project, 1935-38; wrote for the *Daily Worker* and *New Masses.* Mr. Wright was once a Communist, but became disillusioned and left the party.

NATIVE SON. 1940. (IV) Story of the violent life and death of a Chicago Negro boy. "Declares Richard Wright's importance," said P. M. Jack, in the *New York Times*, "not merely as the best Negro writer, but as an American author as distinctive as any now writing."

BLACK BOY; A RECORD OF CHILDHOOD AND YOUTH. 1945. (IV) This autobiography extends only to the point where the youth heads north. "Nowhere except in America could it have been written. Nowhere except in America could such a rebel thrive. But what made him a rebel should be on America's conscience." —*Boston Globe.*

Wycherley, William 1640-1716 English playwright of the Restoration. "Wycherley was ambitious of the reputation of wit and libertinism; and he attained it."—David Hume, 1762.

COUNTRY WIFE. 1773. "There can be no question that the men and women who sat through the acting of *The Country Wife* were past blushing."—George Meredith, in 1897.

THE PLAIN DEALER. 1674. "One of the most brutally cynical, but none the less one of the best constructed pieces which have ever held the stage."—Edmund Gosse, in 1897.

Wylie, Elinor (Mrs. W. R. Benét) 1887-1928 American poet and novelist.

COLLECTED POEMS. 1932. (III) "She recalls the imagery of Blake, the intensity of Emily Dickinson."—*The Dial.* Includes *Nets to Catch the Wind* (1921); *Angels and Earthly Creatures* (1929); etc.

COLLECTED PROSE. 1933 and 1946. Includes *Orphan Angel* (1926) (IV)—a beautiful fantasy about a Shelley rescued after the drowning off Leghorn; *Jennifer Lorn* (1923) (II)—"a comedy of manners recounting the adventures of an Eighteenth-Century titled gentleman"; *Venetian Glass Nephew* (1925)—"an exquisite fairy-tale for grown-ups"; etc.

Xenophon 430(?)-358(?) B.C. Greek man of letters.

MEMORABILIA. (I) Exposition of the moral and practical aspects of the teaching of Socrates, who was Xenophon's friend.

ANABASIS. (I) Called "the most famous of military narratives," this is an account of the retreat from Persia to the Black Sea of ten thousand Greek mercenaries under Xenophon after the battle of Cunaxa.

CYROPAEDIA. (I) A politico-historical romance, with the elder Cyrus, king of Persia, for hero. Contains many of the author's theories regarding education and administration.

Yarmolinsky, Avrahm 1890- editor; Russian-born Chief of the Slavonic Division, New York Public Library.

TREASURY OF GREAT RUSSIAN SHORT STORIES; PUSHKIN TO GORKY. 1944. "Soviet writing does not come within the purview of this book."—Introduction.

Yeats, William Butler 1865-1939 Irish poet, dramatist, critic; leader of the Irish literary revival; awarded Nobel prize for literature in 1923. His belief in fairies was unashamed and absolute.

COLLECTED POEMS. 1933. (III) "The poetry of Yeats . . . is steeped in Irish legend and history, and deeply tinged with oriental philosophy and religious mysticism."—Helen Haines. In these 478 pages Yeats selected the poems he wished to preserve. All were carefully studied and, where he thought necessary, revised.

COLLECTED PLAYS. 1935. (II) There is room in these 617 pages for 22 plays, including all the best ones: *Cathleen ni Houlihan* (1902) (II), *The Hour Glass* (1904) (II), *The Land of Heart's Desire* (1894), *Deirdre* (1907), etc.

AUTOBIOGRAPHY. 3v. in 1. 1938. Includes *Reveries over Childhood and Youth* (II), *The Trembling of the Veil*, and *Dramatis Personae*. "What makes this volume truly invaluable to civilized readers is the unfailing wisdom, penetration and passion for human values apparent on every page."—*New Yorker.*

Yeats-Brown, Francis 1886-1944 English author, soldier, mystic.

LIVES OF A BENGAL LANCER. 1930. (III) Autobiography of a British officer who, in India, led the life of a young subaltern that Kipling made familiar. But, unlike most of his pig-sticking comrades, this one interested himself in Indian life and philosophy.

Yezierka, Anzia 1885- Russian-born American fictionist. An immigrant in 1901, she "worked in factories, sweat-shops, and as cook in private families," and was naturalized in 1912.

HUNGRY HEARTS. 1920. (II) Short stories describing an immigrant's life in New York's ghetto. "Very intense, vivid, and appealing."

Young, Arthur 1741-1820 English traveler and student of agriculture.

TRAVELS IN FRANCE, 1787-89. 1792. Intimate and revealing, though matter-of-fact, picture of social conditions in rural France on the eve of the French Revolution.

Young, Stark 1881- American author, journalist, and teacher —from Mississippi.

So RED THE ROSE. 1934. (III) An attractive picture of a bygone civilization, that of the planter aristocracy. Ellen Glasgow called it "the best and most completely realized novel of the Deep South in the Civil War that has yet been written."

Zangwill, Israel 1864-1924 Anglo-Jewish fictionist and playwright; prominent Zionist.

CHILDREN OF THE GHETTO. 1892. (I and II) Stories of the people who live, or have once lived, in London's Jewish slums.

MELTING POT. New and revised edition, 1914. (I and II) Play about America, the great crucible, where all the races of the earth are mingled and—let us hope—refined.

Zaturenska, Maria 1902- Russian-born wife of Horace Gregory, American poet and critic.

COLD MORNING SKY. 1937. Lyric poems, abounding in symbolism, which were awarded a Pulitzer prize in 1938.

LISTENING LANDSCAPE. 1941. The *New Yorker* considers the poems in this book much superior to those in the prize-winning *Cold Morning Sky.*

Zimmern, Sir A. E. 1879- British political scientist; professor of international relations, Oxford.

GREEK COMMONWEALTH; POLITICS AND ECONOMICS IN FIFTH CENTURY ATHENS. 5th edition, 1937. (II) "Clear, scholarly, and interesting study. . . . The ancient civilization is made very real, the relations of its problems to those of today are clearly shown." —*A.L.A. Catalog,* 1932-36.

Zinsser, Hans 1878-1940 American bacteriologist, whose professional service was worldwide. Member, American Academy of Arts and Sciences.

RATS, LICE AND HISTORY. 1935. (III) There is entertainment as well as instruction in this racy book about unpleasant subjects: typhus, rats, mice, lice, and fleas.

AS I REMEMBER HIM. 1940. (IV) One of those bashful autobiographies in which the author pretends to be writing about some other fellow. "A biography carried through to the ultimate curtain must necessarily have some seriousness. But this one does not become *solemn* at any time. It makes both life and death appear a part of the order of an orderly Nature."—R. L. Duffus, in *New York Times.*

Zola, Émile   1840-1902   French novelist; exponent, not only of realism, but of such naturalism as is likely to upset a queasy stomach, if such frailty is still anywhere to be found. Most of Zola's most important books, including the seven titles listed below, are to be found in the Rougon-Macquart series of 20 volumes, published 1871-93.

L'ASSOMMOIR (THE DRAM SHOP). 1877. (I) Study of the influence of drink on the workingmen of Paris.

NANA. 1884. (I) Coarse picture of the life and death of a courtesan.

GERMINAL. 1885. (I) Describes the life of French miners.

L'ŒUVRE (The Masterpiece). 1886. Dissection of literary and artistic decadents.

LA TERRE (The Soil). 1888. (I) "In which prurient naturalism reaches the zenith of repulsiveness."

L'ARGENT (Money). 1891. (I) Pays its respects to the ways of stockbrokers.

LA DÉBÂCLE (The Downfall). 1892. (I) Novel of the Franco-Prussian War and the fall of the Second Empire in France. The best known of the Rougon-Macquart series.

Zweig, Arnold   1887-   German novelist; author of a tetralogy of stories about World War I. The best two of these are described below.

CASE OF SERGEANT GRISCHA. 1928. (III) Simple-hearted Russian soldier is caught escaping from a German prison camp and condemned to death as a spy. The story demonstrates how pity, justice, and even common sense are often powerless to stop the inexorable wheels of the military steam-roller when they have once been set in motion.

EDUCATION BEFORE VERDUN. 1936. A picture of poor human nature under the stress of war. Another tale of injustice in the German army.

Zweig, Stefan   1881-1942   Playwright, fictionist, biographer. Born in Vienna, of Jewish parents. A pacifist and refugee, he killed himself in Brazil.

MARIE ANTOINETTE. 1933. (III) This psychological study of "an average woman" is a fascinating book without a dull line or a boring paragraph.

WORLD OF YESTERDAY; AN AUTOBIOGRAPHY. 1943. (IV) "The very success with which this book evokes both the beauty of the past and the futility of its passing is what gives it its tragic effectiveness. It is not so much the memory of a life as it is the memento of an age."—Irwin Edman, in *New Republic*.

CLASSIFIED LISTS

CHRONOLOGICAL LIST OF
AUTHORS AND ANONYMOUS CLASSICS *

B.C. 11TH—1ST CENTURIES

Homer	*fl.* 11th cent.
Æsop	*fl.* 6th cent.
Lao-tsze	*fl.* 6th cent.
Æschylus	525
Pindar	522
Sophocles	496
Herodotus	484
Euripides	480
Thucydides	470?
Aristophanes	448?
Xenophon	430?
Plato	427
Demosthenes	385
Aristotle	384
Theocritus	*fl.* 270
Plautus	254?
Polybius	204
Terence	195
Cicero	106
Vitruvius	*fl.* 1st cent.
Mahabharata	1st cent.?
Ramayana	1st cent.?
Caesar	100
Lucretius	96?
Catullus	87
Virgil	70
Horace	65
Livy	59
Tibullus	54?
Ovid	43
Seneca	4

A.D. 1-1000

Petronius	*d.* 66
Martial	43?
Plutarch	46?
Tacitus	55?
Epictetus	60?
Juvenal	60?
Pliny	62
Suetonius	70
Lucian	120?
Aurelius	121
Apuleius	125?
Plotinus	205?
Augustine	354
Kalidasa	*fl.* 450?
Boethius	480?
Confucius	550
Koran	7th cent.
Anglo-Saxon Poetry	650-1000
Bede	673
Beowulf	7th or 8th cent.
Anglo-Saxon Chron.	9th to 12th cent.
Eddas	9th to 13th cent.
Arabian Nights	10th cent.?
Firdausi	940?
Murasaki	978?

A.D. 1001-1500

Chanson de Roland	11th cent.
Kalidasa	11th or 12th cent.
Aucassin & Nicolette	12th cent.
Omar Khayyam	*d.* 1123
Nibelungenlied	12th cent.
Geoffrey of Monmouth	1100?
Francis of Assisi	1182
Sadi	1194?
Joinville	1224?
Aquinas	1225?
Polo, Marco	1254
Dante	1265
Richard de Bury	1278
Mabinogion	14th cent. or earlier
Boccaccio	1313
Mandeville	*d.* 1372
Langland	1330

* The table is arranged by birth date except where otherwise specified. As the birth dates of some twentieth century and nineteenth century authors do not appear in reference books, these writers' names will not be found in this chronological arrangement. Anonymous classics are listed by title in approximately chronological order.

Abbreviations used: *c.*, about; *d.*, died; *fl.*, flourished.

A.D. 1001-1500—*Continued*

Froissart	1337
Chaucer	1340
Thomas à Kempis	1380
Malory	1430?
Villon	1431
Paston Letters	1422-1509
Leonardo	1452
Erasmus	1465
Machiavelli	1469
Copernicus	1473
Ariosto	1474
Castiglione	1478
More	1478
Luther	1483
Rabelais	1483
Everyman	15th cent.
Elyot	1490?
Cellini	1500

SIXTEENTH CENTURY

Hurtado de Mendoza	1503
Calvin	1509
Vasari	1511
Foxe	1516
Holinshed	1520?
Camoëns	1524?
Montaigne	1533
Tasso	1544
Cervantes	1547
Camden	1551
Hakluyt	1552
Raleigh	1552
Spenser	1552
Hooker	1554
Lyly	1554
Sidney	1554
Bacon	1561
Vega	1562
Marlowe	1564
Shakespeare	1564
Nashe	1567
Dekker	1570?
Donne	1573
Jonson	1573
Burton	1577
Fletcher	1579
Smith	1580
Webster	1580?
Grotius	1583
Herbert of Cherbury	1583
Massinger	1583
Beaumont	1584
Ford	1586
Hobbes	1588

Herrick	1591
Herbert	1593
Walton	1593
Descartes	1596
Calderon	1600

SEVENTEENTH CENTURY

Browne	1605
Corneille	1606
Fuller	1608
Milton	1608
Clarendon	1609
Harrington	1611
Butler	1612
Taylor	1613
Evelyn	1620
La Fontaine	1621
Molière	1622
Pascal	1623
Fox	1624
Grimmelshausen	1625
Sévigné	1626
Boyle	1627
Osborne	1627
Bunyan	1628
Dryden	1631
Locke	1632
Spinoza	1632
Pepys	1633
La Fayette	1634
Boileau	1636
Racine	1639
Wycherley	1640
Burnet	1643
La Roche-foucauld	1645
Fénelon	1651
Otway	1652
Defoe	1661
Mather	1663
Swift	1667
Congreve	1670
Cibber	1671
Addison	1672
Saint-Simon	1675
Farquhar	1678
Berkeley	1685
Gay	1685
Law	1686
Pope	1688
Montesquieu	1689
Montagu	1689
Richardson	1689
Butler	1692
Chesterfield	1694
Voltaire	1694
Prévost	1697
Thomson	1700

EIGHTEENTH CENTURY

Wesley	1703
Franklin	1706
Fielding	1707
Goldoni	1707
Johnson, S.	1709
Hume	1711
Rousseau	1712
Diderot	1713
Sterne	1713
Gray	1716
Walpole	1717
Münchhausen	1720
White	1720
Woolman	1720
Smollett	1721
Blackstone	1723
Reynolds	1723
Smith	1723
Kant	1724
Casanova	1725
Cook	1728
Goldsmith	1728
Burke	1729
Lessing	1729
Percy	1729
Cowper	1731
Beaumarchais	1732
Macpherson	1736
Gibbon	1737
Paine	1737
Saint-Pierre	1737
Boswell	1740
Young	1741
Jefferson	1743
Mackenzie	1745
Bentham	1748
Goethe	1749
Sheridan	1751
Burney	1752
Crabbe	1754
Godwin	1756
Blake	1757
Beckford	1759
Burns	1759
Schiller	1759
Radcliffe	1764
Cobbett	1766
Dalton	1766
D'Israeli	1766
Malthus	1766
Staël	1766
Edgeworth	1767
Hegel	1770
Wordsworth, W.	1770
Kleist	1771
Scott	1771
Wordsworth, D.	1771
Coleridge	1772

Ricardo	1772
Southey	1774
Austen	1775
Lamb	1775
Landor	1775
Smith, J.	1775
Porter	1776
Campbell	1777
LaMotte-Fouqué	1777
Hazlitt	1778
Smith, H.	1779
Morier	1780
Trollope	1780
Irving	1783
Stendhal	1783
Hunt	1784
Audubon	1785
De Quincey	1785
Grimm	1785
Manzoni	1785
Peacock	1785
Guizot	1787
Mitford	1787
Barham	1788
Byron	1788
Federalist	1788
Schopenhauer	1788
Cooper	1789
Scott, M.	1789
Faraday	1791
Milman	1791
Ticknor	1791
Keble	1792
Marryat	1792
Shelley	1792
Trelawney	1792
Bryant	1794
Lockhart	1794
Carlyle	1795
Keats	1795
Bulfinch	1796
Prescott	1796
Lover	1797
Shelley	1797
Comte	1798
Alcott	1799
Balzac	1799
Delacroix	1799
Pushkin	1799
Bancroft	1800
Macaulay	1800

NINETEENTH CENTURY

Newman	1801
Dumas	1802
Hugo	1802
Beddoes	1803
Borrow	1803

NINETEENTH CENTURY—
Continued

Emerson	1803
Lytton	1803
Mérimée	1803
Disraeli	1804
Sainte-Beuve	1804
Sand	1804
Andersen	1805
Ainsworth	1805
Tocqueville	1805
Browning, E. B.	1806
Hawthorne	1806
Lever	1806
Mill	1806
Souvestre	1806
Longfellow	1807
Manning	1807
Trench	1807
Whittier	1807
Darwin	1809
Fitzgerald, E.	1809
Gogol	1809
Holmes	1809
Kinglake	1809
Lincoln	1809
Poe	1809
Tennyson	1809
Gaskell	1810
Duruy	1811
Gautier	1811
Thackeray	1811
Browning, R.	1812
Creasy	1812
Dickens	1812
Forster	1812
Goncharov	1812
Lear	1812
Smiles	1812
Stowe	1812
Kierkegaard	1813
Motley	1814
Reade	1814
Dana	1815
Trollope	1815
Brontë, C.	1816
Lewes	1817
Thoreau	1817
Brontë, E.	1818
Froude	1818
Herndon	1818
Marx	1818
Eliot	1819
Kingsley	1819
Lowell	1819
Melville	1819
Ruskin	1819
Whitman	1819
Spencer	1820
Amiel	1821

Baudelaire	1821
Buckle	1821
Burton	1821
Dostoievsky	1821
Eddy	1821
Flaubert	1821
Arnold, M.	1822
Erckmann	1822
Grant	1822
Hale	1822
Hughes	1822
Maine	1822
Masson	1822
Boissier	1823
Fabre	1823
Freeman, E. A.	1823
Parkman	1823
Renan	1823
Smith, G.	1823
Wallace	1823
Collins	1824
Dumas	1824
Ballantyne	1825
Blackmore	1825
Huxley, H.	1825
Lea	1825
Meyer, C. F.	1825

Born 1826-50

Mulock	1826
Scheffel	1826
Coster	1827
Wallace, L.	1827
Ibsen	1828
Meredith, G.	1828
Rossetti, D. G.	1828
Taine	1828
Tolstoi	1828
Verne	1828
Winthrop	1828
Mitchell	1829
Dickinson, E.	1830
Kingsley	1830
Rossetti, C.	1830
Smith, A.	1830
Jackson, H. H.	1831
Alcott, L. M.	1832
Arnold, E.	1832
Björnson	1832
Carroll, L.	1832
Echegaray	1832
Roberts of Kandahar	1832
Stephen, L.	1832
Greenough	1833
Lie	1833
Du Maurier, G.	1834
Halévy	1834

Morris	1834	Eucken	1846
Stockton	1834	Gardner	1846
Whistler	1834	Hall, G. S.	1846
Butler, S.	1835	Sienkiewicz	1846
Clemens	1835	Meynell	1847
Gaboriau	1835	Shaw, A.	1847
Aldrich	1836	Stoker	1847
Besant	1836	Westcott	1847
Gilbert	1836	Harris, J. C.	1848
Burroughs	1837	Jefferies	1848
Eggleston	1837	Rhodes	1848
Green, J. R.	1837	Terry	1848
Howells	1837	Gosse	1849
Swinburne	1837	Henley	1849
Adams, H.	1838	Jewett	1849
Bryce	1838	Riis	1849
Hay	1838	Strindberg	1849
Lecky	1838	Bellamy	1850
Lounsbury	1838	Birrell	1850
Muir	1838	Field, E.	1850
Smith, F. H.	1838	Hearn	1850
Trevelyan, G. O.	1838	Loti	1850
DeMorgan	1839	Maupassant	1850
George	1839	Stevenson	1850
Harte	1839		
Pater	1839		
Clodd	1840	*Born 1851-60*	
Daudet	1840		
Dobson	1840	Brownell	1851
Douglas	1840	Ward	1851
Hardy	1840	Bourget	1852
Mahan	1840	Gregory	1852
Sumner	1840	McMaster	1852
Symonds	1840	Matthews	1852
Verga	1840	Moore, G.	1852
Zola	1840	Van Dyke	1852
Holmes, O. W.,		Caine	1853
Jr.	1841	Page, T. N.	1853
Hudson	1841	Petrie	1853
Bierce	1842	Riley	1853
Brandes	1842	Frazer	1854
Carryl	1842	Howe	1854
Fiske	1842	Isham	1855
James, W.	1842	Page, W. H.	1855
Fogazzaro	1842	Pennell	1855
Lanier	1842	Pinero	1855
Palmer	1842	Repplier	1855
Sullivan, Sir A.	1842	Schreiner	1855
Doughty	1843	Channing	1856
James, H.	1843	Freud	1856
Bridges	1844	Haggard	1856
Cable	1844	Harris, F.	1856
France	1844	Lowell, A. L.	1856
Hopkins	1844	Peary	1856
Nietzsche	1844	Royce	1856
Russell	1844	Shaw, G. B.	1856
Slocum	1844	Taylor, H. O.	1856
Pérez Galdós	1845	Washington,	
Pollock	1845	B. T.	1856
Saintsbury	1845	Wiggin	1856

Born 1851-60—Continued

Wilde	1856
Wilson, W.	1856
Atherton	1857
Bullen	1857
Conrad	1857
Crothers	1857
Darrow	1857
Deland	1857
Gissing	1857
Hough	1857
Howard	1857
Munthe	1857
Nevinson	1857
Osborn, H. F.	1857
Pennell	1857
Sudermann	1857
Tarbell	1857
Veblen	1857
Boas	1858
Brieux	1858
House	1858
Lagerlöf	1858
Pupin	1858
Reinach	1858
Roosevelt, T.	1858
Sabatier	1858
Bergson	1859
Dewey	1859
Doyle	1859
Ellis	1859
Grahame	1859
Hamsun	1859
Housman, A. E.	1859
Lee	1859
Thayer	1859
Thomas	1859
Thompson, F.	1859
Addams	1860
Bashkirtseff	1860
Cahan	1860
Chekhov	1860
Garland	1860
Huneker	1860
Kittredge	1860
Pershing	1860
Wister	1860

Born 1861-70

Hewlett	1861
Quick	1861
Paine	1861
Norris, G. W.	1861
Tagore	1861
Turner	1861
Whitehead	1861
Beveridge	1862

Butler, N. M.	1862
Chapman, J. J.	1862
Cross	1862
Dickinson, G. L.	1862
Freeman, M. E. W.	1862
Grey	1862
Hauptmann	1862
Henry, O.	1862
Parker, G.	1862
Phillpotts	1862
Schnitzler	1862
Wharton	1862
Annunzio	1863
Bok	1863
Bradford, G.	1863
Couperus	1863
Flexner, S.	1863
Fox	1863
Frenssen	1863
Hawkins	1863
Jacobs	1863
Lloyd George	1863
Locke, W. J.	1863
Machen	1863
Newton, A. E.	1863
Quiller-Couch	1863
Robinson, J. H.	1863
Santayana	1863
Sologub	1863
Charnwood	1864
Davis, R. H.	1864
Hichens	1864
Merrick	1864
More, P. E.	1864
Unamuno	1864
Zangwill	1864
Babbitt	1865
Berenson	1865
Breasted	1865
Chambers, R. W.	1865
Cunliffe	1865
Ford, P. L.	1865
Kipling	1865
Merejkowski	1865
Phelps	1865
Sinclair, M.	1865
Slosson	1865
Smith, L. P.	1865
Yeats	1865
Ade	1866
Benavente	1866
Croce	1866
Fry, R.	1866
Lang, P. H.	1866
Marshall, A.	1866
Rolland	1866
Steffens	1866
White, E. L.	1866
Armstrong	1867

Bennett, A.	1867
Blasco-Ibanez	1867
Dunne	1867
Galsworthy	1867
Lowes	1867
Montague,	
C. E.	1867
Pirandello	1867
Russell, G. W.	1867
Stimson	1867
Wald	1867
Wilson, H. L.	1867
Austin	1868
Bell	1868
Cabot	1868
Claudel	1868
Dorsey	1868
Douglas, N.	1868
DuBois	1868
Gorki	1868
Herrick, R.	1868
Jennings	1868
Lucas	1868
Marie	1868
Masters	1868
Milliken	1868
Phillips, S.	1868
Reymont	1868
Rostand	1868
Scott, R. F.	1868
Watts	1868
White, W. A.	1868
Cushing	1869
Dimnet	1869
Dodd	1869
Gide	1869
Leacock	1869
Merriam	1869
Moody	1869
Nexö	1869
Robinson, E. A.	1869
Salten	1869
Tarkington	1869
Wright, F. L.	1869
Baker, R. S.	1870
Belloc	1870
Bevan	1870
Bunin	1870
Hendrick	1870
Johnston	1870
Lenin	1870
Lincoln, J. C.	1870
Lovett	1870
Munro	1870
Norris	1870
Rice	1870
Rostovtzeff	1870

Born 1871-80

Adams, S. H.	1871
Andreyev	1871
Churchill, W.	1871
Crane	1871
Davies	1871
Dreiser	1871
Goodspeed	1871
Hull	1871
Johnson, J. W.	1871
Kennedy	1871
Parrington	1871
Proust	1871
Synge	1871
Amundsen	1872
Beerbohm	1872
Bojer	1872
Deledda	1872
Dunbar	1872
Ferrero	1872
Hughes, R.	1872
Lomax	1872
Russell, B.	1872
Sedgwick, E.	1872
Villard	1872
Baroja	1873
Carrel	1873
"Colette"	1873
De La Mare	1873
Faure	1873
Ford, F. M.	1873
Heiser	1873
Hulbert	1873
Jensen	1873
Sedgwick,	
A. D.	1873
Tomlinson	1873
Trevena	1873
Wassermann	1873
White, S. E.	1873
Barbusse	1874
Beard, C. A.	1874
Chesterton	1874
Churchill,	
W. S.	1874
Davis, O.	1874
Day	1874
Gale	1874
Glasgow	1874
Ickes	1874
Keller, A. G.	1874
Knoblock	1874
Lowell, A.	1874
Magoffin	1874
Maugham	1874
Miller, A. D.	1874
Stein	1874
Sullivan, M.	1874

Born 1871-80—Continued

Weizmann	1874
Woodward	1874
Buchan	1875
Cather	1875
Frost	1875
Greenslet	1875
Grey, Z.	1875
MacKaye	1875
Mann	1875
Overstreet	1875
Quinn	1875
Sabatini	1875
Schweitzer	1875
Siegfried	1875
Starling	1875
Anderson, S.	1876
Beard, M. R.	1876
Briffault	1876
Cobb, I.	1876
Creel	1876
Duun	1876
Fay, S. B.	1876
Hay, I.	1876
Learned	1876
Leonard	1876
London	1876
Ossendowski	1876
Perry	1876
Rölvaag	1876
Service	1876
Tallmadge	1876
Trevelyan, G. M.	1876
Anthony	1877
Beebe	1877
Davis, W. S.	1877
Dickinson T. H.	1877
Douglas, L. C.	1877
Granville- Barker	1877
Hesse	1877
Jeans	1877
Macy	1877
Paxson	1877
Adams, J. T.	1878
Besier	1878
Bowers	1878
Canby	1878
Crothers, R.	1878
Dunsany	1878
Farnol	1878
Fosdick	1878
Gibson	1878
Kelly	1878
Marquis	1878
Masefield	1878
Molnar	1878
Sandburg	1878

Simonds	1878
Sinclair, U.	1878
Zinsser	1878
Bates	1879
Byrnes	1879
Cabell	1879
Einstein	1879
Erskine	1879
Fisher, D. C.	1879
Forster, E. M.	1879
Gerould	1879
James, H., 2d	1879
Lindsay	1879
Lubbock	1879
Parsons	1879
Stevens, W.	1879
Trotsky	1879
Wertenbaker	1879
Zimmern	1879
Asch	1880
Cohen	1880
Grew	1880
Hemon	1880
Hergesheimer	1880
Hutchinson	1880
Keller	1880
Keyserling	1880
Marshall, G. C.	1880
Martin	1880
Mencken	1880
Nock	1880
Noyes	1880
Peterkin	1880
Poole	1880
Richardson, H. H.	1880
Smith, P.	1880
Spengler	1880
Strachey	1880
VanVechten	1880

Born 1881-90

Adams, F. P.	1881
Antin	1881
Bynner	1881
Colum	1881
Ludwig	1881
McFee	1881
Martin du Gard	1881
Neihardt	1881
Papini	1881
Randall	1881
Sherman, S. P.	1881
Stribling	1881
Webb	1881
Young	1881
Zweig, S.	1881

Bent	1882	Lardner	1885
Borgese	1882	Lawrence,	
Burt	1882	D. H.	1885
Drinkwater	1882	Lewis, S.	1885
Glaspell	1882	Mauriac	1885
Hagedorn	1882	Maurois	1885
Hanford	1882	Patton	1885
Hobart	1882	Percy	1885
Joyce	1882	Pound	1885
LaGuardia	1882	Roberts, E. M.	1885
Lewisohn	1882	Roberts, K.	1885
Maritain	1882	Romains	1885
Milne	1882	Rourke	1885
Nathan	1882	Shapley	1885
Perkins	1882	Untermeyer	1885
"Pertinax"	1882	VanDoren, C.	1885
Richardson,		Yezierka	1885
D. M.	1882	Akins	1886
Roosevelt,		Arnold, H. H.	1886
F. D.	1882	Barnes	1886
Skinner	1882	Benét, W. R.	1886
Stephens, J.	1882	Brooks	1886
Undset	1882	Cheney	1886
VanLoon	1882	Doolittle	1886
Wilson, M.	1882	Freeman, D. S.	1886
Woolf	1882	Kilmer	1886
Bell	1883	Lieber	1886
Eastman	1883	Madariaga	1886
Ervine	1883	Sassoon	1886
Flavin	1883	Seabrook	1886
Hackett	1883	Steele	1886
Hasek	1883	Wells	1886
Kafka	1883	Williams, C.	1886
Keynes	1883	Yeats-Brown	1886
Lawes	1883	Brooke	1887
Mottram	1883	Chase, M. E.	1887
Ortega	1883	Dell	1887
Stilwell	1883	Ferber	1887
Williams,		Foerster	1887
W. C.	1883	Geyl	1887
Wilson, F.	1883	Hall, J. N.	1887
Andrews	1884	Hoffman	1887
Clendenning	1884	Hootton	1887
Duhamel	1884	Huxley, J.	1887
Duranty	1884	Jeffers	1887
Feuchtwanger	1884	Kelly, G.	1887
Flecker	1884	Moore, M.	1887
Latourette	1884	Morison	1887
O'Casey	1884	Nordhoff	1887
Perkins,		Osborn, F.	1887
M. E.	1884	Pearson	1887
Roosevelt, E.	1884	Sitwell, E.	1887
Shepard	1884	Williams, K. P.	1887
Swinnerton	1884	Woollcott	1887
Teasdale	1884	Wylie	1887
Walpole, H.	1884	Zweig	1887
Benjamin	1885	Anderson, M.	1888
DeLaRoche	1885	Boyd	1888
Dinesen	1885	Broun	1888
Durant	1885	Byrd	1888
Heyward	1885	Cary	1888

Born 1881-90—Continued

Eliot, T. S.	1888
Chase, S.	1888
Kaye-Smith, S.	1888
Lawrence, T. E.	1888
Mansfield	1888
O'Neill	1888
Parrish	1888
Rusk	1888
Schlesinger	1888
Simonson	1888
Wallace, H. A.	1888
Aiken	1889
Allen, H.	1889
Barbellion	1889
Beer	1889
Benchley	1889
Byrne	1889
Craven	1889
Gaither	1889
Guedalla	1889
Hawes	1889
Hitler	1889
Hurst	1889
Kaufman	1889
Lindsay, H.	1889
Lippmann	1889
Macaulay, R.	1889
Nehru	1889
Page, E.	1889
Toynbee	1889
Waley	1889
Williams, B. A.	1889
Winant	1889
Allen, F. L.	1890
Bush	1890
Capek	1890
Christenson	1890
Connelly	1890
DeKruif	1890
Eisenhower	1890
Fowler	1890
Herbert	1890
Johnson, G. W.	1890
Morley, C.	1890
Nevins	1890
Richter	1890
Roeder	1890
Serge	1890
Stern	1890
Werfel	1890
Yarmolinsky	1890

Born 1891-1900

Arnold, T.	1891
Bacchelli	1891
Bemis	1891

Brown, I.	1891
Ehrenburg	1891
Flynn	1891
Haggard, H.	1891
Hindus	1891
Howard	1891
James, M.	1891
Joad	1891
Lewis, L. D.	1891
Morgenthau	1891
Paul	1891
Aldington	1892
Buck	1892
Coffin	1892
Garnett	1892
Hecht	1892
James, Will	1892
Lamb, H.	1892
Lynch	1892
Lynd, R. S.	1892
MacLeish	1892
Malone	1892
Millay	1892
Miller, D.	1892
Neff	1892
Niebuhr	1892
Plievier	1892
Rice, E. L.	1892
Sackville-West	1892
Sitwell, O.	1892
Suckow	1892
Welles	1892
West	1892
White, N.	1892
Willkie	1892
Behrman	1893
Bishop	1893
Brittain	1893
Buley	1893
Carmer	1893
Conant	1893
Crouse	1893
Damon	1893
Faÿ, B.	1893
Feis	1893
Krutch	1893
Laski	1893
Leech	1893
Marquand	1893
Menninger	1893
Morris, L. R.	1893
Northrop	1893
Oursler	1893
Parker, D.	1893
Scott, E.	1893
Strode	1893
Thomason	1893
Warner, S. T.	1893
White, W. F.	1893
Bainton	1894
Bentley	1894

Cummings	1894	Auslander	1897
Eliot, G. F.	1894	Barr	1897
Field, R. L.	1894	Barton	1897
Forbes	1894	Bowen, C. D.	1897
Frazier	1894	Browne	1897
Green, P. E.	1894	Chamberlin	1897
Gulbranssen	1894	Curti	1897
Huxley, A.	1894	DeVoto	1897
Johnson, O. H.	1894	Faulkner	1897
Kinsey	1894	Goodrich, M.	1897
Morgan	1894	Jessup	1897
Nathan, R.	1894	Knight	1897
Peterson	1894	LaFarge	1897
Porter, K. A.	1894	Lynd, H. M.	1897
Priestley	1894	O'Flaherty	1897
Stallings	1894	Pratt	1897
Thurber	1894	Pringle	1897
VanDoren	1894	Remarque	1897
Burman	1895	Schuster	1897
Chapman, M.	1895	Seagrave	1897
Federova	1895	Sitwell, S.	1897
Fisher, V.	1895	Smith, L.	1897
Graves	1895	Swisher	1897
Giono	1895	Werner	1897
Hillyer	1895	Wilder	1897
Hogben	1895	Benét, S.	1898
Lin Yu-tang	1895	Boyd, T.	1898
Malraux	1895	Bradley	1898
Mumford	1895	Brinton	1898
Papashvily	1895	Douglas, W. O.	1898
Pinckney	1895	Hemingway	1898
Ryskind	1895	Holtby	1898
Schachner	1895	Lewis, C. S.	1898
Sheen	1895	Lyons	1898
Smith, W. B.	1895	Myrdal	1898
Stewart	1895	Peattie	1898
VanPaassen	1895	Smyth	1898
Waln	1895	Tharp	1898
Wilson, E.	1895	Bowen, E.	1899
Barry	1896	Buck, Paul	1899
Blunden	1896	Cobb, H.	1899
Bradford, R.	1896	Coward	1899
Bromfield	1896	Crane, H.	1899
Cronin	1896	Davenport,	
Davis, H. L.	1896	R. W.	1899
Deane	1896	Forester	1899
DosPassos	1896	Hacker	1899
Fischer	1896	Hayek	1899
Fitzgerald	1896	Holt, R.	1899
Jaffe	1896	Josephson	1899
Kennedy, M.	1896	Kimbrough	1899
Larkin	1896	Lilienthal	1899
March	1896	Marshall, B.	1899
Rawlings	1896	Mason	1899
Sherwood	1896	Millis	1899
Spiller	1896	Sheean	1899
Stewart, R.	1896	Tate	1899
Streit	1896	Terhune	1899
Vance	1896	Waller	1899
Willison	1896	White, E. B.	1899
Agar	1897		

Born 1891-1900—Continued

Angle	1900
Arvin	1900
Brogan	1900
Brown, J. M.	1900
Goudge	1900
Hilton	1900
Hughes, R.	1900
Ingersoll, E.	1900
Ingersoll, R.	1900
Mattingly	1900
Mears	1900
Mitchell, M.	1900
O'Faolain	1900
Pyle	1900
Saint-Exupéry	1900
Seghers	1900
Silone	1900
Stettinius	1900
White, W. L.	1900
Winters	1900
Winwar	1900
Wolfe	1900

TWENTIETH CENTURY

Born 1901-23

Beard, M.	1901
Botkin	1901
Brace	1901
Butcher	1901
Dark	1901
Dubos	1901
Gunther	1901
Guthrie	1901
Hicks	1901
LaFarge, O.	1901
Mead, M.	1901
Nansen, O.	1901
Pollard	1901
Sandoz	1901
Skinner	1901
Struther	1901
Wescott	1901
Adler	1902
Cecil	1902
Commager	1902
Covarrubias	1902
Creighton	1902
Daniels, J.	1902
Duguid	1902
Hesseltine	1902
Hughes, L.	1902
Laxness	1902
Levi	1902
Matthiessen	1902
Nash, O.	1902
Sender	1902
Steinbeck	1902

Vogt	1902
Zaturenska	1902
Boothe	1903
Boyle, K.	1903
Caldwell	1903
Chamberlain	1903
Childs	1903
Cozzens	1903
Davenport, M.	1903
Edmonds	1903
Household	1903
Jackson, C.	1903
Kang	1903
Landon	1903
Mallea	1903
Miller, C.	1903
Orwell	1903
O'Sullivan	1903
Simmons	1903
Stone	1903
Taylor, F. H.	1903
Villiers	1903
Waugh, E.	1903
Carroll	1904
Curie	1904
Farrel	1904
Greene, G.	1904
Halper	1904
Kantor	1904
Neruda	1904
Perelman	1904
Shirer	1904
Smith, B·	1904
Vincent	1904
Weston	1904
Burnham	1905
Carr	1905
Ehrlich	1905
Green, H.	1905
Hahn	1905
Howe	1905
Kluckhohn	1905
Koestler	1905
McWilliams	1905
Sharp	1905
Sholokhov	1905
Snow	1905
Valtin	1905
Ward, M. J.	1905
Warren	1905
Crow	1906
Kingsley	1906
Odets	1906
Ottley	1906
Sartre	1906
Steegmuller	1906
Wecter	1906
White, M. B.	1906
White, T. H.	1906
Auden	1907

Baker, D.	1907	Petry	1911
Barzun	1907	Sevareid	1912
Brown, L. A.	1907	Stuart	1912
Butterfield	1907	Bradley, D. J.	1913
Chapman, F. S.	1907	Camus	1913
Deutscher	1907	Graham, G.	1913
DuMaurier	1907	Peters	1913
Fairbank	1907	Rukeyser	1913
Fleming	1907	Shapiro	1913
Flexner, J. T.	1907	Shaw, I.	1913
Fry, C.	1907	Gill	1914
Hutchinson	1907	Hersey	1914
Lea, T.	1907	Heyerdahl	1914
Liebman	1907	Lockridge	1914
Lindbergh	1907	Lauterbach	1914
Llewellyn	1907	Schulberg	1914
Michener	1907	Tilton	1914
Miller, J. C.	1907	Trevor-Roper	1914
Ullman	1907	Ward, B·	1914
Guareschi	1908	Williams, T.	1914
Haines	1908	Gebler	1915
Maxwell	1908	Johnson, W.	1915
Meredith, R.	1908	Kazin	1915
Pennell, J. S·	1908	Merton	1915
Rosten	1908	Miller, A.	1915
Saroyan	1908	Simonov	1915
Scott, R. L.	1908	Stafford	1915
Wright, R.	1908	Bentley, E.	1916
Barnett	1909	Burns, J. H.	1916
Carlson	1909	Hofstadter	1916
Chute	1909	Brown, H. P.	
Clark, W. V.		M.	1917
T.	1909	Lawson	1917
Lowry	1909	Lowell, R.	1917
Schmitt	1909	McCullers	1917
Stegner	1909	Schlesinger, Jr.	1918
Welty	1909	Hargrove	1919
Fischer	1910	Heggen	1919
Halsey	1910	Donald	1920
Johnson, J. W.	1910	Jackson, S.	1920
Miller, G. R.	1910	Link	1920
Gilhreth	1911	Meyer, C.	1920
Hart	1911	Mauldin	1921
Lorton	1911	Mailer	1923
Payne	1911		

SUMMARY

Before Christian Era	31
A.D. 1-1000	25
A.D. 1001-1500	35
A.D. 1501-1600	37
A.D. 1601-1700	50
A.D. 1701-1800	109
A.D. 1801-1825	90
A.D. 1826-1850	110
A.D. 1851-1875	271
A.D. 1876-1900	469
A.D. 1901-1923	178

Authors and Anonymous Classics
Listed by Nationality

American (726)

Adams, F. P.
Adams, H.
Adams, J. T.
Adams, S. H.
Addams, J.
Ade, G.
Adler, M. J.
Agar, H.
Aiken, C.
Akins, Z.
Alcott, A. B.
Alcott, L. M.
Aldrich, T. B.
Allen, F. L.
Allen, H.
Anderson, M.
Anderson, S.
Andrews, R. C.
Angle, P. M.
Anthony, K.
Antin, M.
Armstrong, M.
Arnold, H. H.
Arnold, T.
Arvin, N.
Asch, S.
Atherton, G.
Audubon, J. J.
Auslander, J.
Austin, M.

Babbitt, I.
Bainton, R. H.
Baker, D.
Baker, R. S.
Bancroft, G.
Barnes, M. A.
Barnett, L. K.
Barr, S.
Barry, P.
Barzun, J. M.
Bates, E. S.
Beard, C. A.
Beard, M. R.
Beard, Miriam
Beebe, W.
Beer, T.
Behrman, S. N.
Bell, E.
Bellamy, E.
Bemis, S. F.

Benchley, R. C.
Benét, S. V.
Benét, W. R.
Bent, S.
Berenson, B.
Beveridge, A.
Bierce, A.
Bishop, E.
Bishop, M. G.
Blunden, E. C.
Boas, F.
Bok, E.
Bonnet, T.
Boothe, C.
Botkin, B. A.
Bowers, C. G.
Bowman, P.
Boyd, J.
Boyd, T.
Boyle, K.
Brace, G. W.
Bradford, G.
Bradford, R.
Bradley, D. J.
Bradley, J. H.
Breasted, J. H.
Brinton, C.
Bromfield, L.
Brooks, V. W.
Broun, H.
Brown, H. P. M.
Brown, J. M.
Brown, L. A.
Brown, W. C.
Browne, L.
Bryant, W. C.
Buck, Paul
Buck, Pearl
Buley, R. C.
Bulfinch, T.
Burman, B. L.
Burnham, J.
Burns, J. H.
Burroughs, J.
Burt, M. S.
Bush, V.
Butcher, H. C.
Butler, N. M.
Butterfield, R. P.
Bynner, W.
Byrd, R. E.
Byrnes, J. F.

Cabell, J. B.
Cable, G. W.
Cabot, R. C.
Cahan, A.
Caldwell, E.
Canby, H. S.
Carlson, J. R.
Carmer, C.
Carroll, G. H.
Carryl, C. E.
Cather, W. S.
Chamberlain, J. R.
Chamberlin, W. H.
Chambers, R. W.
Channing, E.
Chapman, J. J.
Chapman, M.
Chase, M. E.
Chase, S.
Cheney, S.
Childs, M. W.
Christensen, E. O.
Churchill, W.
Chute, M. G.
Clark, W. V. T.
Clemens, S. L.
Clendening, L.
Cobb, H.
Cobb, I. S.
Coffin, R. P. T.
Cohen, M. R.
Coit, M. L.
Commager, H. S.
Conant, J. B.
Connelly, M.
Cooper, J. F.
Cortissoz, R.
Cozzens, J. G.
Crane, H.
Crane, S.
Craven, T.
Creel, G.
Cross, W. L.
Crothers, R.
Crothers, S. M.
Crouse, R.
Crow, J. A.
Crum, B. C.
Cummings, E. E.
Curti, M.
Cushing, H.
Damon, S. F.

AMERICAN—
Continued
Winthrop, T.
Winwar, F.
Wister, O.
Wolfe, T.
Woodward, W. E.
Woollcott, A.
Woolman, J.
Wright, F. L.
Wright, R.
Wylie, E.
Yarmolinsky, A.
Yezierka, A.
Young, S.
Zaturenska, M.
Zinsser, H.

ARABIAN (2)

*Arabian Nights' Enter-
tainments*
Koran

ARGENTINE (1)

Mallea, E.

AUSTRALIAN (2)

Dark, E.
Richardson, H. H.

AUSTRIAN (8)

Freud, S.
Hitler, A.
Kafka, F.
Salten, F.
Schnitzler, A.
Wassermann, J.
Werfel, F.
Zweig, S.

BELGIAN (2)

Coster, C. de
Maeterlinck, M.

BRITISH (415)

ENGLISH, SCOTTISH,
WELSH

Addison, J.
Ainsworth, H.
Aldington, R.
Anglo-Saxon Chronicle

Anglo-Saxon Poetry
Arnold, Sir E.
Arnold, M.
Auden, W. H.
Austen, J.
Bacon, F.
Ballantyne, R. M.
Barbellion, W. N. P.
Barham, R. H.
Baron, A.
Barrie, J. M.
Barton, M.
Beaumont, F.
Beckford, W.
Beddoes, T. L.
Bede
Beerbohm, M.
Bell, G.
Belloc, H.
Bennett, A.
Bentham, J.
Bentley, E. R.
Bentley, P.
Beowulf
Berkeley, G.
Besant, W.
Besier, R.
Bevan, E. R.
Birrell, A.
Blackmore, R. D.
Blackstone, W.
Blake, W.
Blunden, E. C.
Bojer, J.
Borrow, G.
Boswell, J.
Bowen, C. D.
Bowen, E.
Boyle, R.
Bridges, R.
Briffault, R. S.
Brittain, V.
Brogan, D. W.
Brontë, C.
Brontë, E.
Brooke, R.
Brown, I.
Browne, T.
Browning, E. B.
Browning, R.
Bryce, J.
Buchan, J.
Buckle, H. B.
Bullen, F. T.
Bunyan, J.
Burke, E.
Burnett, G.
Burney, F.
Burns, R.
Burton, R.

Burton, R. F.
Butler, J.
Butler, S. 1612-80
Butler, S. 1835-1902
Byron, G. G. N. B.,
    Lord
Caine, H.
Camden, W.
Campbell, T.
Carlyle, T.
Carr, J. D.
Carroll, L.
Cary, J.
Cecil, D.
Chambers, E. K.
Chapman, F. S.
Charnwood, G. R. B.,
    Lord
Chaucer, G.
Chesterfield, Earl of
Chesterton, G. K.
Churchill, W. S.
Cibber, C.
Clarendon, Earl of
Clodd, E.
Cobbett, W.
Coleridge, S. T.
Collins, W.
Compton-Burnett, I.
Congreve, W.
Conrad, J.
Cook, J.
Coward, N.
Cowper, W.
Crabbe, G.
Crankshaw, E.
Creasy, E. S.
Cronin, A. J.
Cunliffe, J. W.
Dalton, J.
Darwin, C.
Davies, W. H.
Defoe, D.
Dekker, T.
De la Mare, W.
De Morgan, W.
De Quincey, T.
Dickens, C.
Dickinson, G. L.
Disraeli, B.
D'Israeli, I.
Dobson, A.
Donne, J.
Doughty, C. M.
Douglas, N.
Doyle, A. C.
Drinkwater, J.
Dryden, J.
Duguid, J.
Du Maurier, D.

Du Maurier, G.
Edgeworth, M.
Eliot, G.
Eliot, T. S.
Ellis, H.
Elyot, Sir T.
Evelyn, J.
Everyman
Falkner, J. M.
Faraday, M.
Farnol, J.
Farquhar, G.
Fielding, H.
Fitzgerald, E.
Flecker, J. E.
Fleming, P.
Fletcher, J.
Ford, F. M.
Ford, J.
Forester, C. S.
Forster, E. M.
Forster, J.
Fox, G.
Foxe, J.
Frazer, J. G.
Freeman, E. A.
Froude, J. A.
Fry, C.
Fry, R.
Fuller, T.
Galsworthy, J.
Gardner, P.
Garnett, D.
Gaskell, E.
Gay, J.
Geoffrey of Monmouth
Gibbon, E.
Gibson, W. W.
Gilbert, W. S.
Gissing, G.
Godwin, W.
Goldsmith, O.
Gosse, E.
Goudge, E.
Grahame, K.
Granville-Barker, H. G.
Graves, R.
Gray, T.
Green, H.
Green, J. R.
Greene, G.
Grey of Falloden
Guedella, P.
Haggard, H. R.
Hakluyt, R.
Hardy, T.
Hardy, Mrs. T.
Harrington, J.
Harris, F.
Hawkins, A. H.

Hay, I.
Haydon, B. R.
Hayek, F. A. von
Hazlitt, W.
Henley, W. E.
Herbert, A. P.
Herbert, G.
Herbert of Cherbury
Herrick, R.
Hewlett, M.
Hichens, R.
Hilton, J.
Hobbes, T.
Hogben, L.
Holinshed, R.
Holtby, W.
Hooker, R.
Hopkins, G. M.
Household, G.
Housman, A. E.
Hudson, W. H.
Hughes, R.
Hughes, T.
Hume, D.
Hunt, L.
Hutchinson, A. S. M.
Hutchinson, R. C.
Huxley, A.
Huxley, J.
Huxley, T. H.
Irvine, W.
Jacobs, W. W.
Jeans, J. H.
Jefferies, R.
Joad, C. E. M.
Johnson, S.
Kaye-Smith, S.
Keats, J.
Keble, J.
Kennedy, M.
Keynes, J. M.
Kinglake, A. W.
Kingsley, C.
Kingsley, H.
Kipling, R.
Knight, E.
Knoblock, E.
Lamb, C.
Landor, W. S.
Langland, W.
Laski, H.
Law, W.
Lawrence, D. H.
Lawrence, T. E.
Lear, E.
Lecky, W. E. H.
Lee, S.
Lewes, G. H.
Lewis, C. S.
Llewellyn, R.

Lloyd George, D.
Locke, J.
Locke, W. J.
Lockhart, J. G.
Lowry, M.
Lubbock, P.
Lucas, E. V.
Lyly, J.
Lytton, E. B.
Mabinogion
Macaulay, R.
Macaulay, T. B.
Machen, A.
Mackenzie, H.
Macpherson, J.
Maine, Sir H.
Malory, Sir T.
Malthus, T. R.
Mandeville, Sir J.
Manning, A.
Mansfield, K.
Marlowe, C.
Marryat, F.
Marshall, A.
Marshall, B.
Masefield, J.
Massinger, P.
Masson, D.
Maugham, W. S.
Meredith, G.
Merrick, L.
Meynell, A.
Mill, J. S.
Millar, G. R.
Milman, H. H.
Milne, A. A.
Milton, J.
Mitford, M. R.
Montagu, M. W.
Montague, C. E.
Moore, G.
More, Sir T.
Morgan, C.
Morier, J.
Morley, J.
Morris, W.
Mottram, R.
Mulock, D. M.
Munro, H. H.
Nashe, T.
Nevinson, H. W.
Newman, J. H.
Noyes, A.
Orwell, G.
Osborne, D.
Otway, T.
Parker, G.
Paston Letters
Pater, W.
Payne, R.

BRITISH—*Continued*

Peacock, T. L.
Pearson, H.
Pepys, S.
Percy, T.
Petrie, W. F.
Phillips, S.
Phillpotts, E.
Pinero, A. W.
Pollock, Sir F.
Pope, A.
Porter, J.
Priestley, J. B.
Quiller-Couch, A. T.
Radcliffe, A.
Raleigh, Sir W.
Reade, C.
Reynolds, Sir J.
Ricardo, D.
Richard de Bury
Richardson, D. M.
Richardson, S.
Roberts of Kandahar
Rossetti, C.
Rossetti, D. G.
Ruskin, J.
Russell, B.
Russell, W. C.
Sackville-West, V.
Saintsbury, G. E.
Sassoon, S.
Scott, M.
Scott, R. F.
Scott, Sir W.
Shakespeare, W.
Sharp, M.
Shaw, G. B.
Shelley, M. W.
Shelley, P. B.
Sheridan, R. B.
Sidney, Sir P.
Sinclair, M.
Sitwell, E.
Sitwell, O.
Sitwell, S.
Smiles, S.
Smith, Adam
Smith, Alex.
Smith, G.
Smith, H.
Smith, James
Smith, John
Smollett, T. G.
Southey, R.
Spencer, H.
Spenser, E.
Stephen, Sir L.
Stern, G. B.
Sterne, L.

Stevenson, R. L.
Stoker, B.
Strachey, L.
Struthers, J.
Sullivan, Sir A.
Swift, J.
Swinburne, A.
Swinnerton, F.
Symonds, J. A.
Taylor, J.
Tennyson, A.
Terry, E.
Thackeray, W. M.
Thompson, F.
Thomson, J.
Tomlinson, H. M.
Toynbee, A. J.
Trelawney, E. J.
Trench, R. C.
Trevelyan, G. M.
Trevelyan, Sir G. O.
Trevena, J.
Trevor-Roper, H. R.
Trollope, A.
Trollope, F. M.
Villiers, A. J.
Waley, A. D.
Wallace, A. R.
Walpole, Horace
Walpole, Sir Hugh
Walton, I.
Ward, B.
Ward, Mrs. H.
Warner, S. T.
Waugh, E.
Webb, M.
Webster, J.
Wells, H. G.
Wesley, J.
West, R.
Weyman, S. J.
White, G.
White, T. H.
Whitehead, A. N.
Wilde, O.
Williams, C.
Woolf, V.
Wordsworth, D.
Wordsworth, W.
Wycherley, W.
Yeats, W. B.
Yeats-Brown, F.
Young, A.
Zangwill, I.
Zimmern, Sir A. E.

CANADIAN (6)

Creighton, D. G.
De La Roche, M.

Graham, G.
Hémon, L.
Leacock, S.
Service, R. W.

CHILEAN (1)

Neruda, P.

CHINESE (3)

Confucius
Lao-tsze
Lin Yu-tang

CZECH (3)

Capek, K.
Gebler, E.
Hasek, J.

DANISH (6)

Andersen, H. C.
Brandes, G.
Dinesen, I.
Jensen, J. V.
Kierkegaard, S. A.
Nexö, M. A.

DUTCH (5)

Couperus, L.
Erasmus, D.
Geyl, P.
Grotius, H.
Spinoza, B. de

FINNISH (1)

Kalevala

FRENCH (93)

Amiel, H. F.
Aucassin and Nicolette
Balzac, H. de
Barbusse, H.
Baudelaire, P. C.
Beaumarchais, P. A. C.
  de
Benjamin, R.
Bergson, H.
Boileau, N.
Boissier, G.
Bourget, P.
Brieux, E.

Calvin, J.
Camus, A.
Carrel, A.
Chanson de Roland
Chatrian, A.
Claudel, P.
"Colette"
Comte, A.
Corneille, P.
Curie, E.
Daudet, A.
Delacroix, E.
Descartes, R.
Diderot, D.
Dimnet, E.
Dumas, A. 1802-70
Dumas, A. 1824-95
Duruy, V.
Erckmann, E.
Fabre, J.-H.
Faure, E.
Faÿ, B.
Fénelon, F.
Flaubert, G.
France, A.
Froissart, J.
Gaboriau, E.
Gautier, T.
Gide, A.
Guizot, F. P. G.
Halévy, L.
Hugo, V.
Joinville, J. de
LaFayette, M. M.
LaFontaine, J.
LaMotte-Fouqué,
    F. H. K.
LaRochefoucauld, F. de
Loti, P.
Malraux, A.
Maritain, J.
Martin du Gard, R.
Maupassant, G. de
Mauriac, F.
Maurois, A.
Mérimée, P.
"Molière"
Montaigne, M. E. de
Montesquieu, C. de S.
Pascal, B.
"Pertinax"
Plievier, T.
Prévost, A. F.
Proust, M.
Rabelais, F.
Racine, J.
Reinach, S.
Remarque, E. M.
Rénan, E.
Rolland, R.

Romains, J.
Rostand, E.
Rousseau, J. J.
Sabatier, P.
Saint-Exupéry, A. de
Saint-Pierre, B. de
Saint-Simon, L. de R.
Sainte-Beuve, C. A.
Sand, G.
Sartre, J. P.
Schweitzer, A.
Sévigné, M. de
Siegfried, A.
Souvestre, E.
Staël, Baronne de
"Stendhal"
Taine, H. A.
Tocqueville, A. de
Verne, J.
Villon, F.
"Voltaire"
Zola

GERMAN (30)

Eucken, R. C.
Feuchtwanger, L.
Frenssen, G.
Goethe, J. W. von
Grimm, J.
Grimmelshausen, H. J. C.
Hauptmann, G.
Hegel, G. W. F.
Heine, H.
Hesse, H.
Kant, I.
Keyserling, H. A.
Kleist, H. von
Lessing, G. E.
Ludwig, E.
Luther, M.
Mann, T.
Marx, K.
Münchhausen, K. F.
Nibelungenlied
Nietzsche, F. W.
Scheffel, J. V. von
Schiller, J. C. F. von
Schopenhauer, A.
Seghers, A.
Spengler, O.
Sudermann, H.
Thomas à Kempis
Valtin, J.
Zweig, A.

GREEK (18)

Æschylus
Æsop

Aristophanes
Aristotle
Demosthenes
Epictetus
Euripides
Herodotus
Homer
Lucian
Pindar
Plato
Plutarch
Polybius
Sophocles
Theocritus
Thucydides
Xenophon

HINDU (5)

Kalidasa
Mahabharata and
    Ramayana
Nehru, J.
Tagore, R.

HUNGARIAN (4)

Koestler, A.
Lang, P. H.
Molnar, F.
Nijinsky, R.

ICELANDIC (1)

Laxness, H.

IRISH (16)

Byrne, D.
Colum, P.
Dunsany, Lord
Ervine, St. J.
Gregory, Lady A.
Joyce, J.
Lever, C.
Lover, S.
O'Casey, S.
O'Faolain, S.
O'Flaherty, L.
O'Sullivan, M.
Russell, G. W.
Stephens, J.
Synge, J. M.
Yeats, W. B.

ITALIAN (30)

Annunzio, G. d'
Aquinas, St. T.
Ariosto, L.
Bacchelli, R. de
Boccaccio, G.
Borgese, G. A.
Casanova de S., G. J.
Castiglione, B. de
Cellini, B.
Croce, B.
Dante Alighieri
Deledda, G.
Ferrero, G.
Fogazzaro, A.
Francis of Assisi, St.
Giono, J.
Goldoni, C.
Guareschi, G.
Leonardo da Vinci
Levi, C.
Machiavelli, N.
Manzoni, A.
Papini, G.
Pirandello, L.
Polo, Marco
Sabatini, R.
Silone, I.
Tasso, T.
Vasari, G.
Verga, G.

JAPANESE (1)

Murasaki Shikibu

JEWISH (2)

Bible
Weizmann, C.

MEXICAN (1)

Covarrubias, M.

NORWEGIAN (12)

Amundsen, R.
Björnson, B.
Duun, O.
Eddas
Gulbranssen, T.

Hamsun, K.
Heimskringla
Heyerdahl, T.
Ibsen, H.
Nansen, O.
Rölvaag, O. E.
Undset, S.

PERSIAN (3)

Firdausi
Omar Khayyam
Sadi

POLISH (5)

Copernicus, N.
Deutscher, I.
Einstein, A.
Ossendowski, F.
Sienkiewicz, H.

PORTUGUESE (1)

Camoëns, L. V. de

ROMAN (24)

Apuleius, L.
Augustine, St.
Aurelius Antoninus, M.
Boethius
Caesar, C. J.
Catullus, C. V.
Cicero, M. T.
Horatius Flaccus, Q.
Juvenal
Livius, T.
Lucretius
Martial
Ovid
Petronius
Plautus
Pliny
Plotinus
Seneca
Suetonius
Tacitus
Terence
Tibullus
Virgil
Vitruvius

RUSSIAN (19)

Andreyev, L. N.
Bashkirtseff, M.
Bunin, I.
Chekhov, A.
Dostoievski, F.
Ehrenburg, I.
Gogol, N. V.
Goncharov, I. A.
Gorki, M.
Lenin, N.
Merejkowski, D. S.
Marie, Grand Duchess
Pushkin, A. S.
Serge, V.
Sholokhov, M.
Simonov, K.
Sologub, F.
Tolstoi, L.
Trotsky, L.

SOUTH AFRICAN (2)

Schreiner, O.
Paton, A.

SPANISH (13)

Baroja, P.
Benavente, J.
Blasco-Ibanez, V.
Calderón de la Barca, P.
Cervantes-Saavedra, M. de
Echegaray, J.
Hurtado de Mendoza, D.
Madariaga, S. de
Ortega y Gasset, J.
Pérez Galdós, B.
Sender, R. J.
Unamuno, M.
Vega Carpio, F. de

SWEDISH (4)

Lagerlöf, S.
Munthe, A.
Myrdal, G. K.
Strindberg, A.

SWISS (1)

Meyer, C. F.

Summary

American	726	Dutch	5	Mexican	1		
Arabian	2	Finnish	1	Norwegian	12		
Argentine	1	French	93	Persian	3		
Australian	2	German	30	Polish	5		
Austrian	8	Greek	18	Portuguese	1		
Belgian	2	Hindu	5	Roman	24		
British	415	Hungarian	4	Russian	19		
Canadian	6	Icelandic	1	S. African	2		
Chilean	1	Irish	16	Spanish	13		
Chinese	3	Italian	30	Swedish	4		
Czech	3	Japanese	1	Swiss	1		
Danish	6	Jewish	2				

TOTAL NUMBER OF AUTHORS **1766**

TOTAL NUMBER OF COUNTRIES **35**

List of Authors and Titles Classified by Subject or Literary Form

Scheme of Classification

1. Philosophy (Includes Psychology, Ethics, etc.)

2. Religion and Religions

3. Political Science (Includes Law, World Law, Government, Foreign Relations, Freedom, Democracy)

4. Economics

5. Sociology (Includes Social Work, Crime, Race Problems, etc.)

6. Education

7. Children's Books

8. Folklore, Fables, Fairies, Myths (Includes many titles which are also in Class 7)

9. Language

10. Science

11. Nature Books

12. Art and Architecture, Music

13. Literature: History, Description, Criticism

14. Poetry
    - *a.* American
    - *b.* British and Irish
    - *c.* European and Latin American

    d. Classical (Greek and Latin)
    e. Oriental

15. Drama
    - *a.* American
    - *b.* British and Irish
    - *c.* European
    - *d.* Classical (Greek and Latin)
    - *e.* Indian

16. Fiction
    - *a.* American
    - *b.* British, Canadian, Australian, British-African
    - *c.* French and French-Canadian
    - *d.* German and Austrian
    - *e.* Irish
    - *f.* Italian
    - *g.* Russian
    - *h.* Scandinavian
    - *i.* Spanish and Argentinian
    - *j.* Miscellaneous

17. Essays
    - *a.* American
    - *b.* British
    - *c.* Foreign

18. Speeches

19. Satire and Humor
    - *a.* American

b. British
c. Foreign

20. Description, Travels, Voyages, Geography

21. History
    a. General
    b. Ancient History, Archaeology
    c. Europe in general
    d. England
    e. France
    f. Spain & Latin America

g. Russia
h. Miscellaneous
i. United States & Canada
j. World War I
k. World War II and aftermath

22. Biography
    a. Collective
    b. Individual
    c. Letters. Journals, Diaries, Notebooks, Table Talk

---

1. PHILOSOPHY

(Includes also books on psychology, the mind, reasoning, logic, ethics, aesthetics, living, the good life, etc.)

Aristotle	Works
Aurelius	Meditations
Bacon	Novum Organum
Baker	Adventures of David Grayson
Bennett	How to Live . . .
Bergson	Creative Evolution
Berkeley	Principles of Human Knowledge
Boethius	Consolation of Philosophy
Bridges	Testament of Beauty
Browne	Hydrotaphia
Bynner	Way of Life
Byrd	Alone
Cabot	What Men Live By
Carrel	Man the Unknown
Comte	Positive Philosophy
Confucius	Analects
Confucius	Wisdom of Confucius
Descartes	Discourse on the Method . . .
Dewey	How We Think
Dewey	Reconstruction in Philosophy
Dewey	Human Nature and Conduct
Dewey	Experience and Nature
Dewey	Art as Experience
Dewey	Logic . . .

Dickinson	Greek View of Life
Dickinson	Modern Symposium
Dimnet	Art of Thinking
Dimnet	What We Live By
Dorsey	Why We Behave . . .
Durant	Story of Philosophy
Ellis	Dance of Life
Ellis	Psychology of Sex
Epictetus	Moral Discourses
Eucken	Problem of Human Life
Fosdick	On Being a Real Person
Freud	Basic Writings
Hall	Adolescence
Hegel	Selected Writings
Hume	Human Understanding
Huxley, A.	Eyeless in Gaza
Huxley, A.	Ends and Means
Huxley, A.	Perennial Philosophy
Huxley, J.	On Living in a Revolution
James	Will to Believe . . .
James	Pragmatism
James	Meaning of Truth
Joad	Common Sense Ethics
Joad	Modern Philosophy
Joad	Guide to Philosophy
Kant	Practical Reason
Kant	Pure Reason
Kant	Judgment
Keyserling	Travel Diary . . .
Kierkegaard	Either—Or
Lao-tsze	Reason and Virtue
La Rochefoucauld	Maxims

PHILOSOPHY—*Continued*

Lecky	History of European Morals
Liebman	Peace of Mind
Lin Yu-tang	Importance of Living
Lippmann	Preface to Morals
Locke	Human Understanding
Lucretius	On the Nature of Things
Maurois	Art of Living
Mead	From the South Seas
Menninger	Human Mind
Mill	Logic
Mill	Humanitarianism
More	Shelburne Essays
Nietzsche	Philosophy
Overstreet	Influencing Human Behavior
Overstreet	Mature Mind
Plato	Dialogues
Plotinus	Essence of Plotinus
Robinson	Mind in the Making
Royce	Philosophy of Loyalty
Russell	Conquest of Happiness
Russell	History of Western Philosophy
Russell	Human Knowledge
Russell	Outline of Philosophy
Russell	What I Believe
Santayana	Life of Reason
Santayana	Realms of Being
Santayana	Scepticism and Animal Faith
Santayana	Winds of Doctrine
Sartre	Existentialism
Schopenhauer	World as Will and Idea
Schweitzer	Indian Thought
Seneca	Morals
Spencer	First Principles
Spencer	Principles of Ethics
Spencer	Principles of Psychology
Spinoza	Ethics
Spinoza	Philosophy
Starkey	Devil in Massachusetts
Unamuno	Tragic Sense of Life
Xenophon	Memorabilia

2. RELIGION AND RELIGIONS

Aquinas, St. T.	Summa Theologiae
Augustine, St.	Confessions
Augustine, St.	City of God
Bates	Bible as Living Literature
Bevan	Christianity
Bevan	Symbolism and Belief
Bible	
Browne, L.	This Believing World
Browne, Sir T.	Religio Medici
Bunyan	Grace Abounding
Bunyan	Life. . . of Mr. Badman
Bunyan	Pilgrim's Progress . . .
Butler	Analogy of Religion
Bynner	Way of Life
Calvin	Institutes . . . Christian Religion
Chase	Bible and the Common Reader
Chesterton	Orthodoxy
Claudel	Tidings Brought to Mary
Eddy	Science and Health
Eliot, T. S.	Four Quartets
Eliot, T. S.	Idea of a Christian Society
Eucken	Christianity and the New Idealism
Eucken	Problem of Human Life . . .
Fiske	Destiny of Man
Fosdick	Christianity and Progress
Fosdick	Guide to Understanding the Bible
Fox, G.	Journal
Foxe, J.	Acts and Monuments . . .
Francis of Assisi, St.	Little Flowers
Goodspeed	How to Read the Bible
Goodspeed	Story of the Bible
Goodspeed	Life of Jesus
Herbert	The Temple
Hooker	Laws of Ecclesiastical Polity
James	Varieties of Religious Experience
James	Will to Believe
Kafka	The Castle
Keble	Christian Year
Keyserling	Travel Diary . . .
Kierkegaard	Either-Or
Koran	

Lao-tsze	Book of Reason and Virtue
Law	Serious Call . . .
Lea	History of the Inquisition of Spain
Lewis	Screwtape Letters
Luther	Table Talk
Maritain	Christianity and Democracy
Merton	Seven Storey Mountain
Merton	Waters of Siloe
Milman	History of Latin Christianity
Newman	Apologia pro Sua Vita
Niebuhr	Faith and History
Niebuhr	Nature and Destiny of Man
Oursler	Greatest Story Ever Told
Papini	Life of Christ
Pascal	Thoughts (*Pensées*)
Royce	Problem of Christianity
Ruskin	Praeterita
Sabatier	Life of St. Francis . . .
Sheen	Peace of Soul
Swift	Tale of A Tub
Taylor	Holy Living
Taylor	Holy Dying
Thomas à Kempis	Imitation of Christ
Thompson	Hound of Heaven
Wesley	Journal
Whitehead	Religion in the Making
Woolman	Journal

3. POLITICAL SCIENCE

(Includes Law, World Law, Government, Foreign Relations, Freedom, Democracy)

Aristotle	Politics
Bacon	New Atlantis
Beard	American Leviathan
Beard	The Republic
Bentham	Introd. to . . . Morals and Legislation
Blackstone	Commentaries on Laws of England
Brinton	From Many One
Bryce	American Commonwealth
Burke	French Revolution

Bush	Modern Arms and Free Men
Carlyle	Heroes and Hero Worship
Chamberlain	American Stakes
Dewey	Democracy and Education
Dewey	Freedom and Culture
Fairbank	United States and China
The Federalist	
Flynn	You're the Boss
Grotius	De Jure Belli et Pacis
Harrington	Commonwealth of Oceana
Hayek	Road to Serfdom
Hobbes	Leviathan
Laski	American Presidency
Lilienthal	This I Do Believe
Lin Yu-tang	Between Tears and Laughter
Lippmann	Public Opinion
Lippmann	Principles of a Good Society
Lippmann	United States Foreign Policy
Lowell	Government of England
Machiavelli	The Prince
Maine	Ancient Law
Maritain	Christianity and Democracy
Maritain	True Humanism
Meyer	Peace or Anarchy
Mill	On Liberty
Mill	Representative Government
Milton	Areopagitica
Montesquieu	Spirit of Laws
More	Utopia
Mumford	Culture of Cities
Mumford	Technics of Civilization
Nock	Memoirs of Superfluous Man
Ortega y Gasset	Revolt of the Masses
Orwell	Animal Farm
Orwell	1984
Paine	Common Sense
Paine	Rights of Man
Perry	Puritanism and Democracy
Plato	The Republic
Rousseau	Social Contract
Russell	Power
Russell	Why Men Fight

POLITICAL SCIENCE—*Continued*

Schlesinger, Jr.	Vital Centre
Shaw	Everybody's Political What's What
Shaw	Prefaces
Streit	Union Now
Tocqueville	Democracy in America
Ward	West at Bay
Welles	Time for Decision
Wells	Modern Utopia
West	Meaning of Treason
White, E. B.	Wild Flag
Willkie	One World

4. ECONOMICS

Adams	Our Business Civilization
Arnold	Folklore of Capitalism
Beard	History of the Business Man
Burnham	Managerial Revolution
Chase	Men and Machines
Chase	Rich Land, Poor Land
Chase	Your Money's Worth . . .
George	Progress and Poverty
Hacker	Triumph of American Capitalism
Keynes	Economic Consequences of the Peace
Malthus	Essay on . . . Population
Marx	Capital
Marx	Communist Manifesto
Mumford	Sticks and Stones
Osborn	Our Plundered Planet
Peterson	American Labor Unions
Ricardo	Principles of Political Economy
Russell	Freedom vs. Organization
Shaw	Intelligent Woman's Guide to Socialism
Smith, A.	Inquiry into the . . . Wealth of Nations

Veblen	Absentee Ownership and Business Enterprise
Veblen	Engineers and the Price System
Veblen	Theory of the Leisure Class
Vogt	Road to Survival
Wecter	Age of the Great Depression

5. SOCIOLOGY

(Includes Social Work, Crime, Race Problems, etc.)

Addams	Twenty Years of Hull House
Briffault	The Mothers
Castiglione	The Courtier
Chase	Proper Study of Mankind . . .
Frazier	Negro in the United States
Halsey	Color Blind
Keller	Man's Rough Road
Kinsey	Sexual Behavior in the Human Male
Lawes	20,000 Years in Sing Sing
Lynd and Lynd	Middletown . . .
Lynd and Lynd	Middletown in Transition . . .
McWilliams	Brothers under the Skin
McWilliams	Mask for Privilege
McWilliams	Prejudice, Japanese-Americans
Maine	Village Communities . . .
Mill	Subjection of Women
Mumford	Culture of Cities
Mumford	Technics of Civilization
Myrdal	American Dilemma
Ortega y Gasset	Revolt of the Masses
Osborn	Our Plundered Planet
Ottley	New World A-Coming . . .
Roth	Jewish Contribution . . .
Spencer	Principles of Sociology
Stegner	One Nation . . .

Sumner	Folkways . . .	Clemens	Tom Sawyer
Wald	House on Henry	Defoe	Robinson Crusoe
	Street	De La Mare	Peacock Pie
Wald	Windows on Henry	Field	With Trumpet and
	Street		Drum
Wecter	When Johnny Comes	Grahame	Dream Days
	Marching Home	Grahame	Golden Age
Wiener	Human Use of Hu-	Grahame	Wind in the Wil-
	man Beings		lows
		Grimm	Household Tales
		Harris	Uncle Remus, His
6.	EDUCATION		Songs and His
			Sayings
Bacon	Advancement of	Harris	Nights with Uncle
	Learning		Remus
Barzun	Teacher in Amer-	Harris	Uncle Remus and
	ica		His Friends
Butler	Across the Busy	Hawthorne	Tanglewood Tales
	Years	Hawthorne	Wonder Book
Castiglione	The Courtier	Hudson	Little Boy Lost
Dewey	Democracy and Ed-	Hughes	Tom Brown's School
	ucation		Days
Elyot	Boke Named the	Kipling	Captains Coura-
	Governour		geous
Fisher	Montessori Mother	Kipling	Jungle Books
Harvard	General Education	Kipling	Just So Stories
Univ.	in a Free Society	Kipling	Puck of Pook's
Learned	American Public		Hill
	Library . . .	Kipling	Rewards and Fairies
Locke	Some Thoughts	La Fontaine	Fables
	Concerning Edu-	Lagerlöf	Wonderful Adven-
	cation		tures of Nils
Martin	Meaning of a Lib-	Maeterlinck	Blue Bird
	eral Education	Milne	When We Were
Robinson	Humanizing of		Very Young
	Knowledge	Roosevelt, T.	Letters to His
Rousseau	Émile		Children
Spencer	Education	Ruskin	King of the Golden
Van Doren,			River
M.	Liberal Education	Sandburg	Rootabaga Stories
		Stevenson	Child's Garden of
			Verses
7.	CHILDREN'S BOOKS	Stevenson	Treasure Island
		Swift	Gulliver's Travels
Alcott	Little Women	Tarkington	Penrod
Andersen	Fairy Tales	Van Loon	Story of Mankind
Arabian Nights'		Wiggin	Birds' Christmas
Entertain-			Carol
ments		Wiggin	Rebecca of Sunny-
Barrie	Peter Pan		brook Farm
Bulfinch	Age of Chivalry		
Bulfinch	Age of Fable		
Carroll	Alice in Wonder-	8.	FOLKLORE, FABLES, FAIRIES,
	land		MYTHS
Carroll	Through the Look-		
	ing-Glass		Includes many titles in Class 7,
Carryl	Davy and the Gob-		and also the following:
	lin		
Clemens	Huckleberry Finn	Æsop	Fables
Clemens	Prince and the	Botkin	Treasury of Amer-
	Pauper		ican Folklore

11. NATURE BOOKS

12. ART AND ARCHITECTURE

ART AND ARCHITECTURE—
Continued

Ruskin	Modern Painters
Ruskin	Stones of Venice
Simonson	Stage Is Set
Sitwell, S.	Hunters and the Hunted
Symonds	Renaissance in Italy
Tallmadge	Story of Architecture in America
Taylor	Taste of Angels . . .
Van Loon	The Arts
Vasari	Lives of the Artists
Vitruvius	Concerning Architecture
Wright	Autobiography
Wright	Frank Lloyd Wright on Architecture
Wright	When Democracy Builds

13. LITERATURE: HISTORY, DESCRIPTION, CRITICISM

Adler	How to Read a Book
Aristotle	Poetics
Aristotle	Rhetoric
Auslander	Winged Horse . . .
Babbitt	New Laokoön
Babbitt	Rousseau and Romanticism
Bennett	Literary Taste
Bentley	Bernard Shaw
Boileau	Art of Poetry
Brandes	Main Currents in Nineteenth Century Literature
Brandes	Creative Spirits of the Nineteenth Century
Brooks	Flowering of New England
Brooks	New England: Indian Summer
Brooks	World of Washington Irving
Brooks	Times of Melville and Whitman
Brooks	Ordeal of Mark Twain
Brownell	Victorian Prose Masters
Brownell	American Prose Masters
Cabell	Beyond Life
Canby	Definitions
Canby	Classic Americans

Canby	Thoreau
Canby	Walt Whitman
Chesterton	Charles Dickens
Chesterton	Heretics
Chesterton	Victorian Age in Literature
Coleridge	Biographia Literaria
Coleridge	Lectures on Shakespeare
Commager	American Mind . . .
Conrad	Notes on Life and Letters
Croce	European Literature in the Nineteenth Century
Dickinson, T. H.	Outline of Contemporary Drama
D'Israeli	Curiosities of Literature
D'Israeli	Amenities of Literature
Eastman	Enjoyment of Poetry
Eastman	Literary Mind . . .
Eastman	Artists in Uniform . . .
Eastman	Enjoyment of Laughter
Erskine	Delight of Great Books
Foerster	American Criticism
Foerster	Towards Standards
Forster	Aspects of the Novel
France	On Life and Letters
Geismar	Last of the Provincials . . .
Glasgow	Certain Measure
Granville-Barker	Prefaces to Shakespeare
Hart	The Popular Book
Hazlitt	Characters of Shakespeare's Plays
Hazlitt	Dramatic Literature of the Age of Elizabeth
Hazlitt	Lectures on the English Comic Writers
Hazlitt	Lectures on the English Poets
Hazlitt	Table Talk
Huneker	Iconoclasts
Irvine	Universe of G.B.S.
Kazin	On Native Grounds
Krutch	Edgar Allan Poe
Krutch	Five Masters
Lessing	Laokoön

Lewisohn	Story of American Literature
Lowell, A.	Tendencies of Modern American Poetry
Lowell, J. R.	Among My Books
Lowell, J. R.	My Study Windows
Lowes	Geoffrey Chaucer
Lowes	Convention and Revolt in Poetry
Lowes	Road to Xanadu
Lubbock	Craft of Fiction
Macy	Spirit of American Literature
Macy	Story of the World's Literature
Madariaga	Genius of Spain
Mansfield	Novels and Novelists
March	Two Worlds of M. Proust
Matthews	Molière
Matthews	Study of the Drama
Matthiessen	American Renaissance . . .
Maugham	The Summing Up
Maugham	Writer's Notebook
Maurois	Aspects of Biography
Moody	History of English Literature
More	Shelburne Essays
Mumford	Golden Day
Neff	Edwin Arlington Robinson
Newton	Amenities of Book-Collecting
Newton	Magnificent Farce . . .
Parrington	Main Currents in American Thought . . .
Pater	Greek Studies
Perkins	Editor to Author . . .
Phelps	Advance of the English Novel
Phelps	Essays on Russian Novelists
Phelps	Some Makers of American Literature
Poe	Critical Essays
Pound	Letters
Quiller-Couch	On the Art of Writing
Quiller-Couch	Studies in Literature

Quinn	History of the American Drama
Repplier	Happy Half Century
Richard de Bury	Philobiblon
Ruskin	Sesame and Lilies
Sainte-Beuve	Causeries de Lundi (Monday Talks)
Saintsbury	English Novel
Saintsbury	History of Criticism and Literary Taste
Saintsbury	History of Nineteenth Century Literature
Saintsbury	History of the French Novel
Sedgwick	Happy Profession
Shapiro	Essay on Rime
Sherman	Critical Woodcuts
Sidney	Apologie for Poetry
Smith	On Reading Shakespeare
Spiller	Literary History of the United States
Staël	Germany
Stephen	Hours in a Library
Stevenson	Familiar Studies of Men and Books
Stevenson	Virginibus Puerisque
Swift	Battle of the Books
Symonds	Studies of the Greek Poets
Taine	History of English Literature
Thackeray	English Humorists
Thayer	Art of Biography
Ticknor	History of Spanish Literature
Van Doren, C.	American Novel
Vincent	Trying-out of Moby Dick
Wilson, E.	Axel's Castle . . .
Wilson, E.	To the Finland Station
Wilson, E.	Wound and the Bow
Winters	In Defence of Reason
Winters	Primitivism and Decadence
Woolf	First Common Reader
Woolf	Second Common Reader

14. POETRY

a. American

Aiken	Selected Poems
Benét, S. V.	John Brown's Body
Benét, S. V.	Western Star
Benét, W. R.	Dust Which Is God
Bishop	North and South
Bryant	Poems
Canby	Walt Whitman
Coffin	Collected Poems
Crane	Collected Poems
Cumming	Collected Poems
Davenport	My Country . . .
Dickinson, E.	Collected Poems
Dickinson, E.	Bolts of Melody
Doolittle	Collected Poems
Dunbar	Complete Poems
Eliot	Collected Poems
Eliot	Four Quartets
Emerson	Poems
Frost	Complete Poems
Harte	Poems
Hay	Pike County Ballads
Hillyer	Collected Verse
Hughes	Weary Blues
Jeffers	Selected Poetry
Johnson	Selected Poems
Johnson, ed.	Book of American Negro Poetry
Johnson, ed.	Book of American Negro Spirituals
Kilmer	Joyce Kilmer: Poems . . .
Lanier	Selected Poems
Leonard	Two Lives
Lindsay	Collected Poems
Longfellow	Poems
Lowell, A.	Selected Poems
Lowell, A.	Tendencies of Modern American Poetry
Lowell, J. R.	Complete Poetical Works
Lowell, R.	Lord Weary's Castle
MacLeish	Poems, 1924-1933
MacLeish	Conquistador
MacLeish	Public Speech; Poems
Masters	Spoon River Anthology
Matthiessen, ed.	Oxford Book of American Verse
Millay	Collected Lyrics
Millay	Collected Sonnets
Miller	White Cliffs
Moore	Selected Poems

Nash	Selected Verse
Neihardt	Cycle of the West
Parker	Portable Dorothy Parker
Poe	Poems
Pound	Personae
Pound	Cantos
Riley	Complete Poetical Works
Robinson	Collected Poems
Sandburg	Complete Poems
Sandburg, ed.	American Songbag
Shapiro	V-letters . . .
Shapiro	Essay on Rime
Stevens	Transport to Summer
Tate	Poems, 1922-1947
Teasdale	Collected Poems
Untermeyer, ed.	Treasury of Great Poetry, English and American
Van Doren, M.	Collected Poems
Whitman	Leaves of Grass
Whittier	Complete Poetical Works
Williams	Selected Poems
Williams	Paterson
Wylie	Collected Poems
Zaturenska	Cold Morning Sky
Zaturenska	Listening Landscape

b. British and Irish

Aldington, ed.	Viking Book of Poetry of the English-Speaking World
Anglo-Saxon Poetry: 650-1000 A.D. (Translations)	
Arnold, Sir E.	Light of Asia
Arnold, Sir E.	Song Celestial
Arnold, M.	Collected Poems
Auden	Age of Anxiety
Auden	Collected Poetry
Beowulf	
Blake	Poetical Works
Bridges	Poetical Works
Brontë Sisters	Poems by Currer, Ellis and Acton Bell
Brooke	Collected Poems
Browning, E. B.	Poetical Works
Browning, R.	Works

Burns	Works
Byron	Poems
Campbell	Poems
Chaucer	Poetical Works
Coleridge	Poems
Cowper	Poems
Crabbe	Poems
Colum	Poems
Davies	Collected Poems
De la Mare	Collected Poems
Dobson	Selected Poems
Donne	Complete Poetry . . .
Dryden	Works
Eliot	Collected Poems
Eliot	Four Quartets
Flecker	Collected Poems
Gay	Beggar's Opera
Gay	Trivia . . .
Gibson	Collected Poems
Gilbert	Bab Ballads
Gilbert	Operettas
Goldsmith	Deserted Village
Goldsmith	The Traveller
Gray	Poems
Hardy	Collected Poems
Hazlitt	Lectures on English Poets
Henley	Poems
Herbert	The Temple
Herrick	Poems
Hopkins	Poems
Housman	Collected Poems
Keats	Poems
Keble	Christian Year
Kipling	Rudyard Kipling's Verse
Langland	Vision of Piers Plowman
Lowes	Geoffrey Chaucer
Lowes	Road to Xanadu
Macaulay	Lays of Ancient Rome
Macpherson	"Ossian's" Fingal
Marlow	Plays and Poems
Masefield	Poems: Complete Edition
Meredith	Poetical Works
Meynell	Poems
Milton	Complete Poetical Works
Morris	Earthly Paradise
Morris	Sigurd the Volsung
Noyes	Collected Poems
Percy	Reliques of Ancient English Poetry
Pope	Complete Poetical Works
Quiller-Couch, ed.	Oxford Book of English Verse

Rossetti, C.	Poetical Works
Rossetti, D. G.	Poems and Translations
Russell	Selected Poems
Sassoon	Collected Poems
Scott	Complete Poetical Works
Service	Complete Poems
Shakespeare	Poems
Shelley	Complete Poetical Works
Sidney	Arcadia and Other Works
Sitwell, E.	Canticle of the Rose
Sitwell, E.	Song of the Cold
Spenser	Faerie Queene
Stephens	Collected Poems
Swinburne	Complete Poetical Works
Tennyson	Complete Poetical Works
Thompson	Poems
Thomson	Castle of Indolence
Thomson	The Seasons
Untermeyer, ed.	Treasury of Great Poems, English and American
Wilde	Poems
Wordsworth	Wordsworth Anthology . . .
Yeats	Collected Poems

c. European and Latin American

Ariosto	Orlando Furioso
Baudelaire	Flowers of Evil
Camöens	The Lusiad
Chanson de Roland	
Dante	Divine Comedy
Dante	Vita Nuova
Eddas	
Goethe	Herman and Dorothea
Heimskringla	
Heine	Heinrich Heine: Paradox and Poet: Poems
Kalevala	
Lockhart, trans.	Ancient Spanish Ballads
Neruda	Residence on Earth . . .
Nibelungenlied	
Pushkin	Eugene Onegin
Tasso	Jerusalem Delivered
Villon	Poems

POETRY—*Continued*

d. Classical (Greek and Latin)

Catullus	Poems
Homer	Iliad
Homer	Odyssey
Horace	Poems
Lucretius	De Rerum Natura
Ovid	Metamorphoses
Pindar	Odes
Symonds	Studies of the Greek Poets
Theocritus	Idylls
Tibullus	Elegies
Virgil	Æneid
Virgil	Eclogues
Virgil	Georgics

e. Oriental

Bhagavad Gita (See Arnold, Sir E.	
Firdausi	Shah Namah . . .
Mahabharata	
Omar Khayyam	Rubaiyat
Ramayana (See Mahabharata)	
Sadi	Gulistan
Tagore	Collected Poems and Plays
Waley, *trans.*	Translations from the Chinese

15. DRAMA

a. American

Akins	Old Maid
Anderson	Both Your Houses
Anderson	Elizabeth the Queen
Anderson	High Tor
Anderson	Mary of Scotland
Anderson	What Price Glory?
Anderson	Saturday's Children
Anderson	Winterset
Austin	Arrow-Maker
Barry	Holiday
Barry	Hotel Universe
Barry	Philadelphia Story
Behrman	Biography
Behrman	Second Man
Connelly	Green Pastures
Crothers	Susan and God
Crouse	Life with Father
Crouse	State of the Union
Davis	Icebound
Dickinson	Outline of Contemporary Drama
Glaspell	Plays
Glaspell	Alison's House
Green	House of Connelly
Green	In Abraham's Bosom
Hemingway	Fifth Column
Howard	Silver Cord
Howard	They Knew What They Wanted
Howells	Albany Depot
Howells	Mouse Trap
Kaufman	Of Thee I Sing
Kaufman	Six Plays
Kelly	Craig's Wife
Kingsley	Dead End
Kingsley	Men in White
Kingsley	The Patriots
MacKaye	Canterbury Pilgrims
MacKaye	Jeanne d'Arc
MacKaye	Mystery of Hamlet
MacKaye	Sappho and Phaon
MacKaye	Scarecrow
MacLeish	Fall of the City
Matthews	Molière
Matthews	Study of the Drama
Millay	King's Henchman
Miller	Death of a Salesman
Moody	Great Divide
Nathan	Encyclopedia of the Theatre
Nathan	Theatre Book of the Year . . .
Odets	Six Plays
O'Neill	Anna Christie
O'Neill	Beyond the Horizon
O'Neill	Nine Plays
Quinn	History of the American Drama
Rice	Adding Machine
Rice	Street Scene
Rosten	Hollywood: the Movie Colony . . .
Saroyan	Three Plays
Sherwood	Abe Lincoln in Illinois
Sherwood	Idiot's Delight
Sherwood	Reunion in Vienna
Sherwood	There Shall Be No Night
Simonson	Stage Is Set
Thomas	As a Man Thinks
Thomas	Witching Hour
Wilder	Our Town
Wilder	Skin of Our Teeth
Williams	Streetcar Named Desire

b. British and Irish

Barrie	Admirable Crichton
Barrie	Alice Sit-by-the-Fire
Barrie	Dear Brutus
Barrie	Peter Pan
Barrie	Quality Street
Barrie	Twelve Pound Look
Barrie	What Every Woman Knows
Beaumont and Fletcher	Plays
Beddoes	Death's Jest Book
Bennett	Milestones
Bentley	Bernard Shaw
Besier	Barretts of Wimpole Street
Brown, I.	Shakespeare
Coleridge	Lectures on Shakespeare
Congreve	Selected Works
Coward	Play Parade
Cunliffe	Modern English Playwrights . . .
Dekker	Plays
Drinkwater	Abraham Lincoln
Dunsany	Five Plays
Dunsany	Plays of Gods and Men
Eliot	Cocktail Party
Eliot	Murder in the Cathedral
Ervine	Jane Clegg
Ervine	John Ferguson
Everyman	
Farquhar	Beaux' Stratagem
Ford	Broken Heart
Ford	Perkin Warbeck
Fry	Lady's Not for Burning
Galsworthy	Justice
Galsworthy	Loyalties
Galsworthy	Silver Fox
Galsworthy	Strife
Gay	Beggar's Opera
Gilbert	Operettas
Goldsmith	She Stoops to Conquer
Granville-Barker	Madras House
Granville-Barker	Prefaces to Shakespeare
Gregory	Seven Short Plays
Hardy	The Dynasts
Hazlitt	Characters of Shakespeare's Plays
Hazlitt	Dramatic Literature of the Age of Elizabeth
Jonson	Plays

Kennedy	Servant in the House
Marlowe	Plays and Poems
Masefield	Prose Plays
Masefield	Verse Plays
Massinger	New Way to Pay Old Debts
Milne	Three Plays
O'Casey	Juno and the Paycock
O'Casey	Within the Gates
Otway	Venice Preserved
Phillips	Paolo and Francesca
Pinero	Second Mrs. Tanqueray
Shakespeare	Plays
Shaw	Androcles . . .
Shaw	Arms and the Man
Shaw	Back to Methuselah
Shaw	Caesar and Cleopatra
Shaw	Candida
Shaw	Man and Superman
Shaw	Mrs. Warren's Profession
Shaw	Pygmalion
Shaw	Saint Joan
Sheridan	Plays
Synge	Complete Works
Webster	White Devil
Webster	Duchess of Malfi
Wilde	Plays
Wycherley	Country Wife
Wycherley	Plain-Dealer
Yeats	Collected Plays
Zangwill	Melting Pot

c. European

Andreyev	Life of Man
Annunzio, d'	Daughter of Jorio
Annunzio, d'	La Gioconda
Beaumarchais	Barber of Seville
Beaumarchais	Marriage of Figaro
Benevente	Plays
Björnson	The Gauntlet
Brieux	Damaged Goods
Brieux	Red Robe
Calderón	Life Is a Dream
Calderón	Wonderful Magician
Capek	R. U. R.
Chekhov	Cherry Orchard
Chekhov	Ivanoff
Chekhov	The Sea-Gull
Chekhov	Swan Song
Chekhov	Uncle Vanya
Claudel	Tidings Brought to Mary
Corneille	Plays
Dumas, Jr.	Camille
Echegaray	Great Galeoto
Goethe	Egmont
Goethe	Faust

DRAMA

European—Continued

Goethe	Goetz von Berlichingen
Gogol	Inspector General
Goldoni	Master of the Inn
Gorki	Lower Depths
Hauptmann	Sunken Bell
Hauptmann	The Weavers
Hugo	Hernani
Huneker	Iconoclasts
Ibsen	Brand
Ibsen	Doll'sHouse
Ibsen	Emperor and Galilean
Ibsen	Enemy of the People
Ibsen	Ghosts
Ibsen	Hedda Gabler
Ibsen	Peer Gynt
Ibsen	Rosmersholm
Ibsen	Wild Duck
Lessing	Minna von Barnhelm
Lessing	Nathan the Wise
Maeterlinck	Blue Bird
Maeterlinck	Monna Vanna
Maeterlinck	Pelléas and Mélisande
Matthews	Molière
Molière	Comedies
Molnar	Liliom
Pirandello	Three Plays
Pushkin	Boris Godunov
Racine	Plays
Rostand	L'Aiglon
Rostand	Chantecler
Rostand	Cyrano de Bergerac
Schiller	Dramas
Schnitzler	Stories and Plays
Strindberg	Plays
Sudermann	Magda
Tolstoi	Complete Plays
Vega Carpio	Four Plays in English Versions

d. *Classical (Greek and Latin)*

Æschylus	Tragedies
Aristophanes	Birds
Aristophanes	Clouds
Aristophanes	Frogs
Euripides	Works
Plautus	Comedies
Sophocles	Tragedies
Terence	Comedies

e. *Indian*

Kalidasa	Sakuntala
Tagore	Collected Poems and Plays

16. FICTION

a. *American*

Aiken	Short Stories
Aldrich	Story of a Bad Boy
Allen	Anthony Adverse
Anderson	Dark Laughter
Anderson	Poor White
Anderson	Portable Sherwood Anderson
Anderson	Triumph of the Egg
Anderson	Windy McPherson's Son
Anderson	Winesburg, Ohio
Asch	The Apostle
Asch	Mary
Asch	The Nazarene
Atherton	The Conqueror
Baker	Young Man with a Horn
Barnes	Within This Present
Barnes	Years of Grace
Bellamy	Looking Backward
Benét	Thirteen O'Clock
Bierce	Can Such Things Be?
Bierce	In the Midst of Life
Bonnet	Mudlark
Boyd, J.	Drums
Boyd, J.	Marching On
Boyd, T.	Through the Wheat
Boyle	Plagued by the Nightingale
Boyle	Thirty Stories
Brace	Garretson Chronicle
Bradford	Ol' Man Adam and His Chillun
Bromfield	Early Autumn
Bromfield	Good Woman
Bromfield	Green Bay Tree
Bromfield	Possession
Brown	Walk in the Sun
Buck	Dragon Seed
Buck	Good Earth
Buck	House Divided
Buck	The Mother
Buck	The Patriot
Buck	Sons
Burns	The Gallery
Burt	Delectable Mountains
Burt	Interpreter's House
Cabell	Cream of the Jest
Cabell	Jurgen
Cabell	Rivet in Grandfather's Neck
Cable	The Cavalier
Cable	Dr. Sevier
Cable	The Grandissimes
Cable	Old Creole Days

Cahan	Rise of David Levinsky	Dell	Moon Calf
		Dos Passos	Manhattan Transfer
Caldwell	Tobacco Road	Dos Passos	Three Soldiers
Carmer	Stars Fell on Alabama	Dos Passos	U. S. A. (3 vols.)
		Douglas	The Robe
Carroll	As the Earth Turns	Dreiser	American Tragedy
Cather	Death Comes for the Archbishop	Dreiser	The Financier
		Dreiser	Gallery of Women
Cather	Lost Lady	Dreiser	The Genius
Cather	My Antonia	Dreiser	Jennie Gerhardt
Cather	O Pioneers	Dreiser	Sister Carrie
Cather	Obscure Destinies	Dreiser	The Stoic
Cather	One of Ours	Dreiser	The Titan
Cather	Professor's House	Edmonds	Drums Along the Mohawk
Cather	Sapphira and the Slave Girl		
		Eggleston	Hoosier Schoolmaster
Cather	Shadows on the Rock	Ehrlich	God's Angry Man
Cather	Song of the Lark	Erskine	Private Life of Helen of Troy
Chambers	Cardigan		
Chapman	Happy Mountain	Farrel	Studs Lonigan. 3 vols.
Chase	Mary Peters	Faulkner	As I Lay Dying
Chase	Windswept	Faulkner	Collected Stories
Churchill	The Crisis	Faulkner	The Hamlet
Churchill	The Crossing	Faulkner	Intruder in the Dust
Churchill	Richard Carvel	Faulkner	Sanctuary
Clark	Ox-Bow Incident	Faulkner	The Sound and the Fury
Clemens	Connecticut Yankee at King Arthur's Court		
		Faulkner	The Unvanquished
		Faulkner	Wild Palms
Clemens	Huckleberry Finn	Ferber	Cimarron
Clemens	Mysterious Stranger	Ferber	Show Boat
Clemens	Personal Recollections of Joan of Arc	Ferber	So Big
		Field, E.	Little Book of Profitable Tales
Clemens	Prince and the Pauper	Field, R. L.	All This and Heaven Too
Clemens	Tom Sawyer	Field, R. L.	Time Out of Mind
Cobb, H.	Paths of Glory	Fisher, D. C.	Bent Twig
Cobb, I. S.	Old Judge Priest	Fisher, D. C.	Brimming Cup
Cooper	Leatherstocking Tales. 5 vols.	Fisher, D. C.	Deepening Stream
		Fisher, D. C.	Her Son's Wife
Cooper	The Pilot	Fisher, D. C.	Rough Hewn
Cooper	Red Rover	Fisher, D. C.	Seasoned Timber
Cooper	The Spy	Fisher, V.	Children of God
Cozzens	Guard of Honor	Fitzgerald	The Crack-Up
Cozzens	Just and the Unjust	Fitzgerald	The Great Gatsby
Crane	Red Badge of Courage	Fitzgerald	Last Tycoon
		Fitzgerald	Tender Is the Night
Davenport	Valley of Decision	Fitzgerald	This Side of Paradise
Davis, H. L.	Honey in the Horn	Flavin	Journey in the Dark
Davis, R. H.	Gallegher and Other Stories	Forbes	Paradise
		Forbes	Running of the Tide
Davis, R. H.	Van Bibber and Others	Ford	Honorable Peter Stirling
Deland	Awakening of Helena Richie		
		Ford	Janice Meredith
Deland	Dr. Lavendar's People	Fox	Little Shepherd of Kingdom Come
Deland	John Ward, Preacher	Fox	Trail of the Lonesome Pine
Dell	Briary Bush		

FICTION

American—Continued

Freeman	Humble Romance and Other Stories
Freeman	Jerome, a Poor Man
Freeman	New England Nun and Other Stories
Gaither	Double Muscadine
Gale	Birth
Gale	Friendship Village
Gale	Miss Lulu Bett
Garland	Main Travelled Roads
Gerould	Great Tradition
Gerould	Modes and Morals
Gerould	Vain Oblations
Gill	Trouble of One House
Glasgow	Barren Ground
Glasgow	Deliverance
Glasgow	In This Our Life
Glasgow	Romance of a Plain Man
Glasgow	Romantic Comedians
Glasgow	Sheltered Life
Glasgow	They Stooped to Folly
Glasgow	Vein of Iron
Glasgow	Virginia
Glaspell	Ambrose Holt and Family
Goodrich	Delilah
Grey	Heritage of the Desert
Grey	Lone Star Ranger
Grey	Riders of the Purple Sage
Grey	U. P. Trail
Guthrie	Big Sky
Guthrie	Way West
Haines	Command Decision
Hale	Man without a Country
Halper	Union Square
Harte	Bret Harte's Stories of the Old West
Hawes	Mutineers
Hawthorne	Blithedale Romance
Hawthorne	House of the Seven Gables
Hawthorne	Marble Faun
Hawthorne	Mosses from an Old Manse
Hawthorne	Scarlet Letter
Hawthorne	Twice Told Tales
Hayes	Girl on the Via Flaminia
Heggen	Mr. Roberts

Hemingway	Farewell to Arms
Hemingway	Fifth Column and the First Forty-nine Stories
Hemingway	For Whom the Bell Tolls
Hemingway	Sun Also Rises
Henry, O.	Best Short Stories
Hergesheimer	Bright Shawl
Hergesheimer	Java Head
Hergesheimer	Linda Condon
Hergesheimer	Three Black Pennies
Herrick	Clark's Field
Herrick	Common Lot
Herrick	Together
Hersey	Bell for Adano
Hersey	The Wall
Heyward	Mamba's Daughters
Heyward	Peter Ashley
Heyward	Porgy
Hobart	Oil for the Lamps of China
Hobson	Gentlemen's Agreement
Holmes	Elsie Venner
Holmes	Guardian Angel
Hough	Covered Wagon
Hough	Mississippi Bubble
Howe, E. W.	Story of a Country Town
Howe, H. H.	We Happy Few
Howells	Chance Acquaintance
Howells	Hazard of New Fortunes
Howells	Lady of the Aroostook
Howells	Leatherwood God
Howells	Modern Instance
Howells	Rise of Silas Lapham
Howells	Their Wedding Journey
Howells	Traveller from Altruria
Hughes	Not without Laughter
Hughes	Weary Blues
Hurst	Humoresque
Hurst	Lummox
Irving	The Alhambra
Irving	Bracebridge Hall
Irving	Sketch Book
Jackson, C.	Lost Weekend
Jackson, H. H.	Ramona
Jackson, S.	The Lottery
James	The Ambassadors
James	The American
James	The Bostonians
James	Daisy Miller
James	The Europeans
James	Golden Bowl
James	Portrait of a Lady

FICTION

British—Continued

Dickens	Nicholas Nickleby
Dickens	Old Curiosity Shop
Dickens	Oliver Twist
Dickens	Our Mutual Friend
Dickens	Pickwick Papers
Dickens	Tale of Two Cities
Disraeli	Coningsby
Disraeli	Lothair
Disraeli	Vivian Grey
Douglas	South Wind
Doyle	Micah Clarke
Doyle	Sherlock Holmes Stories
Doyle	Sir Nigel
Doyle	White Company
Du Maurier, D.	Rebecca
Du Maurier, G.	The Martian
Du Maurier, G.	Peter Ibbetson
Du Maurier, G.	Trilby
Edgeworth	The Absentee
Edgeworth	Castle Rackrent
Eliot	Adam Bede
Eliot	Middlemarch
Eliot	Mill on the Floss
Eliot	Romola
Eliot	Scenes from Clerical Life
Eliot	Silas Marner
Falkner	Moonfleet
Farnol	Broad Highway
Fielding	Amelia
Fielding	Jonathan Wild
Fielding	Joseph Andrews
Fielding	Tom Jones
Ford	Parade's End (four vols. in one)
Forester	Captain Horatio Hornblower
Forester	Sky and the Forest
Forster	Passage to India
Forster	Room with a View
Galsworthy	Caravan (Fifty-six short stories)
Galsworthy	Country House
Galsworthy	End of the Chapter (A trilogy)
Galsworthy	Forsyte Saga (Three novels and ten short stories)
Galsworthy	Fraternity
Galsworthy	Modern Comedy (A trilogy)

Garnett	Lady into Fox
Gaskell	Cranford
Gissing	New Grub Street
Gissing	Private Papers of Henry Ryecroft
Godwin	Adventures of Caleb Williams
Goldsmith	Vicar of Wakefield
Goudge	Green Dolphin Street
Graham	Earth and High Heaven
Graves	I, Claudius
Green	Loving
Greene	Heart of the Matter
Haggard	King Solomon's Mines
Haggard	She
Hardy	Far from the Madding Crowd
Hardy	Jude the Obscure
Hardy	Life's Little Ironies
Hardy	Mayor of Casterbridge
Hardy	Return of the Native
Hardy	Tess of the D'Urbervilles
Hardy	Trumpet Major
Hardy	Wessex Tales
Hawkins	Prisoner of Zenda
Hawkins	Rupert of Hentzau
Herbert	Water Gipsies
Hewlett	Forest Lovers
Hewlett	Queen's Quair
Hewlett	Richard Yea-and-Nay
Hichens	Garden of Allah
Hichens	Green Carnation
Hilton	Good-bye, Mr. Chips
Hilton	Lost Horizon
Holtby	South Riding
Household	Rogue Male
Hudson	Green Mansions
Hudson	Little Boy Lost
Hudson	Purple Land
Hudson	Tales of the Pampas
Hughes	Innocent Voyage
Hutchinson, A. S. M.	If Winter Comes
Hutchinson, R. C.	Fire and the Wood
Huxley	After Many a Summer Dies the Swan
Huxley	Brave New World
Huxley	Eyeless in Gaza
Huxley	Point Counter Point
Huxley	Time Must Have a Stop
Isherwood	Goodbye to Berlin
Isherwood	Prater Violet

Jacobs	Cruises and Cargoes	Masefield	Bird of Dawning
Jacobs	The Nightwatchman	Masefield	Jim Davis
Johnson	Rasselas	Masefield	Sard Harker
Kaye-Smith	Joanna Godden	Maugham	Cakes and Ale
Kaye-Smith	Sussex Gorse	Maugham	East and West (30
Kennedy	Constant Nymph		short stories)
Kingsley, C.	Alton Locke	Maugham	Hour Before the
Kingsley, C.	Hereward the Wake		Dawn
Kingsley, C.	Hypatia	Maugham	Moon and Sixpence
Kingsley, C.	Westward Ho!	Maugham	Of Human Bondage
Kingsley, H.	Ravenshoe	Maugham	Razor's Edge
Kingsley, H.	Recollections of Geof-	Meredith	Adventures of Harry
	frey Hamlin		Richmond
Kipling	Captains Courageous	Meredith	Beauchamp's Career
Kipling	Kim	Meredith	Diana of the Cross-
Kipling	Puck of Pook's		ways
	Hill	Meredith	The Egoist
Kipling	Rewards and Fairies	Meredith	Evan Harrington
Kipling	Selected Stories	Meredith	Ordeal of Richard
Kipling	Soldier Stories		Feverel
Kipling	Two Jungle Books	Merrick	Chair on the Boule-
Knight	This Above All		vard
Landor	Imaginary Conversa-	Merrick	Conrad in Quest of
	tions		His Youth
Landor	Pericles and Aspasia	Merrick	While Paris Laughed
Lawrence	Plumed Serpent	Milne	Red House Mystery
Lawrence	Sons and Lovers	Mitford	Our Village
Lawrence	Women in Love	Montague	Disenchantment
Llewellyn	How Green Was My	Montague	Right Off the Map
	Valley	Moore	Brook Kerith
Locke	Beloved Vagabond	Moore	Esther Waters
Lowry	Under the Volcano	Moore	Evelyn Innes
Lucas	Over Bemerton's	Moore	Héloise and Abélard
Lyly	Euphues	Moore	Sister Teresa
Lytton	Last Days of Pom-	Morgan	Fountain
	peii	Morier	Adventures of Hajji
Lytton	Last of the Barons		Baba . . .
Lytton	Rienzi	Mottram	Spanish Farm Tril-
Macaulay	Dangerous Ages		ogy
Macaulay	Potterism	Mulock	John Halifax, Gentle-
Machen	Hill of Dreams		man
Mackenzie	Man of Feeling	Munro	Short Stories of
Manning	Household of Sir		"Saki"
	Thomas More	Nashe	Unfortunate Traveler
Mansfield	Short Stories (Omni-	Orwell	Animal Farm
	bus vol. of 88 sto-	Orwell	Burmese Days
	ries)	Orwell	1984
Marryat	Masterman Ready	Parker	Right of Way
Marryat	Mr. Midshipman	Parker	Seats of the Mighty
	Easy	Pater	Marius the Epicurean
Marryat	Peter Simple	Paton	Cry the Beloved
Marshall, A.	Squire's Daughter		Country
	(Vol. 1 of the Clin-	Peacock	Headlong Hall
	ton Series, in 4	Peacock	Nightmare Abbey
	vols.)	Phelps	Advance of the Eng-
Marshall, B.	Father Malachy's		lish Novel
	Miracle	Phillpotts	Children of the Mist
Marshall, B.	The World, the	Phillpotts	Grey Room
	Flesh, and Father	Porter	Scottish Chiefs
	Smith	Priestley	Angel Pavement

Woolf — Between the Acts
Woolf — Flush
Woolf — Haunted House (18 short stories)
Woolf — Mrs. Dalloway
Woolf — Orlando
Woolf — To the Lighthouse
Woolf — The Waves
Woolf — The Years
Zangwill — Children of the Ghetto

c. French and French-Canadian

Aucassin and Nicolette
Balzac — Country Doctor
Balzac — Cousin Pons
Balzac — Cousine Bette
Balzac — Eugenie Grandet
Balzac — Père Goriot
Barbusse — Under Fire
Benjamin — Private Gaspard
Bourget — The Disciple
Camus — The Plague
Camus — The Stranger
Daudet — Fromont, Jr. and Risler, Sr.
Daudet — Jack
Daudet — Sapho
Daudet — Tartarin of Tarascon
Duhamel — Civilization (1914-17)
Duhamel — Pasquier Chronicles
Dumas — Count of Monte Cristo
Dumas — Forty-Five Guardsmen
Dumas — Three Musketeers
Dumas — Twenty Years After
Dumas — Vicomte de Bragelonne
Erckmann — The Conscript
Erckmann — Friend Fritz
Fénelon — Adventures of Telemachus
Flaubert — Madame Bovary
Flaubert — Salammbô
Flaubert — Sentimental Education
France — At the Sign of the Reine Pédauque
France — Crime of Sylvestre Bonnard
France — Gods Are Athirst
France — Penguin Island
France — Thaïs
Gaboriau — File No. 113
Gaboriau — M. Lecoq

Gautier — Captain Fracasse
Gautier — Mlle. de Maupin
Gautier — Romance of a Mummy
Gide — Counterfeiters
Gide — Strait Is the Gate
Halévy — Abbé Constantin
Hémon — Marie Chapdelaine
Hugo — Les Misérables (5 vols.)
Hugo — Man Who Laughs
Hugo — Ninety-Three
Hugo — Notre Dame de Paris
Hugo — Toilers of the Sea
La Fayette — Princess of Cleves
Loti — Disenchanted
Loti — Iceland Fisherman
Loti — Madame Chrysanthème
Loti — Marriage of Loti
Malraux — Man's Fate
Malraux — Man's Hope
Martin du Gard — World of the Thibaults (10 vols.)
Maupassant — Complete Short Stories
Maupassant — Odd Number (13 stories)
Maupassant — Une Vie
Mauriac — Thérèse
Maurois — Silence of Colonel Bramble
Merimée — Carmen
Merimée — Columba
Prévost — Manon Lescaut
Proust — Remembrance of Things Past
Rolland — Jean Christophe
Romains — Men of Good Will (14 vols.)
Rousseau — Émile
Rousseau — Julie
Saint-Pierre — Paul and Virginia
Saintsbury — History of the French Novel
Sand — Consuelo
Sand — Devil's Pool
Sand — Fanchon the Cricket
Sand — François the Waif
Sartre — Age of Reason
Sartre — Reprieve
Sartre — Troubled Sleep
Staël, Mme. de — Corinne
Stendhal — Charterhouse of Parma
Stendhal — Red and the Black
Verne — Around the World in Eighty Days

Fiction

French—Continued

Verne	From the Earth to the Moon
Verne	Mysterious Island
Verne	Twenty Thousand Leagues under the Sea
Voltaire	Candide
Voltaire	Zadig
Zola	L'Argent (Money)
Zola	L'Assommoir (The Dram Shop)
Zola	La Débâcle (The Downfall)
Zola	Germinal
Zola	Nana
Zola	L'Œuvre (The Masterpiece)
Zola	La Terre (The Soil)

d. German and Austrian

Feuchtwanger	The Oppermanns
Feuchtwanger	Power
Frenssen	Jörn Uhl
Goethe	Sorrows of Young Werther
Goethe	Wilhelm Meister's Apprenticeship
Grimmels- hausen	Adventurous Simplicissimus
Hauptmann	Atlantis
Hauptmann	Fool in Christ
Hesse	Steppenwolf
Kleist	Michael Kohlhaas
LaMotte- Fouqué	Undine
Mann	Beloved Returns
Mann	Buddenbrooks
Mann	Dr. Faustus
Mann	Joseph Tetralogy
Mann	Magic Mountain
Mann	Stories of Three Decades (24 short stories)
Münchhausen	Travels and Adventures
Plievier	Stalingrad
Remarque	All Quiet on the Western Front
Remarque	Arch of Triumph
Remarque	Flotsam
Remarque	Road Back
Salten	Bambi
Scheffel	Ekkehard
Schnitzler	Stories and Plays
Seghers	Seventh Cross

Sudermann	Dame Care
Sudermann	Song of Songs
Wassermann	World's Illusion
Werfel	Forty Days of Musa Dagh
Werfel	Pascarella Family
Werfel	Song of Bernadette
Zweig	Case of Sergeant Grischa
Zweig	Education Before Verdun

e. Irish

Byrne	Blind Raftery
Byrne	Hangman's House
Byrne	Messer Marco Polo
Dunsany	Book of Wonder
Dunsany	Dreamer's Tales
Ervine	Alice and a Family
Ervine	Jane Clegg
Ervine	John Ferguson
Gregory	Cuchulain of Muirthemne
Joyce	Dubliners
Joyce	Finnegan's Wake
Joyce	Portrait of the Artist . . .
Joyce	Ulysses
Lever	Charles O'Malley
Lever	Harry Lorrequer
Lover	Handy Andy
O'Faolain	Nest of Simple Folk
O'Flaherty	Famine
O'Flaherty	The Informer
Stephens	Crock of Gold
Stephens	Deirdre
Stephens	Etched in Moonlight
Stephens	Here Are Ladies
Stephens	Mary, Mary

f. Italian

Annunzio, d'	Flame of Life
Bacchelli	Mill on the Po
Boccaccio	Decameron
Deledda	The Mother
Fogazzaro	The Patriot
Fogazzaro	The Saint
Fogazzaro	The Sinner
Giono	Song of the World
Guareschi	Little World of Don Camillo
Levi	Christ Stopped at Eboli
Manzoni	The Betrothed
Pirandello	Late Mattia Pascal
Silone	Bread and Wine
Silone	Fontamara

Verga	Cavalleria Rusticana and Other Stories	Dinesen	Seven Gothic Tales
Verga	House by the Medlar Tree	Duun	People of Juvik (6 vols.)
		Gulbranssen	Beyond Sing the Woods

g. Russian

		Hamsun	Children of the Age
		Hamsun	Growth of the Soil
Andreyev	He Who Gets Slapped	Hamsun	Hunger
Andreyev	Seven Who Were Hanged	Jensen	Long Journey (3 vols. in 1)
Bunin	Gentleman from San Francisco	Lagerlöf	Emperor of Portugallia
Bunin	The Village	Lagerlöf	Liliecrona's Home
Chekhov	The Bishop and Other Stories	Lagerlöf	Story of Gösta Berling
Chekhov	Little Darling and Other Stories	Lagerlöf	Wonderful Adventures of Nils
Dostoievski	Brothers Karamazov	Laxness	Independent People
Dostoievski	Crime and Punishment	Lie	Pilot and His Wife
Dostoievski	The Idiot	Nexö	Ditte
Ehrenburg	Out of Chaos	Nexö	Pelle the Conqueror
Fedorova	The Family	Rölvaag	Giants in the Earth
Gogol	Dead Souls	Undset	Kristin Lavransdatter (A trilogy)
Gogol	Taras Bulba		
Goncharov	Oblomov		
Gorki	Book of Short Stories		

i. Spanish and Argentinian

Gorki	The Bystander	Baroja	Tree of Knowledge
Gorki	Mother	Blasco-Ibañez	Blood and Sand
Merejkowski	Christ and Antichrist (A trilogy)	Blasco-Ibañez	Four Horsemen of the Apocalypse
Phelps	Essays on Russian Novelists	Blasco-Ibañez	Mare Nostrum
Pushkin	Captain's Daughter and Other Tales	Blasco-Ibañez	Shadow of the Cathedral
Serge	Case of Comrade Tulayev	Cervantes-Saavedra	Adventures of Don Quixote
Sholokhov	The Silent Don (2 vols.)	Hurtado de Mendoza	Lazarillo de Tormes
Simonov	Days and Nights	Madariaga	Heart of Jade
Sologub	Little Demon	Mallea	Bay of Silence
Sologub	Sweet-scented Name	Pérez-Galdós	Doña Perfecta
Tolstoi	Anna Karenina	Sender	Man's Place
Tolstoi	Nine Stories	Sender	Pro Patria
Tolstoi	Resurrection	Sender	Seven Red Sundays
Tolstoi	War and Peace		
Yarmolinski, ed.	Treasury of . . . Russian Short Stories		

j. Miscellaneous

		Apuleius	Golden Ass
		Coster	Tyl Ulenspiegel
		Couperus	Book of Small Souls (A tetralogy)

h. Scandinavian

		Gebler	Plymouth Adventure
Björnson	Arne	Hasek	Good Soldier: Schweik
Björnson	Fisher Maiden	Kafka	The Castle
Björnson	The Gauntlet	Kafka	The Trial
Björnson	Synnove Solbakken	Keller	People of Seldwyla
Bojer	Great Hunger	Koestler	Arrival and Departure

FICTION

Miscellaneous—Continued

Koestler	Darkness at Noon
Koestler	Gladiators
Koestler	Thieves in the Night
Lin Yu-tang	Moment in Peking
Meyer	The Saint
Murasaki	Tale of Genji
Petronius	Satyricon
Reymont	The Peasants
Sienkiewicz	The Deluge
Sienkiewicz	Pan Michael
Sienkiewicz	Quo Vadis
Sienkiewicz	With Fire and Sword
Xenophon	Cyropaedia

17. ESSAYS

a. *American*

Broun	Collected Edition
Burroughs	Works
Cabell	Beyond Life
Cabell	Straws and Prayer Books
Crothers	Among Friends
Crothers	Dame School of Experience
Crothers	Gentle Reader
Emerson	Works
Field	Love Affairs of a Bibliomaniac
Gerould	Modes and Morals
Hemingway	Death in the Afternoon
Huneker	Ivory, Apes and Peacocks
Krutch	Modern Temper
Krutch	Twelve Seasons
More	Shelburne Essays
Morley	Essays, 1919-27
Morley	Letters of Askance
Poe	Essays
Repplier	Eight Decades
Repplier	Fireside Sphinx
Repplier	Happy Half-Century
Repplier	In Pursuit of Laughter
Roosevelt	Strenuous Life
Santayana	Soliloquies in England
Sherman	Critical Woodcuts
Sherman	Main Stream
Smith, L. P.	All Trivia
Van Dyke	Little Rivers
White, E. B.	One Man's Meat
Woollcott	While Rome Burns

b. *British*

Bacon	Essays
Belloc	On Nothing and Kindred Subjects
Birrell	Obiter Dicta
Birrell	More Obiter Dicta
Butler	Note Books
De Quincey	Essays
Dobson	Eighteenth Century Vignettes
Eliot	Selected Essays
Forster	Abinger Harvest
Goldsmith	Citizen of the World
Hazlitt	Table Talk
Lamb	Essays of Elia
Lucas	Selected Essays
Macaulay	Critical and Historical Essays
Meynell	Essays
Pater	Greek Studies
Pater	Studies in the Renaissance
Smith, A.	Dreamthorpe
Stevenson	Familiar Studies of Men and Books
Stevenson	Virginibus Puerisque
Woolf	Death of the Moth

c. *Foreign*

Cicero	Essays
France	On Life and Letters
Koestler	Yogi and the Commisar
LaRochefoucauld	Maxims
Lin Yu-tang	Importance of Living
Lin Yu-tang	Between Tears and Laughter
Montaigne	Essays
Sadi	Gulistan
Saint-Exupéry	Wind, Sand and Stars
Saint-Exupéry	Flight to Arras
Santayana	Winds of Doctrine
Santayana	Soliloquies in England
Seneca	Morals
Tolstoi	Essays and Letters

18. SPEECHES

Burke	On American Taxation
Burke	On Conciliation
Churchill	Blood, Sweat and Tears
Cicero	Orations

Cromwell	Letters and Speeches;
Demosthenes	ed. by Carlyle, *q.v.*
	Orations
Lincoln	Speeches and Letters
Roosevelt,	Public Papers and
F. D.	Addresses

19. SATIRE AND HUMOR

a. *American*

Adams	Innocent Merri-
	ment . . .
Ade	The Permanent Ade
Benchley	20,000 Leagues under
	the Sea . . .
Benchley	Benchley beside Him-
	self
Benchley	Treasurer's Re-
	port . . .
Benchley	Of All Things
Clemens	Works
Day	Clarence Day Omni-
	bus
Dunne	Mr. Dooley at His
	Best
Gilbreth	Cheaper by the Dozen
Halsey	With Malice Towards
	Some
Hargrove	See Here, Private
	Hargrove
Holmes	Autocrat of the
	Breakfast Table
Holmes	Professor at the
	Breakfast Table
Lardner	Portable Ring
	Lardner
Marquis	Best of Don Marquis
Mauldin	Back Home
Mauldin	Up Front
Mencken	Mencken Chrestom-
	athy
Nash	Selected Verse
Parker	Portable Dorothy
	Parker
Perelman	Best of Perelman
Repplier	Happy Half-
	Century
Repplier	In Pursuit of
	Laughter
Rosten	Education of Hyman
	Kaplan
Rourke	American Humor; a
	Study . . .
Skinner	Our Hearts Were
	Young and Gay
Stockton	Casting Away of
	Mrs. Lecks . . .
Thurber	Thurber Carnival . . .

Whistler	Gentle Art of Making
	Enemies
White, ed.	Sub-Treasury of
	American Humor

b. *British*

Barham	Ingoldsby Legends
Beerbohm	Christmas Garland
Beerbohm	And Even Now
Butler	Hudibras
Carlyle	Sartor Resartus
Chesterton	Man Who Was
	Chesterton (Se-
	lected works)
Dekker	Gull's Hornbook
Gilbert	Bab Ballads
Gilbert	Operettas
Hazlitt	Lectures on the
	English Comic
	Writers
Kipling	Just So Stories
Leacock	Last Leaves
Leacock	Leacock Roundabout
Lear	Lear Omnibus
Orwell	Animal Farm
Smith	Rejected Addresses
Sterne	Tristram Shandy
Swift	Gulliver's Travels
Swift	Tale of a Tub
Thackeray	English Humorists

c. *Foreign*

Erasmus	Colloquies
Erasmus	Praise of Folly
France	Gods Are Athirst
France	Man Who Married a
	Dumb Wife
France	Penguin Island
Juvenal	Satires
Lucian	Dialogues of the
	Dead
Martial	Epigrams
Montesquieu	Persian Letters
Münchhausen	Travels and Ad-
	ventures
Rabelais	Gargantua and
	Pantagruel

20. DESCRIPTION, TRAVELS, VOYAGES, GEOGRAPHY

Amundsen	South Pole
Anderson	Tar; a Midwest
	Childhood
Austin	Land of Little Rain
Beebe	Arcturus Adventure
Beebe	Beneath Tropic Seas
Beebe	Edge of the Jungle

Description, Travels—
Continued

Beebe	High Jungle
Beebe	Jungle Days
Beebe	Jungle Peace
Belloc	Path of Rome
Borrow	Bible in Spain
Borrow	Lavengro
Borrow	Romany Rye
Brogan	American Character
Brogan	American Themes
Brown	Story of Maps
Burman	Big River to Cross
Burton	Personal Narrative of a Pilgrimage . . .
Byrd	Alone
Byrd	Little America
Byrd	Skyward
Caldwell	You Have Seen Their Faces
Camden	Britannia
Carmer	Stars Fell on Alabama
Chapman	Jungle Is Neutral
Chase	Goodly Fellowship
Childs	Sweden: the Middle Way
Clemens	Innocents Abroad
Clemens	Life on the Mississippi
Clemens	Roughing It
Cobbett	Rural Rides
Colum	Road Round Ireland
Cook	Voyages
Covarrubias	Island of Bali . . .
Crankshaw	Russia and the Russians
Dana	Two Years Before the Mast
Daniels	Southerner Discovers New England
Daniels	Southerner Discovers the South
Darwin	Voyage of the *Beagle*
De Voto	Mark Twain's America
Dostoievski	House of the Dead
Doughty	Travels in Arabia Deserta
Douglas	Old Calabria
Duguid	Green Hell . . . Bolivia
Emerson	English Traits
Fischer	Why They Behave Like Russians
Fleming	Brazilian Adventure
Gissing	By the Ionian Sea
Gunther	Inside Asia
Gunther	Inside Europe
Gunther	Inside Latin America
Gunther	Inside U.S.A.
Hackett	I Chose Denmark
Hakluyt	Principal Navigations . . . of the English Nation
Hay	Castilian Days
Hearn	Gleanings in Buddha Fields
Hearn	Glimpses of Unfamiliar Japan
Hearn	Japan . . .
Heine	Pictures of Travel
Heyerdahl	Kon-Tiki
Hindus	Humanity Uprooted
Hindus	Red Bread
Huxley	Africa View
Irving	The Alhambra
Irving	Bracebridge Hall
James	American Scene
Johnson	Our English Heritage
Keith	Land Below the Wind
Kinglake	Eothen . . .
Lauterbach	These Are the Russians
Lawrence, D. H.	Plumed Serpent
Lawrence, T. E.	Revolt in the Desert
Lawrence, T. E.	Seven Pillars of Wisdom
Lin Yu-tang	My Country and My People
Lindbergh	Listen! the Wind
Lindbergh	North to the Orient
Lyons	Assignment in Utopia
Madariaga	Genius of Spain
Mandeville	Travels
Mears	Year of the Wild Boar . . . Japan
Mitford	Our Village
Muir	Mountains of California
Muir	My First Summer in the Sierras
Muir	Thousand Mile Walk
Nordhoff and Hall	Bounty Trilogy
Ossendowski	Beasts, Men and Gods
O'Sullivan	Twenty Years A-Growing
Parkman	Journals
Parkman	Oregon Trail
Paul	Last Time I Saw Paris
Paul	Life and Death of a Spanish Town
Peary	North Pole

Perry	Puritanism and Democracy	
Polo	Book of Marco Polo	
Repplier	Philadelphia . . .	
Roberts	Forty-One Years in India	
Saint-Exupéry	Wind, Sand and Stars	
Santayana	Character and Opinion in the United States	
Schweitzer	More from the Primeval Forest	
Schweitzer	On the Edge of the Primeval Forest	
Scott	Scott's Last Expedition	
Seabrook	Magic Island	
Siegfried	America Comes of Age	
Siegfried	France, a Study in Nationality	
Slocum	Sailing Alone Around the World	
Smith, J.	Description of New England	
Smith, W. B.	My Three Years in Moscow	
Snow	Red Star Over China	
Staël, Mme. de	Germany	
Stegner	One Nation	
Stevenson	Travels with a Donkey . . .	
Synge	Aran Islands	
Thoreau	Maine Woods	
Tocqueville	Democracy in America	
Tomlinson	Sea and the Jungle	
Tomlinson, ed.	Great Sea Stories	
Trollope	Domestic Manners of the Americans	
Trumbull	The Raft	
Van Loon	Van Loon's Geography	
Villiers	By Way of Cape Horn	
Voltaire	Letters on the English	
Wallace	Malay Archipelago	
Waln	House of Exile	
Waln	Reaching for the Stars	
West	Black Lamb and Grey Falcon	
Winthrop	Canoe and the Saddle	
Young	Travels in France, 1787-89	

21. HISTORY

a. General

Creasy	Fifteen Decisive Battles . . .
Froude	Short Studies on Great Subjects
Mahan	Influence of Sea Power . . .
Mumford	Culture of Cities
Mumford	Technics of Civilization
Nevins	Gateway to History
Parsons	Stream of History
Spengler	Decline of the West
Toynbee	Civilization on Trial
Toynbee	Study of History
Van Loon	Story of Mankind
Wells	Outline of History

b. Ancient History, Archaeology

Breasted	Ancient Times
Breasted	Conquest of Civilization
Breasted	History of Egypt
Caesar	Commentaries on the Gallic and Civil Wars
Durant	Caesar and Christ
Durant	Story of Greece
Ferrero	Greatness and Decline of Rome
Gibbon	Decline and Fall of the Roman Empire
Herodotus	History
Livy	History of Rome
Magoffin	Magic Spades . . .
Osborn	Men of the Old Stone Age
Petrie	Social Life in Ancient Egypt
Petrie	Making of Egypt
Pliny	Letters
Plutarch	Lives
Polybius	History of Rome
Raleigh	History of the World (To 200 B.C.)
Rostovtzeff	Social and Economic History . . . Roman Empire
Tacitus	Works
Thucydides	Peloponnesian War
Xenophon	Anabasis
Zimmern	Greek Commonwealth

HISTORY—*Continued*

c. Europe in General

Adams	Mont St. Michel and Chartres
Augustine, St.	City of God
Barr	Pilgrimage of Western Man
Beard	Whither Mankind
Brinton	Ideas and Men
Croce	History as the Story of Liberty
Davis	Life on a Medieval Barony
Durant	Age of Faith
Froissart	Chronicles
Guizot	History of Civilization . . .
Lamb	Crusades . . .
Lecky	History of European Morals. . .
Mahan	Influence of Sea Power upon History
Milman	History of Latin Christianity
Pater	Studies in the Renaissance
Smith	History of Modern Culture
Taylor	Medieval Mind
Wilson	To the Finland Station . . .

d. England

Anglo-Saxon Chronicle	
Bede	Ecclesiastical History of the English Nation
Buckle	History of Civilization in England
Burnet	History of My Own Time
Carlyle	Past and Present
Clarendon	History of the Rebellion
Freeman	History of the Norman Conquest
Green	Short History of the English People
Holinshed	Chronicles of England, Scotland and Ireland
Lecky	History of England in the Eighteenth Century

Macaulay	History of England from the Accession of James II
Paston Letters	
Thackeray	The Four Georges
Trevelyan	England in the Age of Wycliffe
Trevelyan	England under the Stuarts
Trevelyan	History of England

e. France

Burke	Reflections on the French Revolution
Carlyle	French Revolution
Duruy	History of France, 1811-1894
Guedalla	Second Empire
Joinville	History of Saint Louis
Saint-Simon	Memoirs on the Reign of Louis XIV . . .
Taine	Ancient Régime
Taine	French Revolution

f. Spain & Latin America

Crow	Epic of Latin America
Irving	Conquest of Grenada
Lea	History of the Inquisition of Spain
Prescott	Conquest of Mexico
Prescott	Conquest of Peru
Prescott	Reign of Ferdinand and Isabella
Roeder	Juarez and His Mexico
Strode	Timeless Mexico

g. Russia

Chamberlin	Russian Revolution, 1917-1921
Crankshaw	Russia and the Russians
Duranty	Duranty Reports Russia
Lenin	Letters
Trotsky	History of the Russian Revolution

h. Miscellaneous

Borgese	Goliath; the March of Fascism
Hitler	Mein Kampf

Latourette	Chinese: Their History and Culture
Latourette	History of Japan
Motley	Rise of the Dutch Republic
Pater	Studies in the Renaissance
Symonds	Renaissance in Italy
Voltaire	History of Charles XII
Weizmann	Trial and Error

i. United States & Canada

Adams	Epic of America
Adams	March of Democracy
Adams	New England in the Republic, 1776-1850
Adams	Provincial Society, 1690-1763
Agar	Price of Union
Allen	Only Yesterday . . . History of the Nineteen-Twenties
Bancroft	History of the United States
Beard	Basic History of the United States
Beard	Rise of American Civilization
Beer	Mauve Decade . . . the End of the Nineteenth Century
Bowers	Beveridge and the Progressive Era
Bowers	Tragic Era
Brinton	From Many One; the Process of Political Integration
Brooks	America's Coming of Age
Buck	Road to Reunion
Buley	The Old Northwest
Butterfield	American Past (1000 pictures)
Channing	History of the United States
Commager	Heritage of America (Collection of 252 documents)
Commager	Short History of the United States
Creighton	Dominion of the North; a History of Canada
Curti	Growth of American Thought
De Voto	Across the Wide Missouri

De Voto	Year of Decision, 1846
Du Bois	Black Reconstruction . . . 1860-1880
Fiske	American Revolution
Fiske	Beginnings of New England
Fiske	Critical Period of American History, 1783-89
Fiske	Discovery of America
Gébler	The Plymouth Adventure
Hacker	Triumph of American Capitalism
Hendrick	Bulwark of the Republic
Hesseltine	Lincoln and the War Governors
Hofstadter	American Political Tradition . . .
Hulbert	The Forty-Niners . . .
Johnson, G. W.	Incredible Tale . . . 1900-1950
Johnson, G. W.	Our English Heritage
Johnson, W.	William Allen White's America
Leech	Reveille in Washington, 1860-65
McMaster	History of the People of the United States
Mather	Magnalia Christi Americana
Miller	Origins of the American Revolution
Millis	Martial Spirit . . . Our War with Spain
Morris	Postscript to Yesterday . . . the Last Fifty Years
Mumford	Brown Decades
Mumford	Golden Day
Nevins	Ordeal of the Union
Parkman	Conspiracy of Pontiac
Parkman	La Salle and the Discovery of the Great West
Parkman	Montcalm and Wolfe
Parkman	Pioneers of France
Paxson	History of the American Frontier
Rhodes	History of the Civil War

HISTORY

United States and Canada— Continued

Rhodes	History of the United States . . .
Rogers	I Remember Distinctly (500 pictures and text)
Roosevelt, T.	Winning of the West
Schlesinger	Paths to the Present
Schlesinger, Jr.	Age of Jackson
Schlesinger, Jr.	The Vital Centre; the Politics of Freedom
Siegfried	America Comes of Age
Skinner	Beavers, Kings and Cabins
Smith, G.	United States; an Outline of Political History
Smith, J.	Newes from Virginia
Starkey	Devil in Massachusetts . . .
Stewart	Names on the Land
Sullivan	Our Times; the United States, 1900-1925 (6v)
Swisher	Growth of Constitutional Power . . .
Trevelyan	American Revolution
Turner	Frontier in American History
Van Doren	Great Rehearsal
Van Doren	Secret History of the American Revolution
Wallace	New Frontiers
Wecter	Age of the Great Depression
Wecter	When Johnny Comes Marching Home
Wertenbaker	The Puritan Oligarchy . . .
Williams	Lincoln Finds a General . . .
Willison	Saints and Strangers
Wilson	History of the American People
Woodward	Way Our People Lived . . . 1640-1908

j. World War I

Barbusse	Under Fire
Benjamin	Private Gaspard
Churchill	The Aftermath
Churchill	World Crisis

Cummings	Enormous Room
Duhamel	Civilization (1914-17)
Fay	Origins of the World War
Hay	First Hundred Thousand
House	Intimate Papers
Keynes	Economic Consequences of the Peace
Lawrence	Revolt in the Desert
Lawrence	Seven Pillars of Wisdom
Lloyd George	War Memoirs
Masefield	Gallipoli
Millis	Road to War; America, 1914-1917
Montague	Disenchantment
Pershing	My Experiences in the World War
Simonds	History of the World War
Stallings	First World War, a Photographic History
Thomason	Fix Bayonets

k. World War II and Aftermath

Boothe	Europe in the Spring
Bowman	Beach Red
Brown	Many a Watchful Night
Butcher	My Three Years with Eisenhower
Byrnes	Speaking Frankly
Carlson	Under Cover
Chapman	Jungle Is Neutral
Churchill	Blood, Sweat and Tears
Churchill	Gathering Storm
Churchill	Grand Alliance
Churchill	Hinge of Fate
Churchill	Their Finest Hour
Curie	Journey among Warriors
Deane	Strange Alliance
Dodd	Ambassador Dodd's Diary
Dos Passos	State of the Nation
Ehrenburg	The Storm
Eisenhower	Crusade in Europe
Eliot	Ramparts We Watch
Feis	Spanish Story
Grew	Ten Years in Japan
Hargrove	See Here, Private Hargrove
Hersey	Hiroshima
Ingersoll, R.	Battle Is the Pay-Off
Ingersoll, R.	Top-Secret

Koestler	Scum of the Earth
Koestler	Yogi and the Commissars
Lawson	Thirty Seconds over Tokyo
Life	Picture History of World War II
Marshall	Winning of the War . . .
Mauldin	Up Front
Millar	Horned Pigeon
Miller	You Can't Do Business with Hitler
Millis	This Is Pearl
Millis	Why Europe Fights
Morgenthau	Germany Is Our Problem
Morison	Battle of the Atlantic
Morison	Rising Sun in the Pacific
Morison	Struggle for Guadalcanal
Nansen	From Day to Day
Patton	War as I Knew It
"Pertinax"	Gravediggers of France
Pratt	Marines' War
Pyle	Brave Men
Pyle	Here Is Your War
Saint-Exupéry	Flight to Arras
Scott	God Is My Co-Pilot
Seghers	Seventh Cross
Sevareid	Not So Wild a Dream
Sheean	Not Peace But a Sword
Sherwood	Roosevelt and Hopkins
Shirer	Berlin Diary . . .
Stettinius	Roosevelt and the Russians
Stilwell	Stilwell Papers
Stimson	On Active Service
Trevor-Roper	Last Days of Hitler
Trumbull	The Raft
Welles	Intelligent American's Guide to the Peace
Welles	Time for Decision
Welles	Where Are We Heading?
White	They Were Expendable
Winant	Letter from Grosvenor Square

22. BIOGRAPHY

a. Collective

Beebe	Book of Naturalists
Bell	Men of Mathematics
Bradford	American Portraits
Bradford	Bare Souls
Bradford	Confederate Portraits
Bradford	Damaged Souls
Bradford	Portraits of American Women
Bradford	Union Portraits
Brooks	Flowering of New England
Brooks	New England: Indian Summer
Brooks	Times of Melville and Whitman
Canby	Classic Americans
Cecil	Poets and Story-Tellers
Emerson	Representative Men
Freeman	Lee's Lieutenants
Fuller	Worthies of England
Greenslet	The Lowells
Hahn	The Soong Sisters
Harris	Contemporary Portraits
Hendrick	Lincoln's War Cabinet
Hendrick	Statesmen of the Lost Cause
Hofstadter	American Political Tradition and the Men Who Made It
Hoover	Forty-two Years in the White House
Jaffe	Crucibles: the Lives . . . of the Chemists
Jaffe	Men of Science in America
Johnson, G. W.	American Heroes and Hero-Worship
Johnson, S.	Lives of the Poets
Josephson	Politicos: 1865-96
Josephson	President Makers: 1896-1919
Josephson	Robber Barons: The Great American Capitalists
Landor	Imaginary Conversations
Matthiessen	The James Family
Peattie	Green Laurels (Lives of great naturalists)

b. Individual

(The names of the persons written about are in the first column, *alphabetically arranged.* In the second column are the titles of autobiographies *or* the authors and titles of biographies.)

Chesterton	Autobiography
Cibber	Apology for His Life
Clemens	Brooks, Ordeal of Mark Twain
Clemens	Mark Twain's Autobiography
Clemens	De Voto, Mark Twain's America
Clemens	Paine, Mark Twain, a Biography
Cleveland	Nevins, Grover Cleveland
Cohen, M. R.	Dreamer's Journey
Coleridge	Lowes, Road to Xanadu
Columbus	Madariaga, Christopher Columbus
Columbus	Morison, Admiral of the Ocean Sea
Conrad	Personal Record
Coolidge	White, Puritan in Babylon . . .
Coward	Present Indicative
Crane, H.	Horton, Hart Crane . . .
Creel	Rebel at Large
Cromwell	Buchan, Oliver Cromwell
Cross	Connecticut Yankee
Curie, M.	Curie, E., Madame Curie
Darrow	Story of My Life
Darwin	Bradford, Darwin
Davies, W. H.	Autobiography of a Super-Tramp
Davis, J.	Hendrick, Statesman of the Lost Cause . . . Jefferson Davis
De Quincey	Confessions of an English Opium Eater
Dickens	Chesterton, Charles Dickens
Dickens	Forster, Life of Charles Dickens
Dickens	Leacock, Charles Dickens
Dickens	Pearson, Dickens . . .
Dickinson	Bianchi, ed., Life and Letters of Emily Dickinson
Disraeli	Maurois, Disraeli
Dostoievski	House of the Dead
Douglas, W. O.	Of Men and Mountains
Doyle	Carr, Life of Sir Arthur Conan Doyle
Duranty	I Write as I Please
Eisenhower	Butcher, My Three Years with Eisenhower
Eleanor of Aquitaine	Kelly, Eleanor of Aquitaine
Eliot	James, H., 2d, Charles W. Eliot
Elizabeth	Strachey, Elizabeth and Essex
Emerson	Brooks, Life of Emerson
Emerson	Rusk, Life of Ralph Waldo Emerson
Erskine	My Life as a Teacher
Ferber	Peculiar Treasure
Fish	Nevins, Hamilton Fish
FitzGerald	Terhune, Life of Edward FitzGerald
Flynn	You're the Boss
Fox	Trevelyan, Early History of Charles James Fox
Francis, St.	Sabatier, Life of St. Francis of Assisi
Franklin	Faÿ, Franklin
Franklin	Autobiography
Franklin	Van Doren, C., Benjamin Franklin
Frederick the Great	Carlyle, Frederick the Great
Gandhi	Fischer, Gandhi and Stalin
Gandhi	Fischer, Life of Mahatma Gandhi
Garland	Daughter of the Middle Border
Garland	Son of the Middle Border
Garrick	Barton, Garrick
Genghis Khan	Lamb, Genghis Khan
Gibbon	Autobiography
Gibbs	Rukeyser, Willard Gibbs
Gissing	Private Papers of Henry Ryecroft
Gladstone	Morley, Life of William Ewart Gladstone
Goethe	Poetry and Truth
Goethe	Lewes, Life of Goethe
Goldoni	Memoirs
Goldsmith	Irving, Life of Oliver Goldsmith
Gorki	My Childhood
Gosse	Father and Son
Grant, U. S.	Personal Memoirs
Grant, U. S.	Lewis, Captain Sam Grant

BIOGRAPHY

Individual—Continued

Villard	Fighting Years . . .
Walker, J.	Fowler, Beau James
Washington, B. T.	Up From Slavery
Washington, G.	Faÿ, George Washington, Republican Aristocrat
Washington, G.	Freeman, George Washington
Washington, G.	Hughes, George Washington
Washington, G.	Irving, Life of Washington
Washington, G.	Woodward, George Washington . . .
Weizmann	Trial and Error (his life and Zionism)
Welch	Flexner, William Henry Welch and . . . Medicine
Wellington	Guedalla, Wellington
Wells	Experiment in Autobiography
Wharton	Lubbock, Portrait of Edith Wharton
Wharton	Backward Glance
Whistler	Pennell, Life of James McNeill Whistler
White, W. A.	Johnson, William Allen White's America
White, W. A.	Autobiography
White, W. F.	Man Called White
Whitman	Arvin, Whitman
Whitman	Canby, Walt Whitman
Whittier	Pollard, John Greenleaf Whittier
Wiggin	My Garden of Memory
Wilde	Pearson, Oscar Wilde . . .
Wilde	Winwar, Oscar Wilde and the Yellow Nineties
Wilson	Baker, Woodrow Wilson . . .
Wilson	Link, Wilson: the Road to the White House
Wilson	White, Woodrow Wilson
Winthrop	Canoe and the Saddle
Woollcott	Adams, Alexander Woollcott . . .
Woolman	Journal of the Life . . . and Christian Experiences

Wright, F. L.	Autobiography
Wright, R.	Black Boy
Yeats	Autobiography
Yeats-Brown	Lives of a Bengal Lancer
Young	Werner, Brigham Young
Zinsser	As I Remember Him
Zweig, S.	World of Yesterday; an Autobiography

c. Letters. Journals, Diaries, Notebooks, Table Talk

Adams	Henry Adams and His Friends (letters)
Alcott, A. B.	Journals
Amiel	Private Journal
Bashkirtseff	Journal
Bell, G.	Letters
Boswell	London Journal
Burney	Journal and Letters
Butler, S.	Note-Books
Chapman	John Jay Chapman and His Letters
Chekhov	Letters . . .
Chesterfield	Letters to His Son
Cicero	Letters (See Cicero and His Friends, by Boissier)
Clemens	Mark Twain's Letters
Conrad	Life and Letters
Cromwell	Letters (See Letters and Speeches, ed. by Carlyle)
Delacroix	Journals
Dickinson, E.	Life and Letters
Dodd	Ambassador Dodd's Diary
Dostoievski	Diary of a Writer
Dostoievski	Letters
Emerson	Letters
Evelyn	Diary
Fitzgerald, E.	Letters
Fitzgerald, F. S.	Crack-up, with Other Uncollected Pieces
Fox, G.	Journal
Gide	Journals
Goethe	Conversations with Eckermann
Gray	Letters
Hay	Life and Letters, comp. by Thayer
Haydon	Autobiography and Journals
Hazlitt	Table Talk
Holmes, O. W., Jr.	Holmes-Pollock Letters

Title Index *

* For technical reasons some biography titles are omitted. If the title sought is not found here the preceding list, classified by subject or form, should also be consulted.